AF478638

MADURA

MAVEN BOOKS

MADURA

W. Francis,

Indian Civil Service

MAVEN BOOKS

Chennai   Trichy   Tirunelveli   New Delhi

An Imprint of **MJP Publishers**

ISBN 978-93-87488-60-1 **Maven Books**

All rights reserved   No. 44, Nallathambi Street,
Printed and bound in India   Triplicane, Chennai 600 005

MJP 323   © Publishers, 2023

Publisher: **C. Janarthanan**

Project Editor: **C. Ambica**

PUBLISHER'S NOTE

The legacy of a country is in its varied cultural heritage, historical literature, developments in the field of economy and science. The top nations in the world are competing in the field of science, economy and literature. This vast legacy has to be conserved and documented so that it can be bestowed to the future generation. The knowledge of this legacy is slowly getting perished in the present generation due to lack of documentation.

Keeping this in mind, the concern with retrospective acquiring of rare books has been accented recently by the burgeoning reprint industry. Maven Books is gratified to retrieve the rare collections with a view to bring back those books that were landmarks in their time.

In this effort, a series of rare books would be republished under the banner, "Maven Books". The books in the reprint series have been carefully selected for their contemporary usefulness as well as their historical importance within the intellectual. We reconstruct the book with slight enhancements made for better presentation, without affecting the contents of the original edition.

Most of the works selected for republishing covers a huge range of subjects, from history to anthropology. We believe this reprint edition will be a service to the numerous researchers and practitioners active in this fascinating field. We allow readers to experience the wonder of peering into a scholarly work of the highest order and seminal significance.

Maven Books

PREFACE.

THE first 'Manual' of this district was *The Madura Country* of Mr. J. H. Nelson, I.C.S., published at Madras in 1868.

The chief features of his work were its sections on the political and revenue history of the district; and these have been freely utilized in the present volume. The early part of the former of them, however, has naturally been largely superseded by the discoveries due to the progress of epigraphy in recent years; and limits of space have necessitated the ruthless condensation of much of Mr. Nelson's picturesque account of the Náyakkan dynasty in the latter part of the same section. Most of the rest of the book is new. It is arranged on the system followed in the other District Gazetteers of the new series now being brought out, and statistical matter appears in a separate Appendix which is to be revised decennially, after each census.

Under instructions, the volume does not deal with the Ramnad and Sivaganga zamindaris, which are to be transferred to another district, and treats the area which will be included in the proposed new Nilakkóttai taluk as though this taluk were already in existence. The absence of statistics for this latter tract has, however, in some cases prevented the consistent carrying out of this method of referring to it.

Thanks to the various gentlemen, non-official and official, who have been kind enough to help with the undertaking have been rendered wherever possible in the body of the volume. The plan of the Madura temple at p. 267 and the early portions of the lists of Collectors and Judges on pp. 203 and 218 were prepared for the revised *District Manual* which was begun by Sir Harold Stuart.

W. F.

PLAN OF CONTENTS.

CHAPTER III.

THE PEOPLE.

CHAPTER IV.

AGRICULTURE AND IRRIGATION.

CHAPTER V.

FORESTS.

CHAPTER VI.

OCCUPATIONS AND TRADE.

PAGE

CHAPTER VII.

MEANS OF COMMUNICATION.

CHAPTER VIII.

RAINFALL AND SEASONS.

CHAPTER IX.

PUBLIC HEALTH.

CHAPTER X.

EDUCATION.

CHAPTER XI.

LAND REVENUE ADMINISTRATION.

CHAPTER XII.

SALT, ABKÁRI AND MISCELLANEOUS REVENUE.

CHAPTER XIII

ADMINISTRATION OF JUSTICE.

CHAPTER XIV.

LOCAL SELF-GOVERNMENT.

CHAPTER XV.

GAZETTEER. .

GAZETTEER

OF THE

MADURA DISTRICT.

CHAPTER I.

PHYSICAL DESCRIPTION.

GENERAL DESCRIPTION—Position and boundaries—Taluks and chief towns--
Etymology of the name—Natural divisions. HILLS—The Palnis—Varusha-
nád and Ándipatti hills—The Nágamalai—Sirumalais —Karandamalais-
Alagarmalais—The Nattam and Ailúr hills—Isolated hills—Scenery. RIVERS
—The Gundár—Tirumanimuttár and Pálár—Kodavanár, Nangánji, Nalla-
tangi and Shanmuganadi—The Vaigai and its tributaries. SOILS. CLIMATE
—Rainfall—Temperature. GEOLOGY—Minerals. FLORA. FAUNA—Cattle
—Sheep and goats—Game.

EXCEPT Tinnevelly, Madura is the southernmost Collectorate of
the Madras Presidency. On the north it is bounded by the
Coimbatore and Trichinopoly districts ; on the east by Trichinopoly, a corner of Pudukkóttai State and the Sivaganga
zamindari; on the south by the Sivaganga and Ramnad
zamindaris ; and on the whole of its western side by the great
range of the Western Gháts, which here is nearly all included in
the Native State of Travancore. Except this last mountain
frontier, none of the boundaries of Madura follow any natural
features, but owe their origin to administrative convenience or the
vicissitudes of history.

Madura is made up of the eight taluks of Dindigul, Kodaikanal (comprising the Upper and Lower Palni hills to be referred
to immediately), Madura, Mélúr, Nilakkóttai, Palni, Periyakulam
and Tirumangalam. The boundaries and position of these will be
evident from a glance at the map in the pocket at the end of this
volume. Statistical particulars regarding them will be found in
the separate Appendix. The chief towns in the district are its

capital, Madura (the largest mufassal municipality in the Presidency); the seven places which are the head-quarters of, and give
their names to, the remaining taluks; and Bódináyakkanúr and
Uttamapálaiyam in Periyakulam. Some account of these, and
also of other localities of interest in the district, will be found in
Chapter XV below.

Etymology
of the name.

The district is named after its chief town. The word is spelt
Madurai in Tamil, and Yule and Burnell say that it is generally
supposed to be the Tamil form of the name of Mathurá (the
modern Muttra), the very ancient and holy city on the Jumna,
30 miles above Agra. They point out that the name Madura
seems to have been a favourite among eastern settlements under
Hindu influence—there being places so called in Ceylon and to
the north of Mandalay and an island of the name near Java—
and suggest that it was perhaps adopted from reverence for the
holy city of the north.

Another etymology is from the Tamil *Madhurai,* meaning
anything sweet, the story being that Siva was so pleased with
the buildings erected round about his shrine by the first Pándyan
king that, as a mark of special favour, he sprinkled the temples,
towers, palaces and houses of the town with drops of sweet nectar
shaken from his locks.

Natural
divisions.

There are five well-marked natural divisions in the district.
The Palni hills are totally unlike any other part of it. Tirumangalam taluk in the south similarly differs widely from the
rest, being a level expanse, dotted with a few granite hills, which
is mainly covered with black cotton-soil and the scanty vegetation
characteristic thereof. The remainder of Madura may be grouped
into three areas; namely, first, the level tracts of rice-land
(mainly irrigated with the water of the Periyár project referred to
on pp. 126–130 below) which cover much of the Nilakkóttai and
Madura taluks and the southern half of Mélúr, and which receive
a high rainfall; secondly, the higher and far drier expanse of red
soil which spreads across the north of Mélúr taluk, all Dindigul
and Palni, and strongly resembles in its general features, soil and
products the adjoining areas in Coimbatore district; and, thirdly,
the long Kambam Valley which makes up the Periyakulam
taluk (see the map) and which, owing to the perennial streams
which flow from its numerous forests and the cool wind which
passes down it from the great hills on the west, is the greenest
and pleasantest part of the district. The low-lying centre of this
valley is occupied by fertile wet land irrigated from the Vaigai,
the Suruli, and the Periyár water flowing down the latter; but
the higher sides of it consist of dry, red land which is cultivated

here and there under wells, but for the most part is as barren and stony as the infertile parts of the Mysore plateau and resembles them markedly in general appearance.

As will be seen from the map, the mountain ranges of Madura include the broad mass of the Palni hills on the west; south of these, on the other side of the beautiful Kambam valley, the narrower, nearly parallel, Varushanád and Ándipatti range; the northern continuation of this, the snake-like Nágamalai which eventually turns south-eastwards in a wide curve nearly as far as Madura town; the Sirumalais north-north-west of that place; and, to the east of these, the Alagarmalais and Karandamalais. Round about Nattam, the town which lies within the triangle formed by these last three ranges, are several groups of smaller heights which are usually called 'the Nattam hills'; and the similar elevations to the northward, round the Ailúr railway-station, are known as 'the Ailúr hills.'

The Palnis are apparently so called from the town of the same name which lies just north of them. Their Sanskrit appellation is Varáhagiris, or 'pig hills,' and to account for it a legend is related of twelve naughty children, who scoffed at a devout rishi who dwelt amid the forests on them, were transformed by him into pigs, were rescued by Siva and were eventually promoted to high office under the Pándya kings. Representations of this story appear among the sculptures in the *Pudu mantapam* at Madura (p. 271). It has led to another derivation of the name, the word Palni being thought by some to be a corruption of Panri-malai, the Tamil form of the Sanskrit Varáhagiri.

The range is an offshoot of the Western Ghâts and is connected with the main part of that great formation. South-west of it runs another offshoot called the Cardamom Hills. These wall in the western side of the upper part of the Kambam valley, but all except their steep slopes is outside Madura and the scope of the present volume.

The greatest length of the Palni range is 40 miles and its maximum breadth 25 miles, and it is divided east and west into two distinct portions, the Upper Palnis and the Lower Palnis, the line between which runs north and south through Neutral Saddle on the map. The forests on both these ranges (as also those on the other hills of the district) are referred to in Chapter V below and the roads up them in Chapter VII.

The Lower Palnis consist of a confused jumble of peaks from 3,000 to 5,000 feet high, separated from one another by steep, wooded valleys of great beauty. In these ravines are a few villages. They are all small (the largest of them, Pannaikádu, contains less than 3,000 inhabitants) and they are picturesquely surrounded with groves of tamarind, jack, mango, orange, lime, citron, sago and other trees. At the approaches to some of them may still be seen remains of the gates which led through the hedges with which they were defended in the turbulent days of old. They usually possess a number of hamlets, perched at haphazard on the slopes of the valleys among dry cultivation and fields of the peculiar aromatic-flavoured plantain for which this country is famous and which goes on bearing for twenty years at a stretch, even without irrigation. The crops include paddy, coffee, cardamoms, ginger, turmeric and most of the usual dry cereals of the plains. Coffee was first planted in these hills by M. Emile de Fondclair about 1846. He obtained the seed from the Sirumalais, where his father had already experimented with the plant. The coffee gardens, like those elsewhere, have now fallen on evil days and several of them have been almost abandoned. Cardamoms and ginger require shade and are grown under the forest trees. The former take five years to come into bearing. Turmeric is planted in the open and is eighteen months before it is ready for gathering.

None of the inhabitants of this part of the range are hill-men in the strict sense of the word, all of them having come up, in some distant past, from the low country. They do not differ greatly from the people of the plains in appearance, dress or physical characteristics. The principal landowners are the Kunnuvans, and the Pulaiyans form the chief labouring caste. Both these communities are mentioned again on pp. 103 and 104 below. Telugu-speaking Chettis and Musalmans are gradually acquiring a good deal of the land which formerly belonged to the Kunnuvans; they trade with these latter, involve them in financial difficulties and then take their fields.

The hill cattle are similarly merely animals which have been taken up from the plains. There are no distinctive breeds like the Toda buffaloes of the Nilgiris.

Parts of this lower range are feverish. March to July are perhaps the worst months in them, but no part of the year can be considered safe.

The Upper Palnis run from 6,000 to 8,000 feet in elevation. The highest point in them (or in the district) is Vembádi Shola hill, which is 8,218 feet above the sea. The sanitarium of Kodaikanal (p. 245) stands on the southern edge of them. They differ from the Lower Palnis in possessing fewer ravines and valleys, much less forest, a colder climate and a more barren soil, and they consist largely of considerable plateaus made up of rolling downs covered with coarse grasses, hidden away in the more sheltered valleys of which are isolated woods called sholas. Except in these hollows, the soil is usually a thin stratum of black peaty earth of varying depth beneath which is a yellow clay, and in many places the underlying rock crops out.

The general fall of the range is to the north, and the slope in that direction is fairly gradual; but on the south the hills terminate abruptly in precipitous cliffs which in parts of the Kambam valley are veritable walls of rock forming scenery of the boldest and wildest description. On the north, two great valleys pierce the range and penetrate southwards through it as far as the villages of Vilpatti and Púmbárai. Up these, in days gone by, led two of the most frequented of all the routes followed by the pack animals of the merchants from Palni, then the chief centre for the trade with the hills. The path from Palni to Vilpatti is interrupted in the middle by precipitous ground over which no horse could travel. The other up the Púmbárai valley is easier. Both these, like other similar tracks on the range, have now been almost deserted in favour of the bridle-path from Periyakulam to Kodaikanal. This bridle-path, Law's Ghát, the new Áttúr Ghát (see pp. 155–6) and the roads within the Kodaikanal settlement are as yet the only really practicable routes on the range. Communication between village and village is by forest roads and rough hill-paths.

The Púmbárai valley is the most remarkable on the range. Its almost parallel sides, up which cultivation climbs amid woods and broken ground, are bounded by precipitous crags which look as if they had been formed by the sudden subsidence of the ground between them. Púmbárai itself stands on a terrace at the head of the valley and (although its inhabitants number less than 1,500) is one of the most important of the Upper Palni villages. It was once suggested as the station of the revenue subordinate in charge of these hills and it boasts a temple to Subrahmanya which is held in much repute.

The houses in this upper range are usually divided by regular paved lanes, are built of wattle and daub, are thatched with grass and possess fire-places. The people are chiefly the Kunnuvans already mentioned, Kárakkat Vellálans and a few of the wild Paliyans referred to again on p. 105 below. In the Upper and Lower Palnis taken together there are in all fifteen Government villages containing a population of just under 20,000 persons.

The crops of the upper range include paddy, coffee, poor varieties of wheat and barley, and garlic. This latter is the great article of export. The frequent torrents pouring down the sides of the hills, which are almost perennial, are often dammed at the top of a slope and thence cunningly led to irrigate paddy planted on a series of narrow terraces ingeniously cut in the hill-side from its brow down to its foot. Manure is supplied to these terraces in liquid form by leading the stream through the manure-heaps. The paddy is a coarse variety and takes eight or ten months to ripen. There are wide extents of land over which the hill folk have no rights of occupation, and the greater part of these has been constituted reserved forest. At present the disposal of unsurveyed and unassessed waste land other than reserves is governed by the provisions of Board's Standing Order No. 20 and not by the rules usual in the low country.

Varushanád and Ándipatti hills.

After the Palnis, the largest area of hill in Madura is the line which, for want of a better name, may be called the Varushanád and Ándipatti range from the Varushanád valley at the southern end of it and the village of Ándipatti near its northern extremity. This (see the map) runs north-eastwards from the south-western corner of the district, almost parallel with the Palnis and Cardamom hills which face it on the opposite side of the Kambam valley. Like them, it is an outlier of the Western Ghâts.

The great Varushanád ('rain country') valley, in which the Vaigai river takes its rise, is so called after the village of the same name, now deserted on account of its malaria, the interesting ruins of which (see p. 318 below) stand on the right bank of a fine bend of the Vaigai near the centre of the lower part of it. Not far off are the remains of Narasingapuram, also deserted. At the uppermost end of the valley stands the prominent Kóttaimalai ('fort hill'), 6,617 feet above the sea and the junction between Madura, Ramnad and Travancore. The valley is quite uninhabited except for a few Paliyans. It was apparently originally Government land, but was quietly annexed by the Gantamanáyakkanúr poligar in the old days before the value of such tracts was properly understood. The poligar gradually exercised wider and wider rights of ownership over it, and when at last, in 1880,[1] the attention of Government was directed to the matter, they reluctantly adopted the view that it was too late to attempt to establish their claims.

The western side of the head of the valley is flanked by the highest portion of the Varushanád and Ándipatti range. This for many years remained unsurveyed, and was merely marked in the atlas sheets as 'a high waving mountain overrun with an

---

[1] See the history of the matter in G.O., No. 917 Revenue, dated 4th August 1880, and connected papers.

impenetrable forest'; whence it is still called 'the High Wavy'. It is the least known part of the hills of Madura. On the top of it is a plateau covered with evergreen forest, and the jungle runs down on both sides of it in great continuous masses to a belt of more barren land consisting of rock and rough grass. Below this again, at the foot of the hill, is a fairly thick line of deciduous forest. The High Wavy is entirely uninhabited except for a few of the miserable Paliyans already referred to, who live in the forest at its foot.

The eastern side of the Varushanád valley is formed by a lower, narrower and more broken line of hills. The most prominent peaks in this are holy Saduragiri in the Sáptúr zamindari (properly Chaturagiri, 'the four-square hill,' from its appearance) which is 4,172 feet high, is declared to be even now the residence of celestial sages and is a favourite place of pilgrimage; and Kudiraimalai ('horse hill') 1,262 feet above the sea. The range is an inhospitable region. It is rugged, gaunt and burnt up, clothed for the most part with only the scantiest sprinkling of thorny trees, euphorbias and cactus, covered often with stupendous blocks of naked granite and visited by no one but a few herdsmen and their flocks. The rock of which it is formed contains numerous narrow dykes of a hard stone which weathers more slowly than the rest, and these stand out in all kinds of curious shapes and from a distance often closely resemble buildings and lines of fortification.

From the extreme northern end of these rugged heights the odd Nágamalai ('snake hill') range strikes off east and then south and runs to within three or four miles of Madura town. It is well named, being a long, straight ridge of barren rock of very uniform height; and local legends declare that it is the remains of a huge serpent, brought into existence by the magic arts of the Jains, which was only prevented by the grace of Siva from devouring the fervently Saivite city it so nearly approaches. All the last part of it consists of granular quartz of a very light colour (pale red or yellow) and this renders it a most conspicuous item in the landscape round Madura.

On the eastern side of the district the most considerable hills are the Sirumalais ('little mountains') which stand some sixteen miles north of Madura. They consist of a compact block almost twelve miles across, and their highest points are a little over 4,400 feet above the sea. On the top of them is a basin-shaped plateau some 3,000 feet high, in the north-eastern corner of which are three small villages inhabited by immigrants from the low country. The climate is very malarious and the only Europeans who have ever attempted to settle on the range (the American missionaries, see p. 250) were speedily compelled to quit it. The fever of 1809-10 committed great havoc in these hills and the Survey Account of 1815-16 says that there were then only 89 people left upon them.

The range has always been noted for its great fertility. The earliest Tamil poems extant speak of the many varieties of fruits which it produced in abundance, and it is still famous for its plantains (which are vociferously hawked at all the neighbouring railway-stations), its coffee and its cardamoms, and grows all the fruit trees already mentioned as occurring in the Lower Palni valleys. The Survey Account speaks with enthusiasm, also, of the timber trees 'of prodigious height and magnitude' which grew upon it in those days; but most of the range belongs to the Ammayanáyakkanúr zamindari and its forests have been so recklessly denuded that much of the great damage done by the floods of 1877-78 (the breaching of roads, of the railway, and of 950 tanks in Mélúr taluk alone) was attributed by the then Collector to the utter bareness of its slopes.

Mr. William Elliott, Judge of Madura from 1838 to 1840, appears to have been the first to start planting coffee on the range, and he is said to have obtained his seeds and young plants from Mysore. His estate (which is still called ' Elliottdale ') eventually passed to M. Faure de Fondclair (father of the M. Emile de Fondclair already mentioned as the pioneer of coffee-planting on the Lower Palnis) and from his family to the Roman Catholic Mission. ' Vans Agnew's estate' is another property on the range which is under European management. The coolies who work on the estates go up every day and return to their villages at night. The coffee grown is considered superior to that from the Palnis. In 1870 Capt. E. A. Campbell, late of the Madras Army, was experimenting on these hills, on behalf of the Cotton and Silk Supply Associations, with mulberry trees and exotic cotton.

The Karandamalais, which stand some eight miles north-east of the Sirumalais, measure about six miles across and are crowned by a little plateau on which are three small villages. From all sides of this run down low ridges enclosing steep valleys each of which has its own local name and gives rise to a small rivulet. On the southern slope are the remains of a fine cocoanut garden and of a hunting-seat of a former poligar.

The Alagarmalais, so called from the famous temple to
Alagarsvámi which stands at the southern foot of them twelve
miles from Madura (see p. 282), consist of a ridge about ten miles
in length and 1,000 feet above the sea at its highest point, from
which lesser ridges branch off in every direction forming valleys
which again have each a local name.

The Nattam and Ailúr hills merit no lengthy description.
They are little, stony ridges and hummocks with steep sides
covered with the shallowest soil, and are of value only for the iron
ore they contain and the scrub they support.

Besides all the above, the district contains a large number
of isolated peaks and heights which belong to no regular range.
Some of these are worthy of passing mention. The Dindigul
rock, the Ánaimalai and the Pasumalai are separately referred
to later on (pp. 232, 254 and 278). Rangamalai (3,099 feet),
on the northern frontier of Dindigul, is exceedingly prominent
throughout most of that taluk and Palni. On one of its
precipitous sides is a temple and a sacred pool into which the
devout throw money and jewellery in performance of vows, and
on top of it is a cauldron which is filled with ghee and lighted at
Kártigai and Dípávali. Karumalai ('black hill,' 2,527 feet)
five miles to the south-south-west, is similarly sacred, people
going up on Saturdays to the spring which issues from its side
from beneath two big boulders leaning towards one another.
Kondrangimalai (2,701 feet), ten miles away on the northern
frontier of Palni, is even more striking in appearance than either
of these. The foot of it is clothed with jungle, and out of this
rises a very steep, tapering, sugar-loaf peak, formed of one mass
of solid rock, bare of any vegetation. On the top of it (as is the
case with so many of the striking peaks in this district) is a tiny
shrine, the ascent to which passes up steps cut in the rock and is
provided with iron stanchions where the climb is steepest. The
hill is a most noticeable landmark for miles in every direction.
It is the handsomest peak of its kind in all Madura, and the
morning mists cling lovingly round it long after they have risen
from the sides of its plainer rivals.

There are surprisingly few noticeable tors among all the
wildernesses of rock with which the district abounds. Perhaps
the most remarkable is that on Sómagiri, a hill four miles east of
the eastern edge of the Alagarmalais. This consists of one huge
stone balanced upon a much slenderer pedestal, the whole being
perhaps 80 feet high. It is visible over half Mélúr taluk and
Mr. Bruce Foote has likened its appearance from the low ground
on the north to that of the head and neck of a beautiful child.

CHAP. I.
HILLS.

Alagar-
malais.

The Nattam
and Ailúr
hills.

Isolated hills

These many ranges and hills make Madura a very picturesque country. They form a background which redeems from the commonplace even its least inviting portion (the black cotton-soil country of Tirumangalam, diversified only by scattered babul trees and shimmering mirages) and which elevates its most charming corner (the deep Kambam valley) into a high position among the entirely delightful localities in the Presidency. Their colouring would exhaust the vocabulary of the most facile word-painter and their outlines vary infinitely from the gentlest of grass-covered slopes to the wildest of precipitous, bare crags. Among them all, the Palnis stand without a rival; whether when at the first dawn a peak here and a shoulder there advance, capriciously, into the warm light, leaving all the rest in mysterious gloom; at evening, when their topmost heights glow with the rose-colour of the fading sunset; or at night, when the big cliffs resume once more their silent watch over the villages below. Perhaps of all the many moods of this range the most memorable is when, during a break in the rains, its summits, looking loftier than ever, remain wreathed in heavy clouds, while its slopes, seamed with a hundred torrents and cascades, gleam in the fitful sunlight with every shade of green and blue, from jade-colour to emerald, from turquoise to lapis lazuli.

RIVERS.

The multiplicity of hills renders the drainage system of the district somewhat complicated. It is enough to mention shortly here the direction and general nature of the various rivers. The irrigation works which depend upon them are referred to below in Chapter IV.

The Gundár.

The Tirumangalam taluk drains south-eastwards away from the Varushanád and Ándipatti range into the Gundár and its tributary the Kamandalanadi, which unite outside the district within the Ramnad zamindari. The Gundár flows through Tirumangalam town, but not until it reaches Kamudi in the Ramnad country is it utilised to any extent for irrigation. The river is very uncertain, being often in high flood one day and nearly dry the next.

Tirumani-muttár and Pálár.

The north of Mélúr taluk drains eastwards into the Tirumani-muttár and the Pálár, which are also fickle streams of little importance within this district but more useful in the lower part of their courses.

Kodavanár, Nangánji, Nallatangi and Shanmu-ganadi.

The red soil plains of Dindigul and Palni in the north of the district drain due northwards into four almost parallel rivers which rise in the Palnis and eventually fall into the Amarávati and so into the Cauvery. These (see the map) are the Kodavanár,

Nangánji, Nallatangi and Shanmuganadi. Like the Gundár, they are often in heavy flood one day and trickling streamlets the next. The picturesque falls of the Nangánji near Virúpákshi are referred to in the account of that place on p. 309 below. The most useful of these four rivers is the Shanmuganadi ('six-faced stream'), which receives the drainage of the great Vilpatti and Púmbárai valleys already mentioned. Six principal torrents flowing down from these combine to form it, and hence its name.

The streams thus far referred to drain the outskirts of the district. The centre is included in the main river system—that of the Vaigai and its tributaries. These latter all rise in the Palni hills or the Varushanád and Ándipatti range, and join the Vaigai in the valley which lies between these two. Thereafter the river receives no tributaries of any importance and flows south-eastwards past Madura town into the Bay of Bengal not far from Ramnad. The geography of this upper part of the Vaigai and the courses of the affluents it there receives can be better grasped from the map than from any quantity of written description.

It will be seen that the river rises in the Varushanád valley already mentioned and at first flows due north in a winding bed. Nearly parallel with it meanders the Suruli, which drains the whole of the upper part of the adjoining Kambam valley. The head waters of this latter fling themselves down from the lower spurs of the High Wavy in a beautiful fall which is visible from the road along the bottom of the valley. Near here are sacred caves (the chief is the *Kailása pudavu*) which are annually visited by many pilgrims, who bathe in the river and sacrifice goats. The water has the property (possessed by several of the Derbyshire streams) of 'petrifying' objects placed in it. The river is almost entirely supplied from the south flank of the Kambam valley (the hills on the other side drain northwards into Travancore) and until lately it was of comparatively small importance. Recently, however, the biggest of the Travancore rivers, the Periyár, has been dammed up (see p. 126), and turned, by a tunnel blasted through the watershed, down into the Kambam valley, where it is led into the bed of the Suruli. In consequence the latter is now full of water for nine or ten months in the year.

About two miles south of Allinagaram the Suruli is joined by the Téni, an almost perennial stream which rises in the deep Bódináyakkanúr valley. Another two miles further on, their combined waters join the Vaigai and they are no more heard of. The Vaigai is now a deep and rapid stream flowing in a narrow channel. It soon changes its direction and runs east-north-eastwards under the northern slopes of the Árdipatti hills and the Nágamalai. In this part of its course it is met by the Varáhanadi ('boar river') and the Manjalár ('yellow river'). The former of these runs down from the Upper Palnis through Periyakulam town, where it unites with the Pámbár, a stream well known at Kodaikanal and the falls of which are a prominent object from the bridle-path leading to that station. The Manjalár (sometimes called 'the Vattilagundu river') dashes down the side of the Palnis just above Dévadánapatti in a splendid cataract 200 feet high which is visible from the main road there, and then races past Vattilagundu, is joined by the Ayyampálaiyam river from the Lower Palnis and flows into the Vaigai. Immediately afterwards, the latter turns and begins the south-easterly course which it continues until it reaches the sea. Just at the point where it runs under the corresponding bend in the Nágamalai it is crossed by the important Peranai and Chittanai dams referred to in Chapter IV, the former of which renders available for irrigation the water of the Periyár which has reached it through the Suruli.

Before the advent of this water the Vaigai used to be in heavy flood for a week or two and dry for almost all the rest of the year ; and its supply was so inadequate that in normal years hardly any water escaped being drawn off by the channels which lead off from either bank, so that at the point where it enters the Bay of Bengal the stream was reduced to the merest trickle. Now, even below the two dams, the flow is more considerable and more constant.

The soils of Madura belong principally to the red ferruginous series, the black varieties being uncommon and the purely arenaceous sorts entirely absent. The marginal table shows the percentage of the assessed area of ryotwari and minor inam land in each taluk which is covered with black and red soils respectively. It will be noticed that, excluding the Palni hills, Tirumangalam is the only taluk in which the proportion of black cotton-soil is considerable, and that the other taluks are almost entirely covered with red earths.

	Percentage.	
Taluk.	Black.	Red.
Kodaikanal ...	36	64
Palni	6	94
Dindigul	4	96
Periyakulam ...	9	91
Madura	14	83
Mélúr	...	100
Tirumangalam ...	61	39
Total .	15	85

The cotton-soil of Tirumangalam differs, however, from that of the Deccan districts ; being more friable, less retentive of moisture and more suited to irrigation. It is, in fact, regularly irrigated from both tanks and wells, and systematically irrigated paddy may often be seen growing side by side with cotton cultivated as a dry crop.

CHAP. I.
SOILS.

The rainfall of the district is referred to in some detail on p. 160 below. The average fall is 33·88 inches (half cf which is received in the north-east monsoon between October and December) and is lightest in Palni and Dindigul and heaviest (excluding the Palni hills) in Madura and Mélúr.

CLIMATE.
Rainfall.

The temperature is officially recorded at Madura and Kodaikanal, but figures for the latter are available for only a short period. The average maxima and minima and the mean for each month at Madura are shown in degrees Fahrenheit in the margin, and alongside is given the daily velocity of the wind in each month. These figures do not, however, give an idea of the extremes which are sometimes reached. The mercury has been known, for example, to fall to 59·2° and to rise to 105·5°.

Temperature.

Month.	Temperature.			Daily velocity of the wind in miles.
	Average maximum.	Average minimum.	Mean.	
	°	°	°	
January ...	87·5	68·6	78·1	129·6
February ..	92·0	69·5	80·8	120·0
March ..	96·7	72·8	84·8	98·4
April ...	99·3	76·4	87 9	86 4
May ...	100·1	77·5	88·8	88·8
June ...	98·2	77·1	87·7	115·2
July ...	97·2	76·4	86·8	110·4
August ...	96 6	75·8	86·2	88·8
September ...	95·3	75·3	85·3	81·6
October ...	91·3	74·0	82 7	69·6
November ...	87·3	72·5	79·9	91 2
December ...	86 0	70·5	78·3	117 6
The year ...	94·0	73·9	83·9	99·8

The annual mean temperature is four degrees higher than in the next recording station to the north, Coimbatore, and in every month in the year the mean in Madura is in excess of the figure at that station. Compared with its other next neighbours, Trichinopoly and Tinnevelly, Madura will be found to be a degree or two cooler than the latter in every month in the year, but slightly hotter than the former in the four months November to February. The worst part of the year is April, May and June, and it is only in November, December and January that the mean temperature is below 80°. Dindigul, however, is considerably cooler than Madura, and during the south-west monsoon the heat in the Kambam valley is reduced by the pleasant breeze which blows down it from the hills. In Madura town, as the figures above show, the only periods when the wind is at all strong are after the north-east, and during the south-west, monsoon.

The annual mean humidity of Madura (70·2) is slightly less than that of Tinnevelly and rather higher than that of Trichinopoly. Of the five-day periods for which the Meteorological department works out averages, the driest in the year (humidity 61·6) is usually that from June 20th to 24th and the wettest (humidity 78·8) from November 7th to 11th.

Geologically, Madura is not interesting. Except a narrow alluvial strip along the Vaigai valley (which generally consists of a very sandy loam) the whole of the district is covered with gneissic rocks. These have not yet been examined in any great detail, especially in the north of the district, but in the centre and south they may apparently be divided[1] into the following six groups :--

1. Lower granitoid gneiss—Tirumangalam group.
2. Lower granular quartz rock—Kokkulam group.
3. Middle granitoid gneiss—Skandamalai group.
4. Middle granular quartz rock—Nágamalai group.
5. Upper granitoid gneiss—Mélúr group.
6. Upper granular quartz rock—Alagarmalai group.

The lowest of this series, the lower granitoid gneiss group, is the set of beds which occur in the Tirumangalam taluk. The next lowest, the lower granular quartz rock, forms a ridge about two miles to the south of the Nágamalai and has been named after the village of Kokkulam (off the Tirumangalam-Sólavandán road) which stands close by one portion of it. This can be traced, despite some gaps, for many miles. Northwards from Kokkulam the ridge runs parallel to the Nágamalai for a great distance and to the south it extends beyond the Skandamalai (or Tirupparankunram hill) before it disappears under the alluvium. The middle granitoid gneiss group is well exemplified in the Skandamalai and in some smaller hills to the north-west of this near the Tirumangalam-Sólavandán road. The fourth of the six groups, the middle granular quartz rock, forms the Nágamalai and its continuation the Pasumalai, and then disappears southwards under the alluvium. The upper granitoid gneiss group

---

[1] See Mr. Bruce Foote's description of them in the *Memoirs* of the Geol. Surv. of India, xx, pt. 1, 11 ff., from which the present account is abstracted.

occupies the country to the north-west of Tiruvádúr in the Mélúr taluk and stretches to the north-east as far as the alluvium of the Pálár and to the south-west down to the valley of the Vaigai. The numerous hills which are formed of this rock in this tract are conspicuous for their boldness of form and beauty of colour. Among them is the curious Ánaimalai referred to on p. 254, below.

The uppermost of the six groups, the upper granular quartz rock, appears prominently in the bold scarp of the south-east side of the Alagarmalai.

In the west of the district charnockite is found, and the Palnis consist entirely of this rock. In the Varushanád hills are hornblende schists and granulites, penetrated by veins of mica-bearing pegmatite.

Minerals are extremely rare. At Tirumál, a village five miles north-east of Kalligudi railway-station in the Tirumangalam taluk, is a broad band of white crystalline limestone which may be traced nearly two miles to the eastward and has been much quarried, and a little to the westward of Kokkulam (two miles north of Tirumál) are two smaller limestone beds. This rock is also scattered through other parts of the district. From the Gópálasvámi hill, in the extreme south of Tirumangalam near the road to Srívilliputtúr, red and white fragments of transparent quartz are obtained. Short and small quartz veins also occur on the western slope of the Sirumalais east and south-east of Ammayanáyakkanúr railway-station. Perhaps the best building-stone in the district is that quarried from the Skandamalai. The iron ore found near Kottámpatti in Mélúr taluk and the gold-washing at Palakkanúttu in Dindigul are referred to in the accounts of those places in Chapter XV (pp. 287 and 241) below.

In 1899 the Geological Survey of India acquired an interesting meteorite which had been found near Kodaikanal. It is only the second *iron* meteorite which has been discovered in India and weighed about 35 lbs. against the 10 lbs. of the other known example, which fell in the Vizagapatam district in 1870. It was composed almost entirely of nickeliferous iron.[1]

Botanically, the most interesting parts of the district are the Palni and Sirumalai Hills. Dr. Robert Wight, the well-known botanist, visited a portion of the former in 1836 and recorded his observations in the *Madras Journal of Literature and Science* for

CHAP I.
GEOLOGY.

Minerals.

FLORA.

[1] See the Survey's General Report for 1899-1900, 4, for more particulars of it.

April 1837; and in the same magazine for January-March 1858
is Colonel Beddome's account of the 'Flora of the Pulney Hill'
which enumerates over 700 species of plants, exclusive of *Compo-
sitæ, Graminæ* and *Cryptogams* which were not determined.
Wight says :—

' The natural productions of the country are sufficiently varied to
give us reason to put a high estimate on its probable capabilities. In
the course of about 15 days I collected little short of 500 species of
plants, and without any attempt on my part to preserve specimens of
all the plants in flower or fruit at this season; many being rejected
merely because 1 was not in want of specimens. It did not in short
occur to me at the time, which it has since, to compare the vegetable
productions of these hills with the recorded ones of the country generally.
This I greatly regret, as I think, were a somewhat perfect collection
formed, it would be found to contain a number of species amounting to
from one-half to four-fifths of the whole peninsula flora, so far as we
are yet acquainted with it, and to present a vast number of species
peculiar to themselves. Among the European forms observed were
two species of *Ranunculus;* two of *Anemone;* three of *Clematis;* two
of *Berberis;* a new *Parnassia;* two of *Drosera* (sun-dew); one *Stellaria,*
and one *Cerastium* (chick-weed); a rose, very abundant; three or four
kinds of rasps or brambles; one *Potentilla;* one *Circæa* (enchanter's
night shade); a tree allied to the Bilberry (*Thibaudia*); one *Anagallis;*
two of *Lysimachia,* both allied to British species; the common dock,
very abundant about the villages; and three kinds of rushes (*Juncus*),
one very nearly allied to the common British rush (*Juncus effusus*).
Among the truly tropical forms, a species of *Magnolia,* the first I
believe that has been discovered in the peninsula, is the most interesting; the *Rhododendron nobilis,* very abundant; a very large and handsome *Ilex* (holly), but without the thorny leaves of the European plant;
a species of *Gordonia,* a tree resembling in its flowers the *Camelia* and
tea plant; a very remarkable species of fig, with a climbing stem,
bearing fruit of the size of large oranges, in clusters along the stems;
besides many other interesting trees which I fear it would be tedious
to mention. Four species of palms are met with on the higher
regions, namely, the sago palm (*Caryota urens*), a wild areca palm, the
Bentinckia condupana, and an alpine species of date. The grasses are
very numerous but the predominant tribe (*Andropogineæ*) are not those
best suited for pasturage, being generally of a coarse nature and
highly aromatic quality. Ferns, moss s, and lichens, abound : among
which, the most conspicuous is a branching variety of the Tree fern
(*Alsophila*) very common in thick jungles on moist banks of streams.'

Dr. A. G. Bourne, F.R.S., and Mrs. Bourne have since studied
the flora in the neighbourhood of Kodaikanal, and the former has
very kindly permitted the reproduction of the following extracts

from his introductory note to the list of plants they observed in that part :—

'I have been able to trace most of the plants mentioned by Wight. *Ranunculus reniformis*, Wall. and *R. Wallichianus*, W. and A. are both very common. The two species of *Anemone* are doubtless merged into *A. rivularis*, Ham. ; that at any rate is the only species I find. The three *Clematis* are *C. smilacifolia*, Wall., *C. Gouriana*, Roxb. and *C. Wightiana*, Wall. The two Berberids are *B. nepalensis*, Spr. and *B. aristata*, DC. The new 'Parnassia' is doubtless *Parnassia mysorensis*, Heyne. The *Droseras* are *D. Burmanni*, Vahl. and *D. peltata*, Sm. The latter literally clothes the banks in certain places. *Stellaria media* occurs and is common in certain places only, while *Cerastium indicum* is abundant in a few spots. *Rosa Leschenaultiana*, W. & A., the only wild rose I found, is common in a few localities only. The 'three or four kinds of rasps or brambles' resolve themselves into *Rubus molluccanus*, L., *R. ellipticus*, Sm. and *R. lasiocarpus*, Sm. The latter is doubtless Roxburgh's *R. racemosus*. *Potentilla Leschenaultiana* is very common. Wight's *Circæa* turns out to be *C. alpina*. With regard to the 'tree allied to the Bilberry,' I have three species of *Vaccinium*. *Anagallis arvensis* is very rare except near Púmbárai. *Lysimachia Leschenaultii*, Duby and *L. deltoides* both abound. *Rumex nepalensis*, Spreng. is the only 'dock' I found and there was not much of that. *Juncus glaucus*, Ehrh. (*J. effusus*, Steud.) and *J. prismatocarpus*, Br. are both common.

With regard to the 'truly tropical forms' the *Magnolia* mentioned by Wight and subsequently by Beddome must be *Michelia champaca*, and this is more frequently met with on the Púmbárai side, which they chiefly explored, than near Kodaikanal; it also occurs on the Sirumalais, but in both places has been doubtless planted, as it is not found far away from the villages. *Rhododendron arboreum*, var. *nilagirica*, *Ilex malabarica*, *I. Gardneriana* and three other species, *Gordonia obtusa*, *Ficus macrocarpa*, with its 'fruit the size of large oranges,' all find a place in my list.

The soil on the hills varies in depth from a few inches to a few feet, while in many places patches of fairly smooth bare rock are exposed; this is sometimes full of cracks and covered with loose boulders. In such places, even where there is not sufficient soil for grass, may be found *Cyanotis arachnoidea*, *Anisochilus*, *Kalanchoe*, *Aneilema Koenigii*, and here and there groups of *Osbekia Wightiana* attaining from five to six feet in height, all rooting in the crevices. Where there is a little soil, the commonest grasses will be *Andropogon contortus* and *A. lividus*, the spikes, stems, and (when mature) the leaves, of which form the chief factor in giving the hill tops their purplish tinge. A little lower down come great tufts of *Pollinia quadrinervis var. Wightii*, with its fascicles of rich brown spikes on stems generally several feet in height, of *Ischæmum ciliare*, with its pairs of thick rich purple spikes, of *Arundinella villosa*, with its solitary untidy-looking spikes, and of *Andropogon zeylanicus* and *A. Wightiana*, both with long graceful panicles—the former mostly purplish in colour with bright yellow anthers and rich purple styles, and the latter a most beautiful grass, the outer glumes of the pedicelled spikelets being salmon-coloured, the sessile spikelets lemon-yellow (as are the anthers and styles) while the awns are over two inches long and yellowish brown in colour. Among these tall species, in addition to those above mentioned, occur *Tripogon bromoides, Arundinella mesophylla* (peculiar, so far as I know, to these hills) and, keeping quite low on the ground, *Eragrostis amabilis*. At rather lower elevations, say 5,000 feet downwards, one may come across miniature forests of *Andropogon Nardus* and, though not usually in the same localities, *A. schoenanthus*, the former readily distinguishable here from the latter by the almost electric green of its leaves. On the ghát are some splendid clumps of *Andropogon halepensis* and *Garnotia*.

To return to the high hills, almost everywhere are to be found among the grass *Brunella vulgaris, Knoxia mollis, Wahlenbergia gracilis, Leucas helianthemifolia, Indigofera pedicellata, Cyanotis Wightii* (in better soil only, than *C. arachnoidea* will grow in—it may generally be found at the bottom of the pits which have been dug for planting trees in if they have been left empty for a year or two), *Polygala sibirica* and, frequently with it and closely resembling it in leaf and habit, *Crotalaria albida*. The small-leaved variety of *C. rubiginosa* is common in some places and commoner still is a *Crotalaria* which I cannot match. This occurs in perfectly glabrous forms in some places; it attains its largest size where it grows in good soil on a road-side bank and its branches hang down. Very common also in similar situations are two Valerians (*V. Hookeriana* on the Kodaikanal side, *V. Beddomei* on the Púmbárai side), *Striga lutea, Gentiana quadrifaria*, to see the azure blue of whose flowers one must go out in the middle of the day, *Micromeria biflora*, the leaves of which are most delicately aromatic, *Bupleurum disticophyllum, Curculigo orchioides*, with its three or four leaves and single yellow flower coming up out of the ground, and, sometimes in great patches making a whole hill-side white, *Anaphalis oblonga* and *A. brevifolia*.

A notable feature of many of these hill-sides is the number of small landslips which have occurred owing to the surface soil slipping on the smooth rock. Sometimes they look like the footsteps of a gigantic animal which has slipped in going up hill; at others they are on a larger scale and an entire hill-side appears to be terraced with steps from three to four feet high and from five to six feet wide; in some places they have occurred on a huge scale and, as suggested by Wight, the whole of the Púmbárai valley with its numerous offshoots looks as though it had been formed in this way. Going down the slopes to the bottoms of the valleys one constantly passes through masses of *Strobilanthes Kunthianus* and below it bracken. At the bottom flourish *Dipsacus Leschenaultii* and alas! huge thistles—*Cnicus Wallichii*—and *Heracleum Sprengelianum* and *H. rigens*. The streamlet at the bottom runs as a rule between six and eight feet underground, showing itself here and there at the bottom of deep holes formed by the falling in of the earth. In the tunnels live jackals and the hill mongoose, *Herpestes vitticollis*. The vertical, or even under-cut, sides of the holes are covered with ferns, and here one may constantly find *Blumea hieracifolia, Parnassia mysorensis, Hydrocotyle, Serpicula indica* and in some places the charming little *Circæa alpina*. Very few other plants grow in these holes, into many of which very little light penetrates.

When there is a large damp area the ground is generally bright with flowers—in contrast to most similar spots on the Nilgiris. In such places grow *Lysimachia Leschenaultii, Pedicularis zeylanica, Impatiens tenella, Osbekia cupularis, Exacum atropurpureum, Satyrium nepalense, Anaphalis Wightiana, Ranunculus reniformis, Dipsacus Leschenaultii, Commelina clavata, Eriocaulon, Lentibulariæ, Xyris, Hypericum napaulense* and *H. japonicum,* and *Drosera.* The commonest plants forming road-side hedges are the species of *Rubus* and in some places *Adenostemma.* Scattered trees are almost sure to be *Photinia, Vaccinium, Eurya* or *Rhododendron.* Other plants which one is pretty sure to meet with here and there in any walk are *Artemisia, Polygonum Chinense, Heracleum Sprengelianum, Pimpinella, Coleus barbatus, Hedyotis Swertioides* and *H. articularis, Sopubia trifida* and *S. Delphinifolia, Gaultheria fragrantissima, Senecio zeylanica* and *S. Lavandulifolius, Anaphalis aristata, Cnicus Wallichii,* various species of *Plectranthus, Campanula fulgens, Emilia Sonchifolia, Flemingia,* etc., etc. *Strobilanthes Kunthianus* forms great patches here and there and even covers whole hill-sides. The commonest ground orchids are *Spiranthes australis,* of which I have counted over fifty spikes while standing in one spot, *Habenaria elliptica* and *H. Galeandra.*'

The flora of the Sirumalais has not yet been examined in detail, but Dr. Bourne's collectors found there a number of plants which do not occur on the Palnis, and the range deserves systematic study.

The indigenous cattle of the district are small and of no special value, and the Káppiliyans of the upper part of the Kambam valley (see below) are the only people who take any trouble to improve the breed. In Mélúr and Tirumangalam ploughing is even done (especially by the Kallans) with cows. In Dindigul and Mélúr' the ryots import animals from Manapárai and Marungápuri in Trichinopoly, while Palni taluk is partly supplied with Coimbatore ('*Konganád*') cattle. The richer ryots in Tirumangalam also purchase Mysore bullocks for ploughing the cotton-soil there, which requires strong animals. In many villages cattle are specially raised for the *jallikats* referred to on p. 83 below, and these have been described[1] as being a special breed.

The chief cattle market in the district is that held at Madura on the occasion of the great Chittrai festival at the temple there. As many as 30,000 head have been counted at this fair and it is perhaps the largest in the southern districts. The majority of the foreign animals brought to it are those reared round about Manapárai and in Coimbatore, but some Mysore cattle from Salem are also offered for sale.

The number of ploughing-bullocks per cultivated acre is, as elsewhere, smallest in the dry taluks and largest where wet lands are most common. The supply is at present insufficient on the land in Mélúr which is being newly irrigated with the Periyár water. Here and there cholam is grown for fodder, being sown very thickly so as to produce a thin stalk, and round Védasandúr in Dindigul grass is cultivated on dry fields; but otherwise no special steps are taken to provide cattle food. Rinderpest is not uncommon and caused great loss in Periyakulam taluk in 1899.

The Káppiliyans of Kambam above alluded to are immigrants from the Canarese country and speak that language. They possess a herd of about 150 cattle of a distinctive breed (small, active, round-barrelled animals, well known for their trotting powers) which they say are the descendants of some cattle they brought with them when they first came to these parts. These deserve a note. They are called the *dévaru ávu* in Canarese or in Tamil the *tambirán mádu*, both of which phrases mean 'the sacred

____

[1] Bulletin No. 44, Vol. II, of the Madras Department of Land Records and Agriculture.

herd.' The cows are never milked and are only used for breeding. Members of the herd which die are buried, and are not
(as elsewhere) allowed to be desecrated by the chuckler's skin-
ning-knife. The leader of the herd is called 'the king bull'
(*pattadu ávu*), and when he dies a successor is selected in a quaint
manner with elaborate and expensive ceremonial. On the
auspicious day fixed for the election the whole herd is assembled
and camphor, plantains, betel and nut and so forth are solemnly
offered to it. A bundle of sugar-cane is then placed before it,
and the attendant Káppiliyans watch eagerly to see which of the
bulls of the herd will approach and eat this. The animal which
first does so is acclaimed as the new 'king bull' and is formally
installed in his office by being daubed with saffron and kunku-
mam and garlanded with flowers. Thereafter he is treated by
the whole caste as a god, is given the holy name of Nandagópála-
svámi, and is allotted, to watch over and worship him, a special
attendant who enjoys the inams which stand in his name and
is the custodian of the jewels and the copper grants which were
presented in days gone by to his predecessors. There are now
nine of these grants, but they do not state the Sakha year in
which they were drawn out and the names of the rulers who
conferred them are not identifiable. The king bulls are credited
with having performed many miracles, stories of which are still
eagerly related, and their opinion is still solicited on matters of
importance. The herd, for example, is not taken to the hills for
the hot weather until its king has signified his approval by
accepting some sugar and milk placed near him. His attendant
always belongs to a particular sub-division of the caste and
when he dies his successor is selected in as haphazard a fashion
as the king bull himself. Before the assembled Káppiliyans,
púja is offered to the sacred herd; and then a young boy is
seized with divine inspiration and points out the man who is to be
the new holder of the office.

The herd receives recruits from outside, owing to the Hindus
round about dedicating to it all calves which are born on the first
day of Tai, but these are not treated as being quite of the elect.
The Káppiliyans have recently raised Rs. 11,000 by taxing all
members of the caste in the Periyakulam taluk for three years,
and have spent this sum in building roomy masonry quarters at
Kambam for the sacred herd. Their chief grievance at present
is that the same grazing fees are levied on their animals as on
mere ordinary cattle, which, they urge, is equivalent to treating
gods as equals of men.

The care they take of their animals suggests the possibility of improving the breed by giving them a good Government bull. This would need to be of one of the lighter breeds, as the cows are all small.

In 1879 and the following years an experiment was made to see how Amrat Mahál cattle would do on the Palnis. A small herd of twelve animals was entrusted by Government to Mr. Vere Levinge, who had retired to Kodaikanal from the Collectorship of Madura, and this was under his charge until his death in 1885. It was then dispersed. While it was on the hills it increased to twenty-six head and—except for one attack of foot and mouth disease—flourished well. Mr. Levinge reported that a mixed herd of his own, consisting of English, Australian, country-bred and Aden cattle, also did well there on no other food than the natural grass of the hills.

Sheep and goats.

The sheep of the district are of two varieties; namely, the hairy, long-legged, red kind which is only useful as a manuring agent and to be turned into mutton, and the black sort which carries a fleece of inferior, wiry, wool. The coarse blankets which are woven from this material by the Canarese-speaking Kurubas are referred to on p. 145 below, and the considerable trade which is carried on in sheep and goat skins is mentioned on p. 151.

The goats of Madura are of the usual kind and, as elsewhere, their numbers constitute one of the difficult problems in forest conservancy.

Game.

Madura is a poor place for small game. Snipe are the only game-birds which can be said to be plentiful. The best spots for these are the tanks round Sólavandán which are periodically filled with the Periyár water. Their foreshores abound with the *kórai* grass which is the bird's favourite cover. Late in the season the Tirupparankunram wet land is also a likely part.

Duck and teal are most easily obtained on the tanks in Tirumangalam, which are smaller, as a rule, than those elsewhere. The other usual game-birds are met with all over the district, but in small numbers. Florican are occasionally seen, round Ándipatti are some sand-grouse, and on the Upper Palnis are woodcock.

Large game is confined to the hill ranges. All the usual south Indian species, from elephant and bison downwards, occur.

Elephants were formerly very numerous all over the Palni range and the old records are full of accounts of the devastation they caused, even as far east as Kannivádi zamindari, and of the steps taken to reduce their numbers. They are seldom seen on this range now, even on the upper parts of it. Lieutenant Jervis, in his *Narrative of a journey to the Falls of the Cauvery,* speaks of a natural pass on the hills near Kambam, which those familiar with that locality may be able to identify, where these animals were regularly caught in pits. The place ended in a narrow gorge between two rocks through which only one elephant could pass at a time, and the herds were driven through this into a network of pits dug on the other side of it in a hollow between two hills. He speaks of 63 elephants being trapped or shot there on one occasion in four hours. Mr. Robert Fischer of Madura possesses a pair of elephant tusks, obtained in the district, of which the larger is 72 inches long, $18\frac{1}{4}$ inches in greatest girth and weighs $72\frac{1}{2}$ lb. and the smaller measures 66 inches in length, $18\frac{1}{4}$ inches in girth and weighs 66 lb.

Bison are fairly plentiful, and two small herds of poor specimens still roam the Alagarmalais. These animals used to be numerous on the Sirumalais, but (with every other sort of large game) they have long since disappeared from there. The Nilgiri ibex (*Hemitrayus hylocrius*) is also found in one or two spots on the Upper Painis. The other game animals present no peculiarities.

The monkeys of the district are numerous and impudent. They used to be such a nuisance in Madura town that people had to cover the roofs of their houses with thorns ; and at length they were all caught and deported. An almost worse pest which has taken their place is the notorious Madura mosquito—a venomous and vindictive breed.

CHAPTER II.

POLITICAL HISTORY.

PREHISTORIC PEOPLES—Palæolithic man—Kistvaens, etc. EARLY HISTORY—The Pándya dynasty—Its antiquity—Appears in early Tamil literature—Its first mention in inscriptions—Its struggles with the Pallavas, 7th century—Decline of the latter—The Ganga-Pallavas, 9th century—Pándya ascendancy—The Chóla revival, 10th to 12th centuries—Pándya rebellions—Pándya renaissance, 12th century—Struggle for the throne—Decline of the Chólas, 13th century—Pándya rule thenceforth—Máravarman Sundara-Pándya I, 1216-35—Arrival of the Hoysalas—Jatávarman Sundara-Pándya I, 1251-61—End of the Hoysala and Chóla power—Máravarman Kulasékhara I (1268-1308) and his successor—Splendour of the Pándya realm. MUSALMAN INVASION, 1310—Musalman dynasty at Madura. VIJAYANAGAR DOMINION, 1365—Its effects—King Achyuta's campaign, 1532. NÁYAKKAN DYNASTY, 1559-1736—Its origin—Visvanátha Náyakkan, 1559-63—His immediate successors—Fall of Vijayanagar kingdom, 1565—Tirumala Náyakkan, 1623-59—He defies Vijayanagar—Calls the Muhammadans to his aid—And becomes their feudatory—His wars with Mysore—His death—Rebellions among his vassals—A curious rumour—Tirumala's capital—His public buildings—Muttu Alakádri, 1659-62—Chokkanátha (1662-82)—His troubles with his neighbours—His conquest and loss of Tanjore—Attacked by Mysore and the Maráthas—The latter seize his country—Ranga Krishna Muttu Vírappa (1682-89)—Matters improve—Mangammál (1689-1704)—Her charities—Her wars—Her tragic death—Vijaya Ranga Chokkanátha (1704-31)—His feeble rule—Mínákshi (1731-36)—Musalman interference—End of Náyakkan dynasty—Character of its rule. MUSALMAN DOMINION—Chanda Sáhib (1736-40)—A Marátha interlude (1740-43)—Musalman authority re-established, 1743—The rival Musalman parties. ENGLISH PERIOD—Siege of Madura, 1751—Col. Heron's expedition, 1755—Mahfuz Khán rents the country—Muhammad Yúsuf sent to quiet it—Mahfuz Khán rebels—Capt. Calliaud's attacks on Madura, 1757—Anarchy again prevails—Yúsuf Khán again despatched—He rebels and is hanged, 1764—His character—Haidar Ali's invasion, 1780—Assignment of the revenue to the Company, 1781—Col. Fullarton's expedition, 1783—Assignment of the revenue cancelled, 1785—Assumption of the revenue, 1790—The Company collects the peshkash, 1792—Story of the Dindigul country—Its cession in 1792—Cession of the rest of Madura, 1801.

<table>
<tr><td valign="top">CHAP. II.
PREHISTORIC
PEOPLES.

Palæolithic
man.</td><td>Of palæolithic or neolithic man, practically no traces have as yet been found in the Madura district. Mr. Bruce Foote says [1] that associated with the shingle which is mixed with the ferruginous gravel to the north of the tank of Tallákulam village (opposite Madura town, across the Vaigai river) occur occasional flakes of different coloured cherts of foreign origin, some of which seem</td></tr>
</table>

---

[1] *Memoirs*, Geol. Surv. India, xx, pt. 1, 49 and *Records*, xii, pt. 3, 154.

certainly to have been trimmed for use as scrapers or knives. He thinks further search would probably reveal unquestionably recognizable specimens of chipped stone instruments, but as yet none seem to have been discovered.

Of the existence of those prehistoric peoples who buried their dead in stone kistvaens and dolmens there is, however, abundant evidence. Instances of these erections are reported from places as widely separated as Kaittiyankóttai and its next neighbour Kalvárpatti in the north of the Dindigul taluk; Rágalápuram and Virálippatti, not far from one another to the south-east of Dindigul town; Mullipallam in Nilakkóttai taluk; Karungálakudi in Mélúr; Kalayamuttúr, Chinnakalayamuttúr (those at the two latter places are regularly worshipped by the villagers!) and Palni in Palni taluk; and Kambam and Márgaiyankóttai in Periyakulam. Pyriform earthen tombs have also been found near Kulasékharankóttai in Nilakkóttai taluk, Paravai and Anuppánadi in Madura, and Senkulam in Tirumangalam. Some of these many remains are referred to again in Chapter XV below, and in the same place (pp. 247–8) are mentioned the most striking of all the prehistoric antiquities of the district, the kistvaens and dolmens of the Palni Hills.

When times which may be styled historical are first reached, the greater part of the Madura country is found to be in the possession of the Pándya dynasty, and the early chronicles of the district are to a large extent the history of that line.

These Pándyas were the rulers of one of three great kingdoms which in the earliest times held sway over the land of the Tamils. Tradition, inscriptions and ancient literature all agree in beginning the history of south India with the story of the three dynasties of the Chéras, the Chólas and the Pándyas, whose eponymous ancestors are fabled to have been three brothers who resided together at Korkai, near the mouth of the Támbraparni river in the Tinnevelly country. They are said to have eventually separated, Pándyan remaining at home, while Chéran and Chólan went forth to seek their fortunes and founded kingdoms in the north and the west respectively. Tradition, which is supported by such history as exists, states that the Chólas ruled in the country which now forms the Tanjore and Trichinopoly districts, the Chéras in Travancore, Malabar and Coimbatore, and the Pándyas in Madura and Tinnevelly.

CHAP. II.
PREHISTORIC PEOPLES.

Kistvaens, etc.

EARLY HISTORY.[1]

The Pándya dynasty.

---

[1] For assistance with this section of this Chapter I am very greatly indebted to Rai Bahádur V. Venkayya, M.A., Government Epigraphist. Mr. F. R. Hemingway, Assistant Superintendent of Gazetteer Revision, compiled most of the original draft up to the end of the Náyakkan dynasty.

The Pándya kingdom can boast a respectable antiquity and is referred to by the classical writers of Greece and Rome.[1] Megasthenes (who was sent as ambassador by Seleucus Nicator, one of Alexander the Great's successors, to the court of Chandra Gupta, king of Pátaliputra near Patna, about 302 B.C.) speaks of a country called Pandaia after the name of the only daughter of 'the Indian Hercules,' or Krishna. To this only daughter Pandaia, says Megasthenes, Krishna 'assigned that portion of India which lies to the southward and extends to the sea.' Pliny (A.D. 77) mentions the Pandae, king Pandion, and the latter's 'mediterranean emporium of Modoura.' That the Pándyas at this period occupied no mean political position is to be inferred from Dr. Caldwell's belief that it was they who sent to the Roman emperor Augustus the Indian embassy mentioned by Strabo (A.D. 20). Ptolemy (A.D. 140) mentions 'Modoura the kingdom of the Pandion.' So many Roman coins have been found in and around Madura that it has been suggested [2] that a Roman colony must once have existed there.

An interesting reference to the Pándyas is also found in an inscription of Asóka,[3] the emperor and militant evangelist of the great Buddhist Mauryan empire of the north, who came to the throne in 269 B.C. and prosecuted extensive conquests in central India. This contains the boast that 'the conquest through the sacred law extended in the south where the Chódas (Chólas) and the Pánidas (Pándyas) dwell, as far as Tamba-panini' (the Támbraparni). This 'conquest' was clearly not a subjugation by force of arms, and the phrase probably means little more than that the Pándyas and Chólas permitted the preaching of the Buddhist religion. Indeed, until the fourteenth century of the present era the Pándyas, the Chéras, and perhaps the Chólas seem to have remained unmolested by the armies of the great empires of the north which from time to time overran the neighbouring country, and their political horizon seems to have been largely limited by their wars among themselves, and their conflicts with neighbouring savage or jungle tribes and with the Singhalese.

Early Tamil literature contains many references to the Pándya dynasty and country. The late Mr. V. Kanakasabhai Pillai in

---

[1] See Bishop Caldwell's *History of Tinnevelly* (Madras, 1881), 15, 16.

[2] Sewell's *Lists of Antiquities*, i, 291 and Tufnell's *Hints to Coin-collectors* (Madras Government Press, 1889), 27–9. A *solidus* of Zeno was found in 1839 in the Tirumangalam taluk (M.J.L.S., xiii, 215) and 63 gold coins of Augustus and other emperors in a small pot in Kalayamuttúr (Palni taluk) in 1856 (M.J.L.S.. xvii, 114).

[3] *Epigraphia Indica*, ii, 471 and *Indian Antiquary*, xx, 240 ff.

his recent work *The Tamils eighteen hundred years ago* [1] gives a series of extracts from such poems as the *Puranánúru*, *Pattupáltu*, *Silappadigáram* and *Manimégalai* which not only present a unique and remarkably interesting picture of the state of art, agriculture, commerce, society and politics during the period when they were written, which Mr. Kanakasabhai places in the first and second centuries of the present era, but also contain a number of historical facts. The value of these latter is discounted by the uncertainty which must be considered to exist as to the dates of the poems [2], and consequently of the events with which they deal, but Mr. Kanakasabhai Pillai has deduced from them the following sequence of five Pándya kings, to whom he assigns the dates affixed below to each :—(1) Nedun-cheliyan I (A.D. 50–75), (2) Verri-vér-cheliyan (75–90), (3) Nedun-cheliyan II (90–128), (4) Ugra-peru-valuti (128–140) and (5) Nan-máran (140–150).

Of the first of these rulers the poems relate that he bore a title which may be taken to imply that he defeated an Áryan army and say that he died suddenly, while sitting on his throne, in the following dramatic circumstances : He had ordered his guards, says the tale, to behead a man on suspicion that he had stolen one of the queen's anklets. The man's wife appeared before him, proved her husband's innocence, and taunted the king with his hastiness. In *her* country, the land of the Chólas, she exclaimed, the kings were of different stuff : one had saved a dove's life by offering his own flesh to an eagle which pursued the bird, and another had executed his own son for driving his chariot over a calf. Stung with shame at the woman's taunts and filled with remorse for his injustice, the king fell fainting from his throne and expired shortly afterwards.

The second of the five kings ruled only a short time and was followed by his son. This latter, Nedun-cheliyan II, was a soldier of much prowess. He repelled a Chóla invasion of his kingdom and afterwards carried the war into the enemy's country and annexed one of their provinces. He was then confronted by a confederacy of the Chólas, the Chéras and five minor chieftains, but defeated them in a great battle which raged all day and in which the flower of all the troops of the Tamil country were engaged.

The fourth king, Ugra-peru-valuti, was the monarch at whose court the *Kural*, the famous sacred poem of Tiruvalluvar, was published in the presence of a brilliant assembly of 48 poets ; and

---

[1] Higginbotham & Co., Madras, 1904.

[2] For the discussion on this point and Dr. Hultzsch's opinion regarding it see *South Indian Inscriptions*, ii, pt. 3, 378.

the well-known Tamil poetess Auvaiyár composed stanzas in his honour. The poems say that he was friendly with the Chéra and Chóla kings, having been present at a sacrifice performed by one of the latter, and that he took a great fortress believed to be impregnable and called Kánappér, ' whose high walls seem to reach the sky, whose battlements gleam like the stars, the ditch surrounding which is deep and unfathomable as the sea, and the jungle beyond it so dense that the sun's rays never penetrate it.'

According to these ancient poems, the capital of the Pándyas was Nán-mádak-kúdal, ' the cluster of four towers,' which is the modern Madura. It was called ' the Northern Madura ' to distinguish it from a previous capital of the same name, in the extreme south of the Peninsula, which had been submerged by the sea.[1]　Another chief town which had shared the same fate was also on the coast and was called Kapádapuram. Even modern Madura was not always in exactly its present position. The original city seems to have been about six miles to the south-east. No vestige of it remains, but the tradition of its existence is strong and the poet Nakkíran speaks of it as being east of Tirupparankunram. It possessed four gates surmounted by high towers, outside its massive stone walls was a deep moat, and surrounding this was a thick jungle of thorny trees. Two of the ' Ten Tamil Idylls ' (the Nedunal-vádai by Nakkíran and the Madurai-kánji of Mámkudi Marutanár, abstracts of which are given in the *Christian College Magazine*, viii, 661 ff.) give most vivid descriptions of the city and its inhabitants in these early days. Korkai in Tinnevelly, which was well known to the writer of the *Periplus Maris Erythræi* (about A.D. 80) and to Ptolemy, was another important town, and the Pándya king is often referred to in ancient Tamil literature (as well as in inscriptions) as Korkaiyáli, or ' the Lord of Korkai.'

The Pándya royal emblem was a fish (that of the Chéras was a bow and of the Chólas a tiger) and it appears on their coins.[2]

---

[1] *Gleanings from ancient Tamil literature*, by the Hon. P. Coomaraswami of Ceylon.

[2] Captain Tufnell, in his *Hints to Coin-collectors in South India*, points out that Madura is a most prolific centre for ancient coins and especially for those of the Pándyas and Chólas. The best local collections have been those of the late Mr. T. M. Scott, barrister at Madura (the pick of which was presented by him to the Madras Museum) and of the Rev. J. E. Tracy of the American Mission. Papers by the latter gentleman on Pándya and Sétupati coins will be found in M.J.L.S. for 1887–88 and 1889–90 respectively, and coins in his possession have thrown much light on the chronology of the Musalman rulers of ' Ma'bar ' (the country facing Ceylon, of which Madura was the capital) between Hijra 737 and 779, who are otherwise only known to us from the narrative of Ibn Batúta (see J.A.S.B., lxiv, pt. 1, No. 1, 1895).

Their warriors wore garlands of margosa when they went to battle, in contradistinction to the chaplets of ' ar ' of the Chólas and the palmyra leaves of the Chéras.

The prevailing religion in early times in their kingdom was the Jain creed. The *Periya Puránam*, a Tamil work dealing with the lives of the 63 devotees of Siva the veracity of which has been established in several instances, says that the Pándya king Nedumáran was converted to Saivism from the Jain faith by the famous Saiva saint Tirugnána Sambandhar, who cured him of a fever upon which none of his own priests could make any impression.

Thus far does Tamil literature enlighten the darkness of the early days of the Pándyas. A wide unbridged gap follows, and it is not until the end of the sixth century of the present era that any continuous history of the line can be said to begin. Inscriptions then take up the tale.

About that time the dynasty of the Pailavas (whose capital was at Kánchi, the modern Conjeeveram) tried to extend their conquests southwards and fell foul of the Pándyas. Two of their kings, Simhavishnu and his grandson Narasimhavarman I, boast in their inscriptions that they conquered the Pándya kingdom.

Almost at once, however, pressure from this quarter was relieved by the sudden appearance of a new line of rulers who gave the Pallavas sufficient employment in the north to divert their attention from their southern neighbours. These were the Chalukyas of Bádámi, in the Bombay Presidency. By 615 A.D. they had driven the Pallavas back to the walls of Conjeeveram, and they even assert that they conquered the Chólas,[1] crossed the Cauvery, and invaded the country of the Pándyas and Chéras.[2] The latter boast is probably an empty one, since there are no traces of Chalukyan conquest in the Chóla or Pándya country at this period ; but a claim which is much more likely to have a foundation in fact, and which is of greater interest for our present purposes, is the statement of the Chalukyan king Pulakésin II (A.D. 610–34) that he induced the Pándyas, Chólas and Chéras to combine and overcome the Pallavas.[3] He had nothing to gain by recording false statements about the success of this combination, as it was due to no merit of his own.

For the next hundred years nothing certain is known of the doings of the Pándyas, but they apparently retained their

----

[1] Sewell's *Lists of Antiquities*, ii, 155.
[2] *Bombay Gazetteer* (Bombay, 1896), i, pt. 2, 188.
[3] *Ind. Ant.*, viii, 245.

CHAP. II.
EARLY
HISTORY.

independence. About 750 A.D. they again came into conflict with the Pallavas, for an inscription of Nandivarman Pallavamalla, who was probably about the last of the latter dynasty who held any real power, states that his general, Udayachandra, gained a victory over the Pándyas at ' Mannaikkudi.'[1] But as this place has not been identified it is not possible to say which of the two combatants was the aggressor.

The Ganga-
Pallavas,
ninth
century.

Shortly after this the power of the Pallavas declined, and their place was taken, though perhaps not immediately, by the Ganga-Pallavas. These latter seem, like their predecessors, to have had their capital at Conjeeveram ; and towards the end of the ninth century they extended their rulé for a few years into the north of the Chóla country.[2]

Pándya
ascendancy.

They do not, as far as is yet known, make any claims to victories over the Pándyas ; and apparently these latter were not only independent, but powerful enough to control the Chóla country as well as their own for a considerable part of the ninth century. For there are inscriptions near Tanjore,[3] in the heart of the Chóla realms, assignable to that century on palæographic grounds, which relate the acts of Pándya kings ; a record in North Arcot mentions a victory of the Pándyas over the Gangas (a Mysore dynasty who seem at this time to have been feudatories of the Ganga-Pallavas) which occurred about the middle of the same century in the very north of the Chóla country, at Tiruppirambiyam near Kumbakónam ;[4] and the Mahávamsa, the Ceylon chronicle, says that the Pándyas made an entirely unprovoked invasion of Ceylon in the time of king Séna I, who reigned from 846 to 866.

Chóla
revival, tenth
to twelfth
centuries.

Towards the latter part of this ninth century, however, the Pándyas must have been forced to retire from at any rate the north of the Chóla dominions before the advance of the Ganga-Pallavas ; and by the end of it the Chólas, who had been under a temporary eclipse, again rose to power and began to lay the foundations of an empire which continued supreme in south India, with slight interruptions, for nearly three centuries.

It would seem to have been in the reign of the Chóla king Parántaka I (about 906–16) that the Pándyas for the first time fell definitely under the Chóla yoke.[5] That monarch assumed

---

[1] *S. Ind. Inscr.*, ii, 364.

[2] Government Epigraphist's Annual Report for 1903-04, para. 12.

[3] Nos. 51 and 10 of the Government Epigraphist's collections for 1895 and 1899 respectively.

[4] *S. Ind., Inscr.* ii, 381.

[5] *Ep. Ind.*, v, 42 and *S. Ind. Inscr.*, ii, 379.

the title of ' conqueror of Madura,' his inscriptions range from
Suchindram near Cape Comorin to Kálahasti in North Arcot, and
he also invaded Ceylon.

A chance of a bid for freedom was afforded the Pándyas
in 949 by the crushing defeat of the Chólas in that year near
Arkónam by the Ráshtrakútas of Málkhéd (in what is now the
Nizam's Dominions) who now occupied the country formerly held
by the Chalukyas of Bádámi. The Pándyas seem to have rebelled
successfully, and their ruler Vira-Pándya defeated the Chóla king
Áditya Karikála and assumed the title of ' he who took the head
of the Chóla.' But later they again succumbed, for the Chóla
king Rájarája I (985-1013) claims to have ' taken away their
splendour,' and the substantial foundation which existed for his
boast and the complete subjection of the Pándya country are
evidenced by the immense number of Chóla inscriptions which
occur in the Madura and Tinnevelly districts, by the very
large number of copper coins of Rájarája which are even now
found in the former of these,[1] and by the fact that the name of
the old Pándya capital of Korkai was changed to the Chóla term
Chóléndrasimha-chaturvédimangalam and that of the Pándya
country itself to Rájarája-Pándi-nádu.[2] The Pándya realms
became, in fact, a province of the Chóla empire.

The position of this empire at this period is a matter which
belongs rather to the history of Tanjore and Trichinopoly[3] than
to that of Madura, and it is not necessary to refer to it here in
any detail. Rájarája extended his rule throughout the Madras
Presidency and in some directions even beyond it : on the west his
sway reached as far as Quilon and Coorg ; on the north-east
to the borders of Orissa ; and his conquests included Ceylon and
the ' twelve thousand ancient islands of the sea.' Parts of
Burma and the Malay Archipelago were added to these dominions by his immediate successors. Their conquests were least
secure in the north-west, and their most formidable rivals at this
period were the Western Chálukyas, a branch of the Chalukyas
of Bádámi above referred to, who had ousted the Ráshtrakútas of Málkhéd and returned to power with their capital at
Kalyáni, in what is now Haidarabad territory.

At first, in the reigns of Rájarája (985-1013) and his succes- Pándya
rebellions.
sor Rájéndra Chóla I (1011-33), the Pándyas appear to have
borne the Chóla yoke quietly enough.

[1] Capt. Tufnell's *Hints to Coin-collectors*, 11.
[2] Government Epigraphist's Annual Report for 1903-04, para. 20.
[3] See Chapter II in the *Gazetteers* of these districts.

During the rule of Rájádhirája I (1018–53), however, trouble began, the Pándyas, the Chéras and the Singhalese uniting to throw off the Chóla yoke. The revolt was sternly suppressed. The Singhalese king was killed in battle, the Chéra ruler captured and put to death, and the Pándya chief driven to headlong flight. The victor's inscription commemorating his triumph[1] says that—

'Of the three allied kings of the south he cut off on the battle-field the beautiful head of Mánábharanan adorned with great gems and a golden crown; captured in fight Víra-Kéralan of the wide ankle-rings, and was pleased to have him trampled to death by his furious elephant Attivárana; and drove to the ancient river Mullaiyár[2] Sundara Pándya of great and undying fame, who lost in the stress of battle his royal white parasol, his fly-whisks of white yak's hair and his throne, and fled, leaving his crown behind him, with dishevelled locks and weary feet.'

The records of the next Chóla king, Rájéndra-Déva (1052–63), do not refer to any trouble with the Pándyas, but his successor, Vira-Rájéndra I (1062–70) had to put down a fresh rebellion of theirs. He captured the Pándya chief and caused him to be 'trampled to death by a furious *mast* elephant,[3]' and he gave the Pándya country to his son Gangai-konda-Chóla, who took the title of Chóla-Pándya.[4]

The death of this Vira-Rájéndra was followed by a fierce domestic contest for the Chóla crown,[5] and it was not apparently till about 1074 that the next king, the great Kulóttunga I, who reigned till 1119, succeeded in establishing himself firmly on the throne. His hands must have been too full during these four years to allow him to keep a proper hold upon the outlying portions of his empire, and a great part of them fell into disorder. Ceylon appears to have cut itself adrift and the Pándyas and the Chéras again united in rebellion. They were again suppressed. An inscription of the fourteenth year of Kulóttunga records that he put the 'five Pándyas' to flight and subdued the Gulf of Manaar, 'the Podiyil mountain' (Agastyamalai in Tinnevelly), Cape Comorin and Kottáru (now in Travancore), the last of which places he took by storm. He limited the boundaries of the Pándya country and placed garrisons at Kottáru and other strategically important places within it.[6]

---

[1] *S. Ind. Inscr.*, iii, 56.

[2] Not identified.

[3] *S. Ind. Inscr.*, iii, 37.

[4] There is, however, evidence to show that the title is earlier than this, and its origin is not wholly clear.

[5] See Chapter II of the Tanjore and Trichinopoly *Gazetteers*.

[6] See the Government Epigraphist's Annual Report for 1900–01, p. 9.

Kings of the Chóla-Pándya line above mentioned seem to have gone on ruling the Pándya country till somewhere about 1136, but the history of both the Chólas and the Pándyas in the next 35 years is at present obscure. During that period the dominions of the former seem to have been considerably curtailed, but it is not possible to say exactly what was their position in the Pándya country. When at length (in the reign of the Chóla king Rájádhirája II, about 1171–72) inscriptions again begin to throw light upon the relations of the two peoples, a struggle for the Pándya throne is found to be proceeding between two Pándya princes who seem to have nothing to do with the Chóla-Pándya line, and the kings of the Chólas and of Ceylon are taking opposite sides in the quarrel. What had happened in the meantime to the Chóla-Pándya dynasty it is impossible to say.

The two rival claimants to the Pándya crown were Parákrama-Pándya and Kulasékhara-Pándya. How they were related, or how the strife arose, is not clear. Chapters 76 and 77 of the Singhalese chronicle Mahávamsa give, however, a fairly detailed, though doubtless one-sided, account of the campaign.[1]

Parákrama was besieged by Kulasékhara in his capital (Madura) and appealed for help to the king of Ceylon. The latter despatched his general Lankápura-Dandanátha with orders to suppress Kulasékhara and establish Parákrama on the throne; but before the Singhalese army could embark, Kulasékhara had captured Madura and put his rival, with his queen and some of his children, to death. Lankápura was ordered by his master to proceed none the less, to recover the Pándya realms, and to hand them over to some relative of the murdered king. He landed in India accordingly, and for some time his troops carried everything before them. He sent for Vira-Pándya, the youngest son of the dead Parákrama (who had escaped when Madura fell), and set him up as claimant for the throne. Subsequently, with the aid of reinforcements from Ceylon, he inflicted such crushing defeats upon Kulasékhara that the latter fled to ' Tondamana,' which is perhaps the Pudukkóttai country, and the Singhalese troops occupied Madura town.

It was at this stage that the Chólas seem to have first given Kulasékhara their support. With their help a stand was made at ' Pon-Amarávati,' a place not yet identified, but the Singhalese

Pándya
renaissance,
twelfth
century.

Struggle for
the throne.

---

[1] Government Epigraphist's Report for 1898–99, paras. 23 ff.

were once more victorious and a space of three leagues was covered with the corpses of the vanquished. Lankápura returned in triumph to Madura, placed Víra-Pándya on the throne and celebrated the event with a great festival.

Supported by the ruler of Tondamana and certain other Chóla chiefs, Kulasékhara again took the field, but was again defeated, this time at Palamcottah, and fled for refuge to the Chóla country. The Chóla king then assisted him with a large army, but he was yet again vanquished, and the Ceylon troops advanced northwards and even burnt some villages in the Tanjore country. After one more victory over the Pándya and Chóla troops the Singhalese returned to Ceylon, leaving Vira-Pándya in possession of his kingdom.

The war did not end there, however. Inscriptions of the Chóla king Kulóttunga III show that that ruler subsequently supported Kulasékhara's successor Vikrama-Pándya in an effort against Víra-Pándya and his son, defeated the Marava army, drove the Simhala (Singhalese) forces into the sea, captured Madura, made over the Pándya crown to his protegé Vikrama, and assumed the title of 'conqueror of Madura and Ceylon.'

These stirring events occurred somewhere about the end of the twelfth century. Early in the thirteenth, the power of the Chólas began to decline. It was during the reign of Kájarája III of that dynasty (1216 to about 1239) that the first fatal blows were received. This king's feudatories revolted on all sides, and one of them, Kópperunjinga, a prince of some power in Tondaimandalam, the present South Arcot, actually had the impudence to kidnap his suzerain (1230–31) and refuse to release him.[1] The unfortunate Rájarája was only rescued by the intervention of the Hoysala Ballálas, a newly-risen dynasty which had recently subverted the Western Chálukyas of Kalyáni and established their capital at Halébíd in Mysore.

The Chóla demoralisation was the Pándyas' opportunity, and they were not slow to avail themselves of it. From this time forth they occupied the throne of Madura in a regular succession, and from astronomical details appearing in inscriptions and supplied by the Government Epigraphist, Professor Kielhorn has fixed the dates of the following of their rulers—the latter year in each case being, not necessarily the last of the king's reign,

---

[1] For details of this exploit, see *South Arcot Gazetteer*, 33.

but the latest date as yet discovered which contains details admitting of verification :—

1. Jatávarman Kulasékhara, 1190–1214.
2. Máravarman Sundara-Pándya I, 1216–35.
3. Máravarman Sundara-Pándya II, 1238–51.
4. Jatávarman Sundara-Pándya I, 1251–61.
5. Víra-Pándya, 1252–67.
6. Máravarman Kulasékhara I, 1268–1308.
7. Jatávarman Sundara-Pándya II, 1275–90.
8. Máravarman Kulasékhara II, 1314–21.
9. Máravarman Parákrama-Pándya, 1334–52.
10. Jatávarman Parákrama-Pándya, 1357–72.
11. Jatilavarman Parákrama-Pándya Arikésaridéva, 1422–61.
12. Jatilavarman Parákrama-Pándya Kulasékhara, 1479–99.
13. Jatilavarman Srívallabha, 1534–37.
14. Máravarman Sundara-Pándya III, 1531–55.
15. Jatilavarman Srívakabha Ativíraráma, 1562–67.

The second of these rulers, Máravarman Sundara-Pándya I, who came to the throne in 1216, invaded the country of the old enemies of his line and captured Tanjore and Uraiyúr, a suburb of Trichinopoly and a former Chóla capital. He boasts that he made himself master of the Chóla realms and in the end graciously returned them as a gift to their owner; [1] and that this was not altogether mere bombast is shown by the frequency of his inscriptions in the Tanjore and Trichinopoly districts [2] and by the fact that his coins bear the title ' he who conquered the Chóla country.'

Máravarman
Sundara-
Pándya I,
1216-35.

But the collapse of the Chólas brought the Pándyas into touch with the Hoysalas, who about this time established themselves near Srirangam in the Trichinopoly district in a new town which the Hoysala king ' had built in order to amuse his mind in the Chóla country, which he had conquered by the power of his arm.' As early as 1222 these Hoysalas were stated to be ' marching against Ranga (*i.e.*, Srirangam) in the south,' and to have ' cleft open the rock that was the Pándya,' and their king assumed the title of ' the establisher of the Chóla kingdom.' Whether he actually came into conflict with the Pándyas it is impossible to say ; but the latter seem to have left the Chóla country, and do not appear to have again interfered with it for some thirty years.

Arrival of the
Hoysalas.

[1] Government Epigraphist's Annual Report for 1899–1900, para. 12.
[2] *Ep. Ind.*, **vi**, 303 ff.

CHAP. II.
EARLY
HISTORY.

Jatávarman
Sundara-
Pándya I,
1251-61.

Of the third of the Pándya kings in the above list, Máravarman Sundara-Pándya II (1238–51), very little is known; but
his successor, Jatávarman Sundara-Pándya I (1251–61), was a
mighty conqueror. He invaded Ceylon, carried off a great booty,
including the celebrated tooth-relic, and assumed in consequence
the title of ' a second Ráma in plundering the island of Lanka ;[1]'
he covered the Srirangam temple with gold; came into conflict
with the rapidly growing power of the Kákatíya kings of Waran-
gal in Haidarabad; extended his conquests as far as Nellore,
where he had himself 'anointed as a hero;' and defeated the
Hoysala king Sómésvara.

End of the
Hoysala and
Chóla power.

The Hoysalas had also been previously worsted about this
time by the Chólas under Rájéndra-Chóla III (1246 to about
1267), who assumed the title of ' the hostile rod of death to
his uncle Sómésvara,' but they appear at Srirangam again in
1256, and their inscriptions and those of the Pándyas overlap and
alternate in the Trichinopoly district in a puzzling manner until
the end of the thirteenth century. The inference is that they
were not permanently weakened by the blows dealt them by the
Chólas and the Pándyas, but continued for some years as the
effective rivals of the latter in that part of the country.

Nor, apparently, were the Chólas at once reduced to an
absolutely subordinate position. Though the Pándyas had penetrated into their territory as far as Nellore before 1261, Rájéndra-
Chóla III seems to have retained some form of independence till
as late as 1267. It was the last flicker of their dying power.
After 1267 they seem to have dropped out of the race; and that
part of their country which was not held by the Hoysalas was
occupied by the Pándyas.

Máravarman
Kulasékhara
I (1268–1308)
and his suc·
cessor.

The sixth and seventh of the Pándya rulers in the list above,
Máravarman Kulasékhara I and Jatávarman Sundara-Pándya II,
were kings of considerable power and are both known to history—
the former as the ' Kalés Déwar ' of Muhammadan historians and
the latter as the ' Sender Bandi ' of Marco Polo.

As will be seen from the overlapping of the dates of the reigns
of these and others of the kings in the list, the chief power in the
Pándya realms was apparently often held jointly by several
members of the ruling family. The Mahávamsa says that the
expedition against Ceylon above mentioned was sent by ' the five
brethren who governed the Pándya kingdom ' and Marco Polo
also alludes to the ' five brothers.' More than one reference,

[1] The Mahávamsa, however, puts this invasion at a later date.

however, shows that one member of ¦the five was always held superior to the others.

Marco Polo, and the Muhammadan, Chinese and Singhalese chronicles, and also the other authorities on the state of the Pándya realm at the end of the thirteenth and the beginning of the fourteenth centuries [1] all agree in extolling its wealth and magnificence. It stretched along the coast from Quilon to Nellore; it was called (according to Marco Polo) 'the greater India;' was the best of all the Indies and indeed 'the finest and noblest province in the world;' its rulers sent an embassy, which is described in the Chinese annals, to the Mongol emperor Kublai Khán in 1286; were on terms of friendliness with the Muhammadans who now begin to interfere in the affairs of southern India; and employed Muhammadan ministers—who, by the way, rose to great influence and wealth. Their chief city was still Madura, but Marco Polo describes with admiration, as a place of great commercial importance, the town of Old Káyal, about a mile and a half from the mouth of the Támbraparni and in the present Tinnevelly district. This seems to have been the centre of a (for those days) very large sea-borne trade which the Pándya kings actively encouraged and which made them widely known. Marco Polo says that all the ships from¦the west touched at Káyal, and the contemporary Persian historian Wassaf states in a flowery passage that all the products of India and China were constantly arriving there, and that all the splendour of the west was derived from the Pándya realm 'which is so situated as to be the key of Hind.'

Early in the fourteenth century a dispute arose about the succession to the Pándya throne and one of the claimants appealed for help to the emperor Allá-ud-dín of Delhi. Perhaps in consequence, followed the great invasion of the south of India by Malik Káfur, the famous general of that monarch, which took place in 1310 and caused the most momentous changes in the political configuration of central and southern India. Having swept away the power of the rulers of the Deccan, Malik Káfur marched on triumphantly into the Carnatic, sacked Madura, and made his way, it is said, as far as Rámésvaram, where he founded a mosque.[2]

Mr. Nelson [3] gives a description, founded on native manuscripts, of the excesses of his troops in Madura town. Life and

CHAP. II.

EARLY
HISTORY.

Splendour of
the Pándya
realm.

MUSALMAN
INVASION,
1310.

---

[1] See Caldwell's *History of Tinnevelly*, 32 ff. and ¦his *Grammar of the Dravidian languages* (London, 1875), 535 ff.

[2] Elphinstone's *History of India* (London, 1857), 340.

[3] *The Madura country*, pt. 3, 81.

property were unsafe, trade and commerce were paralysed, private liberty was so much at an end that one Hindu dared not even converse with another in the street, public worship was suppressed, and the great temple was almost razed to the ground. Its outer wall, with its fourteen towers, was pulled down ; the streets and buildings which it protected were destroyed ; and nothing was left of it but the two shrines of Sundarésvara and Mínákshi and the buildings which immediately surrounded them. Even these apparently owed their escape less to any reverence for them in the victor's breasts than to the outbreak of private dissensions among these Vandals.

Malik Káfur returned almost at once to his own country, but the Pándyas seem to have been prostrated by the invasion. Never again, indeed, did they possess any considerable independent power ; though their kings continued to rule in a spasmodic fashion, with varying authority and over dominions of varying size, for the next two and a half centuries. It is eloquent evidence of the completeness of their collapse that a king of the Chéras, a nation long sunk out of all importance in Indian politics, was able to march right across the peninsula, defeat their ruler, have himself crowned at Madura, and make his way in 1313 to Conjeeveram.[1]

This Chéra occupation of the country must, however, have been very transitory, for a Musalman dynasty was very shortly afterwards established at Madura which existed for about the next 48 years and ruled that district (with Trichinopoly and perhaps South Arcot) first as feudatories of the Delhi emperor and subsequently as independent monarchs. Mr. Nelson[2] gives a traditional list of its kings, eight in number.

It was overthrown about 1365[3] by the power of the new Hindu kingdom of Vijayanagar,[4] which had been founded at Hampe in the Bellary district in 1335 and for the next two centuries stemmed the tide of Muhammadan invasion from the north. Kampana Udaiyár, a prince of this line, drove the Musalmans out of Madura and set up there a little dynasty of his own which was presumably and apparently subordinate to the court of Vijayanagar.

---

[1] *Ep. Ind.*, iv, 146.

[2] Pt. 3, 81.

[3] *Ep. Ind.*, vi, 324.

[4] For the history of this power, see *A Forgotten Empire (Vijayanagar)*, by Mr. R. Sewell, late I.C.S., Swan Sonnenschein, 1900.

Mr. Nelson's authorities [1] give a vivid description of the instantaneous effect in Madura of this victory :—

' Within a few days the temples of Siva and Vishnu had been everywhere re-opened; worship was performed once more with extraordinary solemnity and fervour : and that nothing might be wanting to restore confidence and energy to all classes of men, the Bráhmans contrived a great miracle significant of the pleasure of the god and of his perpetual regard for his faithful worshippers. Kampana was taken on an appointed day to witness the re-opening of the great Pagoda, and on his entering and approaching the shrine for the purpose of looking upon the face of the god, lo! and behold! everything was in precisely the same condition as when the temple was first shut up just forty-eight years previously. The lamp that was lighted on that day was still burning; and the sandal-wood powder, the garland of flowers and the ornaments usually placed before the idol on the morning of a festival day were now found to be exactly as it is usual to find them on the evening of such a day.'

The list of the Pándya kings already given shows that not only during the Musalman occupation, but also throughout the rule of Kampana Udaiyár and his successors, and even, see below, through the time of the later Náyakkan dynasty and down to the overthrow of the Vijayanagar kingdom in 1565, Pándya chiefs remained always in authority in Madura. Dr. Caldwell [2] considers that they probably at first assisted the Vijayanagar forces to expel the Musalmans, and that thereafter they continued in subordination to the power of Vijayanagar. He says that—

Its effects.

' Throughout the greater number of the reigns of these Pándya kings of the later line (that is, those who ruled after the expulsion of the Musalmans), the kings of Vijayanagar appear to have exercised supreme authority, but I think it may be assumed that they did not interfere much in the internal affairs of the country, and that they contented themselves with receiving tribute and occasionally military help.'

Kampana Udaiyár's dynasty only lasted (if we are to credit the vernacular manuscripts on which Mr. Nelson has based his account of them) down to about 1404, and thereafter the administration of the country—subject, no doubt, to the suzerainty of the kings of Vijayanagar—continued for many years in the hands of a number of chieftains, of whom the greater number bore Telugu names and titles (such as Náyakkan) and were apparently the nominees of the suzerain.[3]

---

[1] Pt. 3, 82.

[2] *History of Tinnevelly*, 52.

[3] Their names appear in Mr. Nelson's *Madura Country*, pt. 3, 82 ff. and Mr. Sewell's *Lists of Antiquities*, ii, 223.

The earliest Vijayanagar inscription (other than those of Kampana Udaiyár) as yet discovered in the Pándya country is one of the time of king Déva Ráya II of that line and is dated 1438–39. King Krishna Ráya (1509–30), the greatest of the dynasty, perhaps exercised a closer control over this part of his possessions. Little of note appears, however, to have taken place there until the second quarter of the sixteenth century.

About 1532, however, stirring events occurred. The king of Travancore became aggressive, overran a large part of the Pándya country, and defied the authority of Vijayanagar. To reduce him to submission, and also to defend the Pándya king from the encroachments of two Telugu chieftains (perhaps local governors sent from Vijayanagar who had endeavoured to assume independence) Achyuta, king of Vijayanagar from 1530 to 1542, organised a great expedition into the extreme south of India.

If we are to trust his own inscriptions,[1] he was eminently successful in the campaign. He planted a pillar of victory in the Támbraparni river, exacted tribute from the king of Travancore, suppressed the two troublesome chieftains and married the daughter of the Pándya king. Thenceforth the Pándya country was held more firmly and directly by the representatives of the Vijayanagar empire. The native chronicles, indeed, continue to confuse the authority of these suzerains, their Telugu governors, and the Pándya rulers, treating each in turn as though they were supreme, but there is evidence [2] to show that between 1547 and 1558 the Madura country was in fact ruled by one Vitthala Rája, who was a prince of the Vijayanagar line and invaded Travancore a second time in 1543.

In 1559 was founded the famous Náyakkan dynasty of Madura, which held the country for nearly two centuries until the Musalmans took it in 1736. The origin and early doings of this line are recounted neither in inscriptions nor in really reliable histories, and for light upon both we are driven to depend mainly upon the vernacular manuscripts in the three volumes of the Rev. W. Taylor's *Catalogue Raisonné of Oriental MSS.* (Madras, 1857), in the same author's *Oriental Historical MSS.* (Madras, 1835) and in the collections of manuscripts by Colonel Mackenzie which are now in the Connemara Library. These (in the judgment of so eminent an authority as Bishop Caldwell) are of very doubtful veracity, but happily they are frequently illumined by the letters and periodical reports of the priests of

---

[1] See Government Epigraphist's Annual Report for 1899–1900, paras. 70 ff.

[2] *Ibid.*, para. 78, and Sewell's *Lists of Antiquities*, ii, 224.

the well-known Jesuit Mission at Madura[1], which (though unfortunately incomplete) have been collected and published in four volumes under the title of *La Mission du Maduré*. Mr. Nelson has collated all these authorities with much care in his book, and the ensuing narrative follows closely (though, owing to the exigencies of space, very briefly) his account of this period.

It seems, then, that at about the close of Vitthala Rája's administration the then Chóla ruler invaded the Madura country and dispossessed the Pándya king. Whereupon the latter appealed to the court of Vijayanagar and an expedition under a certain Nágama Náyakkan was accordingly sent to his aid. Nágama easily suppressed the Chóla king and possessed himself of Madura, but he then suddenly threw off his allegiance and, declining to help the Pándya, assumed the position of an independent ruler. The Vijayanagar emperor was furious at his defection, summoned a council, laid the matter before his most faithful officers, and cried out to the assemblage ' Where amongst you all is he who will bring me that rebel's head? ' To the astonishment of every one present, Nágama's own son, Visvanátha, volunteered to do so, and after some natural hesitation the king despatched him with a large force against the rebel. Visvanátha defeated his father in a pitched battle, placed him in confinement, and at length procured for him the unconditional pardon which had doubtless been from the first the object of his action.

He so far obeyed the orders of the Vijayanagar king as nominally to place the Pándya on the throne, but sound policy and his own interests alike deterred him from handing over the entire government of the country to the old feeble dynasty, and he set out to rule on his own account. This was in 1559. Doubtless he held a wide commission as governor from the Vijayanagar court, and perhaps there was little difference between the powers he exercised and those wielded, for example, by Vitthala Rája. But the peculiar characteristic of the new régime was that, whether by accident or design, it developed first into a governorship which became hereditary and then into what was practically an hereditary monarchy. The Náyakkans never, it is true, assumed the insignia or titles of royalty, and were content with the position of lieutenants under Vijayanagar even after they had ceased to pay tribute to that power ; but in essentials their sway was practically absolute and the Pándyas disappear in effect henceforth from history.

Its origin.

___

[1] See Chapter III, p. 75, below.

Visvanátha, then, became the first of the Náyakkan dynasty. The names and dates of its rulers may be conveniently given in tabular form here at once.   They were —

Visvanátha	1559
Kumára Krishnappa	1563
Krishnappa, *alias* Periya Vírappa .. ..⎫ Visvanátha II .. ..⎭	1573
Lingayya *alias* Kumára Krishnappa Visvappa *alias* Visvanátha III	1595
Muttu Krishnappa	1602
Muttu Vírappa	1609
Tirumala	1623
Muttu Alakádri *alias* Muttu Vírappa	1659
Chokkanátha *alias* Chokkalinga	1662
Ranga Krishna Muttu Vírappa	1682
Mangammál (Queen-Regent)	1689
Vijaya Ranga Chokkanátha	1704
Mínákshi (Queen-Regent) .. .. ..1731—	36

Visvanátha is said to have immediately set himself to strengthen his capital and improve the administration of his dominions. He demolished the Pándya rampart and ditch which at that time surrounded merely the walls of the great temple, and erected in their place an extensive double-walled fortress defended by 72 bastions ;[1] and he led channels from the upper waters of the Vaigai—perhaps the Peranai and Chittanai [2] dams owe their origin to him— to water the country, founding villages in the tracts commanded by them.

In his administrative improvements he was ably seconded by his prime minister Árya Náyakka Mudali (or, as he is still commonly called, Árya Nátha,, a man born of peasant Vellála parents. who had won his way by sheer ability to a high position in the Vijayanagar court.   This officer is supposed to have been the founder of ‘ the poligar system, ’ under which the Madura country was apportioned among 72 chieftains—some of them local men and others Telugu leaders of the detachments which had accompanied Visvanátha from Vijayanagar—who were each placed in charge of one of the 72 bastions of the new Madura fortifications, were responsible for the immediate control of their estates, paid a fixed tribute to the Náyakkans, and kept up a certain quota of troops ready for immediate service. Unless their family traditions are uniformly false, these men did much for the country in those days, founding villages, building dams, constructing tanks and

---

[1] See p. 265 and the map attached.
[2] See pp. 124, 125 and 128.

erecting temples. Many of them bore the title of Náyakkan, and hence the commonness of '-náyakkanúr' as a termination to the names of places in this district. They also brought with them the gods of the Deccan, and thus we find in Madura many shrines to Ahóbilam and other deities who are rarely worshipped in the Tamil country. Their successors, the present zamindars of the district, still look upon Árya Nátha as a sort of patron saint.

This man is also credited with having constructed the great thousand-pillared mantapam in the Madura temple, and he is still kept in mind by the equestrian statue of him which flanks one side of the entrance of this, and is even now periodically crowned with garlands by the hero-worshippers of to-day. He lived till 1600 and had great influence upon the fate of the Náyakkan dynasty until his death.

Visvanátha also added the fort of Trichinopoly to his possessions. The Vijayanagar viceroy who governed the Tanjore country had failed to properly police the pilgrim roads which ran through Trichinopoly to the shrines at Srirangam and Rámésvaram, and devotees were afraid to visit those holy places. Visvanátha accordingly arranged to exchange that town for the fort of Vallam (in Tanjore), which was his at that time. He is said to have then vastly improved the fortifications and town of Trichinopoly and the temple of Srirangam, and to have cleared the banks of the Cauvery of robbers.

He had some difficulty with 'the five Pándyas,' who resisted the introduction of his authority into Tinnevelly, but he vanquished them at length (in circumstances set out with much poetic detail in the manuscripts) and then greatly improved the town and district of Tinnevelly. He is also credited with an expedition to subdue a local chieftain at Kambam (in the l'eriyakulam taluk) near the Travancore border.

Visvanátha died full of years and honour in 1563. His name is still affectionately remembered as that of a great benefactor of his country.

He was succeeded by his son Kumára Krishnappa (1563–73), who is represented as a brave and politic ruler. A revolt occurred among the poligars during his reign, but its leader, Tumbichi Náyakkan, was captured while holding the fort of Paramagudi in the Ramnad zamindari, and was beheaded; and the trouble was quenched. Krishnappa is also declared to have conquered Ceylon—an exploit of which heroic details are given in the manuscripts, but of which, in view of the silence of the usually candid annals of that island, the very existence may well be doubted.

He was succeeded in 1573 by his two sons, who ruled jointly and uneventfully till 1595; and they by their two sons, one of whom ruled till 1602.

These were followed by Muttu Krishnappa (1602–09). He is credited with the foundation of the dynasty of the Sétupatis of Ramnad, the ancestors of the present Rája of that place, who were given a considerable slice of territory in the Marava country on condition that they suppressed crime and protected pilgrims journeying to Rámésvaram through that wild and inhospitable region. Mr. Nelson's book (Pt. 3, 109–14 and elsewhere) deals at length with this transaction and other events in the history of the Sétupatis, but these relate to the Ramnad zamindari and the present volume is not concerned with them.

Muttu Krishnappa was succeeded by Muttu Vírappa (1609–23), a hardly more distinct figure.

Fall of
Vijayanagar
kingdom,
1565.

Meanwhile, in 1565, the power of the rulers of Vijayanagar, the suzerains of the Náyakkans, had been dealt an irreparable blow by the combined Musalman kings of the Deccan at the memorable battle of Talikóta, one of the great landmarks in the history of south India. They were forced to abandon a large part of the districts of Bellary and Anantapur to the victorious Muhammadans, to flee hastily from Vijayanagar, and to establish their capital successively at Penukonda in Anantapur and at Chandragiri and Vellore in North Arcot. Their governors at Madura and Tanjore still paid them the usual tribute and marks of respect, but in the years which now follow traces begin to appear of the weakness of the suzerain, and of contempt and finally rebellion on the part of his feudatories.

Tirumala
Náyakkan,
1623-59.

Muttu Vírappa mentioned above was succeeded by the great Tirumala Náyakkan, the most powerful and the best known of his dynasty, who ruled for thirty-six eventful years.[1] He was called upon to play his part in much more stirring times than his predecessors. The peace imposed upon the south by the sway of Vijayanagar had been dissolved by the downfall of that power, and the Pándya country was torn by the mutual quarrels of the once feudatory governors ('Náyakkans') of Madura, Tanjore, Gingee and Mysore; by the unavailing attempts of the last rulers of the dying empire to reassert their failing authority; and finally by the incursions of the Muhammadan kings of the Deccan, who now began to press southwards to reap the real fruits of their victory at Talikóta. An added trouble lay in the

---

[1] For an inscription giving his genealogy, see *Ep. Ind.*, iii, 289.

insubordination of the Sétupatis of Ramnad, who took advantage of the embarrassments of the rulers of Madura to disobey their commands and 'finally to assume independence. The last-named danger was not experienced by Tirumala himself, but was reserved to perplex his successors.

CHAP. II.
NÁYAKKAN
DYNASTY.

Almost the first act of his reign was to withhold the tribute due to the king of Vijayanagar. The letters of the Jesuit priests already mentioned showed that he anticipated trouble in consequence, and accordingly massed large bodies of troops in Trichinopoly and strengthened its fortifications. He none the less still sent annual complimentary messages and presents to his suzerain, and this sufficed for some time to appease the resentment of the incapable representatives of that ancient line. But about 1638 king Ranga, a more resolute prince, succeeded to the throne of Chandragiri; and he soon resolved to put an end to the contumacy of Tirumala and prepared to march south with a large and formidable force. Tirumala had meanwhile persuaded the Vijayanagar governors of Tanjore and Gingee (in South Arcot) to join him in his defiance of their mutual suzerain, and thus Ranga was left with only Mysore, of all his tributaries, to support him. He however continued his preparations, with the result that the governor of Tanjore eventually grew alarmed, sent in his submission, and betrayed the designs of the confederates.

He defies
Vijayanagar.

Ranga advanced upon Gingee, but his plans were frustrated by a desperate move on the part of Tirumala, who, reckless of the claims of a larger patriotism, succeeded in inducing the Muhammadan Sultan of Golconda (one of the confederacy who had been victorious at Talikóta in 1565) to invade the Vijayanagar kingdom from the north.

Calls the
Muham-
madans to
his aid,

Ranga was obliged to retrace his steps to protect his possessions, was defeated by Golconda, and was forced to march south again to implore the help of his rebellious governors against their common foe, the Musalman. They refused, however, to aid him; and in the end Ranga fled, powerless and almost without a friend, to the protection of his only faithful vassal, the viceroy of Mysore.

The Sultan of Golconda was satisfied for some time to consolidate his conquests in the north of the Vijayanagar country, but shortly afterwards (perhaps about 1644) he marched south to subdue its three rebellious governors and advanced upon the great fortress of Gingee. The Náyakkan of Tanjore at once submitted to him, but Tirumala approached a rival Muhammadan, the Sultan of

And becomes their feudatory.

His wars with Mysore.

Bijápur, who sent a force to his assistance. These allies marched to the relief of Gingee, but hardly had they arrived there when the Bijápur troops went over to the enemy, and joined in the siege of the fort they had been sent to deliver. The Golconda king, however, was soon recalled by trouble in other parts of his new conquests, and Tirumala threw himself into the Gingee fortress. Owing to dissensions between his troops and those of the former garrison, however, the gates were opened not long afterwards to the troops of Bijápur and the town fell into the possession of the Musalmans.

Tirumala retreated in dismay to Madura, and the Muhammadans advanced triumphantly southwards, exacted submission from the governor of Tanjore, and proceeded to lay waste the Madura country. Tirumala then submitted, apparently without striking a blow, paid a large sum to the invaders, and agreed to send an annual tribute to the Sultan of Bijápur. Thus, after an interval of nearly 300 years, the Muhammadans were once again recognised as supreme in the district.

Tirumala's next conflict was with Mysore. In the early years of his reign, before his troubles with the king of Vijayanagar and the Muhammadans, he had been involved in a short war with that kingdom. His territories had been invaded by the Mysore troops and Dindigul had been besieged, but the enemy had been eventually driven out and their country successfully invaded in revenge by a general of Tirumala's. Since then, as already noted, the Vijayanagar ruler had taken refuge with the king of Mysore, and now these two monarchs combined to endeavour to recover those portions of the former's territories which had recently been captured by Golconda. They were at first successful; but, whether actuated by jealousy or fear, Tirumala intervened and invited the Muhammadans to attack Mysore from the south, throwing open the passes in his own country for the purpose.

His proposal was accepted, Mysore was invaded, and a general war ensued which resulted in the final extinction of the power of Vijayanagar and the humbling of Mysore. But when returning in triumph from that country, the victorious Muhammadans came down to Madura and levied an enormous tribute from their humble friend Tirumala; and, moving on to Tanjore, treated its Náyakkan in a like manner. So Tirumala profited little from this new treachery to the cause of Hinduism.

It is not clear exactly when these events happened, but they appear to constitute the last interference of the Muhammadans in Madura affairs. Tirumala's only other external war occurred towards the close of his reign and was with Mysore. In this he is represented to have been altogether successful.

The campaign began with an invasion of Coimbatore by the Mysore king—apparently in revenge for Tirumala's contribution to his recent humiliation at the hands of the Muhammadans. That district was occupied by the enemy with ease, and then Madura itself was threatened. The Mysore troops were however beaten off from the town (chiefly by the loyal assistance of the Sétupati of Ramnad) defeated again in the open, and driven in disorder up the ghâts into Mysore. The campaign was known as the ' hunt for noses ' owing to the fact that under the orders of the Mysore king the invaders cut off the noses of all their prisoners (men, women and children) and sent them in sacks to Seringa-patam as glorious trophies.

A counter invasion of Mysore was undertaken shortly after-wards under the command of Kumára Muttu, the younger brother of Tirumala, and was crowned with complete success. The king of Mysore was captured and his nose was cut off and sent to Madura.

Tirumala died before his victorious brother's return. He was between sixty-five and seventy years of age at the time and had reigned for thirty-six eventful years.

His territories at his death comprised the present districts of Madura (including the zamindaris of Ramnad and Sivaganga), Tinnevelly, Coimbatore, Salem and Trichinopoly, with Puduk-kóttai and part of Travancore. Native tradition is persistent in declaring that he met his death by violence. Several stories are current, but two of them are more widely repeated than the others. The first of these says that he so nearly became converted to Christianity that he stopped his expenditure on the temples of the Hindu gods. This roused the Bráhmans, and some of them, headed by a Bhattan (officiating priest of the great temple), enticed him to the temple under the pretence that they had found a great hidden treasure in a vault there, induced him to enter the vault and then shut down its stone trap-door upon him, and gave out that the goddess Mínákshi had translated her favourite to heaven. The second story avers that he had an intrigue with the wife of a Bhattan and that, as he was returning from visiting her one dark night he fell into a well and was killed. The Bhattan was so scared when he found what had happened that he at once filled in the well, but afterwards told the Bráhmans what he had done.

Tirumala's character is summed up, probably with justice, in a letter written by one of the Jesuit priests just after his death and dated Trichinopoly, 1659—

' It is impossible to refuse him credit for great qualities, but he tarnished his glory at the end of his life by follies and vices which nothing could justify. He was called to render account to God for the evils which his political treachery had brought upon his own people and the neighbouring kingdoms. His reign was rendered illustrious by works of really royal magnificence. Among these are the pagoda of Madura, several public buildings, and above all the royal palace the colossal proportions and astonishing boldness of which recall the ancient monuments of Thébes. He loved and protected the Christian religion, the excellence of which he recognised; but he never had the courage to accept the consequences of his conviction. The chief obstacle to his conversion came from his 200 wives, of whom the most distinguished were burnt on his pyre.'

Rebellious among his vassals.

During his reign, two rebellions occurred among his vassals. The first was raised by the Sétupati of Ramnad. It was due to an unjust order of Tirumala's regarding the succession to the chiefship of that country in 1635, which was resisted by the rightful claimant and by the Maravans themselves. Tirumala was successful in placing his nominee on the throne and in imprisoning the rival aspirant, but he was ultimately compelled to allow the latter to succeed. He was rewarded by the loyalty of Ramnad in his last war with Mysore.

The other rebellion was raised by a confederacy of poligars headed by the powerful chief of Ettaiyápuram in the Tinnevelly district. Its cause is not clear. The Sétupati of Ramnad, as chief of all the poligars, was entrusted with the duty of quelling it, and performed this undertaking satisfactorily. The leader was put to death and the others suitably punished; and peace was restored in a few months.

A curious rumour.

The letters of the Jesuits relate a curious event which took place in the Madura country about 1653. The whole territory was thrown into a state of great nervous excitement by the spreading in every direction of one of those mysterious and extraordinary rumours which spring up now and again in India, no one knows where or how. An infant emperor of divine birth, it was declared, would shortly appear from the north and usher in a millennium of peace and plenty. The story obtained universal credence, and large sums of money were collected for the use of the deliverer when he should arrive. But he never did arrive. A woman and child were brought to Bangalore by the perpetrators of the rumour, and vast multitudes flocked thither to pay their respects and offer presents to the supposed emperor; but after squeezing all that was possible out of the pretenders, the Musalman rulers of that town cut off their heads and ordered their followers to disperse immediately.

Tirumala's capital was Madura. The royal residence had been removed thence to Trichinopoly by his predecessor, but Tirumala moved it back again, notwithstanding the fact that Trichinopoly, with its almost impregnable rock, its never-failing Cauvery river and its healthy climate, was by nature far superior to Madura, where the fort was on level ground, the Vaigai was usually dry and fever was almost endemic. The reason given in the old manuscripts for the change is that Tirumala was afflicted with a grievous long-standing catarrh which none of the Vaishnavite gods of Trichinopoly could (or would) cure. One day when he was halting at Dindigul on his way to Madura, Sundarésvara and Mínákshi, the Saivite deities of the latter place, appeared to him in a dream and promised him that if he would reside permanently in their town they would cure him. He vowed that he would do so and would spend five lakhs of *pons* on sacred works. Immediately afterwards, as he was cleaning his teeth in the early morning, the disease left him; and thenceforth he devoted himself to the cult of Saivism and the improvement of Madura. None the less, he resided a good deal at Trichinopoly, and his successors (though they went to Madura to be crowned) generally dwelt there permanently.

It is, however, by his many splendid public buildings in Madura that he is best remembered at the present time. They are referred to in some detail in the account of the place on pp. 257–78 below. The largest and most magnificent of them was the great palace which still goes by his name. Much of this was removed to Trichinopoly in later years by his grandson Chokkanátha, but none the less the portions of it which survive were thought by Bishop Caldwell to constitute the grandest building of its kind in southern India.[1]

The beautiful *Teppakulam* at Madura, the *Pudu mantapam* and the unfinished tower called the *Ráya gópuram* belonging to the great temple there (and doubtless other additions to that building), and (perhaps) the Tamakam, the curious building in which the Collector now resides, were also due to his taste for the magnificent.

[1] *History of Tinnevelly,* 61.

Tirumala was succeeded by his son Muttu Alakádri. It is perhaps surprising that Tirumala's brother—who, as has been seen, had just returned to Madura from Mysore at the head of a victorious army—should not have attempted to seize the crown; but he was prevailed upon to accept the governorship of Sivakási in Tinnevelly district.

Almost the first act of the new king was an attempt to shake off the hated Muhammadan yoke. He tried to induce the Náyakkan of Tanjore to join the enterprise, but only succeeded in involving him in the punishment which the Musalmans meted out when his efforts ended in failure. For though the Tanjore ruler disclaimed all connection with his neighbour's aspirations and attempted to conciliate the Musalmans, the latter none the less marched into his country, took Tanjore and Vallam and drove the Náyakkan to fly into the jungle. The invaders then moved against Trichinopoly and Madura, spreading havoc far and wide, while Muttu Alakádri remained inactive behind the walls of the former of these forts. Fortunately for him, the enemy soon had to retire, for their cruel devastations produced a local famine and pestilence from which they themselves suffered terribly. They accordingly made a half-hearted attempt on Trichinopoly and then permitted themselves to be bought off for a very moderate sum. Muttu Alakádri did not long survive their departure, but gave himself up to debauchery with an abandon which soon brought him to a dishonoured grave.

He was succeeded by his son Chokkanátha (1662-82), a promising boy of sixteen. This young ruler began his reign with a second ill-considered attempt to drive out the Musalman troops, despatching a large army against the Gingee fortress. His general, however, sold himself to the enemy and wasted time and money in a long and unprofitable campaign which was little but pretence. Chokkanátha was also harassed by a domestic conspiracy (in which the same unfaithful general took a prominent part) and though he detected and quashed this, the general went over openly to the Muhammadans and induced them to join in an assault upon Trichinopoly in which they had the countenance (if not the practical assistance) of the Náyakkan of Tanjore. The officers whom Chokkanátha entrusted with the duty of repelling the attack were again disloyal, and it was not until he himself at length took command of the army that the invaders were driven back to Tanjore and eventually to Gingee.

So far things had not gone so badly, but in the next or the following year (1663 or 1664) Chokkanátha paid a heavy price for

his temporary success. The Muhammadans burst into the
Trichinopoly and Madura districts and devastated the country
with almost incredible cruelty. They again besieged Trichinopoly, and this time Chokkanátha had to buy them off with a
large sum. He consoled himself by punishing the Náyakkan of
Tanjore for assisting them, and he attempted similar reprisals on
the Sétupati of Ramnad, who had failed to help him in repelling
them. This latter enterprise was unsuccessful, for though
Chokkanátha succeeded in taking several forts in the Marava
country, he was baffled by the guerilla tactics of his adversary,
and had to retire without obtaining that chief's submission. The
campaign marks a new epoch in the relations of Ramnad and
Madura : from thenceforth the Sétupati aspired to an independent
kingdom.

Chokkanátha's next war was with Tanjore, and it resulted in
the capture of that ancient city and the extinction of its Náyakkan
dynasty. Unluckily the Jesuit letters of the years 1666 to 1673
have been lost, and the only authority upon these exciting events
is a vernacular manuscript. This has been abstracted at length
by Mr. Nelson, but space forbids more than the merest summary
of its contents.

The *casus belli*, says this authority, was the refusal of the
Tanjore Náyakkan to give his beautiful and gifted daughter in
marriage to Chokkanátha. The latter determined to fetch the
maiden by force. His troops invaded the Tanjore country, drove
its forces back into their capital, and successfully stormed that
place. But they did not get the princess : her father placed her
and all the other ladies of the palace in one room, blew this up
with gunpowder and then, with his son and his body-guard,
charged furiously into the thickest of the enemy, was captured
after a desperate resistance, and was beheaded.

Chokkanátha placed his foster-brother Alagiri in charge of
the government of Tanjore, but within a year the latter threw off
his allegiance, and Chokkanátha was now so given up to self-
indulgence and so ill served by his disloyal officers that, after an
outburst of indignation which ended in nothing, he was forced to
acquiesce in the independence of Tanjore.

Alagiri, however, was not long permitted to enjoy his ill-
gotten kingdom. A son or grandson of the last Tanjore Náyakkan
had escaped to the Musalman court of Bijápur and had induced
that power to help to place him on the throne of his fathers. In
1674 the Sultan of Bijápur sent a force commanded by the
Marátha general Venkáji (*alias* Ekóji) to turn out the Madura

usurper and reinstate the scion of the old line. Venkáji ventured little until the occurrence of the rupture between Chokkanátha and Alagiri; but he then defeated the latter with ease, and occupied Tanjore. He did not, however, place his *protegé* on the throne, though he treated him kindly enough, but seized the kingdom for himself. So the outcome of Chokkanátha's feebleness was that a Marátha, instead of a Náyakkan, sat upon the throne of Tanjore.

Venkáji shortly afterwards became embroiled with his famous half-brother Sivaji, and Chokkanátha attempted to take advantage of the circumstance to regain his hold on Tanjore. But he was dilatory in the field and in his negotiations, and Venkáji succeeded in buying off the hostility of Santóji (the son of Sivaji, whom the latter had despatched against him) before Chokkanátha could effect anything. This was in 1677–78.

Attacked by Mysore and the Maráthas.

Soon afterwards, Chokkanátha was forced to turn from aggression to the defence of his own kingdom. The famous Chikka Déva Ráya, king of Mysore from 1672 to 1704, had for some time been massing troops on his frontier, and now burst upon Coimbatore and spread havoc far and wide. Chokkanátha did little to repel him, the country was moreover visited with famine and pestilence, and in despair the ministers of the state deposed their incompetent ruler in favour of his brother.

The change was not for the better, and the parlous state of Madura and its territories in 1678 may be gathered from the following passage in a letter written by one of the Jesuit missionaries in that year :—

'The capital, formerly so flourishing, is no longer recognizable. Its palaces, once so gorgeous and majestic, are deserted and falling to ruin. Madura resembles less a town than a brigand's haunt. The new Náyakkan is essentially a do-nothing king. He sleeps all night, he sleeps all day ; and his neighbours, who do not sleep, snatch from him each moment some fragment of his territories. Nations who would profit from a change of rulers do not trouble to repel invaders, and everything foretells that this kingdom, so powerful twenty years back, will soon be the prey of its enemies, or rather the victim of the insane policy of its own government.'

Chokkanátha was replaced on his tottering throne about 1678 by a Muhammadan adventurer who during the next two years usurped the whole of his authority (and even the ladies of his and his fallen brother's harems) and at last was slain by Chokkanátha himself and a few of his friends. But the Náyakkan's position was still far from enviable. In 1682 his capital was besieged by Mysore ; was shadowed by forces belonging to the Maráthas, who, while pretending to be on his side, were only waiting for a chance to seize his territory for themselves ; and was threatened by a body of Maravans who nominally had hurried to his assistance, but in reality had only come to share in the booty which the sack of Trichinopoly was expected to yield.

While Chokkanátha thus sat helpless behind his defences, matters were taken out of his hands by the more virile actors upon this curious scene. The Maráthas, who were now established in Gingee as well as in Tanjore, inflicted a crushing defeat on the Mysore troops and drove them out of almost every corner of the Madura and Trichinopoly districts. Madura itself they were unable to capture, for the Maravans, regarding the men of Mysore as on the whole more eligible neighbours than the Maráthas, helped the former to hold that fortress. The latter then turned against Chokkanátha, whose friends they had pretended to be, and laid siege to Trichinopoly itself. In despair at their treachery, Chokkanátha died of a broken heart in 1682.

His successor was his son Ranga Krishna Muttu Vírappa, a boy of fifteen, who ruled for seven years. Little enough of his territories remained to him to rule. The greater part of them was held by Mysore, some by the Maravans, some by the Maráthas of Gingee and some by the Maráthas of Tanjore. The country was a prey to complete anarchy and universal pillage, foreign enemies occupying all the forts and robber-chiefs being masters of the rural areas and carrying on their brigandage with impunity.

Matters, however, slowly improved. Mysore was soon distracted by a war with the Maráthas of Gingee, and both the Sétupatis of Ramnad and the Maráthas of Tanjore were occupied by domestic outbreaks in their own countries. A new disturbing factor in south Indian politics had also appeared on the scene in the person of the Mughal emperor Aurangzeb, who in 1686-87 conquered the kingdoms of Madura's old enemies, Golconda and Bijápur, and was for many years engaged in a war with its foes the Maráthas which was most exhausting to both parties. Moreover the young Náyakkan of Madura, though imbued with a boyish love of fun and adventure which endeared him to his courtiers, had also a stock of sound ability and spirit which moved the admiration of his ministers, and he took advantage of his improving prospects. He recovered his capital about 1685, and though he failed in an attempt to reduce the Sétupati in 1686, he gradually reconquered large parts of the ancient kingdom of his forefathers and succeeded in restoring the power of the

Náyakkans of Madura to a position which, though not to be compared with that held by it at the beginning of his father's reign, was still far above that which it occupied at the end of that period. He unfortunately died of small-pox in 1689 at the early age of 22. The story goes that his young widow Muttammál (the only woman, strange to say, whom he had married) was inconsolable at his loss and, though she was far advanced in pregnancy, insisted upon committing *sati* on his funeral pyre. Her husband's mother, Mangammál, with great difficulty persuaded her to wait until her child should have been born, solemnly swearing that she should then have her way. When at length the child (a son) arrived, she was put off day after day with various excuses until, despairing of being allowed her desire, she put an end to her life.

Mangammál, the mother of the late Náyakkan, acted for the next fifteen years as Queen-Regent on behalf of his posthumous son.

She was a popular administrator and is still widely remembered by Hindus as a maker of roads and avenues, and a builder of temples, tanks and choultries. Popular belief unhesitatingly ascribes to her every fine old avenue in Madura and Tinnevelly. Native writers assign a curious reason for her passion for charitable acts. One day, they say, she inadvertently put betel into her mouth with her left (instead of her right) hand, and was warned by the Bráhmans that this offence against manners must be expiated by expenditure of this kind. Mr. Taylor has suggested that this story hides her repentance for some amorous escapade.

She was an able woman as well as a charitable, and under her firm guidance Madura apparently all but regained the proud position it had held in the days of Tirumala Náyakkan. Unluckily, the Jesuit letters from 1687 to 1699, both inclusive, have again been lost and the events of her regency cannot be given with any fullness.

She was less frequently engaged in war than her predecessors, but she did not escape the usual conflicts with her neighbours. In her reign the kingdom of Madura first came into direct touch with the Mughal empire of Delhi, since Zulfikar Khán, the general who was sent by Aurangzeb to attack the Marátha stronghold of Gingee, exacted tribute both from Trichinopoly and Tanjore in 1693, though he did not succeed in taking Gingee till five years later. Trichinopoly was besieged (according to Wilks) by Mysore in 1695, but relieved owing to pressure on the CHAP. II.
NÁYAKKAN
DYNASTY. invader's country from the north.

In 1698 Mangammál had to subdue a rebellion in Travancore. The ruler of that country had of recent years been very remiss in sending his tribute to Madura, and it had been necessary on several occasions to send an army to collect the arrears. In 1697 a force despatched for this purpose was taken off its guard and almost cut to pieces. A punitive expedition was organized in the following year, and after hard fighting Travancore was subdued and an immense booty was brought home. Part of this consisted of many cannon, and these were mounted, says one of the vernacular manuscripts, on the ramparts of Trichinopoly and Madura. Mr. Nelson made many enquiries about these latter, but failed to unearth any tradition regarding their ultimate fate.

In 1700 a desultory war, the origin and course of which are alike obscure, was carried on between Madura and the Maráthas of Tanjore. In the following year the latter were crushingly defeated near their capital, and were glad enough to buy off the invading army with an enormous bribe.

In 1702 Tanjore and Madura united to reduce Ramnad. Strange to relate, they were quite unsuccessful, and the ablest general of the Madura army was killed in battle.

In 1704–05 Mangammál's grandson came of age. Tradition Her tragic
death. says that she refused to make way for him and that she was supported in her intention by her chief minister, a man with whom she was on terms of undue intimacy. A strong party formed against her, seized her and confined her in the building in Madura which is still called 'Mangammál's palace,' was once the District Jail and is now occupied by the taluk cutcherry and other public offices. There, goes the story, she was slowly starved to death, her sufferings being aggravated, with horrible cruelty, by the periodical placing of food outside her prison bars in such a position that she could see and smell, but not reach, it. Some slight confirmation of the tradition is derived from the facts that in the little chapel built by Mangammál on the west side of ' the golden lily tank ' in the Madura temple is a statue of a young man who is declared to be her minister and paramour, and that in a picture on the ceiling of the chapel is a portrait of the same person opposite to one of the queen, who (be it noted) is dressed, not as an orthodox Hindu widow should be, but in jewels and finery appropriate only to a married woman.

CHAP. II.
NÁYAKKAN
DYNASTY.

Vijaya Ranga
Chokkanátha
(1704–31).

Her grandson Vijaya Ranga Chokkanátha (1704–31) enjoyed a long but apparently dull reign of 26 years. It is unfortunate that the Jesuit letters which so greatly illumine previous periods of Madura history now cease altogether, and from this time forth we are driven to rely almost entirely upon native manuscripts and the secondary evidence afforded by English historians. And, curiously enough, the nearer we approach the period of the beginning of British ascendancy in the south, the more meagre and unsatisfactory does our information become.

His feeble
rule.

Judging from such material as is available, it seems that the new ruler of Madura was vain and weak-minded, and unfit to govern either himself or others. His reign was distinguished by the ill-regulated and extraordinary munificence of his gifts to Bráhmans and religious institutions. Every other year he used, it is said, to travel to one or other of the famous shrines within his territories, and on these occasions he lavished gifts on all who could gain access to him. The injustice of his rule caused a serious riot in Madura, the mutiny of the whole of his troops, and incessant internal commotions. It must have been owing solely to their own embarrassments that his neighbours did not attempt to despoil his kingdom.

The only warfare in which he seems to have been engaged was connected with the succession to the throne of Ramnad in 1725. Of the two claimants to that position, one was supported by Tanjore and the other by Madura and the Tondamán of Pudukkóttai. The Tanjore troops won a decisive victory and placed their *protégé* on the throne. A year or two later, however, the Tanjore king himself deposed this very *protégé*, and divided the Ramnad kingdom into the two separate divisions of Ramnad and Sivaganga, which henceforth remained independent Marava powers.

Mínákshi
(1731–36).

Vijaya Ranga Chokkanátha died in 1731, and was succeeded by his widow Mínákshi, who acted as Queen-Regent on behalf of a young boy she had adopted as the heir of her dead husband. She had only ruled a year or two when an insurrection was raised against her by Vangáru Tirumala, the father of her adopted son, who pretended to have claims of his own to the throne of Madura. At this juncture the representatives of the Mughals appeared on the scene and took an important part in the struggle.

Musalman
interference.

It must be remembered that ever since 1693 Madura had been nominally the feudatory of the emperor of Delhi, and that since 1698 the Carnatic north of the Coleroon river had been under direct Muhammadan rule. The local representative of the Mughal was the Nawáb of Arcot, and an intermediate authority was held by the Nizam of Haidarabad, who was in theory the subordinate of the emperor, and the superior of the Nawáb.

How regularly the kings of Tanjore and Madura paid their tribute is not clear, but in 1734—about the time, in fact, that Mínákshi and Vangáru Tirumala were fighting for the crown— an expedition was sent by the then Nawáb of Arcot to exact. tribute and submission from the kingdoms of the south. The leaders of this were the Nawáb's son, Safdar Ali Khán, and his nephew and confidential adviser, the well-known Chanda Sáhib.

The invaders took Tanjore by storm and, leaving the stronghold of Trichinopoly unattempted, swept across Madura and Tinnevelly and into Travancore, carrying all before them. It was apparently on their return from this expedition that they took part in the quarrel between Mínákshi and Vangáru Tirumala. The latter approached Safdar Ali Khán with an offer of three million rupees if he would oust the queen in favour of himself. Unwilling to attack Trichinopoly, the Musalman prince contented himself with solemnly declaring Vangáru Tirumala to be king and taking a bond for the three millions. He then marched away, leaving Chanda Sáhib to enforce his award as best as he could. The queen, alarmed at the turn affairs had now taken, approached Chanda Sáhib with counter inducements to take her side; and had little difficulty in persuading that facile politician to accept her bond for a crore of rupees and to declare her duly entitled to the throne. Mínákshi, says Wilks, required him to swear on the Korán that he would adhere faithfully to his engagement, and he accordingly took an oath on a brick wrapped up in the splendid covering usually reserved for that holy book. He was admitted into the Trichinopoly fort and Vangáru Tirumala—apparently with the good will of the queen, who, strangely enough, does not seem to have wished him any harm—went off to Madura, to rule over that country and Tinnevelly.

Chanda Sáhib accepted an earnest of the payment of the crore of rupees and departed to Arcot. Two years later (1736) he returned, was again admitted into the fort and proceeded to make himself master of the kingdom. Mínákshi was soon little but a puppet. Orme, indeed, suggests that she had fallen in love with Chanda Sáhib and so let him have his own way unhindered.

CHAP. II.
NÁYAKKAN
DYNASTY.

End of
Náyakkan
dynasty.

The latter eventually marched against Vangáru Tirumala, who was still ruling in the south, defeated him at Ammayanáyakkanúr and Dindigul, drove him to take refuge in Sivaganga, and occupied the southern provinces of the Madura kingdom. Having now made himself master of all of the unfortunate Mínákshi's realms he threw off the mask, ceased to treat her with the consideration he had hitherto extended to her, locked her up in her palace and proclaimed himself ruler of her kingdom. The hapless lady took poison shortly afterwards.

Character of
its rule.

With her reign, came to an end the ancient dynasty of the Náyakkans of Madura. The unprejudiced evidence of the Jesuit missionaries already several times referred to enables us to form a more accurate estimate of their administration than is usually possible in such cases. Bishop Caldwell, in summing this up, sardonically remarks that it is unfortunate for their reputation that so much more is known about them and their proceedings than about their Chóla and Pándya predecessors. He concludes by saying[1] that—

'Judged not merely by modern European standards of right and wrong, but even by the standards furnished by Hindu and Muhammadan books of authority, the Náyakkans must be decided to have fallen far short of their duty as rulers. Their reigns record little more than a disgraceful catalogue of debaucheries, treacheries, plunderings, oppressions, murders and civil commotions, relieved only by the factitious splendour of gifts to temples, idols and priests, by means of which they apparently succeeded in getting the Bráhmans and poets to speak well of them, and thus in keeping the mass of the people patient under their misrule.'

MUSALMAN
DOMINION.
Chanda Sáhib
(1736–40).

For a time, Chanda Sáhib had everything his own way. His success was indeed regarded with suspicion and even hostility by the Nawáb of Arcot; but family reasons prevented a rupture, and Chanda Sáhib was left undisturbed while he strengthened the fortifications of Trichinopoly and appointed his two brothers as governors of the strongholds of Dindigul and Madura. It was at this period that he subjugated the king of Tanjore (though he did not annex his territory), and compelled him to cede Káraikkál to the French.

A Marátha
interlude,
1740–43.

Unable to help themselves, the king of Tanjore and Vangáru Tirumala determined to call in the assistance of the Maráthas of Sátára in Bombay. These people had their own grievance against the Muhammadans of Arcot (with whom Chanda Sáhib was still identified) because the latter had long delayed payment

____
[1] *History of Tinnevelly*, 62.

of the *chouth,* or one-fourth of the revenues, which they had pro-
mised in return for the withdrawal of the Maráthas from the
country, and the discontinuance of their usual predatory incursions.
They were also encouraged to attempt reprisals by the Nizam of
Haidarabad, who, jealous of the increasing power of the Nawáb
and careless of the loyalty due to co-religionists, would gladly
have seen his dangerous subordinate brought to the ground.

Early in 1740, therefore, the Maráthas appeared with a vast
army in the south and defeated and killed the Nawáb of Arcot in
the pass of Dámalcheruvu in North Arcot. They then came to an
understanding with his son, the Safdar Ali mentioned above,
recognised him as Nawáb, and retired for a time.

Chanda Sáhib had made a faint pretence at helping the
Nawáb to resist the Maráthas, and he now came to offer his
submission to Safdar Ali. The princes parted with apparent
amity, but at the end of the same year the Maráthas (at the
secret invitation of Safdar Ali) suddenly reappeared and made
straight for Trichinopoly. Their temporary withdrawal had been
designed to put Chanda Sáhib off his guard; and it so far
succeeded that Trichinopoly was very poorly provisioned. They
invested the town closely, defeated and killed the two brothers
of Chanda Sáhib above mentioned as they advanced to his help
from their provinces of Madura and Dindigul, and, after a siege
of three months, compelled the surrender of Trichinopoly. They
took Chanda captive to Sátára, and, disregarding the claims of
Vangáru Tirumala, appointed a Marátha, the well-known Morári
Rao of Gooty, as their governor of the conquered kingdom.

Morári Rao remained there for two years (it is not clearly
known what he did or how far his authority extended) and he
finally retired in 1743 before the invading army of the Nizam,
who marched south in that year, re-established his weakened
authority in the Carnatic, and in 1744 appointed Anwar-ud-din as
Nawáb of Arcot.

The whole of the Madura kingdom now fell under the rule of
this latter potentate. There is reason to believe that he governed
it through his sons Mahfuz Khán and Muhammad Ali, both soon
to play an important part in the history of these districts. It is
said that the Nizam ordered that Vangáru Tirumala should be
appointed king of Madura; but, if such an order was ever made,
it was disregarded; and that feeble individual soon disappeared
finally from the scene, poisoned, some say, by Anwar-ud-din.
As late as 1820, a descendant of his, bearing the same name,
was in Madras endeavouring to obtain pecuniary assistance from

Government. He and his family lived at Vellaikurichi in the Sivaganga zamindari and their children were there until quite recently. It is said that they still kept up the old form of having recited, on the first day of Chittrai in each year, a long account of their pedigree and the boundaries of the great kingdom of which their forebears were rulers.

In 1748, however, Chanda Sáhib regained his liberty and marched south in company with a pretender to the position of Nizam of Haidarabad. The allies were successful, Anwar-ud-dín was slain at the great battle of Ambúr in North Arcot, and Chanda Sáhib succeeded him. One of his sons, Muhammad Ali, fled however to Trichinoply and proclaimed himself Nawáb there, and soon most of the south of India was involved in the struggle between these rivals. The French and the English (who had recently been fighting among themselves, were now nominally at peace, and consequently both had more soldiers than they knew what to do with) took sides in the conflict (the former taking the part of Chanda Sáhib and the latter that of Muhammad Ali) and the campaigns which followed were in reality a disguised struggle for the mastery of south India by these two European nations.

It is not in any way necessary to follow the fortunes of the war in detail, as they are concerned less with Madura than with other districts further north, and we may confine ourselves to some account of the events which directly affected the present Madura country. In these the French had little share. Their energies were chiefly confined to the country further north. The English, however, obtained each year henceforth a more and more predominant share in the government of Madura and Tinnevelly, and the history of these tracts becomes a chronicle of the East India Company's dealings with them.

In 1751, after several startling turns of Fortune's wheel, Chanda Sáhib was very generally recognised as Nawáb of Arcot. Muhammad Ali, however, had many adherents in Tinnevelly and Madura.

In this same year 1751, occurred the first siege of the Madura fort of which any account survives. One Alam Khán, a soldier of fortune who had formerly been in Chanda Sáhib's employ came, says Orme—

'To Madura, where his reputation as an excellent officer soon gained him influence and respect, which he employed to corrupt the garrison, and succeeded so well, that the troops created him governor, and consented to maintain the city under his authority for Chanda Saheb, whom he acknowledged as his sovereign . . . . . The loss of this place, by cutting off the communication between Tritchinopoly and the countries of Tinivelly, deprived Mahomed-ally of more than oue half of the dominious which at this time remained under his jurisdiction. On receiving the news, Captain Cope offered his service to retake it. His detachment was ill-equipped for a siege, for they had brought no battering cannon from Fort St. David, and there were but two serviceable pieces in the city : with one of these, three field pieces, two cohorus, and 150 Europeans, he marched away, accompanied by t00 of the Nabob's [*i.e.*, Nawáb's] cavalry, commanded by another of his brothers Abdul-wahab Khán ; and on the day that they arrived in sight of Madura, they were joined by the army returning from Tinivelly. There were several large breaches in the outward wall; the gun fired through one of them on the iuward wall, and in two days demolished a part of it, although not sufficient to make the breach accessible without the help of fascines. Difficult as it was, it was necessary either to storm it immediately, or- to relinquish the siege, for all the shot of the great gun were expended. The sepoys, encouraged by a distribution of some money, and a promise of much more if the place should be taken, went to the attack with as much spirit as the Europeans. The first wall was passed without resistance, and at the foot of the breach in the second appeared three champions, one of them a very bulky man in compleat armour, who fought manfully with their swords, aud wounded several of the forlorn hope, but were at last with difficulty killed. Whilst the troops were mounting the breach, they were severely annoyed by arrows, stones, and the fire of matchlocks; notwithstanding which they gained the parapet, where the enemy had on each side of the entrance raised a mound of earth, on which they had laid horizontally some palm trees separated from each other, and through these intervals they thrust their pikes. At the bottom of the rampart within the wall, they had made a strong retrenchment, with a ditch ; and three or four thousand men appeared ready to defend this work with all kinds of arms. The troops, wounded by the pikes as fast as they mounted, were not able to keep possession of the parapet, and after fighting until ninety men were disabled, relinquished the attack. Four Europeans were killed : the sepoys suffered more, and four of their captains were desperately wounded. The next day Captain Cope prepared to return to Tritchinopoly, and blew the cannon to pieces, for want of means to carry it away. The troops of Mahomed-ally, encouraged by this repulse, no longer concealed their disaffection, and 500 horse, with 1,000 peons, went over to Allum Khan before the English broke up their camp, and two or three days after, near 2,000 more horsemen deserted likewise to the enemy.'

After ruling Madura for a year, Alam Khán went to Trichinopoly to take part in the fighting which was going on there, and was killed in 1752. Before leaving Madura he appointed one Mayana, a relation, to be governor of Madura, and one Nabi Khán to command Tinnevelly. These two men and Muhammad Barki, son-in-law of the latter of them, were the signatories to a paper which Muhammad Ali afterwards produced as evidence of his title to the sovereignty of Madura and Tinnevelly.

Col. Heron's expedition, 1755.

At the beginning of 1755 Muhammad Ali sent another expedition to reduce these two districts to obedience. It consisted of 500 Europeans and 2,000 sepoys furnished by his ally the English East India Company and commanded by Colonel Heron, and of 1,000 horse led by Mahfuz Khán, Muhammad Ali's elder brother. The 2,000 sepoys were in charge of Muhammad Yúsuf Khán, a distinguished native officer of the Company whom we shall meet again.

This force took Madura without any opposition (Mayana had neglected its fortifications and depleted its garrison) and then seized the temple of Kóvilkudi, east of the town, where Mayana had taken refuge. From this building the English soldiers unthinkingly carried off those little metal images of the gods of the Kallans which brought them so much trouble in the Nattam pass (see the account of this place on p. 289) on their way back.

Mahfuz Khán rents the country.

Before Colonel Heron left, Mahfuz Khán—having, according to Orme, ' contrived every means to make the state of the province appear less advantageous than it really was '—obtained from him a lease of the Madura and Tinnevelly districts at an annual rental of 15 lakhs of rupees. Colonel Heron's consent to the arrangement is declared to have been hastened by the offer of a considerable present.

Muhammad Yúsuf sent to quiet it.

Mahfuz Khán's administration was a total failure, and in 1756 the Company saw that the time for more decisive action had come. Not being able to spare any Europeans, they despatched to the south the Muhammad Yúsuf already mentioned, the commandant of all their sepoys. He was sent with some 1,400 men and given orders to combine them with the troops of Mahfuz Khán and the Nawáb and take command of the whole.

He passed through Madura, on his way to the Tinnevelly country, in April 1756, and the following passage from Orme aptly illustrates the reasons which had led to his being sent to the south and the difficulties with which he had to contend :—

' During this progress Mahomed Issoof had not been able to collect any money from the revenues, for the maintenance of his troops ; because the ravages of the Polygars had ruined most of the villages and cultivated lands of the country through which he passed ; and the real detriment of these devastations was increased by the pretences they furnished the land-holders to falsify their accounts, and plead exemptions for more than they had lost. He found Maphuze Cawn in greater distress than himself, unable either to fulfil the stipulations at which he had rented the country from Colonel Heron, or to supply the pay of the Company's sepoys left with him under the command of Jemaul Saheb, or even to furnish enough, exclusive of long arrears, for the daily subsistence of his own troops. This distress naturally deprived him of the necessary authority over the Jemmadars, or officers of his cavalry, who in Indostan, as the ancient mercenary captains of Italy, hire out their bands, and gain not a little by the bargain. Every kind of disorder likewise prevailed in all the other departments of his administration, at the same time that the indolence and irresolution of his own character confirmed all the evils which had been introduced into his government.'

By July of the same year, the country was to all appearance tranquil, and the two leaders separated—Muhammad Yúsuf going to Tinnevelly town and Mahfuz Khán to Madura. As soon as the latter had arrived 'at that place, his cavalry (2,000 picked men) surrounded his house, headed by the governor of the town, and declared that they would not move until they were given their arrears of pay—some seven lakhs of rupees. At the same time three companies of Madras sepoys who were in Madura were disarmed and turned out; and the brother of the Muhammad Barki already mentioned above entered the fort with 2,000 Kallans whom he had collected in the Nattam country. The standard of revolt was then openly raised and invitations were issued to all the poligars to assist in re-establishing the government of Mahfuz Khán.

These steps were doubtless taken with the knowledge and approval of Mahfuz Khán and were inspired by the fact that in July the Company had farmed out the Tinnevelly country for eleven lakhs of rupees to a certain Mudali, this man being granted plenary civil and criminal jurisdiction within it and being bound to maintain not less than 1,000 of the Company's sepoys.

Hearing what had happened, Muhammad Yúsuf marched at once on Madura, and on the 10th August camped near Tirupparankunram, which was strongly held by the rebels. His whole force was only 1,500 sepoys and six field-pieces, so, seeing that it would be useless to attempt to storm the place, he sent for instructions to Captain Calliaud, who was at Trichinopoly. That officer came over and attempted to negotiate with the rebels. His efforts were vain and a desultory war began which ravaged the whole district.

. In May 1757 Captain Calliaud made a gallant endeavour to carry the Madura fortress by a night surprise, but was repulsed with loss. Orme gives the following account of the affair, which is of interest as containing a description of fortifications which have now utterly disappeared. A reference to the map of the town in 1757 facing p. 265 will make this clearer, and it will be seen that the assault was delivered near where the present maternity hospital stands.

' The inward wall of Madura is 22 feet high, including the parapet, which rises six above the rampart : at the distance of every 100 yards or less (for exact symmetry has not been observed) are square towers. The fausse-bray is 30 feet broad, above which the outward wall rises only five feet, but descending to the bottom of the ditch is 11 on the outside. Midway between every two towers of the inward wall, is a similar projection in the outward, with loop-holes which command the ditch, and flank the intermediate part of the wall, in which are none but the whole parapet of the inward wall has loop-holes, so have some of its towers, and the rest embrasures for cannon. The spot chosen to be attacked was the first tower on the left hand of the western gate-way, being the only part where the fausse-bray was clear of the thick thorny bushes, which had not injudiciously been suffered to overrun it in every other; but the garrison, trusting to this defence, had entirely neglected the ditch, which, by continual drifts after rain, was almost choke 1 up to the level of the plain. The party allotted to the attack were 100 Europeans, and 200 sepoys; the rest of the troops remained in the watercourse [see the map], ready to support the event. Calliaud led the party himself, to whom the method of attack was carefully explained, and strict silence enjoined. The foremost men carried the six shorter ladders intended for the outward wall; the next, the six longer, for the inward; as soon as twenty of the party had got into the fausse-bray, it was intended that they should immediately take over the longer ladders, which they were to plant, as received, against the tower, but not a man was to mount, until all the six ladders were fixed, and then no more than three at a time on each ladder.

' The first ladders were planted, and Calliaud, with the first 20 men, had got into the fausse-bray, had taken over one of the longer ladders, and had planted it against the tower, when their hopes were interrupted by one of those accidents which from their triviality escape the most attentive precaution. A dog, accustomed to get his meals at the messes of some of the soldiers, had accompanied them all the way from Secundermally [Tirupparankunram] into the ditch, and, probably from anxiety at not being able to follow his masters into the fausse-bray, began to bark; which was soon answered by the barking of another dog on the rampart, and the yelps of both awakened the nearest centinal, who, crying out " The enemy ", roused the guard at the gateway, which repaired immediately to the tower. The soldiers in the fausse-bray, finding the alarm taken, instead of continuing to get over the rest of the ladders, endeavoured to mount on that already planted, but crowded on it so many together, that it crushed under

them. This communicated the confusion to those in the ditch, and no
one any longer did what he ought. In the meantime, the garrison
increasing on the rampart hung out blue lights of sulphur, and dis-
covering the whole party began to shower on them arrows, stones,
lances, and the shot of fire-arms. On which Calliaud ordered the
retreat, which was effected with little loss, only one man being killed,
and another wounded; both were sepoys, standing on the glacis.'

In July he made another attempt at the same spot, which was
again unsuccessful. Orme describes it as under :—

'The gabions, fascines, and platforms, were prepared in the camp ;
and as soon as all were ready, the troops allotted marched on the 9th
at night to the watercourse which runs to the west of the city, and
raised the battery against the curtain between the gateway and the
tower which had been attempted by escalade of the 1st of May. It
mounted two eighteen-pounders, with four field-pieces, was finished
before the morning, and at day-break began to fire. The parapet of the
fausse-bray was soon beaten down, and the inward wall, although
strong, was by noon shaken so much, that the parapet of this likewise
fell entirely, and the wall itself was sufficiently shattered, to permit a
a man to clamber to the top : but, in this short time, the garrison had
staked the rampart behind with the trunks of Palmeira trees set on
end : a few shot knocked down some, nor could any of them have been
firmly fixed, and to leave the enemy no more time to prepare farther
defences, Calliaud resolved to storm immediately. Of the Europeans,
only the artillery-men were left at the battery : all the battalion-men,
who were 120, marched, followed by the Company of Coffrees and
they by 400 sepoys. Calliaud led the Europeans, and Mahomed
Issoof the sepoys. The garrison had disciplined 300 of their match-
lockmen as sepoys ; who, although much inferior to these troops, were
improved far beyond their former state ; these were posted on the
western gateway, which projecting beyond the fausse-bray into the
ditch, flanked the tower attacked ; and a multitude were crowded on
the ramparts behind and on each side of the breach. The troops,
although galled, advanced resolutely through the ditch and fausse-
bray, and four of the most active scrambled up the breach to the
rampart, but were immediately tumbled down dead, or mortally
wounded. This repressed the ardour of those who were following:
an officer threw out imprudent words, and the infirmity visibly caught
the whole line, notwithstanding the exhortations and activity of
Calliaud, who was in the fausse-bray directing the assault. Whoso-
ever mounted afterwards came down without getting to the top,
pretending the impossibility, although the danger was as great in the
fausse-bray below; for, besides the shower of other annoyances,
the enemy had prepared bags and pipkins filled with mere powder,
to which they set fire as they tossed them down on the heads of
the assailants, and the scorch of the explosion was inevitable and
intolerable. Nevertheless, Calliaud continued the assault half an

9

hour; when finding that no command was any longer obeyed, and that much loss had been sustained, he ordered the retreat. Four of the bravest serjeants were killed, and as many wounded, and 20 other Europeans were either killed or desperately wounded; of the Coffrees 10, of the sepoys 100 were disabled, but few of this body were killed, and fewer died afterwards of their wounds.'

Eventually the place was given up to Captain Calliaud on his paying the rebels Rs. 1,70,000.

Anarchy again prevails.

The results were small. Disturbances still prevailed every-where; the Kallans ravaged the country in every direction; the great Haidar Ali, the soldier of fortune who was soon to usurp the throne of Mysore, invaded the country round Madura and was with difficulty beaten off; and no revenue worth mentioning could be collected. The Company tried in vain to induce' the Nawáb of Arcot to recall his brother, Mahfuz Khán, who was undoubtedly the cause of all the trouble, and soon afterwards their needs elsewhere compelled them to withdraw Muhammad Yúsuf.

His departure was the signal for wilder anarchy than ever. The Company's garrison in Madura could only just collect, from the country directly under its walls, enough revenue to support themselves; on the north the Kallans, and on the west the poligars, ravaged unchecked; and in the south Mahfuz Khán had thrown himself into the arms of the principal poligars and was beyond the reach of argument or reason.

Yúsuf Khán again despatched.

The Company accordingly sent back Muhammad Yúsuf to the country, renting both Madura and Tinnevelly to him for the very moderate sum of five lakhs annually. He returned in the spring of 1759 and began by teaching the Kallans a wholesome lesson. Cutting avenues through their woods, he shot them down without mercy as they fled, or executed as malefactors any who were taken prisoners. He went on to reduce the rest of the country to order, and soon had sobered all the poligars and made himself extremely powerful. He even had the audacity to make war on the king of Travancore without the knowledge or consent of the Company. In 1761, and again in 1762, he offered to lease Tinne-velly and Madura for four years more at seven lakhs per annum. His offer was refused, and—whether he was enraged at this, or whether he thought himself powerful enough to defy his masters— he shortly afterwards threw off his allegiance and began to collect troops.

He rebels and is hanged, 1764.

In 1763, therefore, a strong force was sent against him and he was besieged in Madura in September. His friends nearly all deserted him, but he held out until October 1764 with great energy and skill, renovating and strengthening the fort at great expense—he is said to have 'entirely repaired' its east face and constantly employed 3,000 labourers about it—and repelling the chief assault with a loss of 120 Europeans (including nine officers) killed and wounded. At the end of that time little real progress against him had been made, except that the place was now rigorously blockaded, but he was treacherously seized by one Marchaud, the officer in charge of the French contingent, and handed over to Major Charles Campbell, who commanded the English among the besiegers.[1] He was ignominiously hanged near the camp, about two miles to the west of Madura, and his body was buried at the spot. A small square mosque was afterwards erected over his tomb. It is still in existence—to the left of the road to Dindigul, a little beyond the toll-gate—and is known as 'Khán Sáhib's *pallivásal.*'

Tradition has many stories to tell of this remarkable man, who is commonly known in Madura as Khánsá, an abbreviation for Khán Sáhib. He was born in the Ramnad country and was originally a Hindu of the Vellála caste. He ran away from his home, took service under a European for three years in Pondicherry, was dismissed, served under another European (who educated him), went to the Nawáb's court, rose rapidly in the army, married a Parangi woman and eventually, as has been seen, became Commandant of all the Company's sepoys. His executive ability is sufficiently indicated in the report (see below) from Colonel Fullarton—dated March, 1785 and entitled 'A view of the English interests in India'—which was republished in Madras in 1867. This says that in Tinnevelly and Madura 'his whole administration denoted vigour and effect. His justice was unquestioned, his word unalterable; his measures were happily combined and firmly executed, the guilty had no refuge from punishment.' It concludes by saying that his example shows that 'wisdom, vigour and integrity are of no climate or complexion.'

After Muhammad Yúsuf's death, the revenue administration of Madura was entrusted to one Abiral Khán Sáhib, who conducted it uneventfully for some six years. He had no military power, and the country was commanded by British officers. The terms of office of his numerous successors were equally devoid of

CHAP. II.
ENGLISH
PERIOD.

His character.

Haidar Ali's invasion, 1780.

---

[1] Vibart's *History of Madras Engineers* (W. H. Allen, 1881), 89. This work gives a detailed account of the operations. Caldwell (*History of Tinnevelly*, 122) seems to give incorrectly the names of both the French and English commanding officers.

episode, and it was not until 1780 that any change of note occurred. In that year Haidar Ali (who had by now made himself king of Mysore) perpetrated his famous invasion of the Carnatic—pillaging, burning and slaying until the country was one blackened waste.

Assignment of the revenue to the Company, 1781.

In the next year the Nawáb Muhammad Ali, assigned to the Company [1] the revenues of the Carnatic to defray the cost of the war with Haidar Ali, and a ' Committee of Assigned Revenue,' consisting of six officials, was appointed to administer them. Under this body, in each of the districts concerned, was a ' Receiver of Assigned Revenue.' The first so sent to Madura— virtually its first Collector—was Mr. George Proctor. His administration was not successful, and he was (apparently) followed in 1783 by Mr. Eyles Irwin. [2]

Colonel Fullarton's expedition, 1783.

But the country required quieting before it could be successfully administered, and in the same year the Colonel Fullarton who has already been mentioned was sent into it with a strong force. His report above cited affords ample evidence of the necessity for this step. It says that—

' Nearly one hundred thousand Poligars and Colleries [*i.e.*,Kallans] were in arms throughout the southern provinces, and, being considered hostile to Government, looked to public confusion as their safeguard against punishment. Your southern force was inadequate to repress these outrages and to retrieve your affairs. The treasury was drained, the country depopulated, the revenues exacted by the enemy, the troops undisciplined, ill-paid, poorly fed and unsuccessfully commanded. During the course of these proceedings, your southern provinces remained in their former confusion. The Poligars, Colleries, and other tributaries, ever since the commencement of the war [with Haidar Ali] had thrown off all appearance of allegiance. No civil arrangement could be attempted without a military force, and nothing less than the whole army seemed adequate to their reduction. While such a considerable portion of the southern provinces remained in defiance of the Company's Government, it was vain to think of supporting the current charges of the establishment, far less could we hope to reduce the arrears, and to prepare for important operations, in the probable event of a recommencement of hostilities. It became indispensable, therefore, to restore the tranquillity of those provinces by vigorous military measures as the only means to render them protective of revenue.'

Colonel Fullarton subdued the poligars of Mélúr and Sivaganga and then passed southwards ; and his principal fighting was in Tinnevelly.

---

[1] See Aitchison's *Treaties, etc.* (1892), viii, 34.
[2] *History of Tinnevelly*, 144, 146.

In June 1785, in consequence of orders from superior authority, the assignment of the revenues was surrendered to the Nawáb of Arcot, the Committee of Assigned Revenue was dissolved, and the civil administration of the Company, with all its numerous advantages, ceased for seven years.

In August 1790 the Madras Government, finding it impossible to induce the Nawáb either to contribute his share of the expenses of the alliance with the Company or to re-introduce the assignment of the revenues, took possession of the country by proclamation, without treaty. A Board of Assumed Revenue, which was a department of the Board of Revenue established in 1786, was constituted to administer the territories, and Collectors were appointed to the various districts. Mr. Alexander McLeod was sent down in 1790 as Collector of Dindigul.

In July 1792 the Nawáb and the Company entered into a new treaty [1] by which the latter undertook to collect at their own expense and risk the whole of the peshkash, or tribute, due from the poligars and with the exception of a few districts—among which were Madura proper and Tinnevelly, which were to remain in the Company's hands till the revenue equalled the arrears which had accrued—the rest of the country was to be restored to the management of the Nawáb on certain conditions.

In the same year (1792) the province of Dindigul came formally into the possession of the Company. The fate of this area had differed for some years from that of the rest of the Madura country. It has been seen above (p. 68) that when Chanda Sáhib seized the latter, he placed one of his brothers in command of Dindigul. About 1742, Birki Venkata Rao, the officer in command of the forces in the adjoining territories of Mysore, invaded the province. The commandant of the Dindigul fort, Mír Imám Ulla, handed it over to him without resistance, and the king of Mysore appointed Birki Venkata Rao as manager of the newly acquired province. It contained a number of pálaiyams, or feudal estates, and its history for the next few years consists largely of the alternate resumption and restoration of these, and of changes in its managers. In 1748 Madúr, one of the pálaiyams, was sequestrated for arrears ; and Venkata Rao was recalled and followed by one Venkatappa. He in his turn was succeeded in 1751 by one Námagiri Rája ; but in the same year Venkatappa was restored and given charge of the pálaiyams, while Srinivása Rao (son of Birki Venkata Rao) was given control of the Government land. In 1755 Venkatappa reported

CHAP. II.
ENGLISH
PERIOD.

Assumption
of the
revenue,
1790.

The Com
pany collects
the pesh
kash, 1792.

Story of the
Dindigul
country.

---

[1] For the text of it, see Aitchison's *Treaties, etc.* (1892), viii, 47.

that the poligars were very contumacious, and Haidar Ali accordingly made a memorable incursion into the country and brought these chiefs to their knees one after the other with extraordinary rapidity, although he had only 1,700 men against the 30,000 whom they might, if they had united, have put into the field to meet him. When he entered the country, only two of the poligars' estates were under resumption; namely, Madúr and Vadakarai; by the time he left it he had resumed all the others except five; namely, Ammayanáyakkanúr, Idaiyankóttai, Kómbai Nilakkóttai and Mámbárai.

Srinivása Rao was now removed for incompetence, and Venkatappa appointed to the charge of both the estates and the Government land. He was shortly afterwards succeeded by one Súrya Náráyana Mudali, who for some reason restored six * of the dispossessed poligars.

* Ambáturai.
Emakkalápuram.
Erasakkanáyakkanúr.
Gantamanáyakkanúr.
Marunúttu.
Tavasimadai.

In 1772 the country was granted to Mír Sáhib, husband of Haidar's wife's sister and a well-remembered individual, on military tenure. In 1773 and 1774 he resumed seven † of the pálaiyams and restored two more (Téváram and Sandaiyúr [1]) to their owners. In May 1783, during the First Mysore War, Dindigul surrendered to the division under Colonel Lang and all the dispossessed poligars were reinstated. But the province

† Ambáturai.
Erasakkanáyakkanúr.
Gantamanáyakkanúr.
Kómbai.
Marunúttu.
Nilakkóttai.
Tavasimadai.

was restored in the next year by the treaty of Mangalore [2] to Tipu Sultan, Haidar Ali's son and successor, and he granted it to Saiyad Sáhib, who is said to have been a nephew of Mír Sáhib, on much the same terms as those the latter had enjoyed. In 1785 and 1786 Saiyad Sáhib resumed five ‡ of the pálaiyams, and in 1788 Tipu himself came to Dindigul and sequestrated fourteen others for arrears, leaving only three of them (Idaiyankóttai, Kómbai and Mámbárai) not under attachment. These fourteen

‡ Eriyódu.
Madúr.
Palni.
Sandaiyúr.
Sukkámpatti.

were taken away from the Dindigul country and attached to the province of Sankaridrug in Salem. In 1790 Sandaiyúr was given back to its owner.

[1] In the present Nilakkóttai taluk; not the existing zamindari of the same name in Tirumangalam.
[2] Aitchison's *Treaties, etc.,* viii, 455.

In August 1790, during the Second Mysore War against Tipu, Colonel James Stuart took the Dindigul fort and district in the manner described on p. 237 below, and all the dispossessed poligars were once more restored to their estates. In 1792, by the treaty which concluded that war,[1] the province was ceded to the Company. The disturbances in it which the various poligars raised in the years immediately following are referred to in Chapter XI below.

The rest of Madura came finally into the hands of the English in 1801, under the following circumstances : When, in 1799, the Third Mysore War ended with the fall of Seringapatam and the death of Tipu Sultan, papers found in the fallen city showed that the then Nawáb of Arcot and his father (the Muhammad Ali already several times mentioned above) had been engaged in treasonable correspondence with Tipu. An enquiry was held, but while it was progressing the Nawáb died. His heir declined to give the security which in the circumstances the Government con_sidered necessary, and the Nawábship was consequently conferred on a junior member of the family, with whom in 1801 [2] an agreement was concluded by which he handed over to the Company in perpetuity ' the sole and exclusive administration of the civil and military governments of all the territories and dependencies of the Carnatic.'

Madura thus passed, with the rest of the Carnatic, under the British, and tasted for the first time for very many years the blessings of settled peace.

[1] Aitchison's *Treaties, etc.,* viii, 460.
[2] *Ibid.,* 56.

CHAPTER III.

THE PEOPLE.

CHAP. III.
GENERAL
CHARACTER-
ISTICS.
—
Density of
the popula-
tion.

THE district is not thickly peopled. Except in the head-quarter taluk, where the population of Madura town raises the figure, the density of the inhabitants is nowhere as much as 400 to the square mile. Details will be found in the separate Appendix to this volume. Excluding Madura again, the density is highest in Palni taluk, and Dindigul comes next. It is lowest in Periyakulam, but the apparent sparseness of the population in that taluk is largely due to the existence within it of large areas of uninhabitable hill and jungle. Where the land is culturable, the density is probably well up to the average.

Its growth.

In the district as a whole, the increase in the population in the thirty years ending with 1901 was 29 per cent., that is, consider-ably more than the averages for the southern districts (21·2 per cent.) or the Presidency generally (22·1 per cent.). In the decade 1871–81, owing to the great famine of 1876-78, a decline of 5 per cent. occurred; in the next ten years the rebound usual after scarcity took place and the advance was as much as 22 per cent.; while in the period 1891–1901 the growth was 11 per cent., or again considerably more than the Presidency average (7·2 per cent.). It would have been larger but for the emigration which took place to Ceylon. Statistics show that in this decade the net result of emigration to, and immigration from, that island was a loss to the district of nearly 80,000 persons On the other hand, the balance of the movement of the population between Madura and the other districts in the Presidency is slightly in its favour, a certain amount of immigration having taken place to the land newly brought under wet cultivation with the water of the Periyár irrigation project.

The increase in the decade 1891–1901 was highest (21·6 per cent.) in Periyakulam taluk, which has benefited considerably from the Periyár water and the opening up to the cultivation of tea and coffee of the Kannan Dévan hills in Travancore to the west of it. It was next highest in Madura and in Palni and Dindigul. The advance was smallest in Méhúr and Tirumangalam. The former of these two taluks will probably do better in future, as soon as the effect of the Periyár water begins to be felt in earnest; but Tirumangalam has hardly any irrigation tanks or channels and but few wells, is more at the mercy of adverse seasons than any other part of the district, and is not likely to exhibit any marked advance. The population there has increased by only 10 per cent. in the last 30 years, against 47 per cent. in Periyakulam and 33 per cent. in both Madura and Dindigul.

The parent-tongue of four-fifths of the people is Tamil. The language is spoken with less purity than in Tanjore, but without that frequent admixture of foreign words which is met with in Chingleput and North Arcot. The Madura people pronounce it with a peculiar jerkiness and a nasal twang which makes it difficult for a man from further north to understand them. They also have a curious trick of inverting consonants, saying, for example, *kuridai* for *kudirai*, *Marudai* for *Madurai*, and so on. Fourteen per cent. of the Madura people speak Telugu, and this language is the home-speech of at least a fifth of the population of four taluks—Dindigul, Kodaikanal, Palni and Periyakulam. These areas are largely peopled by the descendants of the followers of the poligar chiefs who migrated to Madura from the Deccan, in the train of the armies from Vijayanagar which overran the country in the sixteenth century in the circumstances set out in the last chapter.

As many as four per cent. of the people speak Canarese. These are chiefly the weaver communities called Sédans and Séniyans and the cattle-breeding and shepherd castes of the Anuppans, Káppiliyans and Kurubas, all of whom are commonest in the west of the district. No tradition seems to survive regarding the inducements which led these people to immigrate hither from their own distant country, but since authenticated instances are on record of rulers of other parts having, by offers of special privileges, persuaded bodies of artisans and craftsmen to come and settle in their dominions, it is perhaps legitimate to conjecture that the Náyakkan dynasty, finding among the Tamils neither weavers nor herdsmen of talent, induced bodies of these people to come and settle under their protection.

Fifteen in every thousand of the population (a higher proportion than in any other district) speak Patnúli or Khatri, a dialect of Gujaráti. These are the Patnúlkáran silk-weavers, referred to later on in this chapter, who are so numerous in Madura and Dindigul towns.

Education.

The education of the people is dealt with more particularly in Chapter X below, from which it will be seen that in this matter they are rather below the average of the southern districts as a whole. The inhabitants of Madura and Periyakulam taluks are the most advanced and those of Tirumangalam the most backward.

Occupations.

The means of subsistence of the population are discussed in Chapter VI, where it is shown that the proportion of them who live by agriculture and the tending of flocks and herds is even higher than usual.

Religions.

By religion, 93 in every hundred of the inhabitants are Hindus, four are Musalmans and three are Christians.

THE JAINS.

At the census of 1901, not a single Jain was found in the whole of the district, but ample evidence exists to show that in days gone by the followers of this faith were an influential community in Madura. Legends preserved in the *sthala purána* of the great temple at Madura say that the town had three narrow escapes from destruction by a huge elephant, a vast cow and an enormous snake, which were created by the magic arts of the Jains and sent against it, but by the grace of Siva were converted into the three hills in the neighbourhood now known as the Ánaimalai, Pasumalai and Nágamalai. These stories, though wildly apocryphal in details, seem clearly to enshrine the fact that the Jains were once powerful enough to cause the Saivites considerable uneasiness, if not to place their existence in peril. In the account of the village of Tiruvédagam on p. 297 below, is given the traditional embroidered version of a contest between the Jains and the Saivite saint Tirugnána Sambandhar which also is almost certainly an historical fact. The persecutions which the Jains underwent are moreover still referred to in local chronicles, and it is stated that at one of the festivals connected with the Madura temple an image representing a Jain impaled on a stake is carried in the procession. Finally the district contains a number of sculptures and inscriptions which are certainly of Jain origin. References to some of these will be found in the accounts in Chapter XV of Ánaimalai and Tirupparankunram in Madura taluk, Aivarmalai in Palni, Uttamapálaiyam in Periyakulam, and Kóvilánkulam and Kuppalanattam in Tirumangalam.

CHAP. III.
THE JAINS.

On the little granite hills of the district are often found level, rectangular spaces, usually six or seven feet long and two or three feet wide, which have been chipped out on the surface of some flat piece of rock. They look as though the granite had been smoothed to make a sleeping-place, and some of them have a kind of rock pillow at one end, two or three inches higher than the rest of the excavation. The ryots call them *Pancha Pándava padukkai*, or ' beds of the five Pándavas.' They are sometimes found close to images of undoubted Jain origin cut on the rocks, and they perhaps mark the sites of the dwellings of Jain hermits.

THE
CHRISTIANS.

The Christians in Madura numbered at the last census nearly three per cent. of its inhabitants, a figure somewhat below the average for the southern districts as a whole. Relatively to the total population they were most numerous in the taluks of Dindigul (7 per cent.), Kodaikanal (5·8), Periyakulam (2·4) and Madura (2·1) and least so in Tirumangalam (·7 per cent.), Mélúr (·7) and Palni (·6). Nearly the whole of them, as usual, were natives. An overwhelming proportion belonged to the Roman Catholic Church; next in numbers came the nonconformist adherents of the American Mission ; and a few were followers of the Lutheran sect.

Roman
Catholic
Mission.

The Roman Catholic Mission is by far the oldest in the district, and dates from as long back as the beginning of the seventeenth century. Considerations of space prohibit the inclusion here of any detailed account of its doings, but the letters of its priests to their ecclesiastical superiors, which have been collected and published in French in four volumes under the title of *La Mission du Maduré,* depict in a most vivid fashion their struggles and achievements and, incidentally, the political and social conditions of the country at the time.

The earliest missionary to visit Madura was a Portuguese named Father Fernandez, and his congregation consisted largely of Paravas (fishermen) whose forefathers had been converted by Francis Xavier. The first Jesuit was Robert de' Nobili, an Italian of good birth (related to two popes and a cardinal, and the nephew of another cardinal), who began work in 1606 under the control of the Archbishop of Cranganore. Knowing that Fernandez was hopelessly handicapped by the fact that he was one of the detested ' Parangis ' (Portuguese)—a race which was known to all natives to eat beef and consort with the lowest of Paraiyans--de' Nobili (with the concurrence of his superiors) assumed a native name (*Talva Bódayar,* ' the teacher of philosophy ') presented himself as a *sanyási* from Rome, and adopted the characteristic dress and meagre diet of the ascetic class.

His fame soon spread abroad, and those whom he admitted to an interview (he discouraged visitors at first) were charmed with his polished manners, astonished at the purity of his Tamil and captivated by his oriental learning and versatile intellect. Later, he built a church and presbytery and took to the active preaching of the Gospel, and at the beginning scores of persons, including members of all the upper classes, were converted with marvellous rapidity. But the Hindu gurus and priests soon succeeded in stemming the tide, and persecutions followed. Moreover Father Fernandez complained to the authorities of his methods—and especially of his practice of permitting his converts to retain Hindu customs, such as the wearing of the *kudumi* (top-knot) and the thread, and the use of sandal-paste on their foreheads—and in 1613 he was censured and eventually recalled to Goa. It was not until ten years later that the controversy which thus arose was decided in a manner which permitted him to resume his work on the old methods.

In Madura itself he seems never again to have been as successful as he was at the beginning. In 1623 he set out on a long journey through the Salem district and to Trichinopoly, where the converts were chiefly of low castes, and much of his energy was thereafter devoted to the work in this latter town. Persecution, hardship and insults were his daily lot there, and he was even imprisoned. In 1648, after 42 years of labour, he left Madura, utterly broken in constitution and all but blind, and not long afterwards he died at Mylapore.

Two other famous men who belonged to the ' Madura Mission ' which he thus started were de Britto and Beschi. The former was martyred in the most revolting manner in the Ramnad country in 1693. The latter, who was famous for his Tamil poems, which rival those of the best native authors, died in 1746.

Thereafter the Jesuit Mission appears to have languished, and in 1773 it was entirely suppressed by the Pope. In the years which followed much of its work was undone, converts relapsing to Hinduism. The authorities at Rome accordingly appealed to the Society of Foreign Missions, which in 1783 had succeeded the Jesuits in the ' Carnatic (or Pondicherry) Mission,' and in 1795 Monsignor Champenois, Vicar Apostolic of that body, visited the Madura Christians.[1] But difficulties occurred with the priests of the Goanese church, and it was not until 1830 that the then Vicar Apostolic was able to send into the country a first

---

[1] For the account of the fortunes of the mission after 1773, I am indebted to the courtesy of the Rev. J. Pages, S.J., now in charge at Madura.

detachment of three missionaries, Fathers Mehay, James and
Mousset. In July 1836 Pope Gregory XVI created the Vicariate
Apostolic of the Coromandel Coast, which included the Madura
country, and in December of the same year the Madura Mission
was detached therefrom and formed into a separate organization
under the Jesuits.

Four missionaries from the Society of Jesus reached Madura
in 1838. In 1842 one of them, Father Garnier, built the church
there near Tirumala Náyakkan's palace. He died in the town
the next year.

In 1838, the year these four arrived, Pope Gregory XVI, by
his Bull *Multa præclare*, had put an end to the jurisdiction of the
Archbishop of Goa over the mission, but many of the Christians
refused to accept the new state of things. Up to 1847, the mission
was permitted to remain under the jurisdiction of Pondicherry,
but in that year its first Vicar Apostolic, Bishop A. Canoz, was
appointed. In 1857 a Concordat was signed between Rome and
Portugal whereby the Archbishop of Goa was granted authority
over the Goanese Christians in the mission's field, and thence
arose a double jurisdiction within it. This continued until 1886
when, by another Concordat, the difficulty was ended by the
re-establishment of the Bishopric of Mylapore and the grant to it
of that part of the Madura Vicariate Apostolic which lay within
the Tanjore district. By a subsequent agreement the church of
Our Lady of Dolours at Dindigul (built in 1729) and of Our Lady
of the Rosary facing the Perumál Teppakulam at Madura (erected
1770) were left in the hands of the authorities of Goa, who still
possess a few adherents in the district. In this same year 1886,
by the Bull *Humanæ Salutis*, Pope Leo XIII established the
Catholic hierarchy in India and the Madura Vicariate Apostolic
was formed into the Bishopric of Trichinopoly, under the jurisdiction of which its missions are at present conducted.

The largest Roman Catholic congregations are now those in
Madura and Dindigul, but there are 36 churches in other places
in the district, the mission employs sixteen European priests,
keeps up orphanages for boys and for girls at Madura, and is
about to establish a nunnery of Europeans in that town to take
charge of its girls' schools and dispensaries. Its funds are
received principally from France.

The American Madura Mission was established in 1834 as an
off-shoot of the Jaffna Mission in Ceylon.[1] The first workers to

American
Mission

[1] For the materials for the account which follows, I am indebted to the
Rev. J. S. Chandler of the American Mission.

arrive in Madura were **Mr.** and **Mrs.** Todd and **Mr.** Hoisington. Stations were subsequently established in Dindigul (1835), Tirumangalam (1838), Pasumalai (1845), Periyakulam (1848), Vattilagundu (1857), Mélúr (1857) and Palni (1862). The East Gate Church at Madura was begun on part of the glacis of the old fort (see p. 266) in 1843 and finished in 1845.

For several years the policy of the mission was to endeavour to introduce a knowledge of Christianity among the people by means of free schools for native boys, with Hindus as teachers, and boarding-schools with Christian teachers, and its educational institutions were a very prominent part of its work. In 1847, however, great defections were caused by efforts to abolish caste distinctions among the converts, and in 1855 the visit to Madura of a deputation of two members of the American Board resulted in a considerable reversal of the original policy. English education was abandoned, changes were made in the seminary which had been established at Pasumalai (p. 176), the large English school at Madura was closed, and nearly all the boarding-schools except that for girls at Madura were abolished.

Gradually, however, it was realised that this change had not been for the better, and little by little the schools were re-established. The more important of those which the mission now maintains are referred to below in Chapter X.

Another noticeable feature in the policy of the mission has been the combination of medical aid to the natives with its evangelistic work, several of its members being trained medical men. The leader of this branch of its operations was the late Rev. E. Chester, for many years resident in Dindigul. The first lady physician, Miss Root, M.D., arrived in 1885 and her efforts eventually resulted in the erection of the mission hospital for women in Madura. This and the other medical institutions kept up by the mission are referred to in Chapter IX below. The share which the mission took in the foundation of the sanitarium of Kodaikanal on the Palni Hills is mentioned in the account of that place on p. 250.

Its members now include twelve ordained Europeans and a number of missionary ladies, and it possesses 27 churches. Among the best-remembered of its ministers are the Rev. W. Tracy, D.D., for 25 years in charge of the Pasumalai seminary (whose son, the Rev. J. E. Tracy, is still with the mission) and the Rev. J. E. Chandler, whose son is also still working at Madura. The expenditure of the mission is some Rs. 80,000 annually, almost all of which comes from America.

The Lutheran church first began work in the district in the second half of the eighteenth century, in the time of the flourishing Danish Lutheran Missions at Tranquebar and Tanjore. Catechists were sent to Dindigul and other places and succeeded in establishing congregations. The care of all these was eventually, however, transferred to the Society for the Propagation of the Gospel and nothing more was done for many years.

It was not until 1875 that the Leipzig Lutheran Mission began its work in the district. In that year it sent its first European missionary to Madura.[1] In 1882 a second was despatched, and since 1889 he has been living at Dindigul. Three years afterwards another was sent to Madura, but in 1903 he was transferred to Virudupatti in the Tinnevelly district. Two missionary ladies are now working at Madura. The mission possesses eight churches and two more are under construction. It also maintains a number of schools, but none of these are above the primary grade.

The Musalmans in the district number four per cent. of the population, a figure about equal to the average of the southern districts. They are proportionately most numerous in the Mélúr and Palni taluks, and least so in Tirumangalam.

The very great majority of them belong to the community locally known as Rávutans, who are probably the descendants either of Hindus of this part of the world who in former times were forcibly converted to Islám, or of Musalman fathers by the women of this country. They are a pushing and frugal (not to say parsimonious) class. Far from following others of their co-religionists in thinking much of the past, less of the present and least of the future, they conduct the important trade in leather which the district possesses, grow much betel and do a great deal of the commerce of the country, both wholesale and retail. They seldom marry with the Musalmans of pure descent, although there is no religious bar to such alliances, and they often (as in Dindigul town) live in separate streets away from them. They speak Tamil, and not Hindustáni like the Musalmans proper. They also observe, at weddings and similar ceremonies, several customs which are clearly Hindu in origin, such as the use of music and the tying of a táli. The dress and ornaments of both men and women strongly resemble those of Hindus, the men being often only distinguishable by the tartan patterns of their waist-cloths, their beards and their shaven heads, and the women only by their having a loose jacket (instead of a tight bodice) and wearing a

Leipzig
Evangelical
Lutheran
Mission.

THE
MUSALMANS.

Rávutans.

---

[1] The particulars which follow were kindly furnished by the Rev. Th. Bloomstrand, in charge of the mission's affairs at Madura.

series of small rings on the outer edge of the ear. At deaths, they often divide property in accordance with Hindu, and not Muhammadan, law.

They are grouped into a number of sub-divisions which are endogamous in character and usually territorial in origin. Instances of these are the Puliyankudiyár, the men of Puliyankudi in Tinnevelly; the Elaiyánkudiyár, the men of Elaiyánkudi in Ramnad zamindari; the Musiriyár, the men of Musiri in Trichinopoly; the Vaigakaraiyár, the men of the Vaigai banks; and the Eruttukárar, ' bullock-men,' those who used to trade with pack-bullocks.

Relations with Hindus.

The Musalmans live on amicable terms with their Hindu neighbours. They are permitted (see p. 307) to go to the great Hindu temple of Subrahmanya at Palni to make their offerings there, and Hindus flock to the famous tomb of the Musalman fakir on the top of the hill at Tirupparankunram. The followers of the two faiths join in the celebration of the fire-walking which in this district very often follows the Mohurrum.

THE HINDUS.

It remains to refer to the Hindus, the most numerous of the religious communities of the district. A few words may be said about their social and religious ways, and then some account will be given of the castes among them which are found in particular strength in this part of the country.

Villages.

The villages of the district are built in the scattered fashion common in the south. The three polluting castes, the Pallans, Paraiyans and Telugu Chakkiliyans, always live in separate *chéris*, or hamlets, outside them. 'The other communities are more particular about residing together than is usually the case. Even if the Bráhman houses number only two or three, they will generally be found side by side, and the other castes similarly try to collect together, each in their own street. There are usually three wells, one for Bráhmans, one for Súdras and Musalmans, and the third for the polluting castes.

Old records show that in the troubled period before the Company acquired the country almost every village was fortified in some fashion. A mud rampart was the usual defence, and where this was beyond the means of the community a strong live hedge of thorny plants and trees was planted round the village site and provided with a single entrance which was closed at night with a strong gate. In many villages the stone posts which formerly flanked these gateways may still be seen. They are called *vádivásal* and when the village deities are worshipped they often come in for some share of the oblations and offerings which are going. Almost every village has a *mandai*, or piece of open

ground, in the middle of it and in this is nearly always a *chávadi*, CHAP. III.
half club and half court-house, which is kept up at the common The Hindus.
expense and is used as a meeting-place for gossip in the mornings
and evenings, as a spot in which to loaf away the long days in
the hot weather when cultivation is at a standstill, or as a court
for the hearing of disputes or caste questions. In the Mélúr
taluk these *chávadis* are often intimately connected with the
worship of Karuppan, the favourite deity of the Kallans. In big
villages there are often several of them for the use of the different
castes. If the villagers cannot afford a regular building for a
chávadi they will at least put up a masonry platform under some
shady tree to serve the same purposes.

The strong corporate feeling which enables these places to be
built and kept up also exhibits itself in the common (*samudáyam*)
funds which exist in so many villages. These are formed from
the proceeds of land and fruit trees held on common. patta, or
from the sum paid for the right to collect a tax imposed by
common consent on articles of certain classes bought or sold in
the bazaars. The funds are spent for the common benefit on such
objects as repairs to drinking-water sources, ceremonies at the
temples, dramatic performances and so on. In Bódináyakkanúr,
a school is maintained. Sometimes the members of a particular
caste in a village organize similar funds by taxing themselves for
the benefit of their community The Shánáns and the Patnúlkárans
are especially fond of doing this.

Houses are much the same as elsewhere. Where the Kallans Houses.
are most numerous, the fear of incendiarism induces people to try
to afford a tiled or terraced roof instead of being content with
thatch. But as a rule the ryots seem to believe in the poetess
Auvaiyár's saying ' Build small and prosper greatly,' and outside
the towns the stranger is struck with the meanness of the average
type of house. The cattle are always tied up in the houses at
night. Fear of the Kallans prevents them from being left in the
fields, and they may be seen coming into the villages every evening in scores, choking every one with the dust they kick up, and
polluting the village site (instead of manuring the land) for twelve
hours out of every twenty-four. Buffaloes are tied up outside the
houses. Kallans do not care to steal them, as they are of little
value, are very troublesome when a stranger tries to handle them,
and cannot travel fast or far enough to be out of reach of detection
by daybreak.

In the Palni taluk there are fewer Kallans and the ryots are
much keener farmers than elsewhere in the district, and there the
cattle are very usually penned in the fields at night. People who

have a well generally have a house next it, in addition to their ordinary dwelling in the village site, and thus they can stay out on their land at night to watch over the cattle penned on it.

The dress of the people does not differ greatly from that in other southern districts. The prevailing colour of the garments of the women of the poorer classes is red. Three becoming items in their attire which are less common further north are the heavy silver bracelets (*tól káppu*) worn just above the elbow ; the fashion of tying a bunch of white flowers to the centre of the táli necklet, just under the chin ; and the trick of allowing the embroidered end of their cloths to hang squarely down behind from their waists, like a sort of dress-improver. The lowest classes spend more on their dress than is usual in the south—the fine, handsome Pallan women of the Palni taluk being conspicuous in this respect. The *ravikkai*, or tight-fitting bodice, is seldom worn by non-Bráhmans. Indeed the women of the Kallans work in the fields with their bodies above the waist quite bare, and in the west of Tirumangalam taluk they never cover their breasts at all except when going into a town. The Kallans say that an unmarried girl of their caste once used her upper cloth to conceal the fact that she was with child, and that the garment was accordingly tabooed in consequence. The women among the Patnúlkárans of Madura are taking to tying their cloths in the fashion followed by Bráhmans, bunching them up in front and passing one end between their legs and tucking it into the waist behind.

The women of practically all non-Bráhman castes except those of Telugu origin practise the fashion of stretching the lobes of their ears. The Kallan girls are especially noticeable in this respect, their lobes sometimes reaching even to their shoulders. In quarrels between women of the lower castes these long ears form a favourite object of attack, and 'lobe-tearing cases' figure frequently in police records. The boring of the ear is done by Kuravan women as early as the eighth day after birth, and thereafter the stretching is continued by hanging leaden rings from the hole. The ear becomes finally the most bejewelled part of a woman's person. No account of the various ornaments suspended from it by the different castes would be intelligible without illustrations. Some description of the prevalent fashions will be found in Mr. Havell's paper in the *Journal of Indian Art*, v. 32 ff.

Tattooing is as common as elsewhere. Kuravan and Domban women do it. Roman Catholics frequently have a cross done between the eye-brows, on the spot where the sect-mark of the Hindu is usually put.

The food of the mass of the people consists of cholam, ragi and cambu, which rank in public estimation in this order. Varagu and sámai are considered inferior. Rice is eaten only by the wealthier classes. Chutneys and vegetables of the usual kinds are employed to render more palatable the various preparations made from these grains.

The people have fewer amusements than usual. In the dry weather, when cultivation is at a standstill and every one has plenty of leisure, Dombans, Kuravans and (to a less extent) Pallans are invited to the villages to act some of the usual plays, but except these professional companies no one gets up dramatic performances. Cock-fighting is common, especially on the Mélúr side, and is practised by many different castes.

A game which is peculiar to this district and the country immediately to the north of it, and is one of the very few manly sports which survive in southern India, is the jallikat or jellicut. The word *jallikattu* literally means ' tying of ornaments.' On a day fixed and advertised by beat of drum at the adjacent weekly markets a number of cattle, to the horns of which cloths and handkerchiefs have been tied, are loosed one after the other, in quick succession, from a large pen or other enclosure amid a furious tom-tomming and loud shouts from the crowd of assembled spectators. The animals have first to run the gauntlet down along lane formed of country carts, and then gallop off wildly in every direction ; the game consists in endeavouring to capture the cloths tied to their horns. To do this requires fleetness of foot and considerable pluck, and those who are successful are the heroes of the hour. Cuts and bruises are the reward of those who are less skilful, and now and again some of the excited cattle charge into the onlookers and send a few of them flying. The sport has in consequence been prohibited on more than one occasion ; but, seeing that no one need run any risks unless he chooses, existing official opinion inclines to the view that it is a pity to discourage a manly amusement which is not really more dangerous than football, steeple-chasing or foxhunting. The keenness of the more virile sections of the community (especially the Kallans) in this game is extraordinary, and in many villages cattle are bred and reared specially for it. The best jallikats are to be seen in the Kallan country in Tirumangalam, and next come those in Mélúr and Madura taluks.

The sport can boast a very respectable antiquity. A poet of the early years of the present era quoted by Mr. Kanakasabhai Pillai in *The Tamils eighteen hundred years ago* describes in vivid fashion the jallikat practised by the shepherd caste in those days.

The bulls had sharpened horns and the competitors were required to actually capture and hold them. Serious wounds were the order of the day and the young men who most distinguished themselves were awarded the hands of the fairest of the girls of the caste, who watched the game from a kind of elevated grand stand. It is said that even nowadays the swain who would win the favour of a Kallan maiden must first prove himself worthy of her choice by prowess at the jallikat.

Religious life : Bráhman influence small.

Though Madura town itself is a well-known centre of Bráhmanism, the district as a whole is as purely Dravidian in religious sentiment as any in the south. Bráhmans number only 18 in every 1,000 of the population (or fewer than anywhere in the south except Coimbatore, South Arcot and Salem) and their influence upon the religious and social life of the community is small. The famous Bráhmanical temples at Madura, Tirupparankunram, Palni, Alagarkóvil and one or two other places attract attention and create the impression that the people must be generally devoted to the worship of the orthodox gods, but a closer examination shows that there are large areas devoid of any large shrine in the honour of these deities and given over to the cult of the lesser Dravidian godlings. In Dindigul taluk, for example, the Vaishnavite temples at Tádikkombu and Vadamadura are almost the only orthodox institutions to be found.

Saivism is the prevalent form of belief. The rulers of Vijayanagar were of Vaishnavite sympathies, and the poligars who followed their armies into the district brought their own Vaishnavite deities with them and established frequent shrines to them which are still in existence. But the Náyakkan kings were catholic-minded rulers, and their gifts and additions to the Saivite shrines in and around Madura town show how free they were from all narrow bigotry.

One reason why the Bráhmans have been unable to impose their rites to any large extent upon the people of the district is the fact that large sections of the community regard it as in no way necessary that their marriages should be performed, or their funerals attended, by any kind of professional priest. In the accounts of the castes which follow below, it will be seen that the táli is frequently tied, not by a priest, but by the bridegroom's sister. Where custom requires that a priest should do it, this man very usually belongs to the caste himself, and is rather a social, than a religious, leader. Thus the Bráhmans have not the opportunities of impressing their beliefs and rites upon the people which are in some districts afforded by the indispensability of their presence at domestic ceremonies.

CHAP. III.
THE HINDUS.

The non-Bráhmanical deities, as elsewhere, are legion, and space only permits of a reference to one or two of them which are especially characteristic of the district.

Of all of them, Karuppan is the most prominent. He is essentially the god of the Kallans, especially of the Kallans of the Mélúr side. In those parts his shrine is usually the Kallans' *chávadi.* He is said to have been brought 'from the north' and worship to him is done with the face turned in that direction. One of his most famous shrines is that at Manapárai in the Trichinopoly district. He delights in the sacrifice of goats and sheep. His priests are usually Kallans or Kusavans. He has many different names: if his image be large, he will be called Periya (big) Karuppan; if small, Chinna Karuppan; if his dwelling is in the piece of open ground belonging to the village, he will be known as Mandai Karuppan. In the Mélúr taluk his shrine may usually be known by the hundreds of iron chains hung outside it which have been presented to the god in performance of vows. The deity is said to be fond of bedecking himself with chains, and these offerings are usually suspended from a kind of 'horizontal bar,' made of two tall stone uprights supporting a slab of stone placed horizontally upon the top of them. He is also fond of presents of clubs and swords. The curious collection of these weapons at his shrine at the main door of the Alagarkóvil is mentioned in the account of that temple on p 284 below. Bells are also welcome, and in Tirumangalam taluk these are often hung in numbers to the trees round his abode. On the Palni side, Karuppan's shrine is often furnished with little swings for the delectation of the god, and with terracotta elephants, horses and other animals so that he may be able to perambulate the village at night to see that all is well.

Popular deities: Karuppan.

Elsewhere, these images are the sign of a temple to Aiyanár. The biggest examples of them in the whole district are perhaps the brick and mortar erections outside the shrine to that god at Mádakkulam near Madura. Some account of this deity has been given in the *Gazetteer* of South Arcot, in which district he is even more popular, and the description there is generally applicable to Madura and need not be repeated.

Aiyanár.

Another god (or demon) who is common to both districts is Madurai Viran. Curiously enough, this personage, whose history is also given in that *Gazetteer,* is held in much less honour in this, his own, country than in South Arcot. His little shrine just south of the eastern entrance to the great temple at Madura is held in considerable repute and children are often named after him and his famous wife Bommi, but in the villages he is less known.

Madurai Viran.

Another male deity is Sáttán, who is said to reside in trees. Bits of rags are hung on the branches of his dwelling. Several trees covered in this manner may be seen by the road through the Ándipatti pass.

The other minor deities are all of the other sex. The commonest is Máriamman, the well-known goddess of small-pox. The personalities, attributes and likes and dislikes of the others are ill-defined. They go by various flattering names, such as Ponnammál ('golden lady'), Muttammál ('pearl lady') and so forth, and are propitiated at irregular intervals and in varying methods. Several of them require buffaloes to be offered up. The sacrifice of these animals at the festival to Vandikáliamma at Áttúr is referred to in the account of that place on p. 230 below, and similar rites on a smaller scale are performed at numerous other goddess' shrines—those, for example, at Páraipatti in the Kannivádi zamindari, at Pádiyúr in Dindigul taluk, at Dindigul itself and at the two shrines to Alagia-náchiamma in Palni town. The Sapta Kannimár, or seven virgins, are common objects of adoration and their images are very often to be seen in the shrines of the other village goddesses.

Vows to these deities are unusually common, and sometimes take unusual forms. In the north of Mélúr taluk, it is credibly stated, women who are anxious for offspring vow that if they attain their wish they will go and have a cocoanut broken on their heads by the pújári of the temple at Sendurai. In many shrines hang *ex voto* cradles and small painted clay babies placed there by women who have at length been blessed with children. Silver *ex voto* images of parts of the body which have recovered from disease are often presented to the larger temples, such as those at Palni, Tirupparankunram and Alagarkóvil. The mouth-lock vows which are performed at Palni are referred to in the account of that place on p. 307 below. Alagarkóvil is such a favourite place for carrying out the first shaving of the heads of children that the right to the locks presented to the shrine is annually sold by auction! When cattle or sheep are sick, people vow that if they recover they will go and do púja on the top of one or other of several little hills which are thought to be very efficacious in such cases. Gópináthasvámi hill in Kannivádi zamindari is one of these, and others are those at Vádipatti in Nilakkóttai taluk and Settináyakkanpatti near Dindigul. Fire-walking is often performed at Draupadi shrines. In Palni there is an annual feast at the Máriamman temple at which people carry in their bare hands, in performance of vows, earthen pots with a bright fire

blazing inside them. They are said to escape burns by the favour
of the goddess, but it is whispered that immunity is sometimes
rendered doubly sure by putting sand or paddy husk at the bottom
of the pot.

Devils are unusually numerous. Sometimes they haunt land
and render it unlucky, and such fields (*pisásu pidichcha nilam*, as
they are called) are unsaleable. Generally, however, they take up
their abode in a woman. Women thus possessed may be seen at
the great temple at Madura every Navarátri, waiting for release.
There are many professional exorcists, who are often the pújáris
at the local goddess' shrine. Their methods have a family resemblance. At dead of night they question the evil spirit and ask him
who he is, why he has come there and what he wants to induce him
to go away. He answers through the mouth of the woman, who
works herself up into a frenzy and throws herself about wildly.
If he will not answer, the woman is whipped with the rattan which
the exorcist carries, or with a bunch of margosa twigs. When he
replies, his requests for offerings of certain kinds are complied
with. When he is satisfied and agrees to leave, a stone is placed
on the woman's head and she is let go and dashes off into the
darkness. The place at which the stone drops to the ground is
supposed to be the place where the evil spirit is content to remain,
and to keep him there a lock of the woman's hair is nailed with an
iron nail (Madura devils, like those of other parts, dislike iron)
to the nearest tree.

Short accounts will now be given of certain castes which occur
in greater strength in this district than in others. These notes will
clearly show how slight is the influence of the Bráhmans in social
matters. Neither at weddings nor at funerals is their presence
usually required. The various castes employ either priests of their
own community or none at all. Certain other resemblances run
through the customs of all these communities. Endogamous
subdivisions are usual and exogamous septs common; the caste
organization is generally complete and powerful; the ceremonies
performed when a girl attains maturity are elaborate; at weddings
a bride-price is paid and the táli is tied by the bridegroom's
sister; and the rule that a man can claim the hand of his paternal
aunt's daughter in marriage is enforced with a rigour which
sometimes leads to curious complications.

The idea underlying this last custom appears to be the feeling
that a woman is bound to replace the loss to her father's family
occasioned by her marrying out of it, by returning one of her
daughters to that family. The simplest way of making the

restoration is to marry her daughter to her brother's son. But if the brother has no son he can still demand that the girl be restored to his side of the family and can require that she shall marry some other boy belonging thereto. This latter alternative is adopted in some castes where the age of the girl is much greater than that of the mother's brother's son; but in others custom requires that the latter shall marry her however old she may be, and the result is naturally the subversion of all the ordinary rules of morality.

Kallans.

Though slightly inferior in numbers to the Vellálans and Pallans, the Kallans are quite the most prominent of all the castes of the district. They number 218,000 and are in greater strength in Madura (especially in the Mélúr and Tirumangalam taluks) than in any other Collectorate.

They are the 'fierce Colleries' of Orme's history and have always borne a reputation for independence-—not to say truculence. In the time of the Náyakkan dynasty of Madura they steadily refused to pay any tribute[1], arguing always that the heavens supplied the necessary rain, their own cattle did the ploughing and they themselves carried out the rest of the cultivation operations, so there was no possible reason why they should be charged anything. Their conduct at this period was generally so aggressive that bodies of troops marching between Trichinopoly and Madura found it advisable to avoid the Mélúr country and proceed by circuitous routes.

When Vijaya Raghunátha was Sétupati of Ramnad (1710–20) the Kallans raided his territory and carried off 2,000 head of cattle. He forthwith established nine fortresses in their country, lulled them into security by various promises, and then massacred a number of them. They thereafter paid him their respects annually, but they continued to flout the authorities at Madura until 1772. In 1755 they cut up Colonel Heron's expedition in the Nattam pass (see the account of that affair on p. 289 below) and Orme is always referring to their lawlessness.

When Muhammad Yúsuf Khán was in charge of the Madura country (1756–64) he established forts at Mélúr and Vellálapatti (about midway between Mélúr and Alagarkóvil) to overawe them, but he never attempted to collect tribute from them and kept them quiet chiefly by fomenting jealousies among their leaders. He however made one attack against the Nattam Kallans which,

[1] This and one or two other passages below are taken from Mr. Turnbull's notice of the caste, dated 1817, which is prefixed to Vol. III of Captain Ward's account (1821) of the Survey of Madura and Dindigul. This was printed at the Madura Collectorate Press in 1895.

says Orme, 'appeared more like one of the general huntings peculiar to Asia, than a military expedition. Avenues were cut into the forest and the inhabitants shot as they fled.'

After Yúsuf Khán was hanged as a rebel in 1764 the Mélúr Kallans gave so much trouble that the Company sent against them five battalions of sepoys and 1,500 cavalry under Captain Rumley. The force encamped at Mélúr and summoned the Kallan headmen to attend. But they 'would not appear and continued to manifest their licentious character and contemptuously slighted the Detachment.' Captain Rumley accordingly surrounded Vellálapatti and called on its leaders to surrender. Instead of obeying, 'the whole of the Colleries persevered and were preparing for hostility, using insulting language and brandishing their weapons within the hedge that surrounded the village.' Captain Rumley then fired the hedge, the village was soon in flames also, and as the people rushed away from the conflagration his troops set upon them and slew, it is said, about 3,000 of them. The other villages then 'submissively made homage' and formally agreed to pay tribute. The Kallans greatly respected the man who had thus brought them to their knees and called him 'Rumleysvámi.' Renewed instances of contumacy however occurred—ten survey peons, for example, being murdered—and Rumley had to put 2,000 more Kallans to the sword. The country was then surveyed without further opposition.

The war with Haidar Ali in 1781, however, gave the Kallans another chance and they once more got completely out of hand, raiding up to the very walls of Madura and slaying, in an affray outside the fortifications, the officer commanding the town, one Mallári Rao. In 1784 Captain Oliver arrived at Mélúr with another detachment and collected the arrears of tribute by force. A battalion of native infantry continued to be stationed in that town for some years thereafter.

Open rebellion has long since ceased, but the Kallans' inveterate addiction to dacoity and theft ('Kallan' means 'thief' in Tamil) renders the caste to this day a thorn in the flesh of the authorities. A very large proportion of the thefts committed in the district are attributable to them. Nor are they ashamed of the fact. One of them defended his clan by urging that every other class stole—the official by taking bribes, the vakil by fostering animosities and so pocketing fees, the merchant by watering the arrack and sanding the sugar, and so on and so forth—and that the Kallans differed from these only in the directness of their methods.

Dacoity of travellers at night used to be their favourite pastime, and their favourite haunts the various roads leading out of Madura and that from Ammayanáyakkanúr to Periyakulam. The method adopted consisted in threatening the driver of the cart and then turning the vehicle into the ditch so that it upset. The unfortunate travellers were then forced by some of the gang to sit at the side of the road with their backs to the cart and their faces to the ground while their baggage was searched for valuables by the remainder. The gangs which frequented these roads have been now broken up and the caste has practically quitted road dacoity —which was not always profitable and conviction for which meant a long sentence—for the simpler, more paying and less risky business of stealing officials' office-boxes and ryots' cattle. The Kallans have not the courage of such races as the Maravans, and prefer an occupation which needs only slinking cunning to one which requires dash and boldness.

Cattle-theft is now the most popular calling among them. They are clever at handling animals, and probably the popularity of the jallikats already mentioned has its origin in the demands of a life which always included much cattle-lifting. The stolen animals are driven great distances (as much as 20 or 30 miles) on the night of the theft and are then hidden for the day either in a friend's house or among hills and jungles. The next night they are taken still further and again hidden. Pursuit is by this time hopeless, as the owner has no idea even in which direction to search. He therefore proceeds to the nearest Kallan go-between (these individuals are well-known to every one) and offers him a reward if he will bring back the cattle. This reward is called *tuppu-kúli*, or ' payment for clues,' and is very usually as much as half the value of the animals stolen. The Kallan undertakes to search for the lost bullocks, returns soon and states that he has found them, receives his *tuppu-kúli*, and then tells the owner of the property that if he will go to a spot named, which is usually in some lonely neighbourhood, he will find his cattle tied up there. This information is always correct. If, on the other hand, the owner reports the theft to the police, no Kallan will help him recover his animals, and these are eventually sold in other districts or Travancore, or even sent across from Tuticorin to Ceylon. Consequently hardly any cattle-thefts are ever reported to the police.

The Kallan is also an adept at the more ordinary forms of house-breaking and theft. In pursuit of this calling he travels great distances, even as far as Chingleput and Mysore. He does not take his womenkind with him on these expeditions, but is usually accompanied by a Kammálan (goldsmith) to melt down and sell the loot.

In the month of Ádi (July-August) it is the custom for the Kallans' married daughters (especially newly-wedded girls) to go with their husbands to stay a few days with their parents. The extra house-keeping expenses thus incurred by the latter necessitate extra efforts in the way of theft, and the Kallans playfully call these the *Ádi-véttai* or ' Ádi hunting.'

Another important source of income to the Kallan is the *kudi-kával* fees which he levies on other castes. To almost every village or group of villages the Kallans have appointed a *kávalgár*, or watchman, who is remunerated by the villagers in various ways, such as by fees on each plough, proportions of the crop at harvest and so on. In big villages and towns fees of this kind are also paid by each householder of importance, whether he owns land or not. In Madura town, for example, fees are paid to the Kallans of the adjacent village of Kílkudi. In return for these emoluments the Kallans undertake to protect the village or person from thefts by their fellow castemen and to get back any property which may be stolen. In some cases they have even executed a written agreement to do this, and suits have actually been filed for non-performance of the contract !

The fees thus demanded are undisguised blackmail. If any one hesitates or refuses to pay them, he is warned by the Kallan that he must take the consequences and in due course finds his standing crops taken from his field, his straw-stack or his house on fire, or his best pair of bullocks missing. The terrorism thus organised is also used when necessary to obtain meals gratis or to induce jurors and witnesses to help to acquit an accused Kallan.

This state of things has naturally attracted the attention of the authorities and many and various methods of suppressing it have been suggested. It was at one time hoped that the reorganization of the village establishments would give a death-blow to the system by providing in each village a paid watchman who might be substituted for the Kallan *kávalgár*. It has since been suggested, among other remedies, that Government should recognise and properly organize the system ; should provide the Kallans with an honest livelihood by presenting them with land ; should enlist them in Kallan regiments ; fine them all when crime occurred in their neighbourhood ; send them all to school ; register all cattle and all Kallans and prevent either from moving out of their villages without passports; bind over the chief men of the caste to be of good behaviour; hold midnight roll-calls at unexpected intervals in their villages to see who was away; and treat the whole caste under the Criminal Tribes Act.

In 1896 the ryots of Dindigul took the case into their own hands and struck against the Kallans' exactions. The wide-spread movement which followed was known as the ' anti-Kallar agitation.' It actually originated in the anger of certain of the Idaiyans with a Kallan Lothario who enticed away a woman of their caste and afterwards her daughter, and kept both women simultaneously under his protection. But it soon grew into a movement the avowed object of which was to drive the Kallans out of the Dindigul taluk. The leader of it was an Idaiyan called Amayappa Kone. The villagers held meetings at which thousands attended, took solemn oaths to do without the Kallan *kávalgárs*; appointed watchmen of their own; boycotted all the Kallans, refusing them even food and drink; formed a fund to compensate those whose cattle were stolen or houses burnt; provided every village with a horn which was to be blown in case of theft; required every one hearing the horn to hurry to the rescue; and laid down a scale of fines to be paid by those who did not adhere to these rules.

At first the movement was thoroughly successful. It extended to Palni, Periyakulam and the borders of Coimbatore, the Kallans were outnumbered and overpowered, and many of them sold their fields for what they would fetch and fled from the taluk. For about six months crime ceased absolutely. As one deponent put it, ' People even left the buckets at the wells! ' Some of the Kallans, however, showed fight, and in 1896 and 1897 riots occurred in which lives were lost and villages were burnt. The anti-Kallar people lacked efficient leadership, overstepped the limits allowed by law and were prosecuted accordingly. This encouraged the Kallans to renewed efforts, they were often assisted by the existence of factions in the villages, and in the end the greater part of the *kávalgárs* returned once more to their former offices and almost all the good which the agitation had effected was undone again. It was an almost unique instance of the ryots combining to help themselves, and deserved a less melancholy ending.

Hope for the reformation of the Kallan has now recently arisen in quite another quarter. Round about Mélúr the people of the caste are taking energetically to wet cultivation, to the exclusion of cattle-lifting, with the Periyár water which has lately been brought there. In some of the villages to the south-east of that town they have drawn up a formal agreement (which has been solemnly registered and is most rigorously enforced by the headmen) forbidding theft, recalling all the women who have emigrated to Ceylon and elsewhere and — with an enlightenment which puts other communities to shame—prohibiting several other unwise practices which are only too common, such as the removal from the fields of cowdung for fuel and the pollution of drinking-water tanks by stepping into them. The department of Public Works may soon be able to claim that it has succeeded where the army, the police and the magistracy have failed, and made an honest man of the notorious Kallan.

So much for the caste's unfortunate weakness. Its organization and customs may next be considered. It is divided into three endogamous sections: the *Terkunád* ('south country') Kallans of Tanjore, with whom we are not now concerned; the *Kílnád* ('east country') or Mélúrnád Kallans of the Mélúr taluk; and the *Mélnád* ('west country') or *Piramalainád* ('beyond the hills') Kallans who live in the north-west of Tirumangalam taluk to the west of the Nágamalai. These last are often called in the old records 'the Ánaiyúr Kallans' from the village of that name (see p. 325) 3½ miles east of Usilampatti. These main sections are again sub-divided into smaller *náds* called after certain villages which it would be tedious to name in detail. At Sivarátri Kallans go and do *púja* at the temple in the village which gives its name to their *nád*. Tradition says that the caste came originally 'from the north'; the dead are buried with their faces laid in that direction; and when *púja* is done to Karuppanasvámi, the caste god already referred to, the worshippers turn to the north. The Kílnád Kallans were thus the first to reach the district. They came south, say the legends, on a hunting excursion with their dogs and their caste weapon, the *valláritadi* or boomerang, and observing a peacock turn and show fight to one of their hounds saw that the country must be favourable to the development of the manly virtues and decided to settle in it. The Vellálans were then the chief cultivators round Mélúr, and the Kallans took service under them. The masters, however, so bullied the servants that the latter eventually struck and drew up a schedule of money penalties to be exacted for every variety of bodily injury inflicted on them, from the knocking out of a tooth to the causing of death. Later on they grew strong enough to turn the Vellálans altogether out of the taluk, which they then named *tan-arasu-nád* or 'the country governed by themselves.' A section of them then travelled westward beyond the Nágamalai, drove out the Védans who peopled that country and settled there. Branches from this division travelled to Dindigul and Palni. It is said that the poligar of Virúpákshi (p. 310) invited some of them to serve under him as border guards and that Ottaiyúr (' single village ') in Palni, which is now entirely peopled by Kallans, was founded by the descendants of these people.

The organization of the Kílnád Kallans differs from that of their brethren beyond the hills. Among the former an hereditary headman, called the *ambalakáran*, rules in almost every village. He receives small fees at domestic ceremonies, is entitled to the first betel and nut and settles caste disputes. Fines inflicted are credited to the caste fund. The western Kalians are under a more monarchical rule, an hereditary headman called Tirumala Pinnai Tévan deciding most caste matters. He is said to get this hereditary name from the fact that his ancestor was appointed (with three co-adjutors) by king Tirumala Náyakkan and given many insignia of office, including a state palanquin. If any one declines to abide by his decision, excommunication is pronounced by the ceremony of ' placing the thorn,' which consists in laying a thorny branch across the threshold of the recalcitrant party's house to signify that for his contumacy his property will go to ruin and be overrun with jungle. The removal of the thorn and the restitution of the sinner to Kallan society can only be procured by abject apologies to Pinnai Tévan.

Every Kallan boy has a right to claim the hand of his paternal aunt's daughter in marriage. This aunt bears the expenses connected with his circumcision. Similarly the maternal uncle pays the cost of the rites which are observed when a girl attains maturity, for he has a claim on the girl as a bride for his son. These two ceremonies are performed at one time for large batches of boys and girls. On an auspicious day the young people are all feasted and dressed in their best and repair to a river or tank. The mothers of the girls make lamps of plantain leaves and float them on the water and the boys are operated on by the local barber, who gets a fee of from one to five fanams (a fanam is 3 as. 4 ps.) for each. This practice of circumcision, which is not common among Hindu castes, has often been supposed to have been borrowed from, or enforced by, the Musalmans, but argu_ ments in favour of its indigenous origin are the facts that it has a Tamil name and that, as has been said, the maternal aunt pays the expenses.

Polyandry is stated[1] to have prevailed among the western Kallans at one time, but no traces of the practice now survive.

When a girl has attained maturity she puts away the necklace of coloured beads she wore as a child and dons the horse-hair necklet which is characteristic of the Kallan woman. This she retains till death, even if she become a widow. The richer Kallans substitute for the horse-hair a necklace of many strands of fine silver wire. . In Tirumangalam the women often hang round their necks a most curious brass and silver pendant, six or eight inches long and elaborately worked.

Marriage is either infant or adult. Bráhmans have no hand in it. A boomerang should figure among the presents to the bride. The táli is tied by the bridegroom's sister, who then hurries off the bride, weeping piteously, to her brother's house. Widows may re-marry and, if childless, almost invariably do so. The correct match is with the late husband's brother Divorce is a mutual right and is permitted on slight grounds so long as the petitioner pays the usual fines, which are graduated in a complicated manner to meet different cases A man who divorces his wife for unfaithfulness does so by sending for her brothers and formally giving them a piece of straw, the idea being that this is all the fine the lady's value demands. The children of a divorcée conceived after the divorce may be legitimised by the waist-string of the father being cut off at a caste meeting and tied round the woman's neck.

The Kílnád Kallans usually bury their dead. Lamps are periodically lighted on the tomb and it is whitewashed annually. The Piramalaináḍ division usually burn the dead. If a woman dies when with child, the baby is taken out and placed alongside her on the pyre. This, it may here be noted, is the rule with most castes in this district, and in some communities the relations afterwards put up a stone burden-rest by the side of a road, the idea being that the woman died with her burden and so her spirit rejoices to see others lightened of theirs.

It has been stated[2] that in the eighteenth century custom required either party to a Kallan quarrel to perform on his own family whatever cruelties the other chose to inflict on his, and that accordingly one of two disputants had been known to kill his own child so as to have the fiendish delight of forcing his adversary to do likewise. This idea is now apparently quite extinct.

---

[1] Turnbull's notice of the caste already cited.
[2] Orme's history, i, 382, and Turnbull's account.

The fondness of the Kallans for jallikats, their women's fashions of stretching their ear-lobes and dispensing with an upper cloth, and their devotion to Karuppanasvámi have been referred to already in this chapter. Hard things have been said about the Kallans, but points to their credit are the chastity of their women, the cleanliness they observe in and around their villages and their marked sobriety. A toddy-shop in a Kallan village is seldom a financial success.

Idaiyans.

After the Kallans, the Idaiyans are the next most numerous Tamil caste in the district. They number about 154,000. They are the shepherds and cowherds of the community and their title is Kónan. They have an imposing *math* at Palni, near the Tiruvávinangudi temple.

The caste is grouped into numerous sub-divisions which are endogamous but will dine together. Those most commonly met with in this district are the Podunáttu, who mostly live to the south and west of Madura town; the Pancháramkatti, who are in great strength in the same place; the Rájéndra and Kalkatti, both common round Kambam and Gúdalúr in Periyakulam taluk ; and the Valasu and Pendukkumekki, on the borders of the Ramnad zamindari.

The Podunáttu Idaiyans have a tradition that they originally belonged to Tinnevelly, but fled to this district secretly one night in a body in the time of Tirumala Náyakkan because the local chief oppressed them. Tirumala welcomed them and put them under the care of the Kallan headman Pinnai Tévan already mentioned, decreeing that, to ensure that this gentleman and his successors faithfully observed the charge, they should be always appointed by an Idaiyan. That condition is observed to this day.

In this sub-division a man has the same right to marry his paternal aunt's daughter as is possessed by the Kallans. But if the woman's age is much greater than the boy's, she is usually married instead to his cousin or some one else on that side of the family.

A Bráhman priest officiates at weddings and the sacred fire is used, but the bridegroom's sister ties the táli. Divorce and the re-marriage of widows is prohibited. The dead, except infants, are burnt. Caste affairs are settled by a headman called the Náttánmaikáran, who is assisted by an accountant and a peon. All three are elected. The headman has the management of the caste fund, which is utilised in the celebration of festivals on certain days in some of the larger temples of the district,

Among these Podunáttus an uncommon rule of inheritance is in force. A woman who has no male issue at the time of her husband's death has to return his property to his brother, father, or maternal uncle, but is allotted maintenance, the amount of which is fixed by a caste pancháyat. Among the Valasu and Pendukkumekki sub-divisions another odd form of inheritance subsists. A man's property descends to his sons-in-law, who live with him, and not to his sons. The sons merely get maintenance until they are married.

CHAP. III.
PRINCIPAL
CASTES.
———

The Pancháramkatti sub-division consists of two sections, one of which has a number of exogamous septs called *kilais* (branches) and the other has none. Its customs generally resemble those of the Podunáttu Idaiyans, but widows are allowed to marry again. In the first of the two sections above mentioned a widow may re-marry once; in the second there is no restriction. As soon as a widow's táli is removed it is replaced by a gold pendant shaped like a many-rayed sun and having three dots on it. This is called Pancháram and gives the sub-division its name. The story goes that the god Krishna used to tie a similar ornament round the necks of Idaiyan widows of whom he was enamoured as a sign that pleasure was not forbidden them. The dead of the Panchá-ramkatti sub-division are usually buried, and annually at the Pongal feast lights are placed on their tombs.

The Valaiyans are nearly as numerous as the Idaiyans. Their name is derived from *valai*, a net, and they formerly lived chiefly by snaring birds and small animals. Nowadays many of them are cultivators and some of them are thieves. They have a comical fairy tale of the origin of the war which still goes on between them and the rat-tribe. It relates how the chiefs of the rats met in conclave and devised the various means for annoying and harassing the enemy which they still practise with such effect. The Valaiyans are grouped into four endogamous sub-divisions; namely Vahni, Valattu, Karadi and Kangu. The last of these is again divided into Pási-katti, those who use a bead necklet instead of a táli, and Kárai-katti, those whose women wear horse-hair neck-laces like the Kallans. The caste title is Múppan. Caste matters are settled by a headman called the Kambliyán ('blanket man'), who lives at Aruppukóttai and comes round in state to any village which requires his services, seated on a horse and accompanied by servants who hold an umbrella over his head and fan him. He holds his court seated on a blanket. The fines imposed go in equal shares to the *aramanai* (literally, 'palace,' *i.e.*, to the head-man himself) and the *oramanai*, that is, the caste people.

Valaiyans.

A Valaiyan has the right to claim his maternal uncle's daughter as a wife. At weddings the bridegroom's sister ties the táli and then hurries the bride off to her brother's house, where he is waiting. When a girl attains maturity she is made to live for a fortnight in a temporary hut, which she afterwards burns down. While she is there, the little girls of the caste meet outside it and sing a song illustrative of the charms of womanhood and its power of alleviating the unhappy lot of the bachelor. Two of the verses say :—

> What of the hair of a man ?
> It is twisted and matted, and a burden.
> What of the tresses of a woman ?
> They are as flowers in a garland, and a glory.
> What of the life of a man ?
> It is that of the dog at the palace gate.
> What of the days of a woman ?
> They are like the gently-waving leaves in a festoon.

Divorce is readily permitted on the usual payments and divorcées and widows may re-marry. A married woman who goes astray is brought before the Kambliyán, who delivers a homily and then orders the man's waist-string to be tied round her neck. This legitimises any children they may have.

Certain of the Valaiyans who live at Ammayanáyakkanúr are the hereditary *pújáris* to the gods of the Sirumalai hills. Some of these deities are uncommon, and one of them, Pápparáyan, is said to be the spirit of a Bráhman astrologer whose monsoon forecast was falsified by events and who, filled with a shame rare in unsuccessful weather-prophets, threw himself accordingly off a high point on the range.

The ceremonies at a Valaiyan funeral are elaborate. At the end of them the relations go three times round a basket of grain placed under a pandal, beating their breasts and singing—

> For us the *kanji* : Kailásam for thee ;
> Rice for us : for thee Svargalókam,

and then wind turbans round the head of the deceased's heir in recognition of his new position as chief of the family.

When a woman loses her husband, she goes three times round the village *mandai* with a pot of water on her shoulder. After each of the first two journeys the barber makes a hole in the pot and at the end of the third he hurls down the vessel and cries out an adjuration to the departed spirit to leave the widow **and** children in peace.

Kammálan is a generic term applied to the artisans of the Tamil country. The Kammálan caste is divided into five sections; namely, Tattáns or goldsmiths, Kollans or blacksmiths, Kannáns or brass-smiths, Tachchans or carpenters, and Kal Tachchans or stone masons. These all intermarry and dine together. The caste title is Ásári. The Kammálans claim to be of divine origin and say that they are descended from Visvakarma, the architect of the gods. They consequently assume airs of superiority over the Bráhmans, wear the sacred thread and copy many of the Bráhmanical customs. These pretensions are of long standing, but none the less the caste has not yet shaken itself free from several of its Dravidian customs and these reveal its descent. The Kammálans talk, for example, of their *gótras*, but these, unlike real *gótras*, form no guide to the marriages which are permissible, and the caste follows the Dravidian rule that a man is entitled to the hand of his paternal aunt's daughter. Again, though marriage is often performed between infants after the Bráhmanical fashion, yet the Dravidian bride-price is always paid. Widows may not re-marry, but they are allowed to wear jewellery and chew betel and nut and are not required to observe the fasts which Bráhman widows keep. The dead, again, are usually buried and not burnt, and the pollution lasts for the period common among non-Bráhman castes—sixteen days. Vegetarianism is commonly practised and yet animal sacrifices are made to village goddesses.

The caste-goddess is Kámákshiamman, and she has her own temple wherever Kammálans are numerous. In this all caste disputes and affairs are settled. No tradition of this deity's origin appears to survive. The caste-organization is very complete. Each of the five divisions elects its own *náttánmaikáran*, or headman, and his *káryastan*, or executive officer. From the five *náttánmaikárans* a headman of the whole caste, called the *anjuvídu náttánmaikáran* is selected by lot, a little child being made to draw the lots in Kámákshiamman's temple. These officials all serve for life. Local headmen, subordinate to them, are often appointed in big villages where the community is numerous. The caste guru lives in Tinnevelly. He is a householder, and not a *sanyási*, and his authority is limited.

After the Kammálans in numerical strength come the Chettis. Of this great community the only sub-division which is especially prominent in Madura is the Náttukóttai, or wealthy banking, section. The traditions of these people say that they fled to this district from Kávéripattanam, formerly the chief port of Tanjore, because the Chóla king oppressed them ; and that they first settled at Náttarasaukóttai near Sivaganga, whence their name. They are devout Saivites and are usually plentifully marked with holy ash and wear a *rudráksham* seed hung round their necks. They shave their heads completely, not leaving the usual *kudumi*, and their women stretch the lobes of their ears. Consequently ingenious native genealogists have pronounced them to be the offspring of Kallan women by Musalman fathers. The fact that their unmarried girls wear necklaces of cowries has similarly given rise to the story that the caste is descended from unions between Kallans and Kuravans.

The Náttukóttai Chettis have two territorial endogamous sub-divisions, Ilaiyáttakudi and Ariviyúr, called after two villages in the Sivaganga zamindari ; the necklets of the married women of the former of these have two strings, while those of the matrons of the latter have only one. The Ilaiyáttakudi section is further divided into seven exogamous septs called *kóvils*, or temples, which derive their names from seven favourite temples in the seven villages of Ilaiyáttakudi, Máttúr, Iluppaikudi, Súrakkudi, Vairavankóvil, Pillaiyárpatti and Velangudi.

At weddings, garlands are brought from the temple to which the bridegroom's family belongs. A man has a right to the hand of his paternal aunt's daughter and the usual bride-price is paid. The táli is tied by a man of the caste, for choice one who has had many children. Vegetarian families intermarry with those which eat meat. Widows may not re-marry and divorce is forbidden. The dead are burnt. Pollution lasts for fifteen days and is removed by the *gurus*. There are two of these, the heads of the *maths* at Piránmalai and at Padárakudi near Tiruppattúr.

The Náttukóttai Chettis are bankers, money-lenders and wholesale merchants, and do business all over south India and in Burma, Ceylon, the Straits Settlements and Natal. The foreign business is transacted by local agents belonging to the caste, who receive a salary proportioned to the distance of the place from Madura, and also, usually, a percentage on the profits. They generally serve for three-year terms and then return and give an account of their stewardship. In time they amass enough to start business on their own account. The caste has a high reputation in the commercial world for integrity and businesslike habits. These latter they carry even into their domestic affairs. As long as the father is alive, all the sons live together under the same roof with him. Hence the huge houses for which the Náttukóttai Chettis in the Sivaganga zamindari are known. But though the various

component parts of a family reside under one roof, they do not
mess in common; but each one is given a carefully-calculated
annual budget allotment of rice, condiments and other necessaries
and required to cook his meals by himself.

Of the profits of their commercial transactions a fixed percentage (called *magamai*) is usually set aside for charity. Some
of the money so collected is spent on keeping up Sanskrit
schools, but most of it has been laid out in the repair and restoration of the temples of the south, especial attention being paid
to those shrines (*pádal petta sthalangal*, as they are called) which
were hymned by the four great Saivite poet-saints, Mánikya-
Váchakar, Appar, Tirugnána Sambandhar and Sundaramúrti.
Lakhs have been laid out on these buildings, but unluckily the
money has not always been expended with taste, or with a fitting
reverence for the older work.

Vannáns are the washermen of the community. The name is
rather an occupational term than a caste title and, besides the
Pándya Vannáns or Vannáns proper, includes the Vaduga Vannáns,
' northern washermen ' or Tsákalas of the Telugu country, and the
Palla, Pudara and Tulukka Vannáns, who wash for the Pallans,
Paraiyans and Musalmans respectively. The Pándya Vannáns
have a headman called the Periya manishan ('big man') who has
the usual powers and privileges. A man can claim the hand of his
paternal aunt's daughter. At weddings a bride-price of Rs. 10½
is paid and the bridegroom's sister ties the táli. Nambis officiate,
and receive a fee of five fanams. Divorce is freely allowed to
either party on payment of twice the bride-price, and divorcées
may marry again. The caste-god is Gurunáthan, in whose temples
the pújári is usually a Vannán. The dead are generally burnt,
and on the sixteenth day the house is purified from pollution by a
Nambi.

The Kusavans are the potters. They have no caste headmen
and their only sub-divisions are the territorial sections Pándya,
Chóla and Chéra. They say these are descended from the three
sons of their original ancestor Kulálan, who was the son of
Brahma. He prayed to Brahma to be allowed, like him, to
create and destroy things daily ; so Brahma made him a potter.
A Kusavan can claim the hand of his paternal aunt's daughter.
Marriage occurs before puberty. The táli is tied by the bridegroom's sister and the usual bride-price is paid. The ceremonies
last three days. One of them consists in the bridegroom's sister
sowing seeds in a pot, and on the last day of the wedding the
seedlings which have sprouted are taken with music to a river or

tank and thrown into it. When the bride attains maturity a cere-mony is conducted by the caste-priest and consummation follows on the next auspicious day.

Both divorce and the re-marriage of widows are forbidden. The dead, except infants, are burnt. The special deity of the caste is Aiyanár. Kusavans are generally the pújáris in his temples, and they make the earthenware horses and images which are placed before these buildings.

Parivárams. The Pariváram caste are the domestic servants of the Tóttiyan (Kambalattár) zamindars. The word means a retinue, and was no doubt originally merely an occupational term. The community speaks both Tamil and Telugu. It is divided into two endoga-mous sections; the Chinna Úliyam ('little services'), who are palanquin-bearers and have the title Tévan; and the Periya Úliyam ('big services'), who are called Maniyakáran The Kómbai Parivárams, who are the servants of the Káppiliyan zamindars of Kómbai and Téváram in the Periyakulam taluk, are a separate community and do not intermarry with the others. When a girl attains maturity she is kept for sixteen days in a temporary hut which is guarded at night by her relations. This is afterwards burnt down and the pots she used are broken into very small pieces, as there is an idea that if rain-water collects in any of them the girl will be childless. During her subsequent periods the girl has to live in the special hut which is provided for the purpose. Some of the ceremonies at weddings are unusual. On the first day a man takes a big pot of water with a smaller empty pot on top of it and marches three times round the open space in front of the bride's house. With him march the happy couple carrying a bamboo to which are tied, in a saffron-coloured cloth, the nine kinds of grain. After the third journey round, these things are put down at the north-east corner, and the marriage pandal is made by bringing three more poles of the same size. Afterwards the wrists of the couple are tied together and the bridegroom's brother carries the pair a short distance. They plunge their hands into a bowl of salt. Next the husband takes an ordinary stone rolling-pin, wraps it in a bit of cloth and gives it to his wife, saying 'Take the child, I am going to the palace.' She takes it replying 'Yes, give me the child, the milk is ready.' This has to be repeated three times in a set formula. Several other odd rites are observed. Bráhmans officiate and the bridegroom's sister, as usual, ties the táli. Divorce is allowed to both sides. Adultery within the caste or with the zamindar is tolerated. The husbands accept as their own any children their wives may bear to the zamindar. Such children are called Chinna Kambalattár and may marry with Tóttiyans. But adultery outside the caste is most rigorously prohibited and sternly punished with excommunication. A mud image of the girl who so offends is made, two thorns are poked into its eyes and it is thrown away outside the village.

The Kunnuvans are the principal cultivating caste on the Palni hills. They speak Tamil. Their own traditions say that their ancestors were Vellálans from the Dhárápuram and Kángayam country in Coimbatore who went up the Palnis some four or five centuries ago because the low country was so disturbed by war (other accounts say devastated by famine), and they call themselves Kunnuva Vellálans and state that the name Kunnuva is derived from Kunnúr village in Coimbatore. Other traditions add that the Virúpákshi and Áyakkudi poligars helped them to settle on their land in the hills, which up to then had only been cultivated by indolent Pulaiyans. The Kunnuvans ousted these latter and eventually turned them into predial serfs, a position from which they have hardly yet freed themselves. In every village is a headman, called the *mannádi*, who has the usual powers The caste is divided into three endogamous sections, called *vaguppus*; namely, Periya (big) Kunnuvar, Kunnuvar, and Chinna (little) Kunnuvar. These will eat together. The dress of the women is characteristic. They wear rough metal necklets, brass bangles and anklets, silver bangles on their upper arms and rings in their noses; and they knot their upper cloths in front across their breasts and bind them round their waists with a sort of bandage. White cloths used to be forbidden them, but are common enough nowadays.

The claim of a man to his paternal aunt's daughter is rigidly maintained, and the evasions of the rule allowed by other castes when the ages of the parties are disproportionate are not permitted. Consequently a boy sometimes marries more than one of these cousins of his, and until he reaches manhood those of them who are much older than he is live with other men of the caste, the boy being the nominal father of any children which may be born. A boy of nine or ten may thus be the putative father of a child of two or three. The marriage ceremonies are the same as usual, a bride-price being demanded, the bridegroom's sister tying the táli, and the relations being feasted.

When a man has no children except a girl, and his family is in danger of coming to an end, a curious practice called ' keeping up the house ' is followed. The girl cannot be claimed by her maternal uncle's son, as usual, but may be ' married ' to one of the doorposts of the house. A silver bangle is put on her right wrist instead of a táli round her neck, she is allowed to consort with any man of her caste, her earnings go to her parents, she becomes their heir, and if she has a son the boy inherits their property through her. The custom is a close parallel to the system of making girls Basavis which is so common in the western part of Bellary and the neighbouring parts of Dharwar and Mysore.

Divorce is readily obtained on the petitioner paying the amount of the bride-price, but the children all go to the father. Divorcées and widows may re-marry, and they do so with a frequency which has made the caste a byword among its neighbours. The Kunnuvans worship the usual village deities of the plains. They generally burn their dead.

Pulaiyans.

The Pulaiyans were apparently the earliest inhabitants of the Palni hills and had things all their own way until the arrival of the Kunnuvans just referred to. They seem, however, to be merely Tamils from the low country, and not a separate race. They speak Tamil and their customs resemble, generally, those of the people in the plains. The caste has a headman called the Náttánmaikáran, who is assisted by a Sérvaikáran and a tóti, or peon, and whose powers and duties are much the same as elsewhere. The community is grouped into three exogamous sub-divisions, called *kúttams*, which are known respectively as Kólankuppan, Pichi, and Mandiyáman after their supposed original ancestors. Marriages take place after puberty and are arranged by the parents. The ceremonies are simple. A bride-price of Rs. 25 is paid and a táli of white beads is tied round the girl's neck. Divorce can be obtained by either party on payment of a fine equal to the bride-price, and divorcées and widows may re-marry any one they choose. The Pulaiyans' favourite deities are Máyándi (whose shrine is generally on a knoll close to the village), Karumalaiyan, and a goddess called Púvádai. Festivals in their honour occur in Chittrai, and consist largely in much dancing by twelve men who have sanctified themselves for the duty by abstaining from eating beef for the twelve months preceding. On the first day they sacrifice a sheep to Máyándi. On the next, they take a ragi pudding in a pot to the shrine of Karumalaiyan, dance round it and then distribute it. On the third day they begin an eight-day feast to Púvádai. at the end of which is more dancing. The whole caste is extremely fond of dancing, and in Panguni (March–April) both men and women keep it up to all hours, going round and round with great energy to the sound of a drum. Pulaiyans eat beef and pork and even rats. Mr. Turnbull's notice of them embodied in Ward's Survey Account says that when any one is attacked with small-pox his friends and relations all flee and leave him to his fate, and the people of his village are prohibited from holding intercourse with others until the epidemic has abated. Much the same thing occurs among the Malaiyális of the Kalráyan hills.

In the fifties of the last century the Society for the Propagation of the Gospel sent a catechist to work among the Pulaiyans. The work languished afterwards, but has now been revived by the American Mission. The catechist's letters in the *Madras Quarterly Missionary Journal* for 1850–52 give a few details about the ways of the caste. They used to assemble for regular hunting excursions. When any animal was killed, its skin or some other part of it was sent to the nearest temple so that the deity might give them more good sport in future. Anyone who was killed on these occasions was buried in the jungle and his memory treated with much respect. The Pulaiyans were kept in the greatest subjection by their masters, the Kunnuvans, who would not let them have a light at night or sleep on a cot, lent them money at usurious interest and turned them into slaves if they were unable to pay it back. None the less, the Pulaiyans were considered indispensable in all cases of sickness, as they alone knew the powers of the medicinal herbs of the hills ; and also in cases of demoniac possession, as the local devils could only be propitiated through their intervention. They were clever at poisoning tigers, and any man who did so was given a new cloth by public subscription and chaired round the village with dancing and music.

The Paliyans are a very backward caste who reside in small, scattered parties amid the jungles of the Upper Palnis and the Varushanád valley. They speak Tamil with a peculiar intonation which renders it scarcely intelligible. They are much less civilized than the Pulaiyans, but do not eat beef and consequently carry no pollution. They sometimes build themselves grass huts, but often they live on platforms up trees, in caves, or under rocks. Their clothes are of the scantiest and dirtiest, and are sometimes eked out with grass or leaves. They live upon roots (yams), leaves and honey. They cook the roots by putting them into a pit in the ground and heaping wood upon them and lighting it. The fire is usually kept burning all night as a protection against wild beasts and it is often the only sign of the presence of the Paliyans in a jungle, for they are shy folk who avoid other people. They make fire with quartz and steel, using the floss of the silk-cotton tree as tinder. Weddings are conducted without ceremonies, the understanding being that the man shall collect food and the woman cook it. When one of them dies the rest leave the body as it is and avoid the spot for some months. Mr. Thurston has published an account[1], with illustrations and measurements, of a settlement of the caste in the Tinnevelly jungles. There, the dead are buried and a stone is placed over the grave, which is never visited again.

Tóttiyans.

The only Telugu caste which is characteristic of the district are the Tóttiyans, otherwise known as Kambalattár or Kambalattár Náyaks. To this community belong nearly all the zamindars. Most of the men now speak Tamil, but Telugu is commonly used by the women. The caste title is Náyakkan. The usual occupation is cultivation. The traditional story of their migration to this district is given in several of the Mackenzie MSS. and is still repeated by the people of the caste. Centuries ago, says this legend, the Tóttiyans lived to the north of the Tungabhadra river. The Muhammadans there tried to marry their women and make them eat beef, so one fine night they fled southwards in a body. The Muhammadans pursued them and their path was blocked by a deep and rapid river. They had just given themselves up for lost when a *pongu* (*Pongamia glabra*) tree on either side of the stream leant forward and, meeting in the middle, made a bridge across it. Over this they hurried, and, as soon as they had passed, the trees stood erect once more before the Musalmans could similarly cross by them. The Tóttiyans in consequence still reverence the *pongu* tree and their marriage-pandals are always made from its wood. They travelled on until they came to the city of Vijayanagar, under whose king they took service, and it was in the train of the Vijayanagar armies that they came to Madura. Caste matters used to be settled by the Méttu Náyakkan, or headman, and the Kódángi Náyakkan, or priest, so called because he carried a drum. Nowadays they are generally decided by a public assembly the leaders of which seat themselves solemnly on a blanket on which is placed a pot of water containing margosa leaves, an emblem of the presence of the deity. Persons charged with offences are invited to prove their innocence by undergoing ordeals. These are now harmless enough, such as attempting to cook rice in a pot which has not been fired, but Turnbull says that he saw the boiling oil

---

[1] *Madras Museum Bulletins*, Vol. V, No. 1. Other references are *Indian Antiquary*, (1876), v, 60, and *Madras Quarterly Missionary Journal* for October 1851.

ordeal in 1813 in Pudukkóttai territory. Perhaps the most serious caste offence is adultery with a man of another community. Turnbull says that women convicted of this used to be sentenced to be killed by Chakkiliyans, but nowadays rigid excommunication is the penalty.

The caste is divided into eight exogamous septs, which seem .(the information is incomplete) to be totemistic in origin and each of which intermarries only with one of the remaining eight. When a girl attains maturity she is kept in a separate hut which is watched by a Chakkiliyan. Marriage is either infant or adult. A man has the usual claim to his paternal aunt's daughter and so rigorously is this rule followed that boys of tender years are frequently married to grown women. These latter are allowed to consort with their husband's near relations and the boy is held to be the father of any children which may be born. Weddings last three days and involve very numerous ceremonies. They take place in a special pandal erected in the village, on either side of which are smaller pandals for the bride and bridegroom. Two uncommon rites are the slaughtering of a red ram without blemish and marking the foreheads of the couple with its blood, and the pursuit by the bridegroom, with a bow and arrow, of a man who pretends to flee but is at length captured and bound. The ram is first sprinkled with water and if it shivers this, as usual, is held to be a good omen. The bride-price is seven kalams of cambu, and the couple may eat only this grain and horse-gram until the wedding is over. A *bottu* is tied round the bride's neck by the bridegroom's sister. In very rare cases, among certain sections of the caste, the bridegroom sends a dagger to represent him and does not appear himself. This form is apparently only adopted when the bride is of rather inferior social status and the ceremonial is then much simpler. The leading judicial decision upon this form is I.L.R., XVII Madras, 422. After marriage, women are required to bestow their favours upon their husband's nearest relatives, and it is believed that ill-luck will attend any refusal to do so. *Sati* was formerly very common in the caste, and the two caste-goddesses, Jakkamma and Bommayya, are deifications of women who thus sacrificed themselves. Every four years a festival is held in their honour, one of the chief events in which is a bullock race. The owner of the winning animal receives a prize and gets the first betel and nut during the feast. The caste god is Perumál, who is worshipped in the form of a curry-grinding stone. The story goes that when the Tóttiyans were fleeing to the south one of their women found her grinding-stone so intolerably heavy that she threw it away. It however reappeared in her basket. Thrown away again, it once more reappeared and she then realised that the caste god must be accompanying them. The dead are either buried or burnt. In the latter case a tomb is erected at which worship is done for 40 days. The Tóttiyans have mausoleums (*málai*, see p. 320) in which a stone is placed to represent each deceased member of the family, and periodical ancestor-worship is performed in these.

Káppiliyans.

Of the Canarese-speaking castes of the district, two, the Káppiliyans and Anuppans, are worth a note. The former are most numerous in the villages near the head of the Kambam valley. Some of the poligars in this part of the country were Káppiliyans, and they doubtless brought with them a retinue of their own castemen. 'I he Káppiliyans' tradition regarding their migration to this district is similar to that current among the Tóttiyans (whom they resemble in several of their customs), the story being that the caste was oppressed by the Musalmans of the north, fled across the Tungabhadra and was saved by two *pongu* trees bridging an unfordable stream which blocked their escape. They travelled, say the legends, through Mysore to Conjeeveram, thence to Coimbatore and thence to this district. The stay at Conjeeveram is always emphasised, and is supported by the fact that the caste has shrines dedicated to Kánchi Varadarája Perumál.

The Káppiliyans are split into two endogamous sub-divisions; namely, the Dharmakattu, so called because, out of charity, they allow widows to marry one more husband, and the Múnukattu, who permit a woman three husbands in succession. The former are again sub-divided into a number of sections, each of whom may only intermarry with certain of the others.

Caste pancháyats hold court on a blanket and the president is a headman called the Játi Kavundan. Kavundan is the caste title. When a girl attains maturity she is kept in a temporary hut in the village *mandai* (common land) for 15 days, and is waited on, and guarded at night, by her relatives. She is then brought into the village with music, and a saffron-coloured thread is tied round her neck as a badge of her condition. The hut is burnt down and the pots she used are broken to atoms.

A man's right to marry his paternal aunt's daughter is so rigorously insisted upon that, as among the Tóttiyans, ill-assorted matches are common. A woman whose husband is too young to fulfil the duties of his position is allowed to consort with his near relations, and the children so begotten are treated as his. At weddings no táli is tied, but the binding portions of the ceremony are the donning by the bride of a saffron-coloured cloth sent her by the bridegroom and of black *glass* bangles (unmarried girls may only wear bangles made of lac) and the linking of the couple's little fingers. Adultery outside the caste is punished by expulsion and, to show that the woman is thenceforward as good as dead, funeral ceremonies are solemnly performed to some trinket of hers, and this is afterwards burnt. The special deities of the caste are many, and some of them appertain to particular sections and even particular families. In several instances they are women who committed *sati*. The dead are usually burnt, but children, people who have died of cholera, and pregnant women are buried. In the case of the last, as usual, the child is first taken out. The characteristic occupation of the Káppiliyans is cattle-grazing. Their ' sacred herd ' at Kambam has been already referred to on p. 20.

The Anuppans are commonest in the Kambam valley. They have a tradition regarding their migration thither which closely resembles that current among the Káppiliyans and Tóttiyans. Their title is Kavundan. They are divided into six territorial groups called *médus* which are named after three villages in this district and three in Tinnevelly. Over each of these is a headman called the Periyadanakkáran, and the three former are also subject to a guru who lives at Sirupálai near Madura. These three are divided again into eighteen *kilais*, or branches, each of whom intermarries only with certain of the others. Caste pancháyats are held on a blanket on which (compare the Tóttiyan custom) is placed a pot of water containing margosa leaves to symbolise the sacred nature of the meeting. Women who go astray with men of other castes are expelled ; and various ceremonies, including (it is said) the burying alive of a goat, are enacted to show that they are dead to the community. The right of a man to the hand of his paternal aunt's daughter is as rigorously maintained as among the Káppiliyans and Tóttiyans, and leads to the same curious state of affairs. No táli is tied at weddings, and the binding part of the ceremonies is the linking, on seven separate occasions, of the little fingers of the couple. A bride-price, as usual, is paid. Like the Káppiliyans, the Anuppans have many caste and family deities, a number of whom are women who committed *sati*.

Of the castes who speak languages foreign to this Presidency the only one which calls for mention is the Patnúlkáran (' silk-thread-people ') community which is so numerous in Madura and Dindigul towns. Their vernacular is Patnúli or Khatri, a dialect of Gujaráti, and they came originally from Gujarát. An inscription dated 473-71 A.D. at Mandasór in western Málwa relates [1] how the Pattaváyas, as the caste was then called, were induced to migrate thither from Láta, on the coast of Gujarát, by king Kumára Gupta (or one of his lieutenants) to practise there their art of silk-weaving. The inscription says many flattering things about the community, and poetically compares the city to a beautiful woman and the immigrants to the silk garments in which she decks herself when she goes to meet her lover. On the destruction of Mandasór by the Musalmans, the Pattaváyas seem to have travelled south to Dévagiri, the modern Daulatábád, the then capital of the Yádavas, and thence, when the Musalmans again appeared on the scene at the beginning of the fourteenth century, to Vijayanagar and eventually to Madura. A curious ceremony confirming this conjecture is performed to this day at Patnúlkáran weddings in south India. Before the date of the wedding the bridegroom's party go to the bride's house and ask formally for the girl's hand. Her relations ask them in a set form of words who they are and whence they come, and they reply that they are from Sórath (the old name for Sauráshtra or Kathiawar), resided in Dévagiri, travelled south (owing to Musalman oppression) to Vijayanagar and thence came to Madura. They then ask the bride's party the same question and receive the same reply. A Maráthi MS. prepared in 1822 at Salem under the direction of the then Collector, Mr. M. D. Cockburn, contains the same tradition ; Mr. Sewell's *A Forgotten Empire* shows how common silk clothing and trappings were at Vijayanagar in the days of its glory ; most of the Patnúlkárans can still speak Telugu, which raises the inference that they must have resided a long time in the Telugu country, while their Patnúli contains many Canarese and Telugu words; and they observe the feast of Basavanna (or Boskanna) which is almost peculiar to the Bellary country. After the downfall of Vijayanagar some of the caste seem to have gone to Bangalore, for a weaving community called Patvégárs, who speak a dialect similar to Patnúli, still reside there. Patvégár is another form of Pattaváya or Pattaváyaka, and Patnúlkáran is the Tamil form of the same word.

The members of the caste in Madura prefer to be called Sauráshtras. They say that they are Bráhmans. The claim is no new affair, as in the reign of Queen Mangammál (1689-1704)

[1] *Ind. Ant.*, xv, 194-201.

eighteen of the members of the community were arrested by the
governor of Madura for performing the Bráhmanical ceremony
of *upákarma,* or renewal of the sacred thread. The queen con-
vened a meeting of those learned in the Sástras to investigate the
Patnúlkárans' right to perform such ceremonies. This declared
in favour of the defendants; and the queen gave them a palm-leaf
award accordingly, which is still preserved in Madura. The
caste now follows many of the customs of the southern Bráhmans
regarding food, dress, forms of worship and names, and has
recently taken to the adoption of Bráhmanical titles, such as
Aiyar, Áchári and Bhágavatar.

The affairs of the Patnúlkárans at Madura are now managed
by a ' Sauráshtra sabha ' which was started in 1895. This body
collects a *magamai*, a sort of income-tax, from the members of the
caste and spends the proceeds on objects calculated to benefit
the community, among them the maintenance of a high school
and subordinate institutions to feed it, and the upkeep of a caste
temple. The Patnúlkárans have a very strong *esprit de corps* and
this has stood them in good stead in their weaving, which is
more scientifically carried on, and in a more flourishing condition,
than is usual elsewhere.

CHAPTER IV.

AGRICULTURE AND IRRIGATION.

AGRICULTURAL STATISTICS—The different taluks—The various crops. WET CULTIVATION—Paddy—Its cultivation—Its varieties. DRY CULTIVATION—Methods—Cotton—Tobacco. IRRIGATION—Area protected—Wells—Tanks and channels—The Periyár project. ECONOMIC CONDITION OF AGRICULTURISTS.

CHAP. IV.
AGRI-
CULTURAL
STATISTICS.

THE figures appended, which are those for 1903–04, show at a glance the general agricultural position in Madura :—

Taluk.	Percentage of area by survey which is				Percentage of area in village accounts of			
	Ryotwari.	Minor inam.	Whole inam.	Zamindari.	Forest and other area not available for cultivation.	Cultivable waste other than fallow.	Current fallows.	Net area cropped.
Dindigul	66·7	3·0	1·0	29·3	24·6	8·6	14·3	52·5
Kodaikanal	100·0	...	...	...	85·6	4·9	1·6	7·9
Madura	72·2	3·0	21·7	3·1	30·5	12·6	7·0	49·9
Mélúr	93·0	8·8	3·2	...	38·9	9·1	5·3	46·7
Palni	53·7	1·1	0·1	45·1	11·2	6·6	23·5	58·7
Periyakulam	48·9	0·5	0·2	50·4	46·3	8·0	3·4	42·3
Tirumangalam	52·5	3·4	8·1	36·0	18·2	9·8	4·7	67·3
District Total	64·5	2·1	3·7	29·7	36·0	8·6	8·4	47·0

It will be seen that of the total area, 30 per cent. is made up of zamindaris, and that in Periyakulam this proportion rises to one-half of the whole. These tracts and the whole inam villages do not appear in the village accounts. Excluding them, of every 100 acres for which particulars are on record in the accounts, as much as 36 are forest or hill or otherwise not available for cultivation, 47 are cropped, 8 are current fallows and 8½ are other culturable waste.

The different taluks.

The proportion of land not available for cultivation is highest in Kodaikanal and Periyakulam taluks, where so much of the country consists of mountain and jungle, and lowest in Palni and

Tirumangalam. In these latter two taluks there are hardly any forests or hills, and moreover culturable land is seldom left waste in Palni owing to the prevalence of cultivation under wells, or in Tirumangalam owing to the richness of the soil. Fallows would appear to be commonest in Palni and Dindigul, but the reason for this is partly the fact that the year (1903-04) for which statistics are given was unusually dry and consequently less than usual of the unirrigated land was cropped.

The various crops.

The figures below give for the same year 1903–04 the percentage of the total area cultivated, both in the district as a whole and in each of the taluks, which was grown with certain of the more important crops :—

Crops.	District Total.	Dindigul.	Kodaikanal.	Madura.	Mélúr.	Palni.	Periyakulam.	Tirumangalam.
Cereals and pulses—								
Rice	22·8	9·1	10·6	62·2	39·3	10·2	17·1	12·9
Cholam	20·3	30·2	0·9	11·0	9·5	30·0	23·5	15·0
Cambu	6·8	13·6	0·2	1·6	10·3	10·8	1·2	2·1
Ragi	6·6	4·5	12·0	3·8	7·1	9·3	12·8	3·6
Varagu	9·2	9·0	0·1	8·5	10·9	0·6	2·9	21·2
Sámai	7·6	10·5	12·1	2·1	1·2	11·1	16·7	2·0
Horse-gram	5·7	6·7	0·2	1·4	4·1	12·6	9·7	0·9
Others	1·7	0·9	1·8	0·4	4.6	5·0	0·7	0·6
Condiments and spices.	0·8	1·5	1·8	0·5	0·3	0·3	1·0	0·4
Orchard and garden produce	1·1	0·7	15·6	2·1	1·1	0·3	0·5	0·4
Oil-seeds—								
Gingelly	4·3	5·3	...	1·4	4·5	2·0	6·8	4·9
Others	2·2	4·5	0·1	1·1	5·2	1·2	0·1	0·4
Sugar-cane	0·1	0·1	...	0·2	...	0·1	0·1	...
Cotton	6·6	1·7	...	0·9	...	4·0	3·3	28·4
Drugs and narcotics—								
Tobacco	0·5	0 7	...	0·1	...	1·1	1·1	0·2
Betel-vine	0·1	0·1	...	0·3	...	0·1	0·2	0·1
Others	3·6	0·9	*44·6	2·4	1·9	1·3	2·3	0·9

* Includes coffee (28·2 per cent.) ; cardamoms (12·9 per cent.) ; and wheat (3·1 per cent.).

It will be noticed that of the regularly irrigated crops paddy is the only one which occupies any considerable extent, the areas grown with sugar-càne and betel-vine being very small. These two latter, however, are on the increase now that the advent of the Periyár water has rendered irrigation more certain. Of the dry crops, cholam (the black variety) is much the most popular, and then varagu; while cambu, ragi, sámai and horse-gram each occupy about the same proportional extent. Gingelly is the chief oil-seed; cotton is of considerable importance; and tobacco, though occupying only a relatively small area, is of much industrial value.

Paddy is most important in the Madura and Mélúr taluks, which are irrigated by the Periyár channels. It occupies the next laigest area (relatively) in Periyakulam, where again the water of the Periyár is much utilised. In the dry taluks of Dindigul and Palni it is grown on only a tenth of the total cultivated area. Sugar-cane and betel are also most raised in Madura and Mélúr. Cholam occupies 30 per cent. of the cropped area in Dindigul and Palni and a large acreage in Periyakulam. Horse-gram is similarly more grown in these three taluks than in any others. It is the only crop which does well in the red sandy land which is so common in them. Of the other dry grains, cambu is most popular in Dindigul, Palni and Mélúr; ragi in Palni and Periyakulam; varagu in Dindigul, Madura and Mélúr; and sámai in Dindigul, Palni and Periyakulam. Cotton is cultivated in more than a fourth of Tirumangalam and on small areas in Palni and Periyakulam, and the tobacco of the district is mainly raised in these last two taluks and Dindigul. Coffee, cardamoms and wheat are cultivated on Government land only in the Palni hills (Kodaikanal taluk) but the two former are grown on small extents of zamindari land on the Sirumalais. The area under 'condiments and spices' in Kodaikanal is that cultivated with garlic. Most of this is raised for export. The 'orchard and garden produce' which occupies so considerable a relative area in the same taluk is the special plantain for which the Palnis are famous. This is also largely raised on the Sirumalais.

Such is the general agricultural position, and it remains to refer to the methods of the Madura ryots in the cultivation of wet and dry crops.

In Madura and Mélúr, under the Periyár channels, only about one-third of the irrigated land is cropped twice with paddy. In time, two crops may come to be the rule; but at present the area under this comparatively new project is only partly developed; manure, labour and cattle are less plentiful than they should be; and the ryots still adhere to the customs which prevailed before the project was completed and there was usually only water enough for one crop. They often waste so much time by putting off the preparation of the seed-beds and leaving the fields to soak before beginning to plough, that the period left them is insufficient for the cultivation of two crops.

CHAP. IV.
WET
CULTIVATION.

Where two crops are grown, they are called respectively the *kódai* and the *kálam* crops. The cultivation of the former is begun about the middle of June, at which time the Periyár water usually first comes down. Sometimes, however, the seed-beds are started before this, water raised from tanks or wells being used for them. Transplantation from seed-beds is the rule. The seed is usually soaked before being sown. Sowing broadcast is not uncommon, but is looked upon as bad farming.

Its cultiva-
tion.

The actual processes of paddy cultivation are much the same as elsewhere. The land is first manured. Sheep or goats are penned thickly upon it and silt from tanks or channels, village rubbish and farm-yard manure are carted on to it. Cake is very seldom employed.. Then the field is flooded and the manure turned in with the usual wooden plough. In the deep black soil common in Madura taluk the cattle sometimes sink so deeply that much ploughing is impossible, and there the land is turned over with the big hoe called the *mamutti.* When the field has been redúced to a state of slush, green leaf-manure is trodden or ploughed in. No special manurial crops or plants are grown; *áváram* (*Cassia auriculata*), *viráli* (*Dodonœa viscosa*) and *kulinji* (wild indigo) are the leaves usually employed. If the soil is alkaline (*soudu*) more leaves and tank silt are used, and no sweepings or cattle manure. Finally the surface of the field is levelled by dragging over it a log called the *parambu.* The seedlings are then transplanted by hand. A month afterwards, the crop is weeded, also by hand. Harvesting and threshing are performed in the usual manner.

For the *kódai* crop the inferior kinds of rice, which only remain on the ground three months after transplantation, are usually grown. Perhaps the commonest sorts are *sen kár* ('red kár') and *vellai kár* (' white kár') and a two months' crop known as *aruvadán kódai.* When these have been harvested, the *kálam* crop, which ought to have been (but is not always) sown meanwhile in the seed-beds, is planted out. This usually consists of the six months' crops known as *sirumani* ('little grain'), *milagu* (so called because it has a round grain like a pepper-corn), and *vari garudan sambá* (' striped kite-coloured rice ') ; or the five months' varieties called *kamban sambá* (so named from its resemblance to cambu) and *tillaináyakam,* a kind which has been recently imported from

Its varieties.

other districts. *Sirumani* and *garudan sambá* require a great deal more water than the other three, but yield abundantly. *Kamban sambá* fetches a high price, but the yield is less. This does best on red soil, while *sirumani* prefers low-lying black land. A four months' species called *nariyan* ('stunted'), which required less water, used to be much grown, but since the advent of the Periyár water it has given way to the choicer kinds. It seems probable that now that there is an ample and certain supply of irrigation other still better sorts might be introduced and grown with success. This matter and the question of economising water would probably repay investigation. At present the ryots raise the same stereotyped sorts of paddy and swamp their fields in the immemorial manner and are generally casual in their methods. Paddy is commonly raised year after year on the same land without rotation, though recently the ryots have begun to cultivate sugar-cane or plautains every third or fourth year.

The methods of dry cultivation in fashion in Madura differ little either with the nature of the soil or the kind of crop. It has already been seen (p. 12) that Tirumangalam is the only taluk in which any considerable area is covered with any soil except the red ferruginous sorts. The following statistics of the assessments per acre of the dry land of the district show how much more fertile the black land is than the red :—

Taluk.	Percentage of assessed dry land which is assessed at								
	Rs. 3.	Rs. 2.	Re. 1-8-0.	Re. 1-4-0.	Re. 1.	As. 12.	As. 8.	As. 6.	As. 4.
Dindigul	...	...	1	20	53	17	8	1	...
Madura	...	...	2	23	50	16	8	1	...
Mélúr	...	...	...	21	71	7	1	...	...
Palni	...	1	2	22	27	29	15	4	...
Periyakulam	...	1	4	25	36	20	11	3	...
Tirumangalam	...	30	22	21	20	6	1	...	...
District Total	...	5	5	22	42	17	8	1	...

Cultivation methods on this black soil differ in one respect from those adopted on the red. The former requires a thorough soaking before it will raise a crop and thereafter needs no further rain; whereas the latter does not retain moisture well and so wants frequent showers. Consequently on the black soils the sowing season may be deferred to as late as October, when the land has received the heavy showers of the north-east rains; whereas on the red land it must be begun in July or August so that the crops may receive the benefit of both monsoons.[1] With this exception, cultivation on both the red and black soils is conducted in a similar manner. Contrary to the practice in the Deccan districts, the black soils are manured and irrigated (even from wells) in the same way as the red.

Except in the fields cultivated under wells in the Palni taluk by the hard-working Vellálans and those in the cotton country in south Tirumangalam tilled by the Reddis, the methods of cultivating dry crops seem careless and unenterprising. First, the stubble of the last crop is ploughed in. Then such manure as is available is spread. Fields at a distance from the village get practically no manuring at all, being merely left fallow now and again to recuperate. Those nearer at hand are given village sweepings and farm-yard refuse, and sheep and goats are penned upon them; but this only occurs once in every two or three years. Only the fields next the habitations are manured every year. Land under wells in Palni is treated, of course, with more care. The cattle are very usually penned at night on these fields and manure is carted to them from long distances.

The manure having been applied, the land is ploughed three or four times with the usual wooden plough, which is somewhat bigger than that employed on wet land. Then, as soon as sufficient rain has fallen, sowing is effected by scattering the seed broadcast and laboriously ploughing the field again to cover it. Mixed crops are common. The seeds are mixed before they are sown. The larger grains, such as dholl, castor and beans, are dropped separately one by one in a furrow made by the plough and then ploughed in separately. When the crop is about a foot high it is weeded by hand, a small hoe being used. Cholam and cambu are first thinned with the plough. Neither process is carefully carried out and the fields are often choked with weeds. The adoption of the Deccan methods of sowing with a drill, covering the seed with a scuffle and hoeing the crop by bullock-power would seem likely to save much labour, do the work better, and have the additional advantage of allowing larger areas to be sown at the most favourable moment, directly after a heavy shower.

---

[1] Elaborate tables of the dates of seed-time and harvest for the various crops in the different parts of the district will be found in G.O., No. 784, Revenue, dated 15th September 1897.

Cholam is harvested by cutting it off close to the ground and then removing the ears. The straw is considered the best cattle fodder available. Cambu is gathered by cutting off the ears only. If more rain falls the plants will then send out another crop of ears. The straw is thought to be bad for cattle and is seldom given them. Ragi is harvested in the same way, but the straw of this is regarded as nutritious. Sámai and varagu are cut off flush with the ground. The straw of these is also rarely given to the cattle. Two crops in a year are raised on some of the best dry land by growing cambu first and then horse-gram or black gram, and round Védasandúr in Dindigul by sowing coriander or Bengal gram as the second crop; but the practice is not common.

Cholam is said to be an exhausting crop and is not sown twice running on the same land. It is usually followed by varagu, sámai or horse-gram. Cambu does not do well if put in immediately after cholam, but otherwise it will flourish for three years in succession in the same field. Varagu is also an exhausting crop, and cannot be grown successfully two years running on the same land unless manure is given it.

Cotton.

Of the cotton of the district, between 80 and 90 per cent. is grown in the one taluk of Tirumangalam. The methods of cultivating the plant in the neighbouring taluk of Sáttúr to the south are described in much detail in Bulletin No. 19, Vol. I, of the Madras Department of Land Records and Agriculture, and the account there given is applicable to the practice in Tirumangalam. The crop is usually raised on the black soils, but the more clayey kinds of red land suit it also. The black soils are locally divided into four varieties; namely, *karisal* (superior friable), *veppal* (inferior friable), *kakkarai* (stiff) and *pottal* (alkaline). *Kakkarai* resembles the deep régada soils of the Deccan districts, cracking greatly in the dry weather and requiring a good soaking before it can be ploughed. It is regarded as inferior to *karisal*, which requires little moisture to render it fit for ploughing and is so friable that the roots of the cotton penetrate it easily. A local proverb says ' Sell even wet land to buy *karisal*.'

Manure is only given once in six or seven years, and is then generally applied to the crop which follows the cotton, and not to the cotton itself. This is said to make the cotton crop more even, and better able to withstand a scarcity of rain. The tillage begins after the showers of June. Three ploughings are enough on clean land, but they are carried deeper than usual, a big stone being put on the plough to keep the share well down. The seed is generally bought from the dealers. It is sown broadcast from the beginning of August onwards and is ploughed in as usual. Before being sown it is rubbed in a paste of cowdung and water and then dried in the sun. This prevents the seeds from sticking together. Cotton is usually raised every other season, cambu or varagu being grown in the alternate years.

CHAP. IV.
DRY
CULTIVATION.

The crop is weeded once with a pointed stick and hoed twice more afterwards with hand hoes. It is scarcely ever irrigated. The first bolls begin to open about three months after sowing and the first picking begins three weeks afterwards. The first pickings give an inferior sample, as they are mainly bolls which have opened prematurely owing to the attacks of insects. Similarly the last pickings are inferior because the lint is leafy and spoiled by insects. Picking goes on from January to April and then again, after the May rains, up to August. The cotton is carefully stored in places where it will be free from damp, either in rooms, in houses, in circular wattle and daub granaries called *pattarai* or in circular bins made of mud and cambu chaff called *kulukkai*. It is usually sold uncleaned to middle-men, who either get it ginned by women with the ordinary wooden roller-gin or sell it to the steam ginning-factories in the Tinnevelly district. It then passes to the presses at Virudupatti or elsewhere or is disposed of to the steam spinning-mill at Madura. Two varieties are recognised; the *uppam*, which is grown on the best *karisal* lands and yields the better crop, and *náttu*, the indigenous variety, which is cultivated on the inferior soils. But the two are very often found mixed together. In the market the Tirumangalam cotton is known as ' Tinnevellies.' It is one of the most highly prized of Indian cottons, being valued for its colour, which is very white. The staple is not particularly long, but the fibre is strong.

The largest area under tobacco is in Dindigul taluk. Periya- kulam comes next, and then Palni. The plant must be irrigated, and thrives best in red soils under wells. Either the soil or the well-water or both must be alkaline, and if they are not so, alkaline earth is often carted on to the land. The experts are agreed [1] that the methods of cultivation and of collecting and curing the leaf leave a great deal to be desired. The seed is sown in a specially prepared plot of land and the seedlings are afterwards transplanted. The seed-bed is often so carelessly flooded with water that some of the seeds are buried too deep while others are washed out of the ground, and the surface of the bed is so caked all over that

Tobacco.

---

[1] See Bulletin No. 53, vol. iii of the Madras Department of Lands Records and Agriculture, and G.O., No. 1063, Revenue, dated 23rd September 1904.

germination is checked. The seedlings are transplanted when the leaves are three or four inches long. This is done by flooding the seed-bed in the early morning, pulling up the plants, putting them in a covered basket in the shade till the evening, and then dibbling them in. The land is often made so wet that the seedlings rot, or these are dibbled in so loosely that they do not take root properly, or so close together that they damage one another.

For tobacco growing the field must be deeply ploughed and well manured. Cowdung is carted on to it and sheep and cattle are penned on it. The seedlings are watered every day at first, and afterwards at longer intervals. The crop is hoed when it has been about three weeks in the field and after five or six weeks the soil is broken up with a *mamutti*. In some villages liquid manure is applied at this period by throwing cowdung into the irrigation channels. When the plants are nearly three feet high they are topped, and this makes the lower leaves increase in size. The suckers which this topping starts into growth are seldom sufficiently checked, however, and they weaken the plant greatly. After about three months the lowest leaves begin to turn spotted, and the plant is then considered to be ripe and is cut off close to the ground in the evening. Half the leaves are still immature and it would probably be better only to pick the ripe leaves and not cut the whole plant down. The plants are collected early next morning and made into small circular heaps with the leaves inwards and the stalks outside. These are covered with straw and are left untouched for three days. The plants are then spread out on the ground for a short time and next hung up on horizontal poles. Every morning they are moved a little to let the air pass freely through them and at the end of fifteen or twenty days they are considered to be cured. This drying process is carelessly managed and some of the leaves rot and the others are not uniform in colour or dryness. When the leaves are considered to be dry, the plants are taken down from the horizontal poles and made into square heaps about two feet high, the stalks being laid cross-wise over each other in alternate rows. Every two or three days, these heaps are opened and re-made. The leaves ferment and change colour, and when a certain blackish tint is produced the fermentation is considered to be finished and the leaves are stripped from the stalk and made up into bundles for sale. This process really requires most careful watching, to see that the heat reached is not too great and that the process is not stopped too soon or carried too far. But the ryot has no thermometer and leaves matters largely to chance,

The whole subject of the growth and curing of tobacco is now under the consideration of Government, who are endeavouring to procure the assistance of experts to advise as to the directions in which improvements might be possible. The manufacture of the cured leaves into cigars at Dindigul is referred to on p. 149.

CHAP. IV.
DRY
CULTIVATION.

The proportion of the cultivated area of the district which is irrigated is higher than the normal for the Presidency. The statistics say that in ordinary seasons 27 per cent. of it is protected from famine and in all seasons nearly 22 per cent. Details for the different taluks, and figures showing the percentage of the wet area in each of these which is irrigated by the various classes of sources are appended :—

IRRIGATION.
Area
protected.

Taluk.	Percentage of wet area which is irrigated respectively by				Percentage of total cultivated area which is protected	
	Government canals.	Tanks.	Wells.	Other sources.	In ordinary seasons.	In all seasons.
Dindigul	1·1	5·6	9·4	0·2	18·5	15·3
Kodaikanal	1·0	...	...	...	15·4	15·3
Madura	16·7	8·5	0·5	1·0	49·6	44·7
Mélúr	10·2	8·4	0·5	...	35·2	27·0
Palni	1·6	3·0	9·8	0·1	41·5	21·4
Periyakulam	3·8	3·6	4·4	0·1	24·3	21·6
Tirumangalam	0·1	7·9	2·4	0·1	13·7	13·1
District Total ...	34·5	37·0	27·0	1·5	27·2	21·7

It will be seen that the best protected taluks are Madura and Mélúr, which are served by the great Periyár project referred to later. Next come Palni, which is chiefly safe-guarded by its numerous excellent wells, and Periyakulam, which also benefits from the Periyár water. At the bottom of the list is Tirumangalam, where there are hardly any channels and very few wells.

Though a large proportion of Mélúr is now safe from famine, the quality of the wet land in it is the poorest in the district, being mostly sandy red soil. This is clearly shown in the figures below, which give the percentage of the assessed wet land in each taluk which is assessed at each of the standard rates :—

Taluk.	Percentage of assessed wet land which is assessed at							
	Rs. 8-8-0.	Rs. 7-8-0.	Rs. 6-8-0.	Rs. 5-8-0.	Rs. 4-8-0.	Rs. 3-8-0.	Rs. 2-8-0.	Rs. 2-0-0.
Dindigul	...	2	4	13	30	37	12	2
Madura	...	4	13	18	18	27	13	7
Mélúr	...	...	...	1	9	60	27	3
Palni	3	5	10	11	17	43	11	...
Periyakulam ...	1	2	4	22	32	24	11	4
Tirumangalam ...	...	...	6	26	38	24	6	...
District Total ...	...	2	6	14	22	37	16	3

It will be seen that nine-tenths of the Mélúr wet land is assessed as lightly as Rs. 3-8-0 per acre and less. The highly-rated land shown in this table as situated in the Palni taluk is mainly that under the Shanmuganadi, one of the best sources in the district; that in Madura is under the Vaigai channels and that in Periyakulam under anicuts on the Suruli. It will be seen, however, that less than a quarter of all the wet land in the district is charged more than Rs. 4-8-0 per acre. This low figure is due to the generally inferior nature of the irrigation sources. Excluding the Periyár project, the best of these are those depending on the Vaigai and Suruli, and they are only equal to the second best sources in the neighbouring districts of Coimbatore and Tinnevelly.

Wells. Wells water no less than 27 per cent. of the total irrigated area in the district. The figures in the statement above show that the areas so irrigated are proportionally highest in Palni, Dindigul and Periyakulam. Madura and the south of Mélúr require few of these sources, as they are so bountifully supplied with channels, but the north of Mélúr contains a much smaller number of them than its circumstances warrant. The soil there is certainly for the most part rocky, but the sub-soil water is said to lie at no great depth.

The wells in Tirumangalam are usually small affairs, the chief expense connected with which is the necessity of revetting their sides to prevent the loose earth of that part of the district from falling into them. Elsewhere the wells (except the 'supplementary' kind which are dug in wet lands to supplement tank irrigation) are usually deep and large pits sunk at great cost in hard soil or through rock. The only water-lifts in use are the ordinary picottah and double mhote. In the case of the latter the bullocks are always backed up the ramp after drawing up the bucket, and never detached and led round to the top of the slope in the convenient manner so common in the Deccan districts. The buckets are either made of leather throughout or consist of an iron basin with a leather continuation.

CHAP. IV.
IRRIGATION.

Except the Periyár project referred to later, practically the whole of the irrigation works of the district, other than the wells, were made in the days of native rule. Old manuscripts say that very many of them were constructed by the numerous poligars among whom the country was divided up, and there is no record of the central government at Madura ʻhaving constructed any of them. Perhaps for this reason, they are all of them small affairs. There exist none of the bold projects seen here and there in the Deccan districts—the Cumbum and Daróji tanks for instance— where a great embankment has been thrown across a valley and a whole river dammed back. The largest scheme was the Peranai anicut across the Vaigai which has now been replaced by the regulator which controls the irrigation from the Periyár. Except this Periyár project, there is not a single work in all Madura which comes under any of the first three of the four main classes into which irrigation works are divided; and though the numerous small tanks and channels which irrigate the wet land of the district are important collectively, they are individually uninteresting. Statistics of the Revenue department show that out of a total of 4,580 minor works, no less than 2,846 irrigate less than ten acres, and another 1,142 water more than ten but less than 50 acres. The local distribution of these minor works is as under :—

Tanks and
channels.

Taluk.	Under 50 acres.	50 to 500 acres.	Above 500 acres.
Dindigul	1,738	80	1
Madura	217	91	12
Mélúr	1,718	99	1
Kodaikanal	34	19	...
Palni	28	32	11
Periyakulam	75	84	9
Tirumangalam	178	152	1
Total ...	3,988	557	35

It will be seen that the very great majority of them lie in the two taluks of Dindigul and Mélúr. Spring channels, which in some districts are such important sources, are in Madura dug only in the bed of the Vaigai. The other rivers are little more than jungle-streams, and have no underflow worth mention.

The rivers of the district and the areas which they respectively drain have been mentioned on pp. 10-12 above. The distribution among these basins (and the minor basins of which they are made up) of the irrigation works which are supplied from rivers and their tributaries, and particulars of the rivers on which these works severally depend, are shown in the following statement [1] : —

Basin.	Minor basin.	River.	Number of Government anicuts.	Number of Government works.	Irrigable ayacut in acres.
Upper Gundár.	Tirumangalam ...	Gundár	5	193	25,626
	Sivarakóttai.	Kavundanadi ...	9	97	} 7,374
		Varattár	2	2	
Lower Gundár.	Kritimánadi ...	Vaigui	...	38	12,842
Amarávati	Palni ...	Shanmuganadi and its tributaries, the	3	45	13,738
		Varadamanadi ...	1		
		Pálár	2		
		Porandalár and Fachaiyár	2		
			2		
	Nallatangi	Nallatangi and a tributary.	3	5	478
	Nangánji	Nangánji! ...	4	18	1,533
	Lower Kodavanár ...	Kodavanár and tributaries.	3	293	2,466
	Dindigul ...	Do. ...	18	1,033	13,965
Upper Vaigai.	Suruli ...	Suruli	14	67	12,100
	Periyakulam ...	Varáhanadi and tributaries.	13	75	8,132
	Ándipatti	Vaigai and tributaries.	3	13	1,146
	Vattilagundu ...	Manjalár and tributaries.	19	44	4,471
Mid Vaigai.	Sólavandán	Vaigai	...	223	9,061

Included in the first of these minor basins, that of Tirumangalam, is the Nilaiyúr channel, which takes off from the Vaigai below the Chittanai and supplies 5,998 acres directly or indirectly.

[1] Compiled from particulars kindly furnished by M.R.Ry. A. V. Ramalinga Aiyar, B.A., B.C.E., Executive Engineer of Madura district.

The land under this is the only part of the district in which the Voluntary Irrigation Cess is levied.

Connected with the Lower Gundár basin are seven channels from the Vaigai which are supplied by *korambus*, or temporary dams made of brushwood and earth which are renewed every year.

In the Palni minor basin, all but two of the channels have head sluices. The most important of them are the Aiyampalle anicut across the Pálár, which irrigates 3,860 acres, and the Kóttai dam on the Varadamanadi or Varattár, which supplies 2,175 acres. It is proposed to dam up the Porandalár river in this basin and its tributary the Pachaiyár and to form a reservoir which would increase the supply in this area. The scheme, however, is a protective rather than a productive project.

In the Dindigul minor basin, eight of the anicuts have head sluices. The most important of them is the Áttúr dam, which waters 913 acres.

In the Suruli minor basin the chief anicuts are the Uttamúttu, Pálaiyamparavu and Chinnamanúr dams, which irrigate respectively 2,469, 2,451 and 1,666 acres. All but two of the anicuts in this area have head sluices.

In the Periyakulam minor basin, on the other hand, none of the anicuts have any head works. The best of them, that at Talattukóvil, supplies 2,131 acres.

Irrigation from the Varáhanadi in this tract will shortly be improved by the Berijam project recently sanctioned. The Berijam swamp lies on the top of the Palnis about twelve miles south-west of Kodaikanal at an elevation of 7,100 feet. It is about two miles long, runs nearly north and south, and is situated on the water-parting of the Palni range, so that the southern portion of it drains into the Varáhanadi and the northern into the Amarávati. The project, which was first suggested by Col. Pennycuick, C.S.I., R.E., in 1887, consists in throwing dams across both ends of the swamp and forming a reservoir with a capacity of $77\frac{1}{2}$ million cubic feet to increase the supply in the Varáhanadi. The estimate amounts to Rs. 54,500.

In the Ándipatti minor basin lies the uppermost anicut on the Vaigai, that at Kunnúr.

Of the anicuts in the Vattilagundu basin the chief is that at Ayyampálaiyam which supplies 971 acres.

In the Sólavandán minor basin are included the Tenkarai channel which takes off from the Chittanai dam across the Vaigai,

$2\frac{1}{2}$ miles below the Peranai, and supplies land on the south bank of the river, and also several spring channels which are excavated to tap the underflow in the same river.

Particulars similar to those in the above statement are not available for the small area included in the basins of the Tirumanimuttár and Pálár in Mélúr taluk, as this is only now being examined by the Tank Restoration party. Madura was the first district in which the Tank Restoration Scheme was begun, but the Mélúr taluk was not finished at the same time as the rest of it because it was not then clear how much of it would be affected by the Periyár project.

The Periyár project.

The great Periyár project already several times referred to consists, to state the matter very briefly, in damming the Periyár ('big river') which flows down the western slope of the Gháts, through country possessing a superabundant rainfall, and turning the water back, by a tunnel through the watershed, down the dry eastern slope of the Gháts to irrigate the parched up plains on that side of the range. According to Captain Ward's Survey Account of 1815, the first person to suggest this scheme was Muttu Arula Pillai, prime minister of the Ramnad Rája, who in 1798 sent 'twelve intelligent men' to enquire into its possibility. They reported in favour of it, but funds were lacking. In 1808 Sir James (then Captain) Caldwell, the District Engineer, reported, after a cursory examination, that the scheme was impracticable. The matter, however, continued to be discussed, and in 1867 it was brought forward by Major Ryves, R.E., in a practical form. He proposed to construct an earthen dam 162 feet high across the Periyár and turn back the water down a cutting through the watershed. His idea was merely to divert the river, and not to store its waters. He estimated the cost of the matter at $17\frac{1}{2}$ lakhs. From 1868 to 1870 Colonel (then Lieutenant) Pennycuick, R.E., and afterwards Mr. R. Smith, investigated the scheme and a complete project, estimated to cost 54 lakhs, was drawn up which involved important modifications of Major Ryves' proposals, among them the transfer of the site of the dam to a point seven miles lower down the river. Doubts arose as to the practicability of constructing so huge an embankment of earth, and it was not until 1882 that Colonel Pennycuick's proposal to build a masonry dam was accepted, and he was directed to revise the plans and estimates for the whole project. The scheme he drew up included a great masonry dam across the Periyár, a huge lake, and a tunnel through the watershed. It was sanctioned in 1884 and work was begun late in 1887. The estimate for direct charges was 62 lakhs.

The site of the dam and lake are in Travancore territory and it was agreed that the British Government should pay an annual rent of Rs. 40,000 for a certain specified area and certain defined rights, and that the lease should run for 999 years with the option of renewal. Sovereign rights over the tract were reserved by the Travancore State.

The immense difficulties which arose and were overcome during the actual construction of the great project are detailed in the *History of the Periyár Project* (Madras Government Press, 1899) by Mr. A. T. Mackenzie, one of the Engineers who helped to carry it through. The site of the works was an unhealthy jungle 3,000 feet in elevation, where rain and malaria rendered work impossible for a considerable portion of the year, where even unskilled labour was unobtainable, and to which every sort of plant and nearly all material had to be transported at great cost from a railway 76 miles off and up a steep ghát road. A canal was constructed from the top of the ghát to the site of the dam to meet this latter difficulty, and later an overhead wire ropeway, driven by a turbine, was put up from the foot of the ghát to the head of the canal. The difficulty of laying the foundations for a dam in a river of such magnitude (the discharge is equal to half the average flow of Niagara) and liable to such sudden and heavy freshes (one of these registered 120,000 cusecs) was immense, and at first the work was swept away again and again. The operations were described by the Chief Engineer, Col. Pennycuick, as the most anxious, difficult and exhausting of any which had come within his experience. After the foundations were all in, further immense difficulty occurred in passing the ordinary flow of the river and the constant high freshes without damage to the masonry of the dam.

After many expedients had been tried, this was eventually effected through a tunnel or culvert in the body of the dam itself, which was afterwards closed and plugged. On the left of the dam a smaller extension 221 feet long was built to close a dip in the ground, and an escape 434 feet in length was made on the right. The main dam was practically finished by October 1895. Including the parapets, it is 176 feet above the bed of the river, 1,241 feet long, 144 feet 6 inches wide at the bottom and 12 feet wide at the top. The front and rear walls are of rubble masonry and the interior is filled with concrete in surki mortar. The lake impounded by it covers more than 8,000 acres and has a maximum possible depth of 176 feet.

The passage through the watershed consists of an open cutting or approach 5,342 feet long, a tunnel 5,704 feet long, and another open cutting or debouchure 500 feet long. The approach is 21 feet wide. The tunnel is 12 feet wide by $7\frac{1}{2}$ feet high and has a gradient of 1 in 75. It was all blasted through solid rock, machine drills driven by compressed air supplied by a turbine plant being employed. A sluice-gate (Stoney's patent) at the head of it controls the outflow. From the lower end of it the water hurls itself down the face of the hill into a stream called the Vairavanár, whence it flows into the Suruli and thence into the Vaigai. It has long been suggested that the great head obtainable at the outfall, 900 feet in a length of 6,800 feet, might be utilised for driving turbines for the generation of electricity. One difficulty is that the water is only required for irrigation for nine or ten months in the year, whereas for any scheme for the production of electrical power on commercial lines it would need to be passed through the tunnel all the year round. The waste of water which this would involve could, however, be obviated by the construction of a reservoir on the plains, below the outfall and the power-station, and the feasibility of this is under examination.

On the Suruli and Vaigai there are several ancient anicuts, and the supply at these has of course been increased since the Periyár water was passed into the rivers, but the mass of the water is not utilised until it reaches the Peranai ('big dam') anicut which crosses the Vaigai about $5\frac{1}{2}$ miles due south of Nilakkóttai, and 86 miles from the mouth of the tunnel, where the river changes its course to the south-east. This Peranai is an old native work which fed a channel on the north bank of the river called the Vadakarai channel. A great deal of silt collected above it and choked the river bed and the new main channel, and it has now been replaced by a regulator constructed on modern principles and possessing ten vents of 40 feet each, fitted with Colonel Smart's counterbalanced shutters which can be raised to allow the free passage of dangerous floods and lowered at other times to hold up water to the height required. From this regulator leads off the main canal, which passes through a head sluice of six vents of twenty feet span. This runs nearly due eastwards almost as far east as the town of Mélúr, is nearly 38 miles long, is six feet deep and has a carrying capacity of 2,016 cusecs at the head. The courses of the twelve branches which take off from it are shown in the accompanying map of the area served by the project. Their total length is nearly 68 miles.

The project was opened in October 1895 by Lord Wenlock, then Governor of Madras. The construction estimate was closed on the 31st March 1897 and the direct expenditure up to then had

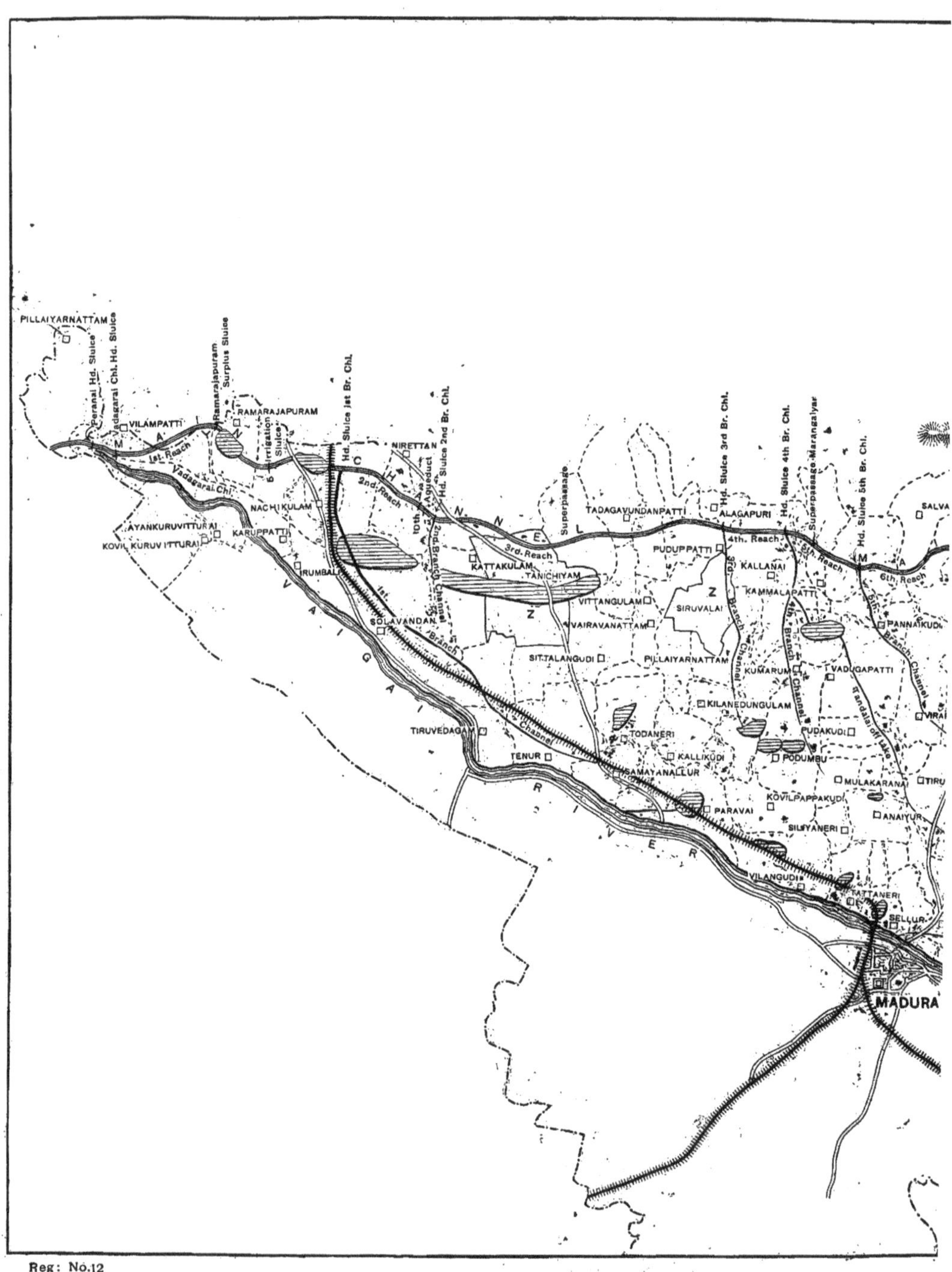

PILLAIYARNATTAM
Peranai Hd. Sluice
Vadagarai Chl. Hd. Sluice
VILAMPATTI
Ramarajapuram Surplus Sluice
RAMARAJAPURAM
Irrigation Sluice
1st. Reach
Vadagarai Chl.
Hd. Sluice 1st Br. Chl.
NIRETTAN
Hd. Sluice 2nd Br. Chl.
Aqueduct
2nd. Reach
10th Br. Channel
NACHIKULAM
AYANKURUVITTURAI
KOVIL KURUV ITTURAI
KARUPPATTI
IRUMBALI
SOLAVANDAN
1st. Branch
VAIGAI
KATTAKULAM
TANICHIYAM
TADAGAYUNDANPATTI
Superpassage
3rd. Reach
VITTANGULAM
VAIRAVANATTAM
SIRUVALAI
PUDUPPATTI
ALAGAPURI
4th. Reach
Hd. Sluice 3rd Br. Chl.
KALLANAI
KAMMALAPATTI
Hd. Sluice 4th Br. Chl.
Superpassage-Marangaiyar
5th. Reach
Hd. Sluice 5th Br. Chl.
SALVA
6th. Reach
PANNAIKUDI
SITTALANGUDI
PILLAIYARNATTAM
KILANEDUNGULAM
KUMARUM
VADUGAPATTI
3rd. Branch Channel
4th. Branch Channel
5th. Branch Channel
Randaimodai off take
VIRAI
TIRUVEDAGAM
TODANERI
PUDAKUDI
PODUMBU
TENUR
KALLIKUDI
SAMAYANALLUR
MULAKARANAI
TIRU
KOVILPAPPAKUDI
PARAVAI
SILUVANERI
ANAIYUR
RIVER
VILANGUDI
KATTANERI
SELLUR
MADURA

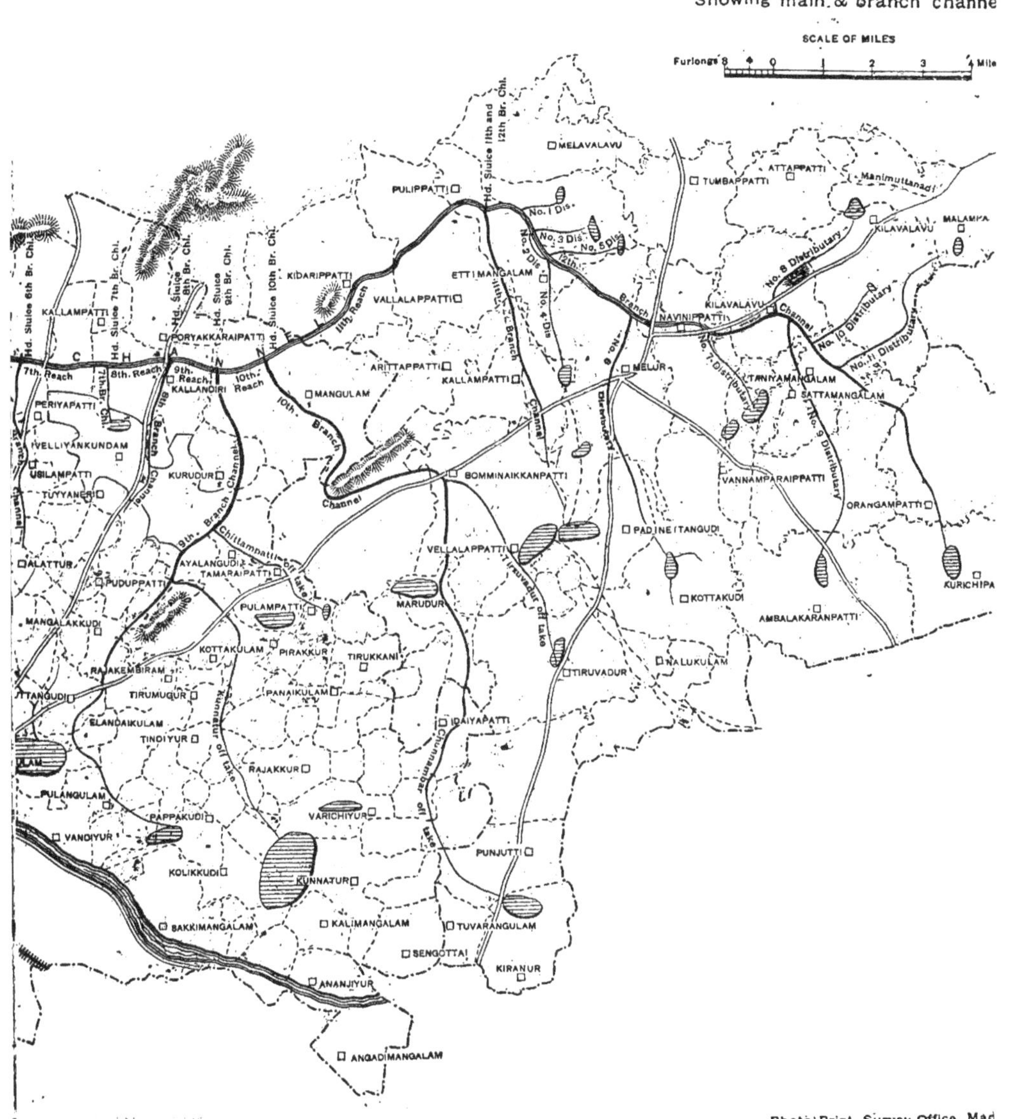

PERIYAR PROJECT
MADURA DISTRICT
Showing main. & branch channe
SCALE OF MILES
Furlongs 8 4 0   1   2   3   4 Mile
MELAVALAVU
ATTAPPATTI
Manimuttanadi
PULIPPATTI
TUMBAPPATTI
KILAVALAVU
MALAMPA
No. I Dis
No. 3 Dis
No. 5 Dis
No. 8 Distributary
Hd. Sluice 11th and 12th Br. Chl.
KIDARIPPATTI
ETTI MANGALAM
KILAVALAVU
NAVINIPPATTI
No. 10 Distributary
No. 11 Distributary
VALLALAPPATTI
No. 2 Dis
No. 4 Dis
12th
11th Branch
Branch
11th. Reach
Hd. Sluice 6th Br. Chl.
Hd. Sluice 7th Br. Chl.
Hd. Sluice 8th Br. Chl.
Hd. Sluice 9th Br. Chl.
Hd. Sluice 10th Br. Chl.
KALLAMPATTI
PORYAKKARAIPATTI
ARITTAPPATTI
KALLAMPATTI
MELUR
TANIYAMANGALAM
SATTAMANGALAM
No. 6 Distributary
No. 7 Distributary
No. 9 Distributary
7th. Reach
7th Br. Chl.
8th. Reach
9th. Reach
10th. Reach
KALLANDIRI
MANGULAM
10th. Branch
Channel
Channel
Channel
PERIYAPATTI
VELLIYANKUNDAM
KURUDUR
BOMMINAIKKANPATTI
VANNAMPARAIPPATTI
ORANGAMPATTI
USILAMPATTI
TUYYANERI
9th. Branch Channel
Chittampatti off lake
PADINEITANGUDI
KOTTAKUDI
AMBALAKARANPATTI
KURICHIPA
ALATTUR
AYALANGUDI
TAMARAIPATTI
VELLALAPPATTI
Tirumadur off lake
PUDUPPATTI
PULAMPATTI
MARUDUR
MANGALAKKUDI
KOTTAKULAM
PIRAKKUR
TIRUKKANI
NALUKULAM
RAJAKEMBIRAM
PANAIKULAM
TIRUVADUR
TIRUMUGUR
ITTANGUDI
Kunnatur off lake
Chinnambar off lake
ELANDAIKULAM
TINDIYUR
IDAIYAPATTI
ULAM
RAJAKKUR
PULANGULAM
VARICHIYUR
PAPPAKUDI
PUNJUTTI
VANDIYUR
KOLIKKUDI
KUNNATUR
SAKKIMANGALAM
KALIMANGALAM
TUVARANGULAM
SENGOTTAI
KIRANUR
ANANJIYUR
ANGADIMANGALAM
Photo-Print, Survey Office. Mad
1906.

amounted to 81·30 lakhs, made up of 42·26 lakhs for the head works (the dam and tunnel), 18·43 lakhs for the main canals, branches and distributaries, and 20·61 for establishment and tools and plant. Other works remain to be carried out which, as far as can at present be foreseen, will bring the total cost to nearly 100 lakhs. The culturable area commanded consists of 106,000 acres of first crop and 51,000 acres of second crop on Government land, and 20,000 and 9,000 acres of first and second crop respectively on zamin and whole inam wet land. The assessment rates on the Government land commanded were raised, in accordance with an announcement made at the time of the last Settlement (see p. 202), to those payable under irrigation sources of the first class adopted for the district, and zamin and whole inam wet lands are charged Rs. 4 per acre for a first wet crop and Rs. 3 for a second. A Special Deputy Collector is in charge of the supply of water to these latter, of the collection of the assessment on them, the disbursement of loans to ryots, and other special matters connected with the project. The total areas actually irrigated since the first year in which the project came into operation are given in the margin. The net profit at present on the existing total capital outlay is 4·08 per cent.

CHAP. IV.
IRRIGATION.

Years.	Area actually irrigated		
	First crop.	Second crop.	Total.
	ACS.	ACS.	ACS.
1896–1897	48,623	11,950	60,573
1897–1898	66,328	18,816	85,144
1898–1899	77,710	25,038	102,748
1899–1900	88,721	29,712	118,433
1900–1901	100,158	31,455	131,613
1901–1902	106,933	36,237	143,170
1902–1903	105,228	35,167	140,395
1903–1904	105,709	36,240	141,949
1904–1905	110,002	36,788	146,790

A project of this magnitude takes some time to attain its utmost extension. Ryots have emigrated from Coimbatore, Tinnevelly and Trichinopoly to the land commanded by it, but the supply of labour and cattle is still unequal to the demand; the obliteration of the former cart-tracks has necessitated the designing of a system of new cross-roads, but these are not yet finished; this difficulty of transport has made manure, which is always scarce in this area, more expensive than ever; drainage channels are required, but have not all been carried out yet; and the ryots, as already explained, have not yet adapted themselves to the new state of affairs but continue to grow one crop where they might raise two, to supersaturate their land to the detriment of the yield, and to avoid, instead of reclaiming, the patches of alkaline land which exist. When the whole area commanded by the project has been taken up and the extension of second-crop cultivation begins in earnest, the project will scarcely be able to supply sufficient water for the demand. In order to increase the storage capacity of the lake and at the same time render the dam safe against extraordinary floods, an estimate has now been sanctioned for lowering the escape on the right, which is at present 14 feet below the crest of the dam, by 8 feet and erecting across it a regulator fitted with movable shutters 16 feet high. These will be raised during dangerous floods and thus increase the waterway on the escape, and lowered at other times. They will raise the full supply level of the lake by eight feet and its storage capacity by 2,361 millions of cubic feet.

In O.S. No. 22 of 1901 on the file of the West Sub-Court of Madura, Mr. Robert Fischer (as proprietor of riparian villages on the Vaigai below the Peranai), the Lessees of the Ramnad and Siva-ganga zamindaris and the minor Rája of Ramnad brought a suit against the Secretary of State in connection with the building of the new regulator at the Peranai and the construction of the new main channel. They claimed that their rights as riparian pro-prietors lower down the Vaigai were injuriously affected by these works, and prayed for a decree declaring, among other things, that Government had no right to erect the regulator or excavate the channel and requiring them to remove the one and either close the other or reduce it to the size of the old Vadakarai channel. The suit was dismissed in October 1903, but an appeal has been preferred to the High Court.

It remains to note the economic condition of the agriculturist of the district. It is sufficient to take his case by itself for the reason that he constitutes nearly three-fourths of the total popula_tion and that the remaining fourth depend for their welfare directly upon his prosperity and spending power. Statistics go to show that the Madura ryot is usually a farmer in a very small way. Of the pattas of the district, as many as 73 per cent. are for amounts as small as Rs. 10 and less, and another 20 per cent. for sums between Rs. 10 and Rs. 30 ; the average size of a holding is under six acres ; and the average assessment thereon is just over Rs. 10. But these figures are probably largely affected by the large number of Kallans who reside within the district. These people seldom farm in earnest, but live largely by blackmailing and theft. They are among the first to feel the pinch of a bad season, and, were they not accustomed to thieve then with more than usual energy and to emigrate light-heartedly with all their belongings to Rangoon and Ceylon, they would constitute a constant source of anxiety. Excluding these people, the Madura ryot appears to be comfortable enough. The wealth of the capital of the district has no doubt led common repute to assess the well-being of the rest of the country at a higher standard than the circumstances warrant ; but the fact that since the famine of 1876–78 no relief-works or gratuitous relief have been necessary is significant. In the quinquennium 1897–1901 the average area cultivated was 22 per cent. greater than the average for the five years 1871–1875 and the land assessment paid was 24 per cent. greater. During this period the population increased by 29 per cent., and it would therefore appear that the people are multiplying dangerously faster than the means of subsistence. But during this same period the Periyár irrigation has rendered available for the cultivation of rice much land which formerly bore only precarious dry crops, and has resulted in two crops being raised on considerable areas where only one grew before. Wells have increased enormously and have not only enabled a crop to be grown with certainty where cultivation was formerly a gamble, but have permitted the planting of such valuable staples as tobacco in place of the dry crops and pulses with which the ryots were formerly content. Credit is sufficiently cheap. The Náttukóttai Chettis abound, and in Madura is the Hindu Permanent Fund, capital Rs. 2,99,964, which was started on 1st February 1894, moved in 1902 into the substantial office near the west *gópuram* of the temple which was opened in March of that year by Lord Ampthill, and possesses a constantly increasing clientèle. *Ela-nidhis*, or chit associations, are also numerous. The members of these agree to subscribe a fixed sum each month for a fixed period and lots are cast monthly to decide who shall take the whole of it. A man who once wins the pool is debarred from competing for it again but is obliged, of course, to go on with his monthly subscription until the end of the fixed period. The parts of the district which stand most in need of improvement at present are the Kallan tracts in the north of Mélúr, the adjoining area in Dindigul and the north-west of Tirumangalam taluk. In the two former of these it seems, from official reports, that much might be done by increasing the number of wells. For the last the best hope at present lies in the chance of the supply in the Periyár lake being sufficiently increased to admit of a channel being led to it from the Peranai regulator.

CHAPTER V.

FORESTS.

CHAP. V.
FORESTS.

Beginnings of
conservancy.

IT was not until the middle of tho last century that any attempt
was made to conserve the valuable forests of the district. Up till
1852, any one was allowed to fell any timber he chose, anywhere,
without let or hindrance, and the jungles were being rapidly
destroyed and stripped of all their choicest trees. In that year
orders were issued prohibiting felling without a license from the
Revenue authorities, but no fee was charged for this permission
and it was freely granted even to the timber-merchants who cut
down wood wholesale and exported it to Tanjore, Trichinopoly and
other districts which had no forests of their own. The only
revenue derived from the forests was the proceeds of the leases cf
jungle produce, and in 1854 the oppression by official underlings
of the hill tribes who collected these products led to the abolition
of even this source of profit.

In 1856 Mr. Parker, the then Collector, brought to notice the
great value of the growth in the Kambam valley and the futility
of the existing orders for its protection, and two years later
Government made a first beginning in conservation by forbidding
the destructive methods by which plantain growing was carried
on in the Palni hills. This cultivation consisted in clearing a
space in the forest by felling and burning every tree within it,
roughly ploughing in the ashes, and putting out the plantain
cuttings in the rich soil thus rendered available ; after a few years
the patch thus cleared was abandoned and another was treated in
the same way; and since the abandoned clearings hardly ever
produced good forest again, but merely relapsed into thorny wastes,
thousands of acres of excellent jungle had thus been ruined.

In 1857 Lieutenant (afterwards Colonel) Beddome, one of the
first of the Assistant Conservators of Forests, visited the Palnis and
sent in a report on the rapid denudation of their forests which

was proceeding and also an elaborate list of their flora.1   He said
that almost all the bigger teak and blackwood trees had already
been felled; that even saplings of these varieties were being
carried off for posts; that *vengai* was similarly carted away in
large quantities; and that, in short, hardly any of the forest on
any part of the range had not been ruthlessly ruined.

In 1860 one forest overseer, salary Rs. 80, was posted to the
Kambam valley and in 1862 he was given a subordinate establishment costing Rs. 100 a month. The meagre scale of this is
sufficiently indicated by the fact that for the whole of the Palni
hills only two peons on Rs. 5 each were proposed, one for the
Upper Range and one for the Lower. The 'Forest department'
thus constituted took charge of the more important woodlands of
the district (including those of the Palnis, the Kambam valley and
the Karandamalais) and its duties were defined to be the accomplishment of strict conservancy and the satisfaction of the timber
requirements of the Public Works department   Some of the
forests were administered entirely by t, and others were worked
on an improved edition of the old license system, permission to
fell being granted by the Forest Officer on payment to the Revenue
department of fees varying with the nature of the tree; trees of
certain varieties reserved for their special value being marked
officially before being cut down (so as to protect saplings); and
the timber felled being checked at certain tannahs by 'Forest
taunah police.'   Ryots were allowed to fell unreserved trees within
their village boundaries free of charge if they wanted them for
agricultural purposes.   Side by side with the forests placed under
the newly constituted establishment were others controlled in a
vague way by the Jungle Conservancy department, as it was
called, under the Collector.

None of these three systems can be said to have worked
successfully.   Much of the duty of conservation was left to the
revenue officers, who had other duties which already engrossed all
their attention and were unable adequately to check frauds by
village officers and others or unauthorised felling by ryots; and
even in the jungles which were specially under the Forest department there was a lack of systematic working and intelligent
provision for the future.   In 1871 the Collector (there was a good
deal of friction in those early days between the Revenue and the
Forest authorities) said that in the west of the district the department's operations ' apparently consisted of purchasing timber at a

---

¹ Both these were published by order of Government in M.J.L.S. (1858), xix,
N.S., 163 ff.

fixed rate per cubic foot from the woodcutters and selling it to the general public at 100 per cent. profit. There was not the slightest check on the woodcutters.'

In the years which immediately followed, the expected needs of the extension of the South Indian Railway (or 'Great Southern India' line as it was called in those days) led to increased interest in the Madura forests, but the reports show that real conservation was far from being attained, illicit felling and the clearing of jungle for plantain gardens on the Lower Palnis going on much as before. A good deal of land was also cleared on this range and on the Sirumalais for coffee gardens of an ephemeral kind which were abandoned soon after they were opened.

In 1871 a small forest establishment was specially sanctioned for the Lower Palnis, and much debate took place regarding the possibility of taking up certain tank-beds in Tirumangalam for plantations of babul (*Acacia arabica*) and *vélvélam* (*A. leucophlœa*) ; of renting on Government behalf the forests on the Palnis which belonged to the Kannivádi and Áyakkudi zamindaris and those on the Sirumalais which were included in the Ammayanáyakkanúr estate; and of inducing the Travancore Darbar to bring some of its timber to a dépôt to be established at Kambam. Confidence in the Forest department was, however, still so small that the Court of Wards, which at that time was managing the jungles in the Gantamanáyakkanúr and Bódináyakkanúr zamindaris during the minority of their proprietors, declined to entrust these areas to the Forest officials. These and the other zamindari jungles were (as, indeed, they still are) a continual source of difficulty. Their exact boundaries were so little known and they so dovetailed with the Government forests that fires started in them spread to the latter ; they rendered smuggling from the reserves a very simple affair ; and they undersold the Forest department by reckless felling whenever a demand for timber or firewood arose. Their boundaries were subsequently ascertained and marked out by the Survey department, but in several cases appeals and suits followed which were not finally settled for a long period.

In 1880 a Committee composed of Mr H. J. Stokes (the Collector), Major Campbell Walker (Deputy Conservator on special duty) and Mr. Gass (Deputy Conservator of the district) definitely selected 21 areas measuring 285 square miles (some of it within zamindaris) which they proposed to constitute reserves and clearly demarcate as such. No very definite action was taken on this body's proposals, but they constituted an important foundation for the proceedings which were subsequently initiated. Grazing-fees were instituted for the first time in accordance with a recommendation by this Committee.

In 1882 the Madras Forest Act was passed into law, the Jungle Conservancy department came to an end, and reservation and conservancy were at last put on a regular footing. As in other districts, the first step taken under this enactment was the ' forest settlement,' or the selection, demarcation, mapping and formal notification of all areas to be reserved, including the enquiry into and adjudication upon all claims over them (such as rights of way, cultivation or pasturage and the like) which were put forward by private individuals.

As elsewhere, it was originally intended to divide all forests into three classes; namely, (1) reserved forests, in which all claims were to be settled under the Act ; (2) reserved lands, which were to be reserved subject to all rights that might be asserted, *i.e* , the claims to rights in them remained unsettled; and (3) village forests, which were intended to meet the requirements of villages in localities where the custom of free-grazing and the free collection of firewood and leaves for manure had long and steadily obtained. In 1890, however, a further step in advance was made, and it was determined that all land which was to be protected at all should be formally settled under the Act and constituted ' reserved forest.' The proposed scheme of village forests was abandoned as impracticable, but villagers were allowed their old privileges over unreserved lands, except that they might not cut reserved or classified trees without permission.

The figures in the margin show the extent and situation of the reserved forests as they have been finally notified under the Act.[1] It will be seen that the largest areas are in the taluks of Kodaikanal, Periyakulam and Mélúr, and the smallest in Tirumangalam and Palni, in both of which latter the extent is quite insignificant. The reserves were nearly all surveyed by the Government of India Survey between 1888 and 1894 on a scale of 4 inches to the mile.

Taluks.	Area in square miles of reserved forest.	Percentage to total area of taluk.
Dindigul ...	88	8
Madura ...	49	11
Mélúr ...	105	22
Palni	3 ⎫	36
Kodaikanal ...	210* ⎭	
Periyakulam.	152	10
Tirumangalam.	13	2
District Total	620	13

* Includes 9 square miles 'proposed for reservation.'

[1] For assistance with the rest of this chapter I am greatly indebted to Mr. H. B. Bryant, District Forest Officer.

CHAP. V.
FORESTS.

Their
position.

The Madura forests differ widely from those in some places (South Coimbatore and Tinnevelly, for example) in that they are not situated all in one block but are scattered about all over the district with cultivation and zamin forests everywhere intervening among them. Broadly speaking, they may be readily and conveniently grouped into four main classes: First, the open and deciduous growth on the plains and slopes of the low hills in the Madura, Mélúr, Dindigul and Tirumangalam taluks in the east and south of the district, which cannot be expected to yield anything in the shape of timber for many years to come, but are of great value for the supply of grazing, leaf manure, firewood, charcoal, and poles and other small building material; secondly, the deciduous forest on the north and south slopes of the Palnis, which formerly contained large quantities of valuable timber trees, especially *rengai,* but has been very extensively felled and damaged by unrestricted lopping and grazing; thirdly, the evergreen forests on the plateaus of the Upper and Lower Palnis; and fourthly (the most valuable, as forests, of the whole) the Kambam valley jungles, yielding teak, *rengai* and blackwood (*Dalbergia latifolia*) and numerous other timber trees only second to them in value.

A very large proportion of these woodlands, however, is unfortunately included in zamindari estates and is not under the control of the Forest department. The plateau and the western slopes of the Sirumalais belong to the Ammayanáyakkanúr estate; large areas on the northern slopes of the Palnis appertain to the Rettayambádi and Áyakkudi zamindaris; all the eastern end of the same range up to the western boundary of Dindigul taluk is the property of the zamindar of Kannivádi; a great slice of the forests on the western side of the Kambam valley belongs to Bódináyakkanúr and Téváram; and, except a comparatively small area at the head of the same valley and another just east of Ándipatti, the whole of the Varushanád and Ándipatti hills are included in the estates of Gantamanáyakkanúr, Erasakkanáyakkanúr, Sáptúr and Doddappanáyakkanúr. The hill ranges and the boundaries of the various proprietary estates are shown in the map at the end of this volume, and roughly it may be said that the Government reserves now occupy the hills of the district less the areas on them which are zamindari land.

Their
characteristics.

A short account may be given of the chief characteristics of the growth in the Government forests in each of the four groups into which they have been above arranged. The hills on which they stand have already been briefly described above on pp. 3 to 9.

The chief forests in the four taluks in the east and south of the district are those on the northern, eastern and south-eastern slopes of the Sirumalais (the rest of this range, as has been said, belongs to the zamindar of Ammayanáyakkanúr), on the Alagarmalais to the east of them, the Perumalais and Manjamalais connecting these two ranges, on the Karandamalais to the north of them, the scattered Nattam hills to the east of these last and the hills just south of the Ailúr railway-station. There are small plateaus on the top of the Sirumalais, Perumalais and Karandamalais, but the other hills consist of narrow ridges with steep, stony sides on which there is no depth of soil and on which, in consequence, any seedlings which may come up are quickly scorched to death in the hot weather. On all these hills the growth (which is all deciduous) was cut to ribbons in the days before conservation began. In 1871 it was reported that almost every stick had been cleared as far as the base of, and for a considerable distance up, the slopes of the Sirumalais. The northern side of the Manjamalais has been largely cleared for plantain-gardens and (judging from the amount of slag still lying about them) the Karandamalais and their immediate neighbours must have suffered much from the cutting of timber for the smelting, in former years, of the iron ore which is found in them.

Almost nine-tenths of the growth on the hills in these eastern and southern taluks is now *Albizzia amara*, which is said to owe its escape from destruction to the fact that goats do not care about it. These enemies of the forests are very numerous in this part of the district, as until recently Dindigul was a great tanning centre, and under recent orders they have been admitted to the reserves in such large numbers that the grazing-fee receipts have bounded up from Rs. 15,000 in 1900–01 to Rs. 29,000 in 1904–05. Next to *Albizzia*, the prevailing species are *Acacias, Wrightia, Cassia, Randia* and *Carissa*, but a stunted growth of certain of the more valuable timber species is found in places. Teak, *vengai*, blackwood, the hard and heavy *Hardwickia binata, Terminalia tomentosa*, satinwood (*Chloroxylon Swietenia*) and other varieties are fairly plentiful, for example, in the 'pole areas,' as they are called, in the Alagarmalais and elsewhere, and many gall-nut trees (*Terminalia chebula*) are found throughout the area. About Ailúr the striking-looking 'umbrella tree' (*Acacia planifrons*) is conspicuous. All these reserves are already greatly the better for the conservation accorded them, the southern slopes of the Alagarmalai, facing Madura, which were formerly quite bare, showing a specially notable improvement. A road has been driven through

CHAP. V.

FORESTS.

In the east and south of the district.

On the slopes
of the Palnis.

the reserves on this hill, eight miles in length, from the forest rest-house at Munúr on the south to that at Patnam on the north.

The forests in the second of the above four groups, those on the slopes of the Palnis, are also deciduous and have also been greatly damaged in past years by indiscriminate felling and burning, so that but little real timber now remains among them. The two best portions of them are probably that in the north-east corner of the range, between the Áyakkudi and Kannivádi estates, where the soil is unusually good, and that at the north-west corner, in the Manjapatti valley, an inaccessible and very feverish tract sloping down from the great Kúkal shola to the Amarávati river. On the prominent Aggamalai spur immediately west of Periyakulam town is a beautiful shola called the Tambirakánal, which affords an uncommon example of a tract of forest which has been able to recover from the felling and burning which accompanies hill cultivation. Land so treated seldom again becomes clad with real forest, but turns into a rank, thorny wilderness of worthless impenetrable scrub. The commonest trees on these Palni slopes are *vengai* (*Pterocarpus Marsupium*) and *vekkali* (*Anogeissus latifolia*), but the white and red cedars and some teak and blackwood occur, and gall-nut trees are numerous.

On the Palni
plateaus.

The third of the three groups, the forests of the Lower and Upper Palni plateaus, are more valuable and contain evergreen trees. The line between the two plateaus is roughly that drawn north and south through Neutral Saddle. The woodlands in the Lower Palnis, as has already been seen, have been greatly cut about for plantain and coffee cultivation. Much cardamom growing also goes on among them; but as this plant flourishes best under heavy shade, the larger forest trees have not been so greatly interfered with in the areas where it is raised. The soil in this tract is a dark loam, especially rich in the valleys, and in this several fine sholas of large extent still survive undamaged and thrive well. Among the more important trees in these are *Vitex altissima*, the so-called 'red cedar' (*Acrocarpus fraxinifolius*), and *Cedrela toona*, the last two of which are very useful for planking and box-making. Gall-nut trees are plentiful everywhere.

To the west, where the ascent to the Upper Palni plateau begins, the soil gradually deteriorates and becomes shallower, and after the low hill lying between the village of Tándikkudi and its neighbour Pannaikádu is left behind, the vegetation gradually changes and the heavier forest soon entirely disappears and is replaced by open, grassy downs dotted with stunted trees and

shrubs with sholas here and there in some of the moister and more
sheltered valleys. Nearly all these woods are included in the
Upper Palni reserves, but scarcely a dozen are of any real size.
Among the best known of them are Tiger shola, near Neutral
Saddle; Perumál shola, on either side of Law's ghát there (this
is full of gall-nut trees); Vanjankánal, further down the same
road; Kodaikanal, in the hill-station of that name; Gundan
shola, about two miles west of this; Doctor's Delight, four miles
west of Kodaikanal and a favourite place for picnics; and Kúkal
shola, some fifteen miles west of that station. None of these
contain any great store of timber trees, the prevailing species
being *Eugenia Arnottiana* and *Elæocarpus*, and they are chiefly
valuable as protectors of the sources of a series of useful streams.
Many of them are thought to show signs of having been greatly
damaged by fire in previous years. The great undulating plateau
on the top of the Palnis, which stretches from the outskirts of
Kodaikanal right away to the Travancore frontier on the west and
Bódináyakkanúr limits on the south, has recently, after considerable discussion,[1] been reserved under the Forest Act and given
the name of the 'Ampthill Downs.' It is over 52 square miles
in extent and about one-fourth of it consists of sholas and three-
fourths of open, rolling, grassy downs. It is diversified with
peaks running up to from 7,000 to 8,000 feet and is one of the
most beautiful tracts in all the Presidency.

The last of the four groups into which the Madura forests may
be divided (those in the Kambam valley) contains the most
interesting and valuable evergreen forests in the district. As has
been said, Government owns only a comparatively small patch of
the immense area of jungle which lines both sides of this valley
and clothes the whole of the Varushanád valley, its next neighbour
to the east. Travelling southwards from Periyakulam along the
west side of the Kambam valley, no Government forest (excepting
a patch on the Aggamalai spur just west of Periyakulam) is
reached until one gets nearly to Kómbai. Even then the growth
from this point to the head of the valley cannot be said to be of
great importance to the streams which rise in it, for it consists of
a narrow belt on hills which rise suddenly and precipitously to
the watershed, the other slope of which is Travancore territory.
On the east side of the lower end of the valley, the only Government reserves of any size are two which lie respectively just north
and south of the road from Ándipatti to Usilampatti. The most
important blocks are those on the eastern side of the head of the

In the
Kambam
valley.

---

[1] See B.P., Forest No. 149, dated 28th May 1903, and connected papers.

Kambam valley—among them the Mélagúdalúr reserve, through which runs part of the Periyár tunnel, and the Vannathipárai reserve, some 24,600 acres in extent and (except the 'Ampthill Downs') the largest in the district. These lie on the top and sides of the 'High Wavy Mountain.' The upper part of this hill consists of an undulating plateau, perhaps fifteen square miles in area, which is covered with a continuous, dense, evergreen forest which is a favourite haunt of elephants and runs down in long irregularly shaped masses for a considerable distance through the deep valleys on either side. Below it is a zone of bare, rocky, grass land, and beneath that again the lower slopes are well covered with deciduous forest. This tract all drains into the Kambam valley, and in it lie the sources of the Suruli river, the beautiful fall of which is a well-known land-mark on the road to the Periyár lake. The upper parts of it contain blackwood (*Dalbergia latifolia*), *Lagerstrœmia microcarpa* and some teak of fair size, while the lower forests produce *Anogeissus latifolia, Adina cordifolia, Dalbergia paniculata, Pterocarpus Marsupium, Schleichera trijuga* and other marketable timber trees, and also the rare *Aquilaria agallocha* (called *akil* in the vernacular) the 'scented eagle-wood' of commerce. But almost every sound tree in the lower levels was carried off in the days before conservation began, and it will be many years before the growth recovers from the treatment it then underwent.

Plantations.　　The artificial plantations in the district are four in number. In 1870 Colonel (then Captain) Campbell Walker started plantations of teak at Velankombai, at the northern foot of the Palnis not far from Palni town, and at Vannathipárai, near the foot of the ghát to the Periyár lake. Each of them now contains some 4,500 trees. The sites were not particularly well chosen, as neither of them receives the full benefit of the south-west monsoon. The former is, moreover, liable to be flooded by an adjoining channel, and the saturation so caused has at different times killed a good many of the trees in it.

In this same year (1870) a plantation of blue gum and Australian blackwood (*Acacia melanoxylon*) was begun at Kodaikanal in order to provide that station with firewood and so save from destruction the fine Kodai shola after which it is named. Here again the site was not well chosen, and the growth has been indifferent. The firewood supply has since been supplemented by a plantation begun in 1887–88 at Gundan shola, about two miles west of the station, which is now an extensive affair. It was partly burnt in February 1895, when considerable damage was done to it, and again in 1905.

The minor produce of the forests includes numerous items of which the chief are, perhaps, gall-nuts (*kadukkáy*, the fruit of *Terminalia chebula*), leaves for manure and cardamoms.

CHAP. V.
FORESTS.
Minor produce.

The principal gall-nut areas are on the Lower Palnis, where the tree abounds in the deciduous forest and is also scattered over the open grass land. In former days the methods of collecting its produce were wasteful in the extreme, trees being lopped, and even felled, to save trouble in picking their fruit. The privilege of collection and sale is now leased out to contractors, but the spread of the chrome process of tanning has caused a great decline in the value of gall-nuts and the revenue from this source in the Palnis has fallen in recent years from Rs. 15,000 to Rs. 2,000.

Leaves for manure are especially sought after in the areas recently brought under wet cultivation with the Periyár water, and are carted great distances by the ryots. In these tracts *Cassia auriculata* shrubs growing on unreserved lands have recently been allowed to be gathered for manure free of charge, and this has caused a further decline in the forest revenue from ' minor produce.'

Areas grown with cardamoms are let out on leases, which usually run for thirty years. The price of the fruit has fallen of late years and the competition for land for growing it has declined. A demand for lemon-grass (*Andropogon citratum*) for the distillation of oil has recently arisen, and this brings in a small income.

The revenue from grazing-fees is inconsiderable in comparison with the extent of the forests. The reserves in the east of the district contain little good grass and many of those in the west are out of favour with the herdsmen because they contain no places suitable for the penning of cattle at night and because water is scarce there in the hot weather. Few cattle are ever driven to the Upper Palni grass lands to graze, but large numbers go to the Travancore forests up the pass leading to the Periyár lake.

Grazing-fees.

Working plans have recently been drawn up and sanctioned for the forests in the four eastern taluks of the district (the Kanavaipatti and Palamédu forest ranges) and also for those in the Kambam valley (the Kambam range). For the remaining two ranges, namely, Kodaikanal, which includes the reserves on the Upper Palnis and their slopes, and Tándikkudi, in which are comprised the Lower Palni woodlands, schemes have not yet been made out.

Working plans: in the four eastern taluks.

The first of the above two working plans includes all the Government reserves in the taluks of Madura, Mélúr, Dindigul and Tirumangalam. It was prepared in 1898–99 and sanctioned in 1900.[1]

Very briefly stated, its proposals are that (with the exception of certain definite tracts containing fair timber and called 'pole areas,' and a few others in which the poverty of the stock is such that there is no probability of there being anything in them worth felling in the next 30 years) the whole area is to be coppiced in the same rotation and on the same method. The large preponderance of he crop consists of *Albizzia amara*, which coppices admirably, and reproduction of the forest by sowing is not thought likely to succeed, for the reasons that almost everywhere the reserves stand on steep slopes where the soil is shallow, stony, scorched up in the hot weather and trodden to pieces by cattle in the rains. The period of rotation is to be 30 years, and each block will be sold once in 30 years, as it stands, by auction, to contractors who will coppice it. It will then have ten years complete rest, grazing being prohibited in it. Thereafter cattle will be allowed to graze in it on payment of the usual fees, and at the end of five years more (by which time the coppice shoots will be fifteen years old) goats will also be admitted at fairly high rates, the area in which they are allowed being, however, changed, every two years and limited in extent.

Provision is made for the supply to ryots of manure leaves, which are highly valued in all the wet land under the Periyár channels, by allowing people to collect them at the usual rates (in those blocks which are not undergoing a complete rest) on a rotation of three years. Three trees—satinwood (*Chloroxylon Swietenia*), *Wrightia tinctoria* and *Ixora parviflora*—which together form about five per cent. of the crop and are of value as timber, are not to be lopped for manure leaves.

The coppicing is expected to produce about five tons an acre and firewood is now supplied, not only to the smaller villages, but to a dépôt in Madura, to the Madura spinning-mill and to the South Indian Railway. The annual output has risen rapidly in the last few years and is now 20,000 tons. The revenue from firewood has increased from less than Rs. 100 in 1900–01 to nearly Rs. 68,000 in 1904–05.

The working plan for the Kambam valley forests, which was sanctioned in 1901,[2] is somewhat more complicated. It divides the

---

[1] See B.P., Forest No. 385, dated 18th September 1900, in which the plan is printed *in extenso*.

[2] See B.P., Forest No. 310, dated 30th September 1901, in which it is printed in full.

total area into six classes of forest; namely, areas to be treated as
(*a*) fuel reserves, (*b*) ground for browsing goats, (*c*) evergreen
forest, (*d*) timber tracts, (*e*) land for grazing cattle, and (*f*) unpro-
ductive and unworkable portions.

The first of these, the fuel reserves, are small and are to be
worked on the system of exploitation known as ' coppice with
standards ' on a rotation of 30 years, browsing and grazing being
prohibited. In the next class of forest, the land provided for
browsing goats, cattle as well as goats are to be admitted, but no
felling is to be allowed. The third class, the evergreen forests,
are to be left untouched as protectors of the sources of streams.
No felling is to be allowed in them nor any grazing nor browsing.
As they contain no grass and are difficult of access, goats and
cattle are as a matter of fact never driven to them even now.

The timber tracts, the fourth of the above classes, are to be
rigidly protected from fire in the hope that in time seedlings may
spring up and reclothe the many open spaces left by former reckless felling, and eventually selected patches are to be planted up.
Previously, fires ran every year through the shrubs and coarse
grass which now covers these gaps, and killed all seedlings ; and
even now the greatest damage is caused by the fires which
annually burn the whole of the Travancore jungles along the
boundary and the violence of which is so great that no ordinary
fire-line is enough to stop them. Goats are to be excluded, but
cattle are to be admitted to help in keeping down the grass and so
minimising the spread of any fires which occur. There is at
present little demand for timber from Government reserves in this
part of the district, as large quantities are imported from Travancore State down the ghát from the Periyár lake.

The last of the workable areas, the land for cattle-grazing,
includes the poorer compartments on the west side of the valley
under the precipitous cliffs already referred to. The trees here
are of inferior species, few in number, widely scattered, and mostly
hacked to pieces by the villagers. Even if the damaged stock
could be cut back and protected for a long period it is thought
doubtful whether it would be of much value, and therefore this
area is to be left open for grazing on the usual terms.

CHAPTER VI.

OCCUPATIONS AND TRADE.

OCCUPATIONS—Agriculture and pasture. ARTS AND INDUSTRIES—Blanket-makin
—Cotton-weaving—Silk-weaving—Appliances—Dyeing—Gold and silver
thread—Wax-printing — Cotton-spinning — Cigar-making — Coffee-curing —
Oils—Tanning—Wood-carving—Metal-work—Bangles—Minor industries.
TRADE—Exports—Imports —Mechanism of trade. WEIGHTS AND MEASURES
—Tables of weight—Measures for grain—Liquids—Land—Distance—And
time—Coinage.

CHAP. VI.
OCCUPATIONS.

Agriculture
and
pasture.

IN every district in this Presidency the number of people
who subsist by agriculture and the tending of flocks and herds
greatly exceeds the proportion employed in all other callings put
together, and in Madura this preponderance is more marked than
usual, nearly three-fourths of the people living directly or indirectly by the land. The census figures of 1901 showed that 87
per cent. of the agriculturists were cultivators of their own land
and that less than 2 per cent. owned land without cultivating it.
Peasant proprietorship thus greatly predominates over all other
classes of tenure. Of those who lived by farm-labour but possessed no fields of their own, nine-tenths were day-labourers and
only one-tenth farm-servants engaged for long terms. This is a
very different state of things from that prevailing in some other
districts, Tanjore for example, where the agricultural cooly is
very commonly the servant of the big land-holder and bound
down to him by numerous pecuniary and other obligations.

Agricultural methods have been referred to in Chapter IV
above, and in Chapter I will be found some account of the
cattle, sheep and goats of the district. It remains to consider
here the callings which are connected with arts and industries and
with trade. The ordinary village handicrafts of the blacksmith,
carpenter, potter and the rest do not differ from the normal, and it
will suffice to refer briefly to the methods of the other artisans.

ARTS AND
INDUSTRIES.

The industry which employs the largest number of hands is
weaving, but the proportion of the people subsisting by it is
smaller than the average for the Presidency as a whole. The
materials employed are wool, silk and cotton, and it will be found
that the greater part of the work is done by people of foreign
castes who have come to the district from elsewhere.

Wool is only used for making coarse blankets. The Kurubas, a Canarese-speaking community who immigrated to the
district in years gone by from the Mysore and Deccan country,
weave these articles from the wool of the black and white sheep.
The industry is practically confined to the Dindigul, Palni and
Periyakulam taluks and (except the actual shearing of the sheep)
is carried out by the women. The sheep are first shorn when
they are six months old and thereafter twice annually, in January
and June, until their death, which generally occurs in their
seventh year. The black wool is sorted by hand from the white,
and the blankets are either black, white, a mixture of the two,
black with white borders, or *vice versâ*. The wool is never dyed.
It is spun by hand and woven on a primitive horizontal loom
fitted with clumsy appliances. The warp threads are first
stiffened with a paste made of crushed tamarind seed and water.
The finished article, the demand for which is entirely local, is
usually six cubits long by three wide and is sold at the weekly
markets at prices varying from As. 12 to Rs. 2.

Cotton is woven into fabrics of very varying quality. The
coarsest of these are the thick white *dupatis* in which the ryots
are wont to wrap themselves in the cold season and which cost
from Re. 1–4 to Rs. 2 apiece. These are woven from machine-
made yarn and are never dyed. They are chiefly made by a few
Kaikólans in Palni and Áyakkudi, and some Rávutans in the
latter place; by Paraiyans in a number of villages in the Kannivádi zamindari and the Védasandúr division of Dindigul taluk;
and by Native Christians (originally Ambattans by caste) and
Rávutans in Sáttangudi and some other places in Tirumangalam.
In Timmarasanáyakkanúr, Sáliyans weave narrow strips of a
similar coarse fabric which are sown together and used for
making native tents and pardahs.

The cloths commonly worn by the women of the middle
and lower classes are made by several different castes in many
different places and vary greatly in quality. In Dindigul taluk
the chief centres are Dindigul and Ambáturai. In Dindigul,
about 100 families of Séniyans (who speak Canarese) make the
coarser varieties from English yarn, and some 600 families of the
Gujaráti Patnúlkárans (see p. 109) weave the better kinds
and also make a peculiar class of cloths for men in which silk
spun with special fineness and silver thread imported from France
are used, and which are mostly exported to Madras. In Ambáturai and two or three neighbouring villages Canarese-speaking
Sédans make the commoner kinds of women's cloths. They buy

CHAP. VI.
ARTS AND
INDUSTRIES

Blanket-
making.

Cotton-
weaving.

the yarn and dye it themselves with imported aniline and alizarine pigments, and export the finished article to Tanjore and Burma. In Tádikkombu, Kaikólans weave similar fabrics.

In Nilakkóttai taluk the chief centres are Mullipallam, Tenkarai (on the opposite side of the Vaigai) and Vattilagundu. At the first of these the weavers are Sédans, some 300 looms are at work and women's cloths are woven from yarn imported from Madura and dyed locally with imported colours. 'They are sent in considerable quantities to Colombo and the Tinnevelly district. In Tenkarai, Kaikólans working at piece-rates for Patnúlkáran capitalists, and in Vattilagundu, Patnúlkárans and Séniyans, carry on a similar industry on a smaller scale.

In Palni taluk the weaving is mainly done in the head-quarter town. There, about 200 Sédan, 150 Séniyan, and 50 Kaikólan families make like stuffs in a similar manner. The Kaikólans usually work at piece-rates for capitalists belonging to the other two communities. Some 300 Patnúlkáran houses are also employed in making cloths with silk borders for men. The silk is obtained from Coimbatore, Kumbakónam and Madras, and the stuffs are exported to the Tanjore, Salem and Coimbatore districts.

In Periyakulam taluk the Sáliyans of Timmarasanáyakkanúr, already mentioned, have lately taken to making coarse cloths for women ; the Sédans and Padmasáles of Vadugapatti, hamlet of Mélamangalam, have each about 100 looms working at similar fabrics ; and the Patnúlkárans of Mélamangalam and Periyakulam turn out the same stuffs and also handkerchiefs with silk borders.

But the most important cotton-weaving centre in all the district is Madura itself, where the industry is in the hands of the Patnúlkárans. The fabrics they make are better woven and of more varied designs than those of any other place and are exported in large quantities to Madras and elsewhere. Their white cloths made from European yarn and ornamented with borders of gold or silver thread are especially famous.

Silk-weaving.   This community is the only caste in the district which manufactures all-silk goods as distinct from those containing merely an admixture of silk or ornamented with silk borders. The industry is practically confined to Madura town, but there it is of much importance. Both cloths and turbans are made and the latter, which usually have borders of gold or silver thread, are in great demand. The raw material is imported from Bombay and, to a less extent, from Calcutta, Kollegál and Mysore State.

Except in Madura, the looms and other appliances used by the weavers are of the kind usual elsewhere and call for no special description. The women and children of the weaver castes do much of the preliminary work, such as preparing the warp.

In Madura the Patnúlkárans have made several attempts to introduce improved machinery. A few fly-shuttle looms have been tried, but they are not popular for use with the higher counts of yarn, as they are apt to break the warp threads. Warping is not usually done in the ordinary method (walking up and down a long line of sticks stuck in the ground and winding the thread off the spindle in and out of these) but the thread is wound on to a series of iron pegs arranged on a square wooden frame. This enables the work to be done indoors and in all weathers. A patent has been taken out for a modification of the country loom which enables it to weave figures on the borders of cloths, and another patent for an entirely new kind of loom has been applied for.

Except in Madura, again, nothing has been done to improve dyeing processes or to prevent the imported aniline and alizarine compounds from ousting the native vegetable pigments.

In Madura a number of Patnúlkáran firms are carrying on dyeing operations on a large scale and on improved lines and vegetable products are generally employed for their silk fabrics. *Kamela* powder (collected from the surface glands of the capsules of the tree *Mallotus Philippinensis*) is used for yellow, lac for red and indigo for blue. The dye called ' Madura red' used once to be very famous, and efforts have chiefly been directed to the production of this. The dye is generally made as follows : The ashes of a plant called *umiri* (*Salicornia Indica*), which grows wild in certain parts of the district, are stirred with cold water and the solution left to stand till the evening. Some of it is then mixed with ground-nut oil (or, if the thread to be dyed is of the finer varieties, with gingelly oil) which becomes emulsified and milky in appearance. In this mordant the thread is soaked all night, and next day it is dried in the sun. This alternate soaking and drying is repeated for ten days, and on the eleventh the thread is taken to the Vaigai (the water of which river is said to be especially favourable to dyeing operations) and left to soak there in running water for some hours. By that time it is beautifully white. Next, the roots of *Oldenlandia umbellata* (chay-root, *imburán* in the vernacular) and the dried leaves of the shrub *Memecylon edule* (*káyam*) are steeped together in water for some time, and to this solution is added some of a German alizarine dye,

Appliances.

Dyeing.

The thread is again soaked in this for a night, and next boiled for two hours; and then it is taken to the river, left in running water for some time and finally dried in the sun. It is now the fine red colour which is so popular. Deeper shades are obtained by giving additional steepings in the dye-solution. For certain special kinds of fabrics, the alizarine dye is sometimes replaced by vegetable pigments, but this is rare.

Gold and silver thread.

Madura used to be famous for the manufacture of the gold and silver thread (or 'lace,' as it is sometimes called) which figures so largely in the borders of the more expensive kinds of cloths and turbans. The local weavers now use the cheaper French and English thread exclusively, but a few Musalmans still carry on the industry to supply a demand which survives in Tinnevelly, Trichinopoly and Travancore. They melt silver and lead in a clay crucible and cast the alloy into thin bars. These are hammered still thinner and then drawn through a series of holes of gradually diminishing size until they are transformed into exceedingly fine wire. The women then hammer this flat to make the thread. Gold thread is made in the same way, the silver bars being coated with gold before being 'drawn' into wire. Gold is so ductile that it continues to cover the silver with a fine coating right through to the end of the process.

Wax-printing.

In Madura town some ten or twenty persons practise the art of wax-printing which is so extensively carried on at Kumbakónam, Conjeeveram and Wallajahbad. This consists in printing designs on the cloth in wax with metal blocks, or drawing them by hand with a kind of iron pen provided with a ball of aloe fibre to act (somewhat on the principle employed in a fountain pen) as a reservoir for the wax. When the designs are finished, the fabric is immersed in the dye-tub, and then, while the body of it takes the dye, the design (being protected by the wax) remains unaffected and retains its original colour. The wax is then melted off by plunging the fabric into hot water and the design appears in white on a coloured ground. If required, the design itself can afterwards be separately dyed by putting the whole cloth into a tub of some other pigment. Cloths for both men and women, and also handkerchiefs, are manufactured in this manner.

A primitive method also employed for producing a rude pattern on a cloth consists in knotting small portions of the stuff at regular intervals with bits of string. These knotted parts are not touched by the dye and remain white while all the rest of the cloth is coloured.

Connected with the weaving industry is the cotton-spinning which is done at Messrs. Harvey's steam mill near the Madura railway-station. This began work in 1892, has a capital of ten lakhs, of which eight are paid up, and in the last year for which figures are available contained 36,000 spindles, employed daily 1,600 men, women and children and consumed annually over $2\frac{1}{2}$ million pounds of cotton.

Of the industries which are concerned with the manufacture of the agricultural products of the district, the most important is the making of the well-known Dindigul cheroots.

Before the railway reached that town, most of the Madura tobacco was sent to Trichinopoly, which was then the centre of the cheroot-trade. The first firm to begin work on any considerable scale in Dindigul were Messrs. Kuppusvámi Náyudu, who started business about 1850. Their cheroots were roughly tied up in plantain leaves, packed in bamboo baskets and exported by cart. Some years later, Captain E. A. Campbell of the Indian Army, who had been growing coffee and exotic cotton and silk on the Sirumalais, entered the trade. He copied the shapes of the Havana and Manila cigars, introduced wooden boxes and made other improvements. Mr. Neuberg of Bombay followed, and eventually transferred his business to his nephew, Mr. J. Heimpel. The latter's factory was in the extensive compound across the road opposite the Roman Catholic church. He was the first to introduce the 'wrappers' of Java, Sumatra and other foreign tobaccos which are now universally used and to substantially raise the price of the cheroots. He closed his business about 1890. His agent, Mr. Mengel, who had already parted from him and established a separate concern, now developed this latter and eventually formed it into a Company with a capital of two lakhs. He died in 1900 and the Company ceased active operations in the next year. About 1890 Messrs. Spencer & Co. entered the field, and they now have practically a monopoly of this trade in the district. In the latest year for which figures are available they employed at Dindigul 1,100 hands daily and made annually 16 million cigars valued at Rs. 4,40,000. The process of manufacture consists in boiling the selected leaves in a specially-prepared 'wash'— boiling has superseded soaking, as it kills the tobacco weevil— 'stripping,' or removing the midrib of the leaf, and 'rolling,' or making the finished cheroot. Each 'roller' works with two or three boys, who make the 'fillers,' or inside part of the cheroot, and hand them to him to roll and cover with the 'wrapper.' The cheroots are finally cut by machinery into the required lengths, examined, bundled and passed to the boxing department.

Coffee is cured at ' Vans Agnew's ' and ' St. Mary's ' estates on the Sirumalais, and at two other properties known as the Manalúr and Pillaiváli estates on the Lower Palnis.

Oils.

The chief oil made in the district is gingelly, which is used by all castes for cooking and by some for oil-baths. It is expressed in the ordinary country mill by Vániyans. In Nattam the people of this caste have three mills of European pattern. Castor-oil, used for lighting, is made on a smaller scale by first roasting the seed and then boiling it with water and skimming off the oil as it rises to the surface. Oil from the seeds of the ním or margosa tree is much employed medicinally, and is used by some few castes, such as Kallans and Valaiyans, for oil-baths. On the Sirumalais, some Labbais from Vániyambádi distil oil from the lemon-grass which grows there. The product is exported to other parts of India.

Tanning.

Tanning was until recently a flourishing industry in the Begampur suburb of Dindigul, where the Rávutans owned about 25 tanneries. Only seven of these now survive, the competition of chrome tanning having resulted in the others being shut up. The workmen mostly come from Pondicherry, and formerly belonged to several tanneries there which were afterwards closed. Hides and skins are now collected at Dindigul and merely dried and sent to Madras for export.

Wood-carving.

The wood-carving of Madura town has more than a local reputation. Good examples of it may be seen over the doorways of some of the better houses, in the *kalyána mahál* in the Mínákshi temple, and on the great cars belonging to this institution which were made about a dozen years ago.

' It is celebrated for its boldness of form, due to the influence of the stone-carvers, for its delicate tracery on flat surfaces, probably first introduced by men from the Bombay side, for the fine carving of panels decorated with scenes from the legend of the Mahábhárata, and for the excellent modelling of the swámis, which suggests the influence of sandalwood carvers from Mysore and Western India. At the present day the best work is done in the Madura Technical School, an institution maintained by the District Board which has done much to revive decadent art industries, and, by finding new markets for the productions of the skilled art workmen, has encouraged them to maintain the old high standard of work.' [1]

Metal-work.

The only work in metals which is known outside the district is the manufacture at Dindigul of locks and safes. The locks are imitations of Chubb's patents and are purchased in con-

---

[1] *Monograph on Wood-carving in southern India*, by Mr. E. Thurston.

siderable quantities by Government. The firm which established
the industry (Sankaralingáchári Brothers) is not now flourishing,
and many of its workmen have left it for younger rivals.

Dindigul also takes the lead in the district in the manufacture
of the usual bell-metal vessels. At Silaimalaipatti also, near
Péraiyúr in the Tirumangalam taluk, about 40 families of
Kannáns make brass platters, water-pots, drinking-bowls, cattle-
bells, etc. The same industry is carried on by the same caste at
Kannapatti near Sandaiyúr in the same taluk, and at Nilakkóttai,
Periyakulam, Uttamapálaiyam and other places. At Nilakkóttai
bell-metal gongs are made.

Bangles are manufactured from lac by Gázula Balijas in
Tirumangalam, Periyakulam, Mélamangalam and a few other
villages. The process consists in melting lac and brick dust,
pounding the result in a mortar, cutting it into strips, moulding
these into bangles over a fire, and finally decorating them, while
still hot, with copper foil, etc.

Minor industries include the making of combs of wood and
buffalo horn by Dommaras at Palni; the weaving of common
mats from *kórai* grass by Rávutans and Kuravans in many
villages; the making of baskets from split bamboo by Médak-
kárans in Palni and the neighbourhood; the turning and
colouring with lac of wooden toys by Tachchans in Airávadanallúr
near Madura; and saltpetre manufacture by Uppiliyans in
Periyakulam, Palni, Sólavandán and other villages.

Statistics of trade are not compiled for each district separately,
and the figures for Madura are lumped with those of Tinnevelly.
It is impossible, therefore, to speak with exactness of the course
of commerce.

The chief exports include cheroots, hides and skins, locks
and safes from Dindigul; plantains, coffee, bamboos and forest
produce (such as dyes, tans, honey, etc.) from the Sirumalais
and Palnis; cardamoms from the Palnis and from the Kannan
Dévan Hills Produce Company's property on the Travancore
range; dry grain from the Palni taluk; cotton from Tirumangalam, which goes to the various presses in Tinnevelly district;
garlic from the Upper Palnis; paddy, and silk and cotton fabrics
from Madura.

The chief imports are articles which the district does not itself
produce, such as European piece-goods, iron and kerosine
from Madras, salt from Tinnevelly, sugar from Nellikuppam and
so forth.

Madura is the chief trade centre and the railway receipts there are larger than at any other station on the South Indian line. Dindigul follows next, and then the head-quarters of the various taluks and Bódináyakkanúr, through which last all the produce of the Kannau Dévan hills travels to the railway at Ammaya-náyakkanúr.

The trading castes are principally Rávutans, Shánáns, Chettis and Lingáyats. Grain-brokers are often Vellálas. The Náttu-kóttai Chettis are the financiers of the district.

The weekly markets are quite a feature of village life, and play a very important part in the collection of goods for export and in the distribution of imports. They are usually controlled by the Local Boards, and the receipts from them are larger than in any other district except Coimbatore. Judged by the amount paid for the right to collect the usual fees at them, the biggest are those at Virúpákshi, Usilampatti, Nilakkóttai and Védasandúr.

The ordinary table of weights is—

6 tolas (·4114 oz.)	=	1 palam (nearly $2\frac{1}{2}$ oz.).
20 palams	=	1 viss (about 3 lb.).
6 viss	=	1 tulám (about $18\frac{1}{2}$ lb.).
8 viss	=	1 maund (about 25 lb.).

In addition, there are certain special weights used for cotton, and the number of viss in a maund differs in a bewildering way both according to local custom and to the substance which is being weighed. Thus in Madura there are 9 viss in a maund of tamarind, $8\frac{9}{16}$ in one of jaggery, $8\frac{1}{2}$ in one of chillies, and so on and so forth.

The usual grain measure is—

135 tolas of rice (heaped)	=	1 measure.
4 measures	=	1 marakkál.
12 marakkáls	=	1 kalam.

The Board of Revenue has directed the stamping department to stamp only multiples and sub-multiples of the Madras measure of 132 tolas, heaped, but the order appears to have had but little effect upon local practice. This varies in the most extra-ordinary manner, as, though the measure is constant in value, the number of measures in a kalam may be anything, according to locality, from two to six. It is reported that in Palni taluk the usual table of measures is—

3 measures	=	1 vallam.
16 vallams	=	1 moda.
$2\frac{1}{2}$ modas	=	1 salagai.

Arrack is sold by the English gallon and dram. Other
liquids, such as curds, buttermilk and so on, are sold by the
sub-multiples of the ordinary grain measure.

Acres and cents are now always used officially as measures of
land, but the ryots themselves still speak of the guli (a square
of 160 feet, or ·5877 acre) and the káni, or 1·32 acre.

The English inch, foot and yard are now very generally
used, but the old native terms are still met with.   These are—

12 fingers' breadth	..	..	..	=	1 span (ján).
2 spans	..	..	..	..	=	1 cubit (mulam).
2 cubits	..	..	..	..	=	1 yard (gajam).
4 cubits	..	..	..	..	=	1 fathom (már).

The English mile is also used in describing long distances,
though the native measures are—

Distance walked in a náligai (24 minutes)	=	1⅓ miles.
Do.	7½ náligais	..	..	=	1 kádam =
				10 miles.

For time also the English style is common.   The native table
is the following—

60	vinádis ..	..	..	..	=	1 náligai =
						24 minutes.
3¾	náligais	..	..	..	=	1 muhúrtam.
2	muhúrtams	..	..	..	=	1 jámam.
8	jámams	..	..	..	=	1 day.

Prior to the conquest of Madura by the Muhammadans, the
coin of highest value in the district was the *pon*, which was
equivalent to 10 *kali-panams* (16½ of which made a star pagoda,
or Rs. 3½) or slightly more than two rupees. This coin was
subsequently superseded by the star pagoda or *pú-varáhan*. The
table was—

80 cash	..	..	=	1 panam (Anglice *fanam*).
45 panams	..	..	=	1 star pagoda = 3·35 *Sica* rupees
				= 3½ British rupees.

The present currency is, of course, the same as in other parts
of the country, but in small transactions the *panam* and *duddu* are
sometimes used instead of annas and pies.   The table is—

2 pies	..	..	..	..	..	=	1 dugáni.
4 pies	..	..	..	..	..	=	1 duddu.
10 duddus	..	..	..	..	=	1 panam.

The value of a *panam* varies, however, in different localities.
In Madura it is 3 annas and 4 pies, and in the Dindigul division
4 annas.

CHAPTER VII.

MEANS OF COMMUNICATION.

CHAP. VII.
ROADS.
——
Their former
state.

LIKE those of most other districts, the metalled roads of Madura are practically a creation of the last forty years. No doubt many regular lines of communication existed as far back as the times of the Náyakkan dynasty, for both Tirumala Náyakkan and Queen Mangammál established and endowed frequent choultries for travellers. But these were almost certainly merely unmetalled tracks very ill-suited to cart traffic in any but the finest weather. The first Collector to carry out any notable improvements in the roads of the district seems to have been Mr. Blackburne, who was officially complimented because he had spent Rs. 1,23,000 on them in the nine years between 1834 and 1842—a sum which nowadays would be considered ridiculously inadequate. Of this outlay, Rs. 70,000 were expended on bridges and culverts, and only Rs. 8,000 on gravelling. In 1854 the Collector reported that only ten miles of road in all the district could be termed metalled; and in 1868, though some 500 miles were returned as 'maintained,' the only route in fair order was that from Trichinopoly, via Mélúr and Madura, to Tirumangalam and Tinnevelly. Even the important road from Dindigul to Madura was 'for the most part in a very ruinous state' and the lesser lines were 'all in a more or less unsatisfactory condition.' Want of money was the reason for this state of things, and it was not until the Madras Local Funds Act of 1871 authorised the levy of a substantial road-cess that any real progress was possible.

Their
existing
condition.

Madura now possesses 800 miles of maintained roads, about half of which are metalled. Except the Áttúr ghát road up the Lower Palnis and the section from Bódináyakkanúr to Kottakudi (both referred to below), which are in the charge of the department of Public Works, these are kept up by the Local Boards.

Considering that the soil through which these pass is for the most part hard and firm and that metal is plentiful almost everywhere, their present condition compares very unfavourably with that of the communications in neighbouring districts.

Most of them are lined with fine avenues. The best of these are always popularly attributed to Queen Mangammál, but though she planted many avenues during her reign, it is doubtful whether the age of any considerable proportion of those now in existence can be as great (over 200 years) as this belief would imply. The receipts from the produce of these trees is higher in Madura (including the Ramnad and Sivaganga zamindaris) than in any other district except Salem and South Arcot.

The chief lines are (*a*) from Trichinopoly district to Tinnevelly, through Mélúr, Madura and Tirumangalam, (*b*) from Madura to Dindigul, and thence to Palni and (*c*) from Dindigul, through Vattilagundu and Periyakulam, to the head of the Kambam valley and the Periyár lake.

From the last of these a branch road has recently been constructed to Bódináyakkanúr and thence to Kottakudi, a village at the foot of the Travancore hills from which a steep track leads to the top of that range. The work was undertaken at the instance of the Kannan Dévan Hills Produce Co. (the owners of a large area of coffee, tea and cardamom cultivation on the range) who have constructed an aërial ropeway from Kottakudi to their estates on the hills to replace the track. This ropeway rises some 4,000 feet, is worked by a turbine driven by a small stream at the foot of the hill, and connects at its upper end with a mono-rail tramway, 22 miles in length, which goes to Munaar, the company's head-quarters. In consideration of Government acquiring and handing over under the Land Acquisition Act the land wanted for the ropeway, the company has entered into an agreement permitting the use of the ropeway, on payment of certain fixed charges, by the general public. The terms of the agreement will be found in G.Os., Nos. 4, W., dated 7th January 1901 and 331, Rev., dated 11th April 1905. The road to Kottakudi is maintained jointly from Provincial and local funds.

Another route of interest is Law's ghát, so called from Major G. V. Law of the Madras Staff Corps who carried it out, which runs for about eleven miles from the hill-station of Kodaikanal to Neutral Saddle, the natural boundary between the Upper and Lower Palnis. It was originally intended to continue it thence down to near Ganguvárapatti, but this lower section was never properly completed, has not been maintained, and is not now practicable for anything but cattle.

The question of opening up roads into the Palni range was first definitely raised in 1875 by the Dindigul taluk board, and Major Law, whose health required a change from the plains, was

The chief routes.

The Kottakudi ropeway.

Law's ghát.

selected to cut the necessary preliminary traces. He found that the only work which had been done up to then was the cutting, by a native surveyor deputed by the District Engineer, Colonel J F. Fischer, R.E., of a trace from Shembaganúr down the Vilpatti valley, north of Kodaikanal, which ended suddenly in an impossible precipice. The remains of this are still visible. He soon saw that Neutral Saddle was the key to the whole position, and in the same year carried a trace to that point from Kodaikanal through Shembaganúr. By 1878, Rs 43,000 had been spent on the work, and the upper ten miles were fit for wheeled traffic, the next thirteen rideable and the last seven partly cleared. In that year an estimate for Rs. 3,20,000 was sanctioned for completing the road down to the plains opposite Ganguvárapatti. On 1st July 1878 Major (then Colonel) Law retired, and in the same year the scarcity of funds resulting from the Afghan War prevented the allotment of the money sanctioned. Nothing more was done in the matter until the Áttúr ghát was begun.

This is a cart-road now under construction by the Public Works department. It will run, with a ruling gradient of not more than one in nineteen, from Áttúr in Dindigul taluk up the Lower Palnis to Neutral Saddle, where it will meet Law's ghát from Kodaikanal. A branch will be made from it to Tándikkudi. It was originally considered that a bridle-path up these hills would be sufficient, and in 1896 an estimate for this was drawn out. The route which should be followed, the rival claims of Áttúr and Ayyampálaiyam as the terminus, and the width of the road subsequently underwent much discussion, and eventually the present scheme was sanctioned. The connecting link between the foot of the ghát and Sembatti (on the Dindigul-Vattilagundu road), five miles in length, is being made from local funds, and it is proposed to continue this $4\frac{1}{2}$ miles further to the Ambáturai railway-station. If this is done, the distance from the railway to Kodaikanal will be about 50 miles by cart-road, as against 33 by road and twelve up a steep bridle-path by the existing route from Ammayanáyakkanúr through Periyakulam.[1]

The only important road-bridge in the district is that across the Vaigai at Madura. Floods in this river used to block all communication between the country on either side of it for days together, and at length in 1889 this work was completed and was opened by the Collector on the 6th December. It

[1] An alternative proposal to carry the Áttúr ghát no further than Tándikkudi and to complete Law's ghát down to Ganguvárapatti is now under consideration. The new railway (p. 159) will pass near this last and Kodaikanal would then be only some 30 miles from the line.

was built by the Public Works Department and cost Rs. 2,75,687 against the estimate of Rs. 3,21,460. Of this sum Rs. 60,000 were contributed from Provincial Funds and Rs. 10,000 by the municipality, and an additional Rs. 20,000 was provided from the unexpended balance of the fund collected for the reception at Madura of the Prince of Wales in 1876. It had been arranged that when Prince Albert Victor was in south India he should visit the town and open the bridge, but his tour was altered in consequence of the prevalence of cholera in the neighbourhood, and the Collector performed the ceremony instead.

The road from Palni to Udamalpet in Coimbatore district formerly crossed the Shanmuganadi and Amarávati on big bridges built at some date before 1868, but both of these have been washed away. The former was destroyed by the inundations of 1877–78. The same floods swept away the bridge over the Tirumanimuttár on the road between Mélúr and the Trichinopoly frontier. A bridge formerly crossed the Pálár on this same road at the point where there is now only a causeway.

The great increase in the volume of the Suruli which resulted when the Periyár water was passed into it necessitated the construction of bridges at Uttamapálaiyam and at Virapándi. These were completed in 1893. The same causes rendered the crossing over the Vaigai at Kunnúr on the Ándipatti-Téni road, where the bed of the river is narrow and deep, a dangerous spot, and a ferry (the only one in the district) has now been established there. The boat is large enough to take laden carts and travels backwards and forwards by means of a block attached to a wire rope slung across the stream.

A list of the travellers' bungalows in Madura, with particulars of the accommodation in each, will be found in the separate Appendix to this volume.

All the main routes to the famous temple at Rámésvaram pass through the district, and it consequently contains a large number of chattrams founded and endowed by the pious for the use of the pilgrims to that shrine. Some of these are controlled by the Local Boards and others are private institutions. Of the former, the most important are Queen Mangammál's chattrams at Sólavandán and opposite the Madura railway-station. When the English first acquired the district, it was found that the proceeds of land granted free of rent for the support of chattrams had in most cases been appropriated to their own private use by the grantees. Mr. Hurdis, the Collector, wrote in 1802 that—

'The establishment of Choultries, which was made with the view of accommodation to travellers, has since the time of Yúsuf Khán been appropriated by the present incumbents, as their own private property. The rapacity of the former managers had winked at this assumption, so long as it was profitable to them : but the discovery of their aggression, instead of causing retributive justice to the sufferer, enriched progressively the Renters' treasury by fixing as a tribute all that had been discovered taken by previous compulsion. And the holders of the property, formerly *public*, are, by the yearly receipt of the rent specified, in quiet possession of their impudent usurpations.'

Mr. Hurdis accordingly resumed most of these chattram inams and assigned to the institutions tasdik allowances in place of them. The land given by Mangammál to the Sólavandán chattram was treated in this manner, and the institution is now paid an annual allowance of Rs. 3,160 from Provincial Funds.[1] When the new road from Madura to Dindigul through Tádampatti was opened, it diverted part of the pilgrim traffic from Sólavandán, and a branch of the chattram was accordingly opened, and is still kept up, at Tádampatti. Later on, when the railway was brought to Madura, Sólavandán became of less importance than ever as a halting-place for pilgrims to Rámésvaram, and, with the approval of Government, a portion of its endowment was diverted in 1894 to the founding and upkeep of the chattram opposite the railway-station at Madura, and this was called after Queen Mangammál.

The only railway in the district is the South Indian Railway, the main line of which (metre gauge) enters it near Ailúr in the Dindigul taluk, runs in a wide curve (to avoid the Sirumalais) through Dindigul to Madura town (crossing the Vaigai there on a bridge of 15 spans of 70 feet each), and thence passes south-west and south, through Tirumangalam into Tinnevelly district. The section up to Madura was opened in 1875 and that beyond it in the next year.

From Madura a branch line, also metre gauge, was built in 1902 to Mandapam, on the neck of land which runs out to meet Pámban island. This is to be eventually carried across the Pámban channel to the island, where it is proposed to establish a large port for ocean-going vessels. Schemes are also afoot to continue it thence over Adam's Bridge to Ceylon. Details of these matters are beyond the scope of this volume, but if they are ever brought to completion Madura will be a more important town than ever.

Other lines have been projected. One proposed route would run from Dindigul, through Palni, to join the Madras Railway at

---

[1] For further particulars, see G.Os., Nos. 252, Revenue, dated 7th February 1872 and 1095, L., Mis., dated 14th June 1894.

Tiruppúr in the Coimbatore district. Another would similarly CHAP. VII.
start from Dindigul and pass through Palni, but thence would RAILWAYS.
run westwards to join the Madras Railway at Palghat. Neither
scheme has yet got beyond the stage of surveys and estimates.

In 1899 Messrs. Wilson & Co. of Madras were granted a
concession to make a 2′ 6″ tramway from Ammayanáyakkanúr on
the South Indian Railway to Kuruvanúth, at the extreme upper
end of the Kambam valley, with branches to Kottakudi mentioned
above and to Kistnama Náyak's tope at the foot of the ghát to
Kodaikanal. The order of Government granting this concession
contained the conditions that the work should be begun within
twelve months thereafter, and completed within three years.
The Company, however, were unable to raise the necessary funds
and eventually relinquished the concession. In August 1905 the
District Board decided to levy a cess of three pies in the rupee of
land revenue to be spent upon the construction of railways within
the district and it is now proposed that the proceeds of this should
be laid out in making a metre-gauge line, to be constructed and
worked by the South Indian Railway Co., from Dindigul[1] to
Uttamapálaiyam, passing through Sembatti (at the end of the new
Áttúr ghát road), Vattilagundu, Dévadánapatti, Periyakulam,
Téni (Allinagaram), Bódináyakkanúr and Chinnamanúr. This
would run through much rich country and would tap every pass
to the Upper and Lower Palnis along which any considerable
traffic is ever likely to travel.

[1] It has since been decided that the line shall start from Ammaya.
náyakkanúr.

CHAPTER VIII.

RAINFALL AND SEASONS.

CHAP. VIII.
RAINFALL.

STATISTICS of the average rainfall at the various recording stations in the district, and for the district as a whole, are given below for the dry weather (January to March), the hot season (April and May), the south-west monsoon (June to September), the north-east monsoon (October to December) and the whole year :—

Taluk.	Station.	Years recorded.	January to March.	April and May.	June to September.	October to December.	Total.
Dindigul ...{	Dindigul	1870-1903	1·55	5·00	9·37	14·18	30·30
	Védasandúr ...	1887-1903	1·64	5·81	6·74	13·83	28·02
Nilakkóttai ...	Nilakkóttai ...	Do.	1·45	5·49	8·24	14·86	30·04
Kodaikanal ...	Kodaikanal ...	1874-1903	6·43	11·44	21·00	26·50	65·37
Madura	Madura	1870-1903	1·70	5·11	12·34	15·85	35·00
Mélúr	Mélúr	Do.	1·44	4·80	15·33	16·31	37·88
Palni	Palni	Do.	1·30	4·69	4·94	15·13	26·06
Periyakulam ...{	Periyakulam ...	1880-1903	3·58	5·38	6·19	14·13	29·28
	Uttamapálaiyam .	Do.	1·82	4·85	5·25	15·50	27·42
Tirumangalam ...{	Tirumangalam ...	1870-1903	1·41	5·58	9·93	14·89	31·81
	Usilampatti ...	1880-1903	1·56	5·69	7·43	16·87	31·55
	Average for the district	...	2·17	5·80	9·72	16·19	33·88

It will be noticed that the average fall for the district as a whole is nearly 34 inches. This is less than is received in neighbouring areas, and moreover the supply is very irregular. The extreme variations on record are the 47·41 inches of 1877 and the 18·60 of 1876, but in 1898 the fall was over 40 inches and in 1870, 1873, 1881 and 1892, it was under 25 inches.

Excluding Kodaikanal, the circumstances of which are pecu- CHAP. VIII
liar, the highest amounts are received in Mélúr and Madura RAINFALL.
taluks and the lowest in Dindigul, Periyakulam and Palni. The
figures show that the difference occurs almost entirely in the
supply registered during the south-west monsoon. The last
three taluks are robbed of the moisture brought by this current
by reason of their position close under the highest portions of
the whole range of the Western Ghâts, while Madura and Mélúr
stand farther away from the shelter of those hills and opposite a
lower portion of them, and thus receive a somewhat larger supply.
The average fall in the district as a whole during the south-west
monsoon is smaller than in any other district except Tinnevelly.
All the taluks share about equally in the rain brought by the
north-east current.

The average number of wet days in a year is 53, so that the Liability to
average fall per rainy day works out to ·64 inch, which, though famine and
quite a good shower, is considerably less than is necessary to fill floods.
tanks in a country containing as much porous red soil as does this
district. Consequently Palni and Dindigul taluks depend greatly
upon their wells to bring crops to maturity and Tirumangalam,
where there are no wells, is at the mercy of the seasons. On the
other hand the disastrous floods which periodically sweep through
some of the Madras districts are rare in Madura.

Of the famines and scarcities which visited the country in the FAMINES AND
days before the British occupation, no exact record survives. SCARCITIES.
Such things were little accounted of in those days. Native MSS. In pre-Brit-
mention them incidentally, but give no details. A Jesuit letter ish days.
of 1622 says that famine had then been so bad for some years
that the numerous corpses of those who had died of starvation
were left unburied. Mention is made of other famines; namely,
in Tirumala Náyakkan's time; after the troubles of 1659–62,
when 10,000 Christians alone are said to have perished from want;
in 1675, after Venkáji's incursion, which was so severe that, says
one of the Jesuits, nothing was to be met with in any direction
save desolation and the silence of the tomb; in 1678, following a
deluge caused by excessive rain on the Western Ghâts; in 1709,
when another great storm was succeeded by a famine which
seems to have lasted right up to 1720; and in 1781 in consequence of Haidar's invasion of the year before.

In 1799 there was considerable distress round Dindigul and In 1799.
the Collector was authorised to purchase grain on Government
account and distribute it to the people.

The district again suffered greatly in the three years 1812–14, and in the early part of the last of these it was found necessary to give employment to 42,000 of its people and to advance 2,000 pagodas to the grain-merchants to enable them to import foodstuffs from elsewhere. The expenditure on relief in the five months from January to May was nearly Rs. 3,25,000.

The next famine occurred in 1832–33. This is generally known as the Guntúr famine, as it was most acute in that district; but it was also severe in Madura, Salem, North Arcot and Cuddapah. Four years later, in 1836, there was another scarcity in the district. The late rains of that year failed altogether and led to a prolonged drought. Large remissions had to be granted, a number of the poor were employed on public works, and the Collector (Mr. Blackburne) ordered relief to be distributed from the funds belonging to the Madura temple, which were under his administration.

The loss of population caused by these two famines must have been considerable. In 1822 the inhabitants of the Government taluks of the district numbered 788,196, while at the census taken in 1838 they were only 552,477. It is true that these enumerations were probably very defective, but there is no reason to suppose that the former was more accurate than the latter; the presumption, indeed, is just the opposite. The decrease in the population must, therefore, be real; and though it is possible that some of it was due to emigration, the greater part of it must be ascribed to starvation and epidemic diseases, especially cholera. Allowing for the natural increment of population from 1822–38, the decline was at the rate of 39·8 per cent. Seven other districts suffered a loss during the same period.

Though a number of the subsequent years were distinctly unfavourable and high prices caused much suffering, the next really bad season was in 1857. The south-west monsoon of that year failed and the north-east gave no rain after October. Prices continued at a high level, numbers of people were in receipt of relief, and over 40,000 persons emigrated to Ceylon. The next year was not much better, but the failure of the crops was due to excessive, rather than deficient, rainfall. High prices continued and the people suffered much from both cholera and fever.

The famine of 1866 was more severe. The monsoons were very late, prices rose rapidly, and in September rice was selling at 4·2 measures a rupee, ragi was 66 per cent. dearer than in the corresponding month of the previous year, and in some parts grain was not procurable at any figure. The statistics below indicate the course of events :—

Year and month.	Number relieved.		
	Gratuitously.	On works.	Total.
1866.			
August	4,313	...	4,313
September	5,375	...	5,375
October	5,540	60	5,600
November	3,892	310	4,202
December	4,203	310	4,513
1867.			
January	3,407	6,161	9,568
February	2,071	5,313	7,384
March	1,077	739	1,816
April	1,355	768	2,118
May	800	739	1,539
June	...	763	763

A sum of Rs. 14,000 was raised by local subscription and Rs. 24,000 were spent on gratuitous relief and Rs. 19,000 on works. The taluks worst affected were Mélúr, Dindigul and Tirumangalam.

But the most serious visitation which Madura has ever had to face was the ' great famine ' of 1876–78, which affected disastrously so many other districts in this Presidency.

The south-west and north-east monsoons of 1876 both failed. The latter began propitiously enough with a fall of nearly three inches, but then ceased altogether. By November 15th matters were critical and by the end of the year not only were all agricultural operations at a standstill, but in many places the water available was insufficient even for domestic purposes. Sheep and cattle in Palni began to die, although the forest reserves were thrown open for grazing. The ryots began to sell their cattle and other property and to emigrate in thousands to Ceylon and elsewhere, leaving their children and womenkind behind them. So great was the crowd at Pámban waiting to get away, that the food supplies there ran out, and Government authorised the Collector to buy grain and sell it at cost price to the emigrants. Cholera, small-pox and other epidemics also appeared. Between July 1876 and June 1878, it may here be noted, 120,000 persons emigrated from the district (including the Ramnad and Sivaganga zamindaris) and 20,000 died of cholera.

On 11th December 1876 Government placed a first instalment of Rs. 5,000 at the disposal of the Collector for the opening of relief-works, and the Sub-Collector started three centres for gratuitous relief round Dindigul on his own responsibility.

In the early part of 1877 the numbers on relief increased so considerably that for purposes of famine administration the district was arranged into four divisions; Mr. C. W. W. Martin, the Sub-Collector, taking Dindigul and Palni; Mr. E. Turner, Extra Assistant Collector, Tirumangalam and Periyakulam; and two Deputy Collectors (Messrs. P. Subbaiyar and Tillaináyakam Pillai) being in charge of Madura and Mélúr respectively. The District Engineer's staff was also strengthened by the addition of several European Assistant Engineers, and a number of subordinates of the Survey department were transferred to famine duty.

The figures subjoined (which have been worked out for the district without the Ramnad and Sivaganga zamindaris) show graphically the progress of the famine from that time forth:—

Month and year.	Number of persons on last day of month on			Expenditure on		
	Works.	Gratui-tous relief.	Total.	Works.	Gratui-tous relief.	Total.
1876.				RS.	RS.	RS.
December ...	6,281	1,015	7,296	6,309	772	7,081
1877.						
January ...	3,554	331	3,885	11,844	372	12,216
February ...	5,245	230	5,475	12,801	244	13,045
March	8,447	1,179	9,626	20,206	992	21,198
April	11,631	5,458	17,089	21,534	5,725	27,259
May	12,314	7,553	19,867	26,346	11,012	37,358
June	7,086	12,622	19,708	39,989	25,942	65,931
July	22,559	34,537	57,096	43,211	47,868	91,079
August	24,594	50,990	75,584	62,034	87,337	1,49,371
September ...	14,199	81,470	95,669	87,921	1,56,987	2,44,908
October ...	12,565	40,910	53,475	63,955	1,34,541	1,98,496
November ..	9,977	27,930	37,907	24,598	63,034	87,632
December ...	2,407	15,249	17,656	17,411	49,685	67,096
1878.						
January ...	4,251	9,818	14,069	7,788	20,122	27,910
February ...	250	936	1,186	3,283	8,071	11,354
March	...	265	265	946	1,624	2,570
April	...	106	106	..	393	393
May	...	24	24	...	145	145
June	...	24	24	...	97	97
July	...	...	...	...	55	55
Total ...	...	...	...	4,50,176	6,15,018	10,65,194

It will be seen that things quickly went from bad to worse. Everyone, however, lived in the hope that the south-west monsoon of 1877 would be plentiful and put an end to the distress. When, therefore, it again turned out a failure, the numbers both on works and gratuitous relief increased very seriously, the latter quadrupling between June and August. Grain was poured into the district by the railway, which had just been opened, but there remained the difficulty of getting it distributed to the outlying parts. Weavers were relieved in Dindigul and Palni by giving them advances of raw material and paying them the market value of the fabrics woven therefrom. Many people died of sheer starvation and the records of the time are full of tales of horror—children deserted by their mothers, corpses lying unburied by the road-sides and so forth. Crime also naturally increased by leaps and bounds. Every effort was made to reach the worst cases of destitution with the money provided by the Mansion House Fund, and when at length, in September and October 1877, good rain fell, this same money was utilised in assisting ryots to start the cultivation of their fields.

Thereafter the numbers both on works and gratuitous relief rapidly declined, but in November and December the little progress which had been made with the new crop was checked by excessive rain ending (in Ramnad) with the most disastrous floods which had been known for years.

On the last day of the February following, however, matters had improved sufficiently to enable the distinction between famine and budget works to be revived, and village relief was ordered to be discontinued from the last day of March 1878.

During the fifteen months which had elapsed since operations began in December 1876, Rs. 6·15 lakhs had been spent on gratuitous relief in the district and 4·50 lakhs on works. Besides these amounts, large sums from the Mansion House Fund had also been expended. The indirect cost of the famine to the State included over $6\frac{1}{4}$ lakhs granted in remissions of assessment, as under :—

CHAP. VIII.
FAMINES AND
SCARCITIES.

Fasli.	Remissions.		
	Wet.	Dry.	Total.
	Rs.	Rs.	Rs.
1286	2,03,291	2,80,720	4,84,011
1287	11,814	93,381	1,05,195
1288	40,203	......	40,203
Total ...	2,55,308	3,74,101	6,29,409

Thus the total cost to the Government, direct and indirect, of the famine in this district may be put at 17 lakhs.

The loss to the people themselves was, of course, infinitely greater. It was reported that in Palni there were practically no cattle left alive.

At the census of 1881, taken three years after the famine was over, the people of the district were 5 per cent. fewer than they had been in 1871, five years before it began. Tirumangalam taluk evidently suffered more severely than any other, for the decline in the population there amounted to no less than 15 per cent. In Palni and Madura it was 7 per cent. and in Dindigul 6 per cent. Since then no famine or serious scarcity has visited Madura.

FLOODS.

Few floods have occurred in the district. We are told that in December 1677 an extraordinary superabundance of rain on the Western Ghâts caused a kind of deluge, which swept away many low-lying villages with all their inhabitants. On the 18th December 1709 a tremendous cyclone appeared. The tempest began at 7 A.M. with a strong north-easterly gale and very violent rain. This lasted till nearly noon, when the wind and rain suddenly ceased and a profound calm followed which continued until 5 P.M. The wind then got up again with great suddenness from the opposite quarter, the south-west, and blew for most of the night with even greater force than in the morning. The wind and the rain breached tank after tank until at last a mighty wave of water was surging through the district carrying everything before it ; and by morning the country was one vast sheet of water with only the higher ground appearing above it here and there.

In November 1814 a terrific storm from the south-east swept over the neighbourhood of Madura town and destroyed nearly 3,000 cattle and some 50 herdsmen.

In December 1843 extraordinary freshes occurred in the Vaigai and many tanks were breached.

In the same month in 1877 the Gundár came down in a most unexpected and dangerous flood. The Special Assistant Collector then in charge of Ramnad zamindari under the Court of Wards described in a graphic way how he was riding along through jungle when he suddenly heard a noise of rushing water and in a few minutes was struggling with his horse in a torrent three feet deep. The details of the matter belong to the history of Ramnad, and it is enough to mention here that the river swept during the night through the famine camp which had been pitched

in its bed at Tiruchuli and drowned about 20 people there before
they could escape; travelled to Kamudi and washed away the
wall of the temple and a thousand yards of the big embankment
there; and then rushed across country, breaching nearly every
tank in the south-west of the zamindari, until the whole of that
side of the district was covered with one wide sheet of water.

In 1884 an unusually high flood in the Vaigai topped the road
to the west of Madura and flowed into the Anuppánadi channel,
but no great damage was done except to the newly-opened
water-works mentioned on p. 223.

CHAP. VIII.

Floods.

CHAPTER IX.

PUBLIC HEALTH.

CHAP. IX.
GENERAL
HEALTH.

THE frequency of cholera and fever in Madura is at present too great to warrant the inclusion of the district among those which are clearly healthy to native constitutions. Europeans have the advantage of Kodaikanal as a haven of refuge from the usual effects of a tropical climate, but otherwise do not find the district invigorating. To both classes the high and dry land round about Dindigul and Palni is better suited than the Vaigai valley, and both find the atmosphere of Madura town itself debilitating and unwholesome. Hence the movement of the residences of the head-quarter officials (see p. 261) to the new site on the race-course on the opposite side of the river.

Cholera.

Cholera is an ancient enemy of the country. A letter from the Jesuit missionary Robert de' Nobili, dated as far back as April 1609, speaks of the ravages of a virulent epidemic disease which he calls *mordechin*, and Father Martin, writing in 1701, gives an account of this which makes it clear that it was none other than cholera. Yule and Burnell say that *mordechin* is a fanciful French corruption of *modachi*, the Konkani and Maráthi name for the disease. The remedy favoured by the Jesuit fathers for the cure of choleraic attacks was the application of a red hot sickle to the soles of the patient's feet. If he did not move when this was applied, they naively observe, his case was hopeless.

Severe epidemics of cholera are reported to have occurred in 1815, 1818, 1819, 1820, 1831 to 1837, 1839, 1843, 1850 to 1852, 1853, 1858, 1859, 1861, 1864 and 1865. In 1875, 11,600 persons died of the disease and 15,600 in 1877. Since then, the worst years have been 1891 (6,800 deaths), 1897 (8,300) and 1900 (5,800), but in no single year since 1871, with the two solitary exceptions of 1874 and 1886, has Madura been entirely free from this scourge. The festivals at the temples at Madura, Palni, and Rámésvaram used to be the great centres for its propagation, but these are now more carefully watched than formerly. Statistics of the deaths from cholera and certain other causes in recent years will be found in the separate Appendix to this volume.

Malarial fever is endemic in most of the country close under the numerous hill-ranges of the district, such as the tracts lying among the Nattam hills, at the head of the Kambam valley and at the foot of the Palnis. The Sirumalai hills are also themselves exceedingly malarious.

In the early years of the last century, however, some sort of fever created havoc all over the district and not only in the country near the hills. It was especially virulent in the three years 1809 to 1811, and is constantly referred to in the old records. In his jamabandi report for fasli 1221 the Collector said that 13,000 people had died of it in ten months, and that those who had escaped with their lives were almost all prostrated from its effects. Cultivation and business had everywhere been interrupted; the ryots were unable to work in the fields; the náttamgárs could hardly crawl to the cutcherries for their pattas; the gumastahs were too ill to prepare the accounts; and he himself was not strong enough to write the report and had been obliged to order his Head Assistant to do it for him.

A Committee investigated the disease and reported in 1816 at great length upon its nature and its supposed causes. It reappeared in that year and again, in a severe form, in 1818, 1819, 1820, 1839, 1840, 1845, 1850, 1851, 1854 (when it was especially malignant), 1855, 1856, 1858, 1859, 1861, 1863, 1864 and 1865. But in some of these years it was confined to limited areas. Sometimes, it was said, whole villages were decimated by it in a few days. Since that time it has not visited the district. Over one-third of all the deaths in Madura since 1883 have, it is true, been attributed to 'fever,' but probably (as elsewhere) many diseases are so entered which are beyond the powers of diagnosis possessed by the heads of villages who are responsible for the returns.

Small-pox is not particularly common. The worst years since 1871 have been 1872 (4,491 deaths), 1877 (3,161) and 1891 (2,783). In the decade 1883–1892 the disease caused 555 deaths out of every 10,000 and in the quinquennium 1898–1902, 343 out of the same number. Vaccination is compulsory in all the unions and municipalities.

A disease worth special mention is 'Madura foot,' or mycetoma. In this Presidency it is especially common in the Madura district and (in the same way that elephantiasis is often called ' Cochin leg ') it gets its popular name from this fact. It consists in a marked swelling of the foot (or occasionally of the hand) and is popularly supposed to be confined to the tracts covered with black cotton-soil.

The earliest notice of the disease was by Kæmpfer in 1712.[1] Its more modern history began with Godfrey, of Madras, who gave a description of several undoubted examples of it in the *Lancet* of June 10th, 1843. The merit of bringing the disease prominently to notice, of distinctly describing its clinical and anatomical features, as well as of suggesting its probable pathology, belongs entirely to Vandyke Carter, who, from 1860 to 1874, in a series of important papers, furnished the information on which all later descriptions have been principally founded.

The disease is not confined to India, but occurs with some degree of frequency in Senegambia and, more rarely, in Algeria, Italy and Cochin-China. In India, it is endemic in more or less limited areas which are scattered over a wide extent of country and separated by tracts which are almost completely immune. Besides Madura, it is said[2] to be prevalent in the Proddatúr, Jammalamadugu and Pulivendla taluks of the Cuddapah district (chiefly on the cotton-soil areas in them) and it is common in the Punjab, Kashmir and Rajputana. It appears to be acquired only in rural areas, the inhabitants of towns being exempt.

Mycetoma begins usually, but by no means invariably, on the sole of the foot, the first indication of its presence being a small round painless swelling perhaps half an inch in diameter. After a month or more, this swelling will soften and rupture, discharging a peculiar viscid fluid containing in suspension minute round particles (compared by some to fish-roe) which are either grey, yellow or black. In time other similar swellings appear and go through the same process, leaving sinuses which do not heal. Gradually the foot enlarges to two or three times its normal size, the sole becomes convex so that the toes do not touch the ground, the tissues soften and the whole of the member is covered with the discharging sinuses.

As the foot enlarges, the leg atrophies from disuse, so that in advanced cases an enormously swollen foot is attached to a leg which is little more than skin and bone. Unless treated, the patient dies after ten or twenty years, worn out by the continued drain.

Three varieties of the disease have been recognised—the white, the black and the red—of which the last is very rare. It is due to a ray fungus which is allied to the actinomyses which in some places causes an affection (actinomycosis) among cattle which has

---

[1] See Manson's *Tropical Diseases* (Cassel & Co., 1898), from which the following particulars are abstracted.

[2] *Cuddapah District Manual*, 193.

been communicated to man. How this enters the foot is not yet certain. It is conjectured that it may be a usual parasite on some plant, and that it finds its way into the tissues through a wound in the skin. This theory is supported by the facts that the disease occurs almost invariably on the feet and hands, and principally among the barefooted ryots. If the harm has not proceeded far, free excision of the affected parts will stop it; but in more advanced cases amputation is the only remedy yet known.

Statistics of the recorded rates of births and deaths will be found in the Appendix. Registration of these events is now compulsory in all the unions and municipalities in the district. The figures are probably as reliable as elsewhere. They show, among other things, that the hot weather is much more healthy than the rains.

The medical institutions of the district comprise five municipal, three local board, and two mission, hospitals, and three municipal, twelve local board, and one mission, dispensaries. Statistics of the attendance at, and expenditure on, the municipal and local board institutions are given in the Appendix.

The mission hospitals are that for women and children in Madura town, near the site of the east gate of the old fort, which was opened by the American Mission in 1898 (the cases treated in which numbered 15,500 in 1904) and the well-equipped Albert Victor hospital (commonly known, from the name of the surgeon who originated it, as the Van Allen hospital) belonging to the same body, where there is accommodation for 48 in-patients and the out-patients treated in which numbered 20,800 in 1904. This latter was erected at a cost of Rs. 42,000 (nearly all subscribed by natives of the district), was opened by Sir Arthur Havelock in 1897, and is supported by annual subscriptions from the Náttu-kóttai Chettis, the Lessees of Sivaganga and others, aided by grants from the municipality, the District Board and the mission. The mission also maintains a dispensary at Pasumalai.

Of all the medical institutions the oldest is the municipal hospital at Madura. It was opened in May 1842 in the old guard-room over the remains of the west gate of the Madura fort (see p. 266) where the maternity hospital (opened in 1863) is now located. In 1843 the rooms on the north side of the platform over this, gateway, behind the guard-room, were erected for it. In 1862 the Collector, Mr. Vere Levinge, set on foot a public subscription for the provision of proper accommodation for the institution and for a maternity hospital. About Rs. 67,000 were collected among the natives of the district and part of this was spent in putting up new buildings and part in constructing, as an investment for the hospital, the bungalow in which the European Club at Madura is now located. The land round the site on which this stands had, it was said, been used for Sir Thomas Munro's camp when he once came to Madura as Governor, and ever afterwards it had continued to be reserved in case another Governor might similarly require it. Mr. Levinge levelled it with convict labour, sold part of it by auction and reserved one portion for the new bungalow. This last was apparently transferred to the municipal council, which now receives the rent of it, when the two hospitals were vested in that body in 1872 The erection of the excellent range of buildings in which the hospital is now located was sanctioned in May 1903, the estimate amounting to Rs 1,03,500. The cost of two of the wards was borne by M.R.Ry. A. L. A. R. Arunáchala Chetti of Dévikóttai and M.R.Ry. P. L. R. M. Shanmuga Chetti of Moraiyúr, the District Board contributed Rs. 10,000, and the municipal council provided the remainder. From 1875 to 1887 a medical school for training hospital assistants existed in connection with the institution. In addition to this and the maternity hospital, the municipality keeps up a branch dispensary, opened in July 1876, and a dispensary for women and children, originated in 1894.

The Dindigul hospital.

After that at Madura, the next most prominent hospital in the district is that maintained by the municipality of Dindigul. For many years the Rev. E. Chester, M.D., of the American Mission, who was engaged in medical work in the town from 1860 until his death there in 1902, managed a hospital in Dindigul which was aided from local and municipal funds. In 1899 the municipality started an institution of its own in a rented building. Five years earlier a dispensary for women and children had been opened, also in a rented house. Both these buildings were repeatedly condemned as unsuitable, and the Government has recently sanctioned Rs. 21,000 from Provincial Funds for the erection of a new building to hold both institutions. To this a sum of about Rs. 3,000, which has been collected towards a memorial to Dr. Chester, is to be added and, at the suggestion of the municipal council, the building is to be called the 'Chester hospital.'

Other institutions.

The municipalities of Palni, Periyakulam and Kodaikanal also maintain hospitals. The first two of these institutions were opened in 1872 and the last in 1873. Hospitals are kept up by the local boards in Bódináyakkanúr (started in 1880), Uttamapálaiyam (1873) and Usilampatti (1876).

In addition to the three municipal dispensaries at Madura and Dindigul already mentioned, others have been maintained from local funds at the places, and since the dates, noted below : In Dindigul taluk, Kannivádi (1884) and Védasandúr (1879); in Kodaikanal, Tándikkudi (1891); in Mélúr taluk, Mélúr (1879) and Nattam (1888); in Nilakkóttai taluk, Nilakkóttai (1891); Sólavandán (1888) and Vattilagundu (1881); in Palni, Sattirapatti (1897); in Periyakulam, Ándipatti (1891) ; and in Tirumangalam, Sáptúr (1888) and Tirumangalam itself (1873). Except those at Mélúr, Nattam, Nilakkóttai, Sólavandán and Tirumangalam, all these are located in rented buildings.

CHAP. IX.
MEDICAL
INSTITUTIONS.

CHAPTER X.

EDUCATION.

CHAP. X.
EARLY
HISTORY.

The three
Sangams.

MADURA was famous as a seat of learning in very early times. Tradition says that the Pándya capital was the home, at different periods, of three different Sangams, or bodies somewhat similar to the existing French Academy, which sat in judgment on literary works submitted for their approval and without whose *imprimatur* no composition could hope for a favourable reception. The first of these was at the old capital of the Madura country which (see p. 28) was swept away by the sea; the second at Kapádapuram, its successor as the chief town of the Pándyas; and the third was at the present town of Madura.

Fabulous stories are told of this last. The Madura *sthala puràna* recounts a long tale of how Sarasvati, the goddess of learning, was impudent to Brahma and was accordingly visited by him with a curse compelling her to undergo forty-eight successive births on earth. Afterwards, relenting somewhat, he allowed the sentences to run concurrently; and a forty-eighth part of her soul was thereupon transfused into each of forty-eight mortals who became poets of transcendent excellence, were received with honour by the Pándyan king, and formed the Sangam. They were, however, constantly annoyed by the absurd pretensions of others who claimed to be their equals, and at length Siva gave them a diamond bench which contracted and expanded so as just to accommodate those of the forty-eight who were present and no more, and thus prevented any unworthy aspirant from attempting to take his seat among them. When at last, says another tale, Tiruvalluvar, the Paraiyan composer of the famous *Kural*, brought his work for the approval of the Sangam, its members declined to 'crown' it ; but the miraculous bench, knowing the worth of the book, expanded to make room for it, and the book then in its turn grew bigger and bigger and pushed all the forty-eight off their eat.s

Native literary critics of much repute have held that it is doubtful whether any Sangam ever existed at all; but the weight of opinion is in favour of the theory that the third of them is an historical fact and that it flourished in the early years of the present era. Mr. Kanakasabhai Pillai [1] gives the sober version of its reception of the *Kural* in the time of the Pándyan king Ugra-peru-valuti (see p. 27 above).

The 'New Madura Tamil Sangam,' a flourishing literary society, was established in 1901. Its object is the improvement of the Tamil language; its income from endowments is returned as Rs. 4,850, and from subscriptions Rs. 10,974; its supporters include the Rája of Pudukkóttai and many well-known natives of Madura, and the members number 525; it maintains a boarding institution in Madura where Sanskrit, Tamil and English are taught; possesses a library of 3,800 books and manuscripts in these three languages; issues a monthly journal from a press of its own; holds examinations and awards medals to those who are successful in them; and conducts original research and the editing of ancient Tamil works.

Under the Náyakkan rulers, the education of Bráhmans (apparently other classes were neglected) was subsidised by the state on an unparalleled scale. The Jesuit missionary Robert de' Nobili wrote in 1610 that more than ten thousand Bráhmans were being taught, boarded and lodged at the public cost in Madura, and that the courses of tuition provided not only for the instruction of boys, but for the education of adults in philosophy and theology. Sanskrit, and not Tamil, was the medium of instruction. The fall of the Náyakkans put an end to these classes, and in the disturbed times which followed education seems to have been almost entirely neglected. When the English first acquired the country hardly any one in rural parts except a few hereditary village accountants and headmen seems to have been able to read and write, and the Tamil Bráhmans in the towns were so ignorant that, as elsewhere, Maráthas and other foreigners had to be called in by the Government to do its work, the records were kept in Maráthi, and this tongue became almost the official language. The American Mission (see below) were the first to re-introduce systematic education in the district, and it was not until 1856 that the first Government Zilla school, referred to later, was established.

In the separate Appendix to this volume will be found the chief statistics of the last census and of the Educational department

CHAP. X.
EARLY
HISTORY.

The new Sangam.

Education under the Náyakkans.

CENSUS STATISTICS.

---

[1] *The Tamils eighteen hundred years ago*, 138–140.

regarding the present state of education in Madura. The census showed that in the literacy of the males among its population the district ranked sixth in the Presidency, but that it came only fourteenth in the education of its girls. Taking both sexes together, the number of people in it who know how to read and write is slightly below the average of the southern districts and numbers just over seven per cent. Tamil is the language most generally known and only three persons in every thousand can read and write English. Among the eleven towns in the Presidency which contain over 50,000 inhabitants, Madura ranks sixth in the education of its males and eighth in the literacy of the other sex.

Figures by religions and taluks.

Figures of education among the followers of the different religions show that (as in several other districts) the males among the Musalmans are better educated than those of any other faith. The Madura Musalmans are mainly Rávutans, a pushing commercial class to whom a knowledge of reading and writing is essential. Next to them, but a long way behind, come the males among the Christians, and the Hindus of that sex bring up the rear. In the literacy of their girls, however, the Christians, as usual, easily take the first place among the three religions, neither the Musalmans nor the Hindus even approaching their standard.

Education is most advanced, as is natural, in the head-quarter taluk of Madura. Excluding Kodaikanal, the conditions in which are exceptional, Periyakulam comes next. Between the other taluks there is not much to choose, but Tirumangalam is at the bottom of the list.

EDUCATIONAL INSTITUTIONS.

The educational institutions of the district include two colleges; namely, that formerly maintained by the American Mission at Pasumalai, 2½ miles from Madura, but now transferred to Madura itself, and the Madura College.

The Pasumalai College.

The former is the older. It originated in a seminary which was opened at Tirumangalam in 1842 and moved to Pasumalai three years later. The original object of the mission was to provide in this school a high class education for youths of all religions, the Bible and the tenets of the Christian faith being included in the curriculum. But alterations and re-alterations of this plan took place, owing to changes in the views of the authorities upon the question whether the work of the institution should be confined to the instruction of candidates for missionary labours, or so extended as to include non-Christian students as well. In 1875 it was resolved that the latter of these plans should be followed, and subsequently the department for the training of missionary agents was separated from the rest of the institution.

In 1882 the school was raised to the position of a second-grade college, but the high and middle school classes were retained. In 1886 a normal school with a primary practising branch was added, and in 1892 the first of its hostels was opened. The institution now stands on a site some 50 acres in extent, which includes tennis courts and a field for football and cricket, and is accommodated in buildings which have cost over Rs. 80,000. It has a consulting and general library, its own press, and an endowment fund the interest of which is devoted to scholarships. The college classes have very recently been moved to the mission's high school building in Madura, as Pasumalai is so far from the town, and a proposal is on foot to construct, from the mission's share of Mr. Rockefeller's recent munificent gift in furtherance of education, a new college building on a site belonging to the mission near the Collector's residence.

CHAP. X.
EDUCATIONAL
INSTITUTIONS.

The Madura College is a development of the Government Zilla school which was established in March 1856 as an outcome of the Directors' famous despatch of 1854 on education. It was at first located in the north-east corner of the great arcade of Tirumala Náyakkan's palace ; and, on this being pronounced likely to fall down, was moved to the Naubat khána, or music pavilion of the palace, which then stood near the Ten Pillars (see p. 274), was afterwards used as the Police head-quarter office, was eventually pulled down because it was unsafe, and the site of which is now occupied by the Patnúlkárans' primary school. About 1865 the Zilla school was moved to a building near the railway-station (apparently erected partly from public subscriptions) which now forms part of the existing college. In March 1880 a college department was opened in the institution, but this was abolished in 1888. In the next year the school building and library were lent to the committee which was managing the then Native High School and this body started the present college. The institution was affiliated to the University in the same year. In 1891 the extension of the premises at a cost of Rs. 11,750 was sanctioned and in the following year the new block was opened by Lord Wenlock. The attendance in the college classes is about 120. The institution is now managed by a committee of native gentlemen. Attached to it are three lower secondary branches located in rented buildings.

The Madura
College.

The upper secondary schools of the district are six in number ; namely, that maintained at Dindigul by the municipality, those in Madura kept up by the American Mission, the Patnúlkáran community and the committee of the Madura College (the ' Sétupati

Upper
secondary
schools.

23

High School '), the American Mission's school for girls in the same town, and the school maintained at Periyakulam by M.R.Ry. V. Rámabhadra Náyudu, the present representative of the old poligars of Vadakarai (see p. 323).

Lower
secondary
schools.

Lower secondary schools for boys number twelve, and comprise those kept up by the American Mission at Dindigul and Mélúr and by the Roman Catholic Mission at Madura, the Dindigul Muhammadan school, the schools at Sólavandán, Madura, Palni, Mélamangalam (near Periyakulam), Uttamapálaiyam, Bódináyak-kanúr and Tirumangalam, and the general education branch of the local board's Technical Institute at Madura. Schools of the same grade for girls are three in number; namely, the Government school at Dindigul, the American Mission practising institution at Madura and the South Indian Railway's school for European girls in the same town.

Other
schools.

Government maintains a training school for masters at Madura, the local boards have a sessional school, and the American Mission keeps up a training school for masters at Pasumalai and another for mistresses at Madura.

Excluding classes for book-keeping, type-writing and the like, the only technical instruction obtainable is that given in the local board's Technical Institute opposite the railway-station at Madura. There, besides those learning drawing, about 100 pupils are being taught cabinet-making, metal-work, etc.

Some 190 boys are instructed in the Védas and Sástras in a number of *páthasálas* kept up in various parts of the district at the cost of the Náttukóttai Chettis and others.

Newspapers,
etc.

Five newspapers or periodicals are published in Madura. The American Mission issues a fortnightly English and Tamil paper and a monthly Tamil periodical, both of which are devoted mainly to religious matters; the Tamil Sangam has its own organ (a Tamil monthly); and there are two newspapers, namely, the Tamil monthly *Vivéka Bhánu* with a circulation of about 800 copies and the *South Indian Mail*, an English weekly with a circulation of 400.

CHAPTER XI.

LAND REVENUE ADMINISTRATION.

REVENUE HISTORY—Native revenue systems—Methods of the Náyakkans—Of
the Maráthas—And of the later renters—British administration : in the
Dindigul country—Mr. McLeod, first Collector, 1790—His incapacity—Mr.
Wynch and his maladministration, 1794—Commission of enquiry, 1796—Mr.
Hurdis' Collectorship—Order restored and survey and settlement begun,
1800—Principles of these—Miscellaneous taxes—The financial results—
Mr. Parish becomes Collector—The district declines, 1805—Mr. Hodgson's
report upon it—Triennial village leases, 1808-10 —Mr. Rous Peter's reductions
in the assessments, 1823—Further reductions, 1831—Abolition of *vánpayir*
assessments, 1854—Unsettled pálaiyams—British administration in the
Madura country—Difficulties at the outset—Formal cession of the country,
1801—Early settlements in it—The various land tenures—Government land
—*Hafta dévastánam—Sibbandi poruppu—Jívitham—Poruppu* villages—
Church *mániyams*—Chattram land—*Arai-kattalai—Arai-kattalai* villages—
Ardhamániyam, etc.—Defects of the settlement—Triennial leases and the
ryotwari system—Reductions in assessments. THE EXISTING SURVEY AND
SETTLEMENT, 1885-89—Principles followed—Rates prescribed—Resultant
effects—Settlement of hill villages. INAMS. EXISTING DIVISIONAL CHARGES.
APPENDIX, List of Collectors.

OF the details of the revenue systems in force under the various
native governments which held the Madura country before it came
into the possession of the English, exceedingly little is known.
Besides the land-tax proper, there were several smaller imposts on
the soil. Among these (in Tirumala Náyakkan's time at least ;
no continuous particulars are available) were the plough-tax, which
required owners of land to furnish the Náyakkan when called upon
with one labourer, free of charge, for every plough they owned ;
the ferry tax for the upkeep of the public ferries on the rivers ; the
kávali-vari, or tax for providing crop watchers ; and the *tér-úliyam*,
or car-service, which required each village to provide a fixed quota
of men to drag the great temple cars. Also every kind of art and
profession was taxed.

'Every weaver's loom paid so much per annum; and every iron-
smelter's furnace ; every oil-mill; every retail shop ; every house
occupied by an artificer ; and every indigo vat. Every collector of wild
honey was taxed ; every maker and seller of clarified butter ; every
owner of carriage bullocks. Even stones in the beds of rivers, used by

CHAP. XI.
REVENUE
HISTORY.[1]

Native
revenue
systems.

---

[1] The early part of this chapter is for the most part an abridgment of the
full account of the matter given by Mr. Nelson in the 190 pages of Part IV of
his book.

CHAP. XI.
REVENUE
HISTORY.

Methods of
the Náyak-
kans.

washermen to beat clothes on, paid a small tax. In the towns there were octroi duties on grain and other commodities brought through the gates. And lastly there were the land customs.'

The revenue from the land was however always the chief main-stay of the public exchequer. Tradition [1] says that under the Vijayanagar kings (it is useless to attempt to trace matters further back) the state was held to be entitled to one-half of the gross produce of all land cultivated. This revenue was realised by parcelling out the greater part of the country—the Náyakkan's private estates and the favourable grants to temples, charities and Bráhmans were excepted—among the poligars already (p. 42) referred to, and entrusting them with the collection of it subject to certain payments and services. The rapacity of these men and their servants was usually limited only by the inability of the ryot to pay, or by his success in deceiving or bribing the collecting staff; and oppression was rampant.

After the disruption of the Vijayanagar dynasty in 1565 at the battle of Talikóta, these methods still continued; but they were complicated by the fact that the Náyakkans of Madura frequently declined to pay their dues to their nominal suzerains, the fallen kings of that line. The system and its deplorable results are graphically described in a letter from a Jesuit priest, dated Madura, 30th August 1611, which is preserved in *La Mission du Maduré* and may be rendered as under :—

'The king, or great Náyakkan, of Madura has only a few estates which depend immediately upon him, that is to say which are his own property (for in this country the great are the sole proprietors and the common people are merely their tenants) and all the rest of the land belongs to a crowd of small princes or tributary poligars. These last have, each in his own estate, the entire administration of the police and of justice—if justice it can ever be called—and they levy the revenue (which comprises at least half the produce of the soil) and divide it into three parts. Of these, the first is set aside as tribute to the great Náyakkan, the second is allotted for the upkeep of the troops with which the poligar is obliged to furnish him in case of war and the third goes to the poligar himself. The great Náyakkan of Madura, and also those of Tanjore and Gingee, are themselves tributary to the king of Vijayanagar, to whom they have each to pay annually from six to ten million francs. But they are not regular in sending these amounts, often make delay, sometimes even refuse insolently to pay at all; and then the king of Vijayanagar appears, or sends one of his generals, at the head of 100,000 men to collect the arrears with interest. When this happens (as it often does) it is once more the poor common people who pay for the fault of their princes;

---

[1] Sir Thomas Munro's report cited in the *Bellary Gazetteer*, 150.

the whole country is devastated, and the inhabitants are pillaged or massacred.'

After the Maráthas came into power, things were even worse; for John de Britto, an eye-witness of what he described, wrote of the neighbouring Tanjore country in 1683 that—

'Ekóji (the Marátha king) levies four-fifths of all the produce. As if that were not enough, instead of accepting this share in kind he makes the ryots pay in money. And since he is careful to fix the price himself at a figure much above that which the cultivator can get, the proceeds of the sale of the whole of the crop are insufficient to meet the land assessment. Thus the ryots linger under the weight of a crushing debt and are often put to cruel tortures to prove their inability to pay. You will hardly be able to realize such oppression, and yet I must add that the tyranny in the Gingee kingdom is even more frightful and revolting. But I will say no more on the matter, for words fail me to express its horrors.'

Under the Musalmans, the Madura country (like other parts of the Presidency) was usually rented out to farmers for fixed sums, the farmers being left to make what profits they could by grinding the faces of the ryots.

About 1742, as has been seen above (p. 69), the province of Dindigul was leased in this manner by the Rája of Mysore to Birki Venkata Rao; in 1755 Madura proper and Tinnevelly were similarly rented by Colonel Heron to Mahfuz Khán for fifteen lakhs of rupees and in 1758 to Muhammad Yúsuf for five lakhs; in 1772 Haidar Ali of Mysore leased the Dindigul country to his brother-in-law Mír Sáhib, and in 1784 Tipu Sultan leased it to Mír Sáhib's nephew Saiyad Sáhib. In fact the land revenue in most of the area which now makes up the district was administered in this way up to the time when the British obtained final possession of it. These renters were usually tyrants of the worst description. Colonel Fullarton wrote that the object of each of them—

'Too frequently was to ransack and embezzle, that he may go off at last enriched with the spoils of his province. The fact is, that in every part of India where the Renters are established, not only the ryot and the husbandman, but the manufacturer, the artificer, and every other Indian inhabitant, is wholly at the mercy of those ministers of public exaction. The established practice throughout this part of the Peninsula has for ages been, to allow the farmer one-half of the produce of his crop for the maintenance of his family, and the re-cultivation of the land; while the other is appropriated to the Circar. In the richest soils, under the cowle of Haidar, producing three annual crops, it is hardly known that less than forty per cent. of the crop produced has been allotted to the husbandman. Yet

Renters on the coast have not scrupled to imprison reputable farmers, and to inflict on them extreme severities of punishment, for refusing to accept of sixteen 'in the hundred, as the proportion out of which they were to maintain a family, to furnish stock and implements of husbandry, cattle, seed, and all expenses incidental to the cultivation of their lands. But should the unfortunate ryot be forced to submit to such conditions, he has still a long list of cruel impositions to endure. He must labour week after week at the repair of water-courses, tanks, and embankments of rivers. His cattle, sheep, and every other portion of his property is at the disposal of the Renter, and his life might pay the forfeit of refusal. Should he presume to reap his harvest when ripe, without a mandate from the Renter, whose peons, conicopolies, and retainers attend on the occasion, nothing short of bodily torture and a confiscation of the little that is left him, could expiate the offence. Would he sell any part of his scanty portion, he cannot be permitted while the Circar has any to dispose of; would he convey anything to a distant market, he is stopped at every village by the collectors of Sunkum or Gabella, who exact a duty for every article exported, imported, or disposed of. So unsupportable is this evil, that between Negapatam and Palghaut-cherry, not more than three hundred miles, there are about thirty places of collection, or, in other words, a tax is levied every ten miles upon the produce of the country; thus manufacture·and commerce are exposed to disasters hardly less severe than those which have occasioned the decline of cultivation.

' But these form only a small proportion of the powers with which the Renter is invested. He may sink or raise the exchange of specie at his own discretion; he may prevent the sale of grain, or sell it at the most exorbitant rates; thus at any time he may, and frequently does, occasion general famine. Besides maintaining a useless rabble, whom he employs under the appellation of peons, at the public expense, he may require any military force he finds necessary for the business of oppression, and few inferior officers would have weight enough to justify their refusal of such aid. Should any one, however, dispute those powers, should the military officers refuse to prostitute military service to the distress of wretched individuals, or should the Civil Superintendent remonstrate against such abuse, nothing could be more pleasing to the Renter; he derives, from thence, innumerable arguments for non-performance of engagements, and for a long list of defalcations. But there are still some other not less extraordinary constituents in the complex endowments of a Renter. He unites, in his own person, all the branches of judicial or civil authority, and if he happens to be a Bráhman, he may also be termed the representative of ecclesiastical jurisdiction. I will not enlarge on the consequences of thus huddling into the person of one wretched mercenary all those powers that ought to constitute the dignity and lustre of supreme executive authority.'

After the district came into British possession in 1790 the revenue history of the Dindigul country differed altogether for many years from that of Madura proper, and it may conveniently be dealt with first.

The Dindigul territory, as has already (p. 71) been seen, was obtained by conquest from Mysore in August 1790, and ceded formally in 1792. When first it was acquired it consisted of four * estates or pálaiyams ('pollems') which were in the possession of their owners ; four † which had been sequestered in 1785–86 by Saiyad Sáhib ; and some inconsiderable extent of Government land included in which were four ‡ more which had been resumed many years before. Shortly after the acquisition, fourteen § estates which had been resumed by Tipu in 1788 on account of the arrears of tribute in them, and had been temporarily attached by him to the province of Sankaridrug (in Salem district), were restored to their former owners and re-annexed to the Dindigul country, and this therefore at that time comprised 26 estates making up roughly the present Dindigul, Palni and Periyakulam taluks and the west of Nilakkóttai.

* Idaiyankóttai.
Kómbai.
Mámbárai.
Sandaiyúr.

† Eriyódu.
Madúr.
Palni (apparently including Áyak-
kudi and Rettayambádi).
Sukkámpatti.

‡ Dévadánapatti.
Gúdalúr.
Kambam.
Vadakarai.

§ Ambáturai.
Ammayanáyakkanúr.
Bódináyakkanúr.
Emakkalápuram.
Erasakkanáyakkanúr.
Gantamanáyakkanúr.
Kannivádi.
Marunúttu.
Nilakkóttai.
Palliyappanáyakkanúr (now called
Kúvakkápatti).
Tavasimadai.
Téváram.
Tóttiyankóttai.
Virúpákshi.

Some account of the various pálaiyams will be found in Chapter XV below. The Mysore Government had apparently not interfered in the management of the four which were in the possession of their owners, but had leased out the others, and also the Sirkar land, to renters.

Immediately after the acquisition of the province, General Medows, who was commanding in the south, placed it temporarily in the charge of one Venkatappa Náyakkan, who made hay while the sun shone and went off at once with all the accounts.

On the 6th of the following month (September 1790) Mr. Alexander McLeod[1] arrived and took charge as Collector. His

[1] In the Appendix to this chapter will be found a list of the various Collectors of Madura from this time forth up to date.

position was one of much difficulty, and he was quite unequal to it; and the four years during which he endeavoured to administer the country were marked by confusion bordering on anarchy.

Each year, he assessed the peshkash due from the various estates, the amounts purporting to be fixed on the basis of established usage and of estimates of the outturn of crops furnished by the poligars and their officials; but, as Venkatappa had made off with such accounts as there were, it seems clear that these payments were regulated more by chance than by precedent or equity. The Government land (which was divided into the six taluks of Tádikkombu (the kasba), Periyakulam, Vattilagundu, Ándipatti, Uttamapálaiyam and Kambam) was annually leased either in blocks for fixed sums to renters, or village by village to the headmen. The renters treated the ryots after the barbarous manner of their kind already described above, but the headmen lessees paid (as elsewhere) fixed money rates (the details of which are not now ascertainable) for dry land, and for wet land one half of the gross produce after the *swatantrams* (or fees due to village officers and others) had been deducted therefrom.

His incapacity.

But the whole country was constantly in disorder. In June 1791 it was stated that troops were required to maintain the Collector's authority; in November of the same year Coimbatore and the surrounding tracts on the north were in the hands of the Mysore forces; in February 1792 the neighbouring Palni and Idaiyankóttai poligars were plundering in the same area; the Rája of Travancore was at the same time preventing the Collector from taking possession of Kambam and Gúdalúr, though these tracts (which had once been pálaiyams, but had been confiscated by Haidar Ali of Mysore in 1755) undoubtedly belonged to the Dindigul district; and the Kallans had quarrelled with the Madura renter and were committing every kind of excess. The poligars naturally took advantage of this confusion to withhold payment of their dues, and the renters followed their example.

In September 1793 the Board of Revenue endeavoured to improve the class of renters by directing the Collector to lease villages to their headmen instead of to strangers; but though the system was introduced in part, the headmen of villages which were especially exposed to the attacks of the Kallans of Ánaiyúr, the notorious centre of this caste in the Tirumangalam taluk, naturally declined to have anything to say to it.

In May 1794 Mr. McLeod went on leave to the seaside to recruit his health, and was succeeded by his Head Assistant, Mr. John Wrangham. A Board's Proceedings of August of this

year comments in a caustic manner on Mr. McLeod's maladminis- CHAP. XI.
tration, which had reduced the district to disorder and its revenues REVENUE
HISTORY.
to a very low ebb. It appears that not only had the poligars,
Kallans and renters been permitted with impunity to exhibit open
contumacy, but misappropriations of inams and swatantrams had
occurred, the assessments had not been collected, large remissions
had been obtained on the plea that tanks were out of order,
Kambam and Gúdalúr had not been recovered, the customs had
been mismanaged and the Collector's accounts were worthless.

In December of this same year Mr. Wrangham was replaced Mr. Wynch
and his
maladminis-
tration, 1794.
by Mr. George Wynch, but the year and a half during which the
latter remained in charge witnessed even worse confusion than
ever. He had scarcely taken charge when Captain Oliver, the
officer commanding the district, reported that the Palni poligar
was engaged in open hostilities with his neighbour the poligar of
Áyakkudi, while one of Tipu Sultan's officers complained that the
former was looting across the boundary in Coimbatore ; several of
the other poligars disobeyed the Collector's summons to appear
before him in Dindigul ; the poligar of Sandaiyúr laid claim to the
pálaiyam of Dévadánapatti, the owner of which had recently died,
and refused to enter into any engagement for the payment of his
arrears until his claim was allowed ; the Palni poligar objected to
the proposal to detach and assess separately the Áyakkudi estate
which had once been an appanage of his pálaiyam, and not only
refused to pay his peshkash but armed a thousand of his followers ;
the Virúpákshi poligar declined to receive the Collector's sanad
and customary presents and laid claim to the Kannivádi estate ;
the Travancore manager kept on committing every sort of excess
in Kambam and Gúdalúr ; in April the Collector himself and his
escort were stopped on the boundaries of Bódináyakkanúr and his
peons were fired on ; and in May the Vadakarai poligar joined
Bódináyakkanúr, both Palni and Áyakkudi began arming, Virúpákshi opposed the Collector's progress, and Kómbai set himself
to stir up disturbances in the Kambam valley.

In June, Government issued a proclamation to the poligars
forbidding them to arm themselves and requiring them to obey
the Collector. This had some temporary effect, but the country
went rapidly from bad to worse and in June 1796 Government
appointed a Commission, consisting of Mr. William Harrington
and Captain William McLeod, to take charge of the district and to
investigate the causes of the disorder which existed.

On the last day of the following August the two Commissioners Commission
of enquiry,
1796.
sent in a voluminous report on the matter and handed over the

24

district to a new Collector, Mr. Thomas Bowyer Hurdis. They
stated that not only was the district a prey to the political confusion just described, but that its revenue administration was defective
throughout. The karnams and amildars (or tahsildars) had combined to produce false revenue accounts; the former had entered
large areas of land as 'inams' in the accounts, so that they might
be able to appropriate the produce of them; poligars who had
been nominally dispossessed for contumacy went about none the
less with armed bands, annoying the ryots on their old estates;
the land-customs were maladministered, certain individuals (for
example) being exempted without authority from paying them; the
lessees of the five taluks (these had been rented out for five years
in November 1794; Kambam alone was kept under amáni) had
fabricated false returns and kept the authorities in ignorance of the
real value of these tracts; one of them, Appáji Pillai, moreover
caused all the ryots to leave their lands when the Commission
came round to measure and appraise them, lest they should give
information prejudicial to his interests; these renters were not
only in arrears, but so bullied their tenants and let the lands fall
into such disrepair that numerous ryots had emigrated; numerous
unauthorised alienations of Government land had been made by
subordinates; the above Appáji Pillai and his father Kumára
Pillai had fraudulently effected many of these and had systematically colluded with the Collector's understrappers to undervalue
Government land and bring about other irregularities; the peshkash collected from the poligars was from 14 to 23 per cent less
than it ought to have been, and than it had been in the time of
the Mysore renters Mír Sáhib and Saiyad Sáhib mentioned above;
and so forth and so on.

Government and the Board considered the report and ordered,
among other things, that unauthorised alienations of land made
since the country came into British hands should be resumed;
that inamdars who were not in possession at the same date should
be dispossessed; that Kumára Pillai and Appáji Pillai should be
banished the district; that triennial, instead of annual, agreements
should be made with the poligars; that troops should be sent to
Dindigul; and that the Palni poligar should forfeit his estate for his
repeated misbehaviour. They stated that they looked to the new
Collector, Mr. Hurdis, to bring the district back again into order.

For several years this officer was only partially successful in
doing so. Unlike Sir Thomas Munro in the Ceded districts, he
had no body of troops at his command sufficient to enable him
forcibly to compel the poligars to behave themselves. These men

had already become angry and disaffected ; some of them had been ousted from their ancestral estates and were wild with grief and indignation; the others found themselves expected to give up for ever the independence and power they had always enjoyed and to settle down to live virtuously and tamely on the produce of their properties in entire subjection to the orders of the new Government.

In 1797 this inflammable material was ignited by a revolt in the Ramnad country, and the more daring and rebellious of the Dindigul poligars began to raise disturbances in every quarter. The records of this year and of 1798 are full of accounts of their misdeeds. The one matter for congratulation was the fact that they acted independently, each in what he conceived to be his own interests, so that Mr. Hurdis was usually able to deal with them one by one.

In May 1799 the news reached Dindigul of the British successes in the Third Mysore War against Tipu Sultan, of the fall of Seringapatam, that ruler's capital, and of his death during the attack. This produced the happiest results. Those of the poligars who were secretly disaffected were awed into obedience to the British, while those who were more deeply implicated lost all heart and relaxed their efforts to create trouble.

By November 1799 order had been sufficiently restored to enable the Collector to begin a task which he had always set before himself, namely, the systematic survey and assessment, field by field, of his charge. He eventually completed this undertaking and sent in a monumental report thereon (dated 6th April 1803) which came to be quoted as an authority for years afterwards; and it is not too much to say that the prosperity of the district dates from the time of his administration, and that (while the settlement which he effected was ultimately modified in many of its details) the revenue system now in force is Mr. Hurdis' original system, developed and improved.

About this time the policy of concluding permanent settlements of the land revenue was being strenuously advocated, and Mr. Hurdis was directed so to survey and report upon his charge that the Board of Revenue might be able at once to effect such a permanent settlement of its assessments. His charge, it may be here noted in parenthesis, included, from the 31st July 1801 (the date on which the Nawab of Arcot concluded the arrangement already referred to on p. 71 above) the Madura country proper as well as the province of Dindigul ; but as the revenue history of the former is distinct from that of Dindigul, it will be separately dealt with later.

Mr. Hurdis, then, proceeded to survey and assess the Dindigul country in much detail; and at the end of each subsequent year the area completed up to then was rented out on triennial leases on progressive rents which were so arranged that by the end of the third of the three years they would reach the figure at which Mr. Hurdis considered that a permanent settlement might with justice be concluded. These operations were carried out not only in Government land but in twelve of the twenty-six estates included in the district and named on p. 183 above, which twelve had come under Government management owing to their having been forfeited for rebellion, escheated in default of heirs, or attached for arrears of revenue. The other fourteen estates were left in the hands of their owners and assessed at a peshkash equal to 70 per cent. of their value as ascertained by the survey and settlement of fasli 1212 (1802–03).

By the end of fasli 1214 (1804–05) all the Dindigul country had been thus surveyed and assessed, the triennial leases had all expired, and the permanent settlement came into full operation throughout it. With the exception of the fourteen palaiyams above mentioned and of a few hill villages which had never formed part of any of the poligars' estates and were likely to become refuges for bad characters if removed from Government control, the whole district was cut up into 40 different zamindaris or estates. The annual peshkash payable on each of these was definitely fixed, and eight of them, which had been formed from six estates forfeited for arrears, were handed over to their former owners ; 31 were sold to new purchasers; and the remaining one, being unsold, remained in the Collector's hands.

The principles upon which Mr. Hurdis effected this memorable survey and settlement were, very briefly, as under : ---

Excluding poramboke (that is, areas such as tank beds, the sites of forts and so on which could never be cultivated) the land of the district was primarily classed as being either (a) dry (unirrigated) or (b) wet, that is, land capable of being regularly irrigated.

Dry land was again sub-divided into (i) *bághayat,* or garden, and (ii) ordinary dry land. On the former, the Government assessment—which seems to have been fixed after considering what not only the settlement staff, but also the proprietor of the land and the ryots themselves had to say on the matter—was one-third

ot the estimated gross produce after a certain deduction had been
made for the cost of manuring. On the latter, the assessment was
usually two-fifths of the estimated gross produce. In neither case,
apparently, was any allowance made for ordinary cultivation
expenses.

Wet land was sub-divided into (i) *pánmalá*, or betel-growing
land, and (ii) ordinary wet land. 'I he former was assessed in
accordance with the estimated produce, the excellence of the
irrigation available and the cost of cultivation; and the revenue
varied from as little as 20 per cent. of the gross produce to as much
as 40 per cent. The latter, ordinary wet land, was assessed
according as it was capable of growing (*a*) sugar-cane, turmeric
and similar valuable crops, (*b*) two crops of paddy, or (*c*) one crop
of paddy. In the first of these cases due deductions were made
from the value of the estimated gross produce for cultivation
expenses, and the assessment was then fixed at the value in money
of one half of the remainder. In the other two cases a similar
method was followed, except that for some reason no allowance
was apparently made for cultivation expenses, while on the other
hand a deduction from the gross produce of $12\frac{1}{2}$ per cent. for
swatantrams was made before the hypothetical division between
Government and the ryot was made.

In addition to the above four main kinds of dry and wet land
there were also *nanjai taram punjai* and *pilluvari* land. The
former of these was wet land which was so poorly supplied with
irrigation that it would not produce wet crops, and its assessment
was fixed at rates calculated to give the Government 40 per cent.
of the gross produce. The latter was pasturage, and was assessed
on very easy terms.

In addition to the land revenue, part of which was paid in kind
and part in money, there were a number of other and curious taxes
which were styled *swarnadáya*, or payable in money. Some of
these (such as *pontkádu*, a customary rent levied on small patches
on the hills, the tope tax, derived from sixteen sorts of trees, and
poruppu, a small quit-rent on inams) were held to be such as might
be properly levied by the proprietors of the estates which were
being newly formed, but others of them were reserved by Government for its own management and disposal. These last included
the shop tax, on the estimated value of the dealings of merchants;
the house tax, a somewhat similar impost on petty traders and
artificers; the loom tax, assessed on the outturn of each loom; the
oil-mill, iron-furnace and indigo-vat taxes, which were rated on
similar principles; the Pallar tax, levied on men of certain castes

in proportion to the wages they obtained at harvest-time; the honey tax, on the amount of wild honey collected; the Patna Chetti and Bógári tax, levied on two rival factions as a payment for protection and religious supervision; the ghee-tax, paid for the monopoly of the retail sale of ghee in each village; and, lastly, the carriage-bullock tax, which was proportioned to the profits derived from the hire of those animals.

The financial results.

On the whole, the total increase in the assessment of the Dindigul country amounted to no less than 67 per cent., the average collections in the years preceding 1790 having been 43,543 star pagodas; [1] those from 1790–91 to 1795–96 (faslis 1200 to 1205) 59,180 pagodas; those from 1796–97 to 1801–02 (faslis 1206 to 1211) 86,543 pagodas; and those for the twelve years of British possession, from 1790–91 to 1801–02 (faslis 1200 to 1211), 72,851 pagodas. Mr. Hurdis considered that by the end of fasli 1214 (1804–05), when the whole of the district would have come under the new settlement, the revenue would be as much as 1,13,315 star pagodas. He explained, however, that a very large proportion of this was due to the increase in the area in occupation brought about by the survey, which had disclosed an enormous extent of concealed cultivation. He reported that in the thirteen of the forty zamindaris where the new rates had already been introduced, 'the increase thus levied was cheerfully agreed to by the ryots . . . . and, as made, has hitherto been fully and regularly collected.' He also believed that it was possible to count upon a great future increase in the wealth of the country from the extension of cultivation. Only some thirty-four per cent. of the whole culturable area in the Dindigul country was actually under tillage, and though the waste land was unavoidably very unequally divided among the different zamindaris (some containing much and others hardly any) and though ryots and capital were both lacking at the moment, he anticipated that ' under a vigilant superintendence and firm, yet almost imperceptible, guidance of the labours of the inhabitants (if peace continue) the revenues from the increase of population, and the habits of industry which may be then expected to be confirmed in the ryots, will in the course of ten years be nearly doubled.'

Mr. Parish becomes Collector.

In December 1803 Mr. Hurdis was promoted and Mr. George Parish became Collector of Madura. He held the post until 1812. He at first continued, generally, the policy which Mr. Hurdis had inaugurated but had not remained to see carried out in its entirety. The orders of the Board of Revenue were

---

[1] A star pagoda was equivalent to Rs. 3–8.

meanwhile received on that officer's great report on his survey and settlement. While the Board approved the figure of **1,31,315** star pagodas which had been arrived at as the ultimate revenue on all the cultivated lands in the Dindigul country, they considered that the deduction of some ten per cent. from the gross value of the province which Mr. Hurdis had proposed to allow the zamindars as their profit should be increased to 16 per cent., and that the permanent revenue should be 1,09,189 star pagodas.

But hardly had the division of the district into these forty estates come completely into operation than (from 1805 onwards) the state of the country rapidly became alarmingly serious. The owners of the various zamindaris fell heavily into arrears, the total balance at the end of fasli 1216 (1806-07) against twenty-six estates then under attachment being 39,909 star pagodas; the capitalists became bankrupt ; and at last in 1808 Mr. Hodgson, a Member of the Board of Revenue, was deputed to visit and inspect the country and ascertain the causes of its rapid decline.

He travelled all around the district and eventually submitted a most elaborate report upon the case. He considered that though Mr. Hurdis' rates of assessment were not in themselves excessive, nor his calculations for commuting produce into money anything but fair, yet his settlement had in some respects been based on incorrect principles. Too much stress had been laid upon the possible future profits to the zamindars from the cultivation of the waste land included in their estates, and instead of taking (as had been done elsewhere) the average collections of a number of years as the basis upon which the revenue should be collected, all that had been done was to deduct 16 per cent. from the proposed total revenue of fasli 1214, which was a higher figure than had ever been actually collected while the country was under the Company. Consequently the margin of profit left to the zamindars was very small, and as a series of bad seasons had followed the completion of the permanent settlement they had collapsed under the losses which these had involved. Mr. Hodgson concluded by recommending that as the permanent settlement had thus failed it should be replaced by the system of leasing out each village separately for a fixed term.

The Government approved his conclusions and suggestions, and wrote a despatch on the matter to the Directors which largely reproduced them both. From fasli 1217 (1807-08) the system of renting out the various villages for a term of three years was introduced under Mr. Parish's supervision. The result was a slight increase in the amount of the revenue realised over that

The district declines, 1805.

Mr. Hodgson's report upon it.

Triennial village leases, 1808-10.

which would have been received under the permanent settlement, but this was counterbalanced by the higher charges of management and collection which the more detailed system involved.

From 1812, the year when the triennial village leases expired, to 1828 (with the exception of one short interval) the Collector of the district was Mr. Rous Peter, a gentleman who made himself extremely popular among the natives of the district and is still (see p. 259) well remembered in Madura.

The triennial leases had been almost as serious a failure as the attempted permanent settlement; and on their expiry a ryotwari settlement, based on Mr. Hurdis' survey, was introduced. This system has continued to the present day. In 1823 Mr. Rous Peter proposed to the Board of Revenue that the assessments of the Dindigul country should be revised and lowered. He considered that they had proved themselves to be higher than the ryots could afford, and that they were moreover unequal in their incidence owing to imperfections in the land classification effected by Mr. Hurdis. He was of opinion that to remedy matters a reclassification of the whole country was necessary.

His suggestions were sanctioned by the authorities at Madras with but little discussion, and were carried out.

They were, however, insufficient to meet the needs of the case; and in October 1831 the then Collector, Mr. Viveash, submitted for the consideration of the Board of Revenue yet another scheme for the reduction of the Dindigul assessments which he appears to have carried out in part in anticipation of sanction. He pointed out that Mr. Hurdis' rates had been prescribed without ever considering whether the result of them was to bring the revenue demanded from any particular tract or zamindari above the figures prevailing under former governments, so that in many cases, when compared with such figures, they were clearly excessive. He instanced the case of kasba Tádikkombu, the amount collected from which had been 4,637 chakrams in fasli 1183 under the renter Mír Sáhib already mentioned; 4,508 chakrams on an average during six years under the renter Saiyad Sáhib; 3,296 chakrams on an average in the eighteen years from fasli 1194; but 4,999 chakrams in fasli 1212 under Mr. Hurdis.

Mr. Viveash said he had followed the methods and rules which had been adopted in the Ceded districts, and had assembled before him the village headmen, karnams and ryots of each zamindari or estate, together with experienced ryots of neighbouring taluks to

act as arbitrators, and had required them to revise the classification
of all land cultivated in fasli 1236 (1826–27), a good year, with
reference to such sets of accounts as were available, to the assessments of neighbouring tracts and to their own personal experience.
He went on to say that—

‘After the rates of Mr. Hurdis had thus been revised, I considered,
with reference to the collections of Fusly 1236, the average collections
of former years, and the opinions of the experienced Natamgars,
whether any, and if any, what addition should be made to the total
revenue of each taluq resulting from the revised rates of the ryots in
Cutcherry, and the addition was then made to the villages, and the
fields of each village, by the Natamgars, Kurnums, and Ryots, who,
aware that what one gained another would lose, took special care that
the additional revenue was fairly imposed. The accounts were then
brought to me, the revised rates read over, the ryots were questioned
if any of the villages or lands had been favoured, and, on their
expressing themselves and signing a document to the contrary, they
were dismissed. . . . . The basis of the revised assessment
is the Hooloos assessment of Mr. Hurdis revised and corrected by
the instrumentality of the ryots themselves; whilst loss of revenue was
prevented by fixing the total bereez of the district with reference to
average collections, and checks were provided against inequality in
the assessment by leaving the ryots themselves to distribute the total
reduction.’

Apparently no definite orders were ever passed on this report of
Mr. Viveash’s.

In March 1854 Mr. Parker, the then Collector, submitted for
the consideration of the Board a plan for the abolition of an
exceptional tax known as *vánpayir* which was levied on the cultivation of certain specially valuable kinds of produce (such as
betel, plantains, turmeric, chillies and brinjals) when grown on
wet land, and a similar extra assessment which was levied on
garden dry land planted with these same crops. The rates at
which the *vánpayir* tax was imposed varied in a complicated
manner from taluk to taluk and with the nature of the crop. Mr.
Parker considered that only the ordinary wet land and garden dry
land assessments, respectively, should be charged in these two
cases. He urged that the extra rate was objectionable on the
ground that it violated the accepted principle that the land, and
not the particular product raised, should be taxed, that it restricted
the ryots’ methods, that it raised the price of very necessary articles
of food and that it occasioned vexatious inquisitions into the
ryots’ doings and complications in the accounts. The Board
agreed with him, and shortly afterwards also sanctioned the

Abolition of
vánpayir
assessments,
1854.

discontinuance of an extra tax which was being similarly levied on tobacco in certain parts of the district.

In 1861 Government asked the Board to report on certain questions which had been left undetermined for many years; namely, the position of what were termed the ' unsettled pálaiyams' (also spelt ' poliems ' and ' pollams ') in this and other districts, the expediency of granting them permanent sanads, and the terms on which this might be done.

It will be remembered (see p. 183 above) that when the Din. digul country was first acquired by the Company it contained 26 pálaiyams or zamindari estates. By 1803, when Mr. Hurdis wrote his great report on the settlement of the district, twelve of these had come under Government management – three of them (Eriyódu, Palni and Virúpákshi) having been forfeited for rebellion; three more (Dévadánapatti, Madúr and Rettayambádi) having escheated for want of heirs; and six (Idaiyankóttai, Nilakkót-tai, Palliyappanáyakkanúr, Sandaiyúr, Sukkámpatti and another) having been resumed for arrears. These twelve, together with the Government lands, were carved up into the forty zamindaris already mentioned, and were either handed over to their former owners or were sold to sundry purchasers under the idea that a permanent settlement would thus be established. Their fate has already been sketched above.

The other fourteen estates were left in the hands of their owners and charged a peshkash assessed at 70 per cent. of their value as ascertained by Mr. Hurdis' survey and settlement of fasli 1212. Similar arrangements were made by Mr. Hurdis and his successor Mr. Parish with respect to the sixteen other pálai-yams in the Madura country proper—' the ten poliems of Madura and the six poliems of Manapara,' as they are called in the old records. In 1816, several of these thirty estates were in arrear with their peshkash and Government authorised the Collector in future to take such properties under his own management and allow the ejected poligars a málikhána allowance of ten per cent. on the net proceeds of the pálaiyams. This course continued to be followed until 1840. In that year Government called upon the owners of estates thus under attachment either to pay up the arrears or to agree to surrender their properties on condition of continuing to receive the málikhána they were then getting; and said that the pálaiyams of those who would not consent to either alternative would be sold in satisfaction of the arrears due upon them. Several of the poligars accordingly gave up their estates

* Ammayanáyakkanúr.
Áyakkudi.
Bódináyakkanúr.
Erasakkanáyakkanúr.
Gantamanáyakkanúr.
Idaiyankóttai.
Kannivádi.
Mámbárai.
Téváram.
Doddappanáyakkanúr.
Jótilnáyakkanúr.
Kílakkóttai.
Mélakkóttai.
Nadukkóttai.
Puliyankulam.
Sirupálai.
Uttappanáyakkanúr.
Velliyakundam.

and the owner of Kannivádi paid up the arrears due by him. Such of the other pálaiyams as neither escheated on failure of heirs nor were resumed for arrears, continued to pay the peshkash originally fixed by Messrs. Hurdis and Parish, even though this had not been formally declared permanent and though no sanads had been granted for them.[1] By 1865 eighteen * of the original thirty pálaiyams, as well as the mittahs of Vélúr and Rettayambádi in the Palni taluk, were still in existence.

In that year (in answer to the orders of Government above mentioned) the Board of Revenue reviewed in an elaborate proceedings [2] the history and position of these estates and recommended that permanent sanads should be granted to the owners of such of them as were willing to accept such grants and to execute the corresponding kabúliyats ; and that, for reasons stated, the peshkash should in no case be enhanced. Government agreed.

The owners of one † of the two mittahs and of fourteen ‡ of the eighteen pálaiyams accepted this invitation and applied for sanads.

† Vélúr.
‡ Ammayanáyakkanúr.
Áyakkudi.
Bódináyakkanúr.
Erasakkanáyakkanúr.
Gantamanáyakkanúr.
Idaiyankóttai.
Kannivádi.
Téváram.
Doddappanáyakkanúr.
Jótilnáyakkanúr.
Nadukkóttai.
Sirupálai.
Uttappanáyakkanúr.
Velliyakundam.

In August 1867 Government ordered that the case of Vélúr should receive further consideration, postponed orders in the cases of Bódináyakkanúr, Gantamanáyakkanúr, Uttappanáyakkanúr, and Sirupálai (the owners of which were minors) and also of Kannivádi (which, see p. 239, was exceptionally situated), but sanctioned the issue of sanads in the remaining nine cases. In

[1] Forty blank sanads (with their corresponding kabúliyats) were sent to Mr. Parish in 1805 for distribution to 'the mittahdars in Dindigul,' but the estates were continually being resumed and resold and Mr. Parish as a fact never even filled up these documents—much less issued them. Except one which was lost and another which had been abstracted by the record-keeper and made over to a pretender to the Kílakkóttai estate, the whole of them lay in the Collector's records until 1838, when they were torn up.

[2] Printed in G.O., No. 2730, Revenue, dated 10th November 1865.†

subsequent years sanads were also granted to all the other estates except (apparently) Sirupálai. Statistics regarding the various zamindaris now in existence will be found in the separate Appendix to this Gazetteer and some account of each of them is given in Chapter XV below. Of the eighteen estates and two mittahs mentioned above as being included in the district in 1865, all except five* have been declared impartible and inalienable by the Madras Impartible Estates Act, 1904, and the same declaration has been made regarding three † others which were transferred to the district from Tinnevelly in 1859.

* Kannivádi.
Kílakkóttai.
Sirupálai.
Velliyakundam.
Vélúr.

† Péraiyúr.
Sandaiyúr.
Sáptúr.

British administration in the Madura country.

We may now turn to the revenue history of the Madura country from the time when it came into British hands.

As has already (p. 69) been seen, this practically became part of the territories of the British in 1790, when the Company assumed its revenues from the Nawáb by proclamation and Mr. McLeod was appointed Collector of it.

Difficulties at the outset.

His responsibilities within it appear to have been limited at first to receiving the rent from the man, Muttu Irulappa Pillai, to whom it had been leased, and to watching the Company's pecuniary interests, but the difficulties in Madura soon became almost as serious as those which had been experienced at the outset of the administration of the Dindigul country.

Early in 1791 the renter appears to have been guilty of tyrannical and extortionate conduct and to have provoked the Kallans to commit a series of outrages. The Collector reported that it was necessary to station sufficient troops at Ánaiyúr (in Tirumangalam) and Mélúr (at which latter place there were already two companies of sepoys) to keep these people in order, and that the Ánaiyúr Kallans were in the habit of making predatory excursions through both the Dindigul and Madura provinces because there was no force there which was adequate to overawe them. In June 1791 the renter was deprived of his farm and much correspondence ·followed regarding his conduct and pecuniary liabilities. Government resolved that thenceforth the country should be leased out in a number of small farms and not again to a single individual.

Three years later, in June 1794, Mr. McLeod seems to have ceased to be Collector at Madura, and to have been in charge of

Dindigul only. Apparently, indeed, Madura was left for a time without any Collector at all, for in October 1795 the Collector of Dindigul complained of the outrages committed by the Kallans, stated that the turbulent individuals all belonged to the Madura country, and urged that the faujdar of the Nawáb of Arcot, who was in charge of that tract, ought to be required to keep them in order. He said that the road from Dindigul to Kambam was altogether unsafe, and that it was necessary to station troops along it in the Kambam valley.

In July 1801, as has already (p. 71) been seen, the Madura country, which was then under the management of the amildar of the Nawáb of Arcot, was formally ceded by treaty by the Nawáb to the Company ; and a proclamation was issued constituting Mr. Hurdis, the Collector of Dindigul, as Collector of the whole of the Madura district. Government informed that officer that there was no reason to expect any opposition to the transfer, but that the troops quartered in the south of the Presidency would be at his disposal if necessary ; and directed him to use his own discretion as to maintaining for a time or disbanding at once the regular troops and *sibbandi*, or armed police, which had been kept up by the Nawáb. Mr. Hurdis set a native commandant named Nattam Khán to watch the Kallans, kept on the Nawáb's tahsildars for a time, obtained the revenue accounts from these and others of that potentate's officers and organized taluk establishments in all parts except Mélúr, where the Kallans were apparently exceptionally troublesome.

His first jamabandi of the country was begun towards the end of 1801 (fasli 1211) and merely retained the customary rates of assessment and avoided any sweeping changes. His report on this, his letter of 20th July 1802 on the improved settlement he afterwards introduced in this same fasli, and a third report, dated 4th May 1803, and dealing with the jamabandi of fasli 1212 (1802–03), are the chief authorities regarding his administration of the country. They cannot be said to be perspicuous documents. Mr. Nelson spent much labour in the ' endeavour to illumine to some little extent their dark and apparently unfathomable depths ' and came to the conclusion that ' the mode in which its (the Madura country's) settlement was effected is to this day a mystery.'

The reports speak of the following different kinds of lands and land tenure, some of which are of interest : (1) Sirkar, or ordinary Government, land, (2) *Hafta dévastánam*, (3) *Sibbandi poruppu*, (4) *Jívitham*, (5) *Poruppu* villages, (6) Church *mániyams*, (7) Chattram, (8) *Arai-kattalai*, (9) *Arai-kat alai* villages, (10) *Ardhamániyam*, (11) Pálaiyam, and (12) Inam.

Government
land.

The first of these, ordinary Government land, was divided into (a) wet, (b) dry, and (c) betel, land.

The revenue on wet land was collected according to one of two methods. Under the former of these, which was called *áttu-kál-páshanam* and was followed only in the case of land watered from a river channel, the customary *swatantrams* and *rassums* (which **Mr.** Hurdis, after much enquiry, had fixed at 12½ per cent. of the whole) were first deducted from the gross produce of each field and distributed to their owners, and then the remaining produce was divided in equal shares between Government and the cultivator. The Government share was either handed over in kind, or paid for in cash at a price fixed by the Collector. Under the latter of the two methods of collecting the revenue on wet land, which was called *mánaváripat* and was applied only to land under rain-fed tanks, the gross produce was equally divided between Government and the cultivator without any deduction for *swatantrams* being made.

The revenue on dry land was collected in money and was either assessed on the acreage cultivated (at what rates does not appear) or in a lump sum on each village as a whole, without reference to the area tilled therein. These latter villages were called *kattu-kuttagai*, or fixed rent, villages.

Betel land was reported to have been assessed on the principles followed under the Nawáb's government, but what these were was not explained. The assessments collected in this year 1801 on the various fields, calculated almost at haphazard though they were, were duly recorded and remained for years afterwards the revenue always demanded on those fields.

Hafta dévastánam.

The *hafta dévastánam* (seven temples) land was land granted for the upkeep of the worship and ceremonies at the following seven temples : those of Mínákshi at Madura (the great temple), Kallar Alagarsvámi and Kúdal Alagarsvámi, and those at Tirupparankunram, Tenkarai, Tiruvédagam and Kuruviturai. Who originally made these grants is not now ascertainable. It was perhaps Tirumala Náyakkan. Nor is their subsequent fate clear, as accounts differ. Perhaps some of them were usurped during the troublous times immediately following the disruption of the Vijayanagar empire. When Chanda Sáhib obtained possession of the Madura kingdom (see p 58) he is said to have seized what remained of them ; and his proceedings rendered it necessary for the managers of the Mínákshi temple to close that institution and to hurriedly remove the idols and the entire establishment to Mánamadura in the Sivaganga zamindari, where, it is said, they remained for two years and three months, the expenses of maintain-

ing the customary worship being met by the Sétupati of Ramnad.
After the capture of Chanda Sáhib (see p. 59), Morári Rao, it is
stated, effected the return to Madura of the idols and establishment
and the restoration of part, if not all, of the land which Chanda
Sáhib had taken from the temple. Subsequently much of the
property was again lost, but when Muhammad Yúsuf Khán (who
was by birth a Vellála and therefore, though by faith a Musalman,
kindly disposed towards Hindu temples) came to Madura (see
p. 66), he is declared to have retained possession of the whole of
it, but to have made, in his first year, a grant of 12,000 chakrams
for the support of the seven temples and, in the succeeding years,
an allotment of 6,000 chakrams. When Mr. Hurdis took charge
of the country he found that what was then called the *hafta
dévastánam* land yielded the Government a revenue of Rs. 50,292,
and he proposed to the Board that it should be retained in the
hands of Government and that an annual permanent allowance
of 12,000 chakrams should be made to the seven temples.

The Board ordered the Collector to restore to the temples 'the
lands resumed from the pagodas by the late government,' but
for some reason not now traceable Mr. Hurdis never carried out
these instructions and (though the question of its disposal was
raised in 1849 and again in 1859) the *hafta dévastánam* land
remains in the hands of Government. It had long ceased to be a
religious endowment, and formed part of the resources of the
State at the time of the cession of the district.

Sibbandi poruppu land was that in the occupation of indivi- *Sibbandi*
duals belonging to the establishment (*sibbandi*) of the great *poruppu.*
Mínákshi temple at Madura. It is said that Yúsuf Khán imposed
on this a *poruppu*, or fixed tribute, of an arbitrary nature in
order to make up the grant of 6,000 chakrams which he accorded
to the great temple at Madura. In Mr. Hurdis' time this
poruppu amounted to as much as 5,506 chakrams, and it was
excluded by him from his revenue demand.

Jívitham land was that which had been held by military *Jívitham.*
peons for subsistence. Holding the opinion that the peons were
no longer required, Mr. Hurdis resumed it all and added its
assessment to the revenue demand.

Poruppu villages appear to have been those which were *Poruppu*
originally granted free to Bráhmans but were afterwards taxed *villages.*
with a quit-rent, or *poruppu*, by later rulers.

'Church *mániyams*' seem to have included in a general way *Church*
all land which was held by the temples, or by Bráhmans or others *mániyams.*
connected therewith, and was not subject to the ordinary full
land-tax.

*Chattram
land.*

Chattram land was that granted for the purpose of perpetually maintaining certain chattrams, or rest-houses, for travellers. As has been mentioned on p. 157 above, the grantees had in many instances altogether ignored their trusts and treated the land as their private property, guarding themselves by bribes to the authorities against interference with their dishonesty.

Arai-kattalai.

Arai-kattalai land was apparently ˌthat granted and added to temple property to pay for the performance of certain religious acts, among them the celebration of worship for the benefit of the soul of the departed grantor. Mr. Hurdis found that, as in the case of the chattram land, many of these grants had been improperly alienated by the dishonest servants of their nominal managers, and that the proceeds of them were no longer devoted to the purposes for which they were originally intended.

*Arai-kattalai
villages.*

Arai-kattalai villages were said to be those which had been granted rent-free to individuals in order that they might transfer them to the temples and thus obtain credit for a religious act. The transfers effected in accordance with the grants had in most cases been merely nominal and colourable, and the villages remained the property of the grantees. The fiction of transfer had, however, the advantage of obtaining for the villages that protection which was often accorded to temple property, though in some cases this had had to be bought by the payment of a *poruppu*, or quit-rent. Following the rules laid down by the late Nawáb, Mr. Hurdis recommended that these grants should be resumed unless they could be proved to have been made by Tirumala Náyakkan.

*Ardha-
mániyam,
etc.*

Ardha-mániyams comprised a small extent of land which had been granted on payment of half (*ardha*) the usual assessment.

Of the two remaining sorts of land, pálaiyams were the poligars' estates, ana ínams were fields or villages granted on the usual favourable terms for the usual multiplicity of reasons.

*Defects of the
settlement.*

Mr. Hurdis set himself to survey and settle the Madura side of the district just as he had done the Dindigul portion, but the work was far less carefully done in the former, than in the latter, area. Madura was never surveyed, like Dindigul, by skilled men. The area under cultivation in 1802,ˈand that ˌalone, wasˌhastily and incompletely surveyed by the karnams and other village officers in that year. The work was never finished, and that part of it which was done was never revised until the existing survey was carried out.

The settlement which followed was also defective. No provision seems to have been made, as'ˌin Dindigul, for the case of double-crop wet land, and therefore fields sufficiently well watered to raise two crops paid only single assessment if only one crop was raised. Again, neither wet nor dry land was ever classed as garden and assessed according to the class of crop grown on it, as had been done in Dindigul. This was no doubt a very liberal and proper arrangement, but it was clearly due to the happy accident of Mr. Hurdis' forgetfulness rather than to economic sagacity and forethought on the part of him and his successors.

As in Dindigul, the Government revenues in Madura included a number of money taxes, known generically as *swarnadáya*, and the land customs.

Mr. Hurdis, as has already been seen, left the district in 1803 and was succeeded by Mr. Parish. As in Dindigul, so in the Madura country, the latter adhered generally to the system which he found in operation. His report on the jamabandi of fasli 1213 (1803–04) showed that since the preceding year there had been a healthy extension of cultivation to the extent of 8 per cent., and that there was every prospect that this would further develop.

In 1804–05, it appears, a settlement 'formed upon the money assessments introduced by Mr. Hurdis' was made with each ryot separately. In 1805–06, apparently, the villages were leased out, as in Dindigul, either singly or in groups, to renters. In fásli 1218 (1808–09) these leases were made triennial. They were not a success, and when they expired (in fasli 1220) the system of settling with each ryot separately was reverted to. This was temporarily continued for a year or two more, and was formally adopted, as in Dindigul, in 1814–15.

Between that year and 1821–22 Mr. Rous Peter on several occasions granted unauthorised reductions in the assessments of some 52 villages situated in the then taluks of Mádakkulam, Sólavandán, Mélúr and Tirumangalam. These were carried out on no fixed principles and without any regard for the characteristics of each village. Mr. Peter was repeatedly called upon by the Board to explain on what grounds he had granted them, but neither he nor his successor Mr. Viveash ever replied. Eventually, however, in 1843 the Board ordered them to be cancelled.

The existing survey of the whole district was begun in 1872. Between then and 1875 it was carried on in a desultory manner by detachments from a survey party mainly employed in other districts, while between 1876 and 1878 work was seriously delayed by the great famine. From 1879, however, a full party was employed and the operations were completed in 1884. The whole of the six taluks were entirely re-surveyed, but the work was done in detail in Government land only, and not in the zamindaris or whole inam villages.

CHAP. XI.

REVENUE
HISTORY.

Triennial
leases and
the ryotwari
system.

Reductions in
assessments.

THE EXISTING
SURVEY AND
SETTLEMENT,
1885-89.

The Settlement department began operations in the district in 1881, and in 1884 submitted a settlement scheme. This was sanctioned by Government in 1885 and its introduction was begun in 1885 86 and completed in March 1889. It did not extend to the whole inam villages or the zamindaris.

It proceeded on the usual principles and was based on elaborate enquiries undertaken in the five taluks other than Tirumangalam. The soils were classified, and were grouped under the two main headings of régada, or black cotton-soil, and red ferruginous. The extent to which each of these occurs in each of the taluks has already been shown on p. 12 above. There are none of the arenaceous, or sandy, soils found in some districts. These main varieties were then again sub-divided according to their fertility into 'classes' and 'sorts.'

For the purposes of wet assessment, the irrigation sources of the district were divided into four classes. These were (to give them in the order of their superiority) first, permanent anicuts or head sluices on the main rivers and tanks directly fed by channels led therefrom; second, channels led direct from the main rivers without permanent anicuts or head sluices, permanent anicuts on the minor rivers, tanks fed directly from the above, and spring channels and rain-fed tanks of six months' capacity and upwards; third, channels from minor rivers without permanent anicuts and tanks fed by them, and spring channels and rain-fed tanks of from three to six months' capacity; and, fourth, other rain-fed tanks and hill and jungle streams. Notice was given that on the completion of the Periyár Project (pp. 126–130) all irrigation affected thereby would be included in the first group.

In some districts villages are classified, for the purposes of dry assessment, into groups in accordance with their facilities for getting their produce to favourable markets, but in Madura no distinction of this kind was drawn.

The money assessments were calculated on the estimated value of the calculated outturn of standard grains on wet and on dry land. For wet land, paddy was taken as the standard grain; the outturn was calculated to vary from 1,000 to 400 Madras measures per acre; and the 'commutation price,' fixed for commuting the money value of the estimated outturn on different classes of soil, was taken at Rs. 123–8–0 per Madras garce of 3,200 Madras measures—this being the lowest figure touched during the preceding twenty non-famine years and some Rs. 30 less than the average price for those years (Rs. 171·35), even when reduced by ten per cent. to allow for the difference between the figure obtainable by the ryot and that commanded by the merchant. For dry land, cholam and cambu, each in the proportion of a half, were taken as the standard grains; the outturn of the two together was estimated to vary from 275 to 100 Madras measures per acre; and the commutation price of the two was taken at Rs. 108-8-0 per Madras garce—the lowest figure reached in the preceding twenty non-famine years, and a value much less than the average for such years (Rs. 160·75), even when a deduction of ten per cent. for merchants' profits had been made therefrom.

From these commutation prices the gross value of the outturn on an acre of each of the different varieties of soil was calculated; from this a deduction of one-fifth was made to compensate for vicissitudes of season and the inclusion within the survey fields of unprofitable patches, such as paths, banks and channels; and a further deduction, based on experiment and enquiry, for cultivation expenses. The remainder was assumed to be the net yield per acre; and one half of this, rounded to the next lowest of the standard rates of assessment, was taken to be the value of the Government share of the crop and the money assessment per acre.

The rates per acre so arrived at for wet and dry land respectively are given in the margin. The percentage of each class of land which is assessed in each taluk at each of these rates is given on pp. 122 and 116, and in the separate Appendix to this volume will be found figures showing by taluks the actual area under each money rate and the classes and sorts of soils included under each. Less than one per cent. of

Rates prescribed.

Wet.		Dry.	
RS.	A.	RS.	A.
8	8	3	0
7	8	2	0
6	8	1	8
5	8	1	4
4	8	1	0
3	8	0	12
2	8	0	8
2	0	0	6
		0	4

the total wet area of the district is charged the highest rate, and only 2 per cent. of it the next highest, while 59 per cent. is assessed at either Rs. 4-8-0 or Rs. 3-8-0. Of the total dry area, less than thirty acres is similarly charged the highest dry rate, and only 5 per cent. the next highest, while 64 per cent. is assessed at either Re. 1-4-0 or Re. 1. It had long been recognised that the old wet assessments were too low and the dry rates too high. This was sufficiently evident from the figures of occupation, which showed that while only seven per cent. of the assessed wet land was unoccupied, the unoccupied portion of the assessed dry land was as high as 37 per cent. The Director of Revenue Settlement found that some of the most fertile wet land in the whole of the Periyakulam taluk (then the best irrigated in the district) was assessed at only some Rs. 2 per acre. The dry land was accordingly treated with especial leniency, but the wet rates were frequently enhanced. There remained, at the time of the settlement, 253,794 acres of dry land assessed at Rs. 2,17,519 and 10,050 acres of wet land assessed at Rs. 31,770 which was still unoccupied. Most of the latter was in Madura and Mélúr taluks.

Resultant
effects.

The figures below give at a glance the general effect of the survey and settlement on wet and dry land respectively ; namely, the increase in the cultivated area in each taluk disclosed by the survey, and the enhancement or reduction of the assessment brought about by the settlement. It should however be noted that the figures for Palni, Dindigul and Periyakulam compare the old wet assessment, which was a consolidated rate on the two crops, with the settlement assessment on a single crop. If the compulsorily registered and compounded second-crop charges and the additional assessment levied where second crops were grown are taken into account, the increase will be larger :—

	Wet land.		Dry land.	
	Percentage difference in		Percentage difference in	
Taluk.	Extent.	Assessment.	Extent.	Assessment.
Dindigul	+ 10	+ 12	+ 9	− 6
Madura	+ 9	+ 10	+ 7	− 18
Mélúr	+ 15	+ 11	+ 12	− 20
Palni	+ 5	− 7	+ 7	− 11
Periyakulam	+ 3	+ 4	+ 8	− 5
Tirumangalam	+ 8	+ 10	+ 3	− 7
District Total ...	+ 9·3	+ 7·7	+ 7·5	− 9·5

It will be seen that though the survey showed that the irrigated area in occupation was 9·3 per cent. more than was entered in the accounts, the settlement only increased the assessment on it by 7·7 per cent. ; and whereas the survey showed the similar excess in the dry land in occupation to be 7·5 per cent., the settlement brought about a decrease of no less than 9·5 per cent. in the amount charged on this. Taking both wet and dry land together, the survey disclosed an increase of 8 per cent. in the occupied area, while the settlement resulted in a net decrease of 2½ per cent. in the assessment, or, including the charge for second crop, an increase of ·45 per cent. The settlement cannot therefore be said to have dealt harshly with the Madura ryot.

The *pilluvari* tax already referred to, which was a light assessment collected in the Palni and Dindigul taluks on land used for pasturage, was discontinued after the settlement.[1]

The settlement of the villages on the Palni hills, which were sixteen in number (six on the Upper Palnis, and ten on the Lower), covering an area of 413 square miles and containing 18,000 souls, was separately undertaken in the latter half of 1893. These villages, as has already (p. 188) been stated, were not included in Mr. Hurdis' original settlement. Besides the *ponikádu* already referred to, which was a customary rent on patches in the hills which were cultivated with hoes, a tax of from Rs. 3 to Rs. 9 was at one time charged on each plough kept there and another of from As. 8 to Rs. 3 on every hatchet. Taxes on wild honey, dammar, ginger and other jungle products collected were also levied. In Mr. Hurdis' time and for many years afterwards, the hill villages were farmed to renters who lived on the plains and only occasionally visited their farms. The villagers repeatedly represented the intolerable exactions of these men (and of the *mannádis*, or headmen of hill villages, who afterwards were made the renters in some cases) and at length, in 1837, karnams were appointed in each village to enquire into the modes of taxation in vogue and the methods of the renters. In 1842, on the representations of Mr. Blackburne, the then Collector, the farming out was formally abandoned in favour of the ryotwari system, and the land was taxed, as elsewhere, according as it was dry or wet.[2] At the time of the settlement, of the total occupied area, 4 per cent. was dry and 15 per cent. wet in the Upper Palni villages, and 78 per cent. dry and 3 per cent. wet in those in the Lower Palnis. The old rates of assessment had varied from Rs. 3–9–9 (for plantains) to Re. 0–5–9 on dry land, and from Rs. 3–9–9 (again for plantains) to Re. 1–4–8 on wet. The new rates ranged respectively from Rs. 2 to As. 4 and from Rs. 5–8–0 to Rs. 2. The survey disclosed an increase in the dry land of 38 per cent. and the settlement imposed an enhancement of 25 per cent. in the assessment. In the case of wet land the corresponding figures were 25 and 148. The old wet rates were admitted on all hands to have been much too low. In calculating the assessments the same standard grains and the same commutation prices were taken as on the plains. All the irrigation sources were placed in the fourth class, as they had all been made by the ryots themselves.

[1] A history of this impost will be found in the papers read in B.P., No. 1362, Revenue, dated 16th June 1886.

[2] For further particulars, see the interesting report of Mr. Clarke, the Sub. Collector, dated 10th May 1853.

The inams of Madura are not of particular interest. As has already been seen, the poligars and karnams more than once endeavoured, when the district was first taken over by the British, to get the best fields into their possession by showing them in the accounts as inams. On receipt of the report of the Dindigul Commission of 1796, Government passed the very liberal order that every inamdar who was in actual legal possession at the time when the British arrived should be confirmed, and that any of them who were denied confirmation under this rule should be given a money allowance for life. Mr. Hurdis made enquiries into most of the inams and compiled a list of them. Those which he proposed to confirm amounted in extent to rather more than three per cent. of the whole cultivable area of the Government lands and were mostly granted for religicus purposes. He proposed to resume 'those given by the heads of villages, or by amildars and renters to dancing-girls, poets, musicians, heroes and others contributing to the pleasure of their immediate employers.'

The inam settlement was based on his accounts of fasli 1211 and on two other sets of faslis 1217 and 1222, and proceeded on the usual lines. Details of the grants then in existence will be found in the Inam Commissioner's letter read in G.O., No. 545, Revenue, dated 19th March 1863.

In 1860, in consequence of Mr. Pelly's scheme for the reorganization of the village establishments, the taluks of the district were re-named and re-arranged as under :—

Former taluks.	*New taluks.*
Tádikkombu. ⎱ Nilakkóttai. ⎰	Dindigul.
Mádakkulam.	Madura.
Mélúr.	Mélúr.
Aiyampalle.	Palni.
Tenkarai.	Periyakulam.
Tirumangalam.	Tirumangalam.

On the 17th October 1861 a sub-magistrate was first appointed at Kodaikanal, but revenue jurisdiction over the Palni Hills remained unchanged, and they continued to be included partly in Periyakulam, and partly in Palni, taluk.

In 1889 the existing Kodaikanal taluk was formed and a deputy tahsildar was appointed to the charge of it. Besides this officer and the tahsildars of the other seven taluks, there are deputy tahsildars at Védasandúr in Dindigul taluk, at Uttamapálaiyam in Periyakulam, at Usilampatti in Tirumangalam and two (one sanctioned temporarily in 1904 for two years) in Madura town.

The existing divisional charges are as under: Dindigul, Kodaikanal, Palni and Periyakulam taluks are under the care of the Divisional Officer of Dindigul ; Madura and Mélúr are under the Madura (or Head-quarter) Deputy Collector, who also does the magisterial work arising in Madura town ; and Nilakkóttai and Tirumangalam are in charge of the Tirumangalam division Deputy Collector.

In 1903 an additional Sub-Collector and Joint Magistrate was appointed temporarily to assist the Collector and District Magistrate, who was greatly overworked, and his appointment still continues.

A special Deputy Collector is engaged in the introduction of the Proprietary Estates Village Service Act in the whole inam and zamin villages in the district, and another in attending to various matters connected with the introduction of the Periyár water, such as the sale of land commanded by the Project, the levy of water-rate on inam and zamin land, the acquisition of land for the series of cross-roads which are being made in the Periyár area, and so forth.

APPENDIX.

List of Collectors.

Date of taking charge.		Names.
6 Sept.	1790.	Mr. Alexander McLeod, Principal Collector.
13 May	1794.	Mr. John Wrangham, Acting Collector.
27 Dec.	1794.	Mr. George Wynch, Principal Collector.
22 June	1796.	{ Mr. William Harington, Captain William McLeod, } Acting Collectors.
Sept.	1796.	Mr. Thomas Bowyer Hurdis, Principal Collector.
Dec.	1803.	Mr. George Parish, Principal Collector.
1S March	1812.	Mr. Rous Peter, Principal Collector.
13 Jan.	1815.	Mr. George Cherry, Acting Collector.
17 May	1815.	Mr. Rous Peter, Principal Collector.
9 Aug.	1828.	Mr. Jonathan Gleig (Sub-Collector in charge).
10 Sept.	1828.	Mr. Henry Viveash, Principal Collector.
15 Jan.	1830.	Mr. Henry Morris (Sub-Collector in charge).
15 Feb.	1830.	Mr. Henry Viveash, Principal Collector.
20 Dec.	1831.	Mr. John Chardin Wroughton (Sub-Collector in charge).
23 Jan.	1832.	Mr. Henry Viveash, Principal Collector.
30 April	1833.	Mr. John Chardin Wroughton, Acting Collector.
17 Feb.	1834.	Mr. John Blackburne, Acting Collector.
13 March	1834.	Mr. John Blackburne, Principal Collector.
14 Oct.	1836.	Mr. Robert Davidson (Sub-Collector in charge).
8 Nov.	1836.	Mr. John Blackburne, Principal Collector.
20 Dec.	1842.	Mr. George Dominico Drury (Commissioner in charge).
19 April	1843.	Mr. William Elliott (Sub-Collector in charge).
4 May	1843.	Mr. William A. Morehead, Acting Collector.
27 June	1843.	Mr. William Elliott (Sub-Collector in charge).
27 July	1843.	Mr. John Blackburne, Principal Collector.
1 April	1847.	Mr. Robert Deane Parker, Acting Collector.
13 July	1847.	Mr. Robert Deane Parker, Collector.
7 July	1852.	Mr. Thomas Clarke (Sub-Collector in charge).
7 Aug.	1852.	Mr. Robert Deane Parker, Collector.
24 Aug.	1852.	Mr. Thomas Clarke (Sub-Collector in charge).
23 Oct.	1852.	Mr. Robert Deane Parker, Collector.
1 April	1853.	Mr. Thomas Clarke, Acting Collector.
8 Oct.	1853.	Mr. Robert Deane Parker. Collector.
16 Oct.	1856.	Mr. John Rennie Cockerell (Sub-Collector in charge).
22 Oct.	1856.	Mr. Richard James Sullivan, Acting Collector.
21 Oct.	1857.	Mr. John Rennie Cockerell (Sub-Collector in charge).
11 Nov.	1857.	Mr. Arthur Hathaway, Acting Collector.
9 March	1858	Mr. Robert Deane Parker, Collector.
7 April	1858	Mr. Arthur Hathaway, Acting Collector.
8 Nov.	1858.	Mr. Arthur Pemberton Hodgson (Sub-Collector in charge).
19 Nov.	1858.	Mr. Thomas Clarke, Collector.
17 March	1860.	Mr. Charles Herbert Ames (Sub-Collector in charge).
7 May	1860.	Mr. Vere Henry Levinge, Collector.
11 Jan.	1864.	Mr. Æneas Ranold McDonell, Acting Collector
11 April	1864.	Mr. Vere Henry Levinge, Collector.
15 Jan.	1867.	The Honourable David Arbuthnott, Acting Collector.
9 April	1867.	The Honourable David Arbuthnott, Collector.
13 May	1868.	Mr. John Robert Arbuthnott, Acting Collector.
13 Aug.	1868.	The Honourable David Arbuthnott, Collector.
7 Jan.	1869.	Mr. John Robert Arbuthnott, Acting Collector.
8 April	1870.	Mr. Henry William Bliss, Acting Collector.
2 July	1870.	The Honourable David Arbuthnott, Collector.

List of Collectors—cont.

Date of taking charge.	Names.
12 May 1871.	Mr. William McQuhae, Acting Collector.
6 May 1872.	Mr. William McQuhae, Collector.
2 Sept. 1873.	Mr. Henry William Bliss, Acting Collector.
16 Nov. 1873.	Mr. William McQuhae, Collector.
5 Sept. 1874.	Mr. Henry William Bliss, Acting Collector.
5 Oct. 1874.	Mr. William McQuhae, Collector.
16 Sept. 1875.	Mr. Henry William Bliss, Acting Collector.
3 Sept. 1876.	Mr. Jeremiah Garnet Horsfall, Acting Collector.
11 Dec. 1876.	Mr. William McQuhae, Collector.
24 Nov. 1877.	Mr. Henry John Stokes, Acting Collector.
30 Sept. 1878.	Mr. Charles William Wall Martin, Acting Collector.
16 April 1879.	Mr. Henry John Stokes, Acting Collector.
18 June 1879.	Mr. Charles Kough (Acting Sub-Collector in charge).
24 June 1879.	Mr. Henry John Stokes, Collector.
13 March 1881.	Mr. Charles Kough, Acting Collector.
13 June 1881.	Mr. Henry John Stokes, Collector.
26 March 1882.	Mr. Charles Stewart Crole, Acting Collector.
24 Nov. 1883.	Mr. Charles Stewart Crole, Collector.
11 Jan. 1885.	Mr. Charles Kough, Acting Collector.
5 Feb. 1885.	Mr. Charles Stewart Crole, Collector.
4 Jan. 1886.	Mr. Edward Turner, Collector.
23 July 1889.	Mr. William Henry Welsh, Acting Collector.
23 Oct. 1889.	Mr. Edward Turner, Collector.
15 March 1891.	Mr. Rámachaudra Rao, Acting Collector.
4 April 1891.	Mr. Sydenham Henry Wynne, Acting Collector.
5 March 1892.	Mr. Charles James Weir, Acting Collector.
28 March 1892.	Mr. Edward Turner, Collector.
28 April 1894.	Mr. Leslie Creery Miller, Acting Collector.
1 Feb. 1895.	Mr. John Twigg, Collector.
3 Jan. 1898.	Mr. John George Denman Partridge, Acting Collector.
2 Nov. 1898.	Mr. Charles James Weir, Acting Collector.
30 Jan. 1899.	Mr. John George Denman Partridge, Acting Collector.
14 Aug. 1899.	Mr. Llewellyn Eddison Buckley, Acting Collector.
15 Nov. 1899.	Mr. John George Denman Partridge, Acting Collector.
16 July 1900.	Mr. John Arthur Cumming, Acting Collector.
3 Oct. 1901.	Mr. Alexander Gordon Cardew, Collector.
3 Feb. 1903.	Mr. Charles George Todhunter, Acting Collector.
3 Dec. 1903.	Mr. Mathew Young, Acting Collector.
25 Dec. 1903.	Mr. Arthur Rowland Knapp, Acting Collector.
30 Oct. 1904.	Mr. James Perch Bedford, Acting Collector.
11 Nov. 1905.	Mr. Edward Labouchere Thornton, Acting Collector.

CHAPTER XII.

SALT, ABKÁRI AND MISCELLANEOUS REVENUE.

Salt—Earth-salt—Saltpetre. Abkári and Opium—Arrack—Foreign liquor—
Toddy—Opium and hemp-drugs. Income-tax. Stamps.

CHAP. XII.
Salt.

THE salt consumed in Madura comes chiefly from the factories in the Tinnevelly district. The lighter Bombay product has not so far entered into competition with this. The fact that the frontiers of Pudukkóttai and Travancore States both march in places with those of Madura occasions no difficulty in the maintenance of the Government monopoly, for the Durbar of the former State consented in 1887 to entirely prohibit the manufacture of salt and salt-earth within its limits on condition of receiving from the British Government an annual compensation of Rs. 38,000; while that of the latter agreed, by a Convention of 1865, to adopt within the State the British Indian selling price. In the one case, therefore, there is no salt to smuggle across the frontier into Madura, and in the other there is no inducement to smuggle it.

Earth-salt.

Earth-salt has never been largely manufactured illicitly in any part of Madura except Mélúr taluk, where alone salt-earth occurs with any frequency. In this area, however, the temptation to make it is considerable, as there are many places on the numerous rocky hills which serve as admirable evaporating-pans and the local salt-earth makes very pure and white salt. Formerly the Kallans and Valaiyans of this part regularly made this illicit product, and murderous affrays occurred in consequence between them and the Police; and only a few years ago some 70 cases of illicit manufacture were detected in and about the one village of Karaiyapatti, about eight miles north-west of Mélúr.

The process of manufacture was the same as elsewhere, the salt-earth being placed in a chatti in the bottom of which was a small hole plugged with a bit of rag. Water was then stirred with it, and the brine so formed filtered through the hole into a smaller pot placed beneath, and was eventually evaporated in the sun in shallow pans made on the rocks.

Saltpetre.

Saltpetre is only refined at one place in the district (a factory owned by a Shánán at Kusavapálaiyam, a hamlet of Anuppánadi, just south of Madura town) and operations there are on a small scale, less than 500 maunds being made in the latest year for which figures are available.

Round about Palni and Áyakkudi a good deal of crude salt-petre is made by the ordinary process of lixiviating the alkaline efflorescence of the soil, and this is sent to be refined at Dhárá-puram in the Coimbatore district, whence a good deal of it is ultimately exported to the Nilgiris to be used as a manure on the coffee-estates there.

The abkári revenue of the district consists of that derived from arrack, foreign liquor, toddy and hemp-drugs. Statistics regarding each of these items, and also concerning opium, will be found in the separate Appendix to this Gazetteer.

The arrack revenue is managed under what is known as the contract distillery supply system, under which the exclusive privilege of manufacture and supply of country spirits throughout the district is disposed of by tender, and the right to open retail shops is sold annually by auction. The successful tenderer at present is M.R.Ry. T. Ratnasvámi Nádár, who makes the arrack from palmyra jaggery at his distillery at Tachanallúr in Tinnevelly and supplies the district from a warehouse in Madura town.

No difficulties occur with Pudukkóttai State. The arrack made in the distillery there is about the same strength as the Tachanallúr brand, and the duty levied is nearly as high as in British territory; so prices on both sides of the frontier are fairly equal. The case of Travancore is less simple, but the existing rate of duty on this side of the boundary is not high enough to encourage smuggling.

The supply of foreign liquor is controlled in the usual manner, licenses to vend wholesale or retail being issued on payment of the prescribed fees. This liquor all comes from Madras. It appears to be growing in popularity with the richer of those classes which are not prohibited by caste custom from touching strong waters, and to be in some degree ousting the cheaper but harsher country spirit.

Since October 1895 the toddy revenue has been managed on the tree-tax system, under which a tax is levied on every tree tapped and the right to open retail shops is sold annually by auction. The toddy is obtained chiefly from cocoanut, but to some extent from palmyra, palms. The number of the former tapped is eight or ten times as many as that of the latter. Date trees are never utilised, nor, except here and there in the Lower Palnis, are sago palms. Cocoanut and palmyra toddy are never blended in the shops, but are sold separately, some consumers preferring one, and some the other. The best cocoanut palms are those in the neighbourhood of Madura town, and along the banks of the Vaigai, and toddy is sent from these, in casks by rail and road, as far as Mélúr in the north-east, Ramnad in the south-east and Virudupatti in the south-west.

The toddy-drawers are all Shánáns by caste, and their methods do not differ from the ordinary. They employ Pallans, Paraiyans and other low castes to help them transport the liquor, but Musalmans and Bráhmans have in several cases sufficiently set aside the scruples enjoined by their respective faiths against dealings in potent liquors to own retail shops and (in the case of some Musalmans, at least) to serve their customers with their own hands.

Toddy shops sometimes proclaim their presence by a sign consisting of the small earthen pot which is specially used for toddy inverted on a long stick, while arrack shops similarly display a glass bottle.

No smuggling appears to take place from Pudukkóttai or Travancore States. The former has adopted the tree-tax system and the selling price of toddy differs but little on the two sides of the frontier. The boundary of the latter, where it adjoins Madura, consists of a high range of hills on which toddy-producing trees do not grow and across which it would be a difficult matter to smuggle a drink which keeps good for so short a time.

The consumption of toddy is usually heaviest at the periods of the year when paddy seedlings are transplanted into the fields and when the paddy harvest is reaped. The cooly classes, the chief consumers of this drink, have money in their pockets at those seasons and moreover are so continuously at work that they require a pick-me-up in the evening. Judged from the official statistics of the incidence of the revenue therefrom per head of the population, the consumption of toddy in Madura is comparatively small, and the similar incidence of the revenue from toddy and arrack together is lower in this district than in any other in the south except Tinnevelly.

A little sweet toddy and some palmyra jaggery is made at Páganattam and Nallúr in the Dindigul taluk and at Sandaiyúr in Tirumangalam, where palmyra trees are plentiful, but practically nowhere else.

Opium and
hemp-drugs,
    The sale of opium, ganja and poppy heads is controlled on the usual system.

Opium is supplied from the Madras storehouse, bhang from the storehouse at Daggupád in the Guntúr district and ganja from this latter and that at Kaniyambádi in North Arcot, where the crop from the Javádi hills is kept. The consumption of ganja in the district is considerable, owing chiefly to the number of north-country *bairágis* (who are greatly addicted to it) who pass through on their way to the sacred shrines at Madura, Palni and Rámésvaram. Neither Pudukkóttai nor Travancore produce either opium or hemp-drugs, and they are supplied with both from the British storehouses. Consequently no difficulties about smuggling arise.

Income-tax is levied and collected in the usual manner; statistics will be found in the separate Appendix to this volume. Including the zamindaris of Ramnad and Sivaganga (separate figures are not available for the other taluks by themselves) the incidence of the tax per head of the population and per head of the tax-payers both in the triennium ending with 1901–02 and in that ending with 1904–05 was higher in Madura than in any other district in the Presidency but the Nilgiris and the Presidency town, the circumstances of both of which are exceptional. This, however, is largely due to the presence, in the Tiruppattúr and Tiruvádánai divisions of Sivaganga, of large numbers of the wealthy Náttukóttai Chettis. A special Deputy Collector has recently been appointed to relieve the deputy tahsildars and the Divisional Officer of the heavy work connected with the assessment to the tax of these people, whose accounts and methods of business are complicated and who trade all over India, Burma, Ceylon and the Straits Settlements. The collection of the tax under Part II of the Act (profits of Companies) is increased by the existence in the district of a large number of 'Ela nidhis,' or auction chit associations.

Both judicial and non-judicial stamps are sold on the system usual elsewhere: statistics of the receipts will be found in the separate Appendix. The amount of the revenue from stamps in a district has with justice been held to be an index to its prosperity, and judged by this criterion Madura is a wealthy tract; for (including again the Ramnad and Sivaganga zamindaris) the receipts within it from the sale of judicial stamps in the latest year for which figures are available were higher than in any other district in the Presidency except Tanjore and Malabar, and those from non-judicial stamps were in excess of the figures of any district excepting Malabar.

CHAP. XII.
ABKÁRI AND
OPIUM.

INCOME-TAX.

STAMPS.

CHAPTER XIII.

ADMINISTRATION OF JUSTICE.

FORMER COURTS. CIVIL JUSTICE—Existing courts—Amount of litigation—
Registration. CRIMINAL JUSTICE—The various tribunals—Crime—Criminal
castes. POLICE—Previous systems—The existing force. JAILS. APPENDIX,
List of Judges.

CHAP. XIII. IN the days before the Company acquired the district, there were
FORMER no regular courts, either civil or criminal. In the time of the
COURTS. Náyakkans the poligars to whom (see below) the responsibility for
the suppression of crime within their estates had been delegated
administered criminal justice in a rough and ready way and also
constituted the only civil tribunal available in rural parts. Suits
were also settled by arbitration, by the intervention of the friends
of both parties, by ordeals by fire, oil and water, or by one of the
sides swearing to the truth of his case before the god of some
temple. The Náyakkans appear, from native MSS., to have themselves held a kind of court at their capital in which quarrels were
settled, with the aid of learned Bráhman assessors, as far as
possible in accordance with the known customs of the caste or castes
concerned. Thus it is recorded that the king decided a dispute
between the Sédan weavers and another caste as to which of them
was entitled to precedence in receiving betel on public occasions,
and settled a quarrel between the Saivites and the Vaishnavites
regarding the placing of a certain image in the *Pudu mantapam*
at Madura.

CIVIL Under the Muhammadan governors who followed the Náyakkans,
JUSTICE. matters were apparently managed on an even more casual system.

For some time, too, after the British acquired the country there
were no regular courts. Rebels and freebooters seem to have been
dealt with by martial law, and other criminals were punished by the
Collector, who also settled such civil cases as were brought before
him. By the Regulations of 1802 which introduced Lord
Cornwallis' judicial system into Madras, the first Zilla Court was
established at Ramnad and the Collector's judicial powers were
abolished. In the Appendix to this chapter will be found a list
of the Judges who thenceforward administered justice in the
district. Appeals from the Zilla Court lay to the Provincial Court
at Trichinopoly. The former was soon moved from Ramnad to
Madura. Subsequent changes in the judicial system were the
same in principle as elsewhere, and it is not necessary to trace

them in detail. In 1816 district munsifs were established in a few places under Regulation VI of that year. Act VII of 1843 effected important alterations in the system, the Provincial Courts of Appeal being abolished and new Zilla Courts established with far wider powers than their predecessors. The existing District and Sessions Court was established by the Act of 1873.

Besides this last tribunal there are in the district two Sub-Courts, those of Madura (East) and Madura (West), the usual district and village munsifs, and revenue courts for the trial of suits under the tenancy law, Act VIII of 1865.

The district munsifs are four in number; namely, those of Dindigul, Madura, Periyakulam and Tirumangalam.

More village munsifs hear civil cases in Madura than in any other district, and the Bench Courts established in 1895 under Act I of 1889 at the various taluk head-quarters also try more suits than the similar bodies in any other Collectorate.

Madura is one of the most litigious areas in the Presidency. Including the Ramnad and Sivaganga zamindaris, the ratio of suits to population is higher in this district than anywhere else except Tanjore, Malabar and Tinnevelly.

The registration of assurances is effected in the usual manner. A District Registrar is located at Madura and there are eighteen sub-registrars. The latter are stationed at the eight taluk head-quarters and also at Védasandúr in Dindigul, Ponméni and Sólavandán in Madura, Nattam in Mélúr, Sattirapatti in Palni, Bódináyakkanúr and Uttamapálaiyam in Periyakulam, and Kalligudi, Péraiyúr and Usilampatti in Tirumangalam.

The criminal tribunals are of the same classes as in other districts. Special magistrates exercise powers under the Towns Nuisances Act in Nattam and Bódináyakkanúr and benches with second-class powers sit at Dindigul and Madura.

The district is one of the most criminal in all Madras. An average of ten years' statistics shows that the number of persons who were convicted in it of the graver classes of crime was higher than in any other Collectorate, and that in respect to offences against the public tranquillity it stood at the head of all the districts; in regard to thefts was second among them; in respect to murders, hurts and assaults and cattle thefts, ranked third; was fourth in other offences against property; and fifth in culpable homicides and dacoities.

The position of Madura in these tables is no doubt adversely affected by the facts that the figures are absolute, and not worked out proportionately to the population, and that including the Ramnad and Sivaganga zamindaris the district is one of the most populous in the Presidency. But none the less the results are striking. Dacoities of travellers on the public roads used until recently to be common, but the gangs which infested the most unsafe of the roads, that from Ammayanáyakkanúr to Periyakulam, have now been broken up and this class of crime is comparatively rare. Special 'road talaiyáris,' paid from Police Funds, still patrol the Dindigul-Palni road.

Criminal castes.

Jail statistics amply prove that a very large proportion of the crime is committed by one caste, the Kallans, and it is not too much to say that if these people could by any miracle be reclaimed from their evil ways the district would immediately lose the unenviable reputation it now possesses. Some account of the community and its methods has already been given on pp. 88–96 above.

The other criminal castes may be dismissed in a few words. The Maravans and Agamudaiyans, who are prominent in the Ramnad zamindari and the north of Tinnevelly, commit but little crime in Madura. The Kuravans and Valaiyans give some trouble in Palni taluk, the former being addicted chiefly to theft and the latter being daring at house-dacoity, especially on the Coimbatore border. A certain number of wandering gangs, composed of castes who are generally classified as criminal, visit the district, but their share of the crime committed is small. They are chiefly Oddes (Woddahs) from Salem and Anantapur, Valaiyans from Coimbatore, Dásaris from the Nellore country and Tógamalai Kuravans from Trichinopoly. The last two, especially the Tógamalai Kuravans, are often prominent at festivals, where they commit much skilful petty theft among the pilgrims. Several other sub-divisions of the Kuravans, such as those which practise ear-boring and basket-making, are common in the district, but they are usually harmless folk.

POLICE.
Previous systems.

As in the other southern districts of the Presidency, the only police force in Madura in the days before the Company acquired the country was that supplied by what was known as the *kávali* system. This was arranged as follows: In the days of the Náyakkans, as has been explained in Chapter XI (p. 180) above, the district was divided into a number of feudal estates which were handed over to chiefs called poligars on condition that they collected the revenue, sent a certain proportion of this to the royal exchequer, spent a part on maintaining a fixed quota of troops ready for immediate active service, and were responsible for *kávali* or the maintenance of law and order, in their charges.

The last of these duties was usually fulfilled by appointing a head *kávalgár*, or watchman, who was given land free of rent, and was authorized to collect certain periodical fees in money or kind from the inhabitants on the understanding that he put down crime and made good any property which was stolen. Under this head *kávalgár* were a number of subordinate *kávalgárs* who received similar emoluments and undertook a similar responsibility in each village or group of villages.

After the downfall of the Náyakkans, the system was less rigorously enforced, and it degenerated by degrees into little less than the organized extortion of black-mail.

When the British took over the country they accordingly resumed the inams and emoluments of the head *kávalgárs*, and themselves took over their duties by appointing talaiyáris and peons to guard the villagers from thefts. The system was a failure. The talaiyáris were badly paid and worse supervised, and the conflict between their revenue and police duties resulted in the neglect of the latter.

The present police force, like that in other districts, was established by Act XXIV of 1859. It is under the control of a superintendent. As elsewhere, it includes a ' reserve ' of picked men at head-quarters who are better drilled and armed than the main body and would be of use in case of open disturbance of the public peace.

The prisons of Madura comprise the District Jail at the head-quarters, and the sub-jails at the stations of the tahsildars and deputy tahsildars elsewhere.

The present District Jail stands (see the map facing p. 258) to the north-east of Madura town and just north of the road thence to Dindigul. The building was begun in 1866 with convict labour and was finished, at a cost of about Rs. 65,000, in December 1869. A proposal to locate it on the race-course was thought to be dangerous, since if an outbreak occurred among the convicts when the Vaigai was in flood it would not in those days have been possible to cross the river to suppress it. The old District Jail was in the building near the north-west corner of the temple which is usually called ' Mangammál's Palace,' and the civil prisoners remained in this even after the convicts had been transferred to their new quarters.

In August 1872 the construction of separate wards at the new jail for civil debtors was sanctioned, and these were completed in 1874–75 at a cost of nearly Rs. 20,000. In 1882–83 separate wards and solitary cells for female prisoners were built. They cost Rs. 10,000.

APPENDIX.

List of Judges.

No.	Date.*	Name.
1	20 Oct. 1805.	Mr. D. Cockburne.
2	5 June 1806.	Mr. W. R. Irwin.
3	25 Sept. 1806.	Mr. J. D'Acre (Acting).
4	31 Oct. 1806	Mr. W. R. Irwin.
5	18 Jan. 1808.	Mr. T. A. Oakes (Acting).
6	13 May 1808.	Mr. W. R Irwin.
7	21 May 1810.	Mr. E. Powney (Acting).
8	21 July 1810.	Mr. G. F. Cherry (Acting).
9	17 Aug. 1810.	Mr. E. Powney (Acting).
10	15 April 1811. (No records.)	Mr. J. Long.
11	14 Sept. 1812.	Mr. W. O. Shakespeare (Acting).
12	11 Nov. 1812.	Mr. J. Long.
13	6 Aug. 1813.	Mr. J. Riddell.
14	26 May 1814.	Mr. W. O. Shakespeare (Acting).
15	7 March 1815. (No records.)	Mr. W. O. Shakespeare.
16	17 Jan. 1822.	Mr. G. W. Saunders (Acting).
17	23 Feb. 1822. (No records.)	Mr. W. O. Shakespeare.
18	18 July 1827.	Mr. S. Nicholls.
19	31 Aug. 1827.	Mr. H. Wroughton (In charge).
20	24 Oct. 1827.	Mr. S. Nicholls.
21	14 Feb. 1828.	Mr. W. R. Taylor (Acting)
22	22 Dec. 1828.	Mr. E. Bannerman (Acting).
23	27 March 1830.	Mr. A. E. Angelo (Acting).
24	2 June 1830.	Mr. E. Bannerman.
25	26 Dec. 1832.	Mr. J. C. Scott (Acting).
26	7 May 1833.	Mr. G. S. Hooper (Acting).
27	19 Feb. 1835.	Mr. R. H. Williamson (In charge).
28	17 March 1835.	Mr. J. C. Scott (Acting).
29	28 July 1835.	Mr. G. S. Hooper.
30	May 1836.	Mr. E. P. Thompson (Acting).
31	5 Oct. 1837.	Mr. D. R. Limond (In charge).
32	20 Aug. 1838.	Mr. T. A. Anstruther (Acting).
33	6 Oct. 1838.	Mr. W. Elliott (Acting).
34	3 July 1840.	Mr. H. Babington.
35	24 Feb. 1841.	Mr. J. Horsley (Acting).
36	1 June 1841.	Mr G. F. Bishop (Acting).
37	6 July 1841.	Mr. J. Horsley.
38	16 Oct. 1841.	Mr. F. Copleston (In charge).
39	20 Oct. 1841.	Mr. J. G. S. Bruere (Acting).
40	2 March 1842.	Mr. W. Elliott (Acting).
41	9 June 1842. (No records.)	Mr. W. A. Forsyth (Acting).
42	9 Jan. 1843.	Mr. W. Douglas.
43	6 Sept. 1843.	Mr. W. Elliott (Acting).
44	10 Oct. 1843.	Mr. G. S. Hooper.
45	Dec 1844.	Mr. G. S. Greenway.
46	Dec. 1846.	Mr. C. R. Baynes.

* The entries Nos. 1 to 44 were prepared from the records available in the Collector's office, and the date given against each officer is the date of the first of the letters written by him to the Collector, and not that of his appointment.

List of Judges—cònt.

No.	Date.		Name.
47	Feb.	1855.	Mr. A. W. Phillips.
48	14 April	1855.	Mr. T. Clarke.
49	Oct.	1855.	Mr. H. D. Cook.
50	April	1856.	Mr. A. W. Phillips.
51	18 Jan.	1858.	Mr. D. Mayne.
52	11 March	1858.	Mr. R. R. Cotton.
53	17 Feb.	1864.	Mr. J. D. Goldingham.
54	1 March	1864.	Mr. C. R. Pelly.
55	1 Feb.	1865.	Mr. J. D. Goldingham.
56	May	1865	Mr. C. N. Pochin.
57	Oct.	1865.	Mr. R. R. Cotton.
58	April	1867	Mr. E. C. G. Thomas.
59	June	1868.	Mr. G. P. Sharpe.
60	28 Sept.	1868.	Mr. J. R. Daniel.
61	1 Oct.	1868.	Mr. J. D. Goldingham.
62	23 Oct.	1872.	Mr. P. P. Hutchins.
63	13 March	1874.	Mr. F. H. Woodroffe.
64	30 July	1875.	Mr. H. W. Bliss.
65	1 Sept.	1875.	Mr. W. H. Glenny.
66	15 Dec.	1875.	Mr. P. P. Hutchins.
67	16 June	1879.	Mr. W. A. Happell.
68	1 Sept.	1879.	Mr. P. P. Hutchins.
69	28 March	1881.	Mr. E. Turner.
70	1 May	1881.	Mr. P. P. Hutchins.
71	6 July	1881.	Mr. C. W. W. Martin.
72	17 Nov.	1881.	Mr. E. Turner.
73	28 Feb.	1882.	Mr. P. P. Hutchins.
74	7 Dec.	1882.	Mr. E. Turner.
75	1 Sept.	1884.	Mr. T. Weir.
76	10 Sept.	1886.	Mr. L. Moore.
77	23 Oct.	1886.	Mr. T Weir.
78	2 March	1888.	Mr. H. T. Ross.
79	1 Sept.	1890.	Mr. J. Twigg.
80	1 Jan.	1891.	Mr. T. Weir.
81	27 July	1891.	Mr. S. Russell (Additional Sessions Judge).
82	5 March	1892.	Mr. S. H. Wynne.
83	9 Jan.	1893.	Mr. J. W. F. Dumergue.
84	8 April	1896.	Mr. G. E. L. Campbell.
85	22 June	1896.	Mr. A. F. Pinhey.
86	24 Oct.	1896.	Mr. S. Russell.
87	28 Feb.	1899.	Mr. H. Moberly.
88	7 April	1905.	Mr. J. Hewetson.
89	9 March	1906.	Mr. A. F. Pinhey.

CHAPTER XIV.

LOCAL SELF-GOVERNMENT.

CHAP. XIV.
THE LOCAL
BOARDS.

OUTSIDE the five municipalities referred to below, local affairs are managed by the District Board and the four taluk boards of Dindigul, Madura, Mélúr and Tirumangalam. The jurisdictions of the first and last of these latter correspond with those of the divisional officers of Dindigul and Tirumangalam, and the Madura and Mélúr taluk boards have charge respectively of the taluks after which they are named. When the Local Boards Act of 1884 was first introduced into the district, the three taluks of Dindigul, Palni (which then included Kodaikanal) and Periyakulam had each their own taluk board; the charge of the Tirumangalam board included so much of the Madura taluk as lay south of the Vaigai; and the rest of Madura and all Mélúr were directly under the District Board. Early in 1887 the part of Madura south of the Vaigai was transferred to the care of this latter body, and later in the same year the Madura and Mélúr taluk boards were constituted. The Dindigul, Palni and Periyakulam boards were amalgamated in 1894.

The Unions.

Nineteen of the larger villages have been constituted unions. Under the Dindigul board are those at Ayyampálaiyam, Áyakkudi, Bódináyakkanúr, Chinnamanúr, Gúdalúr, Kalayamuttúr (Neikkára-patti), Kambam, Kílamangalam, Mélamangalam, Uttamapálaiyam and Védasandúr; under the Méhír board, those at Mélúr and Nattam; and under the Tirumangalam board those at Nilakkóttai, Péraiyúr, Sólavandán, Tirumangalam, Usilampatti and Vattila-gundu. Of these, Nilakkóttai was established in 1888, Gúdalúr in 1901, and all the rest in 1885. As elsewhere, the chief item in their income is the house-tax, and this is levied at the maximum rates allowed by the Act in all of them except Sólavandán and Tirumangalam (where it is collected at three-quarters of this maximum) and Péraiyúr and Usilampatti, in which only half rates are charged. The incidence per house is lowest (nine annas or less) in Kalayamuttúr and Áyakkudi, and highest (Re. 1–10–2) in the flourishing town of Bódináyakkanúr. In 1905 the Collector suggested that the last-named place, sanitary conditions in which have long been unsatisfactory, should be constituted a municipality, but Government vetoed the proposal.

The separate Appendix to this volume contains statistics of the receipts and expenditure of the boards and unions. Including the figures for the Ramnad and Sivaganga zamindaris, the incidence of local taxation per head of the population, both including and excluding the receipts from tolls, and also the similar incidence of the total local fund receipts, are greatly below the average for the Presidency as a whole, or the level in the adjoining districts of Tanjore and Tinnevelly. The figure is brought down by the unusually low incidence in the country under the Dindigul and Tirumangalam boards, and the inference arises that these areas are by no means overtaxed.

The chief source of the receipts is the land-cess, which is levied at the usual rate of one anna per rupee of the land assessment. Next comes the house-tax, and then the tolls, which are fixed at three-fourths of the maximum rates allowed by the Act. Other conspicuous items are the income from markets, which is larger than in any other district except Coimbatore, and that from the produce of the avenue trees, which is exceeded only in South Arcot and Salem.

The principal objects on which local funds are expended are (as usual) the roads, the hospitals and dispensaries, and the schools. These have already been referred to in Chapters VII, IX and X respectively.

The five municipal towns are Madura, Dindigul, Palni, Periyakulam and Kodaikanal. The first two of these places were originally constituted municipalities on 1st November 1866 under the old Towns Improvement Act X of 1865, and continued as such under that enactment's successors, the Towns Improvement Act III of 1871 and the present District Municipalities Act. The Palni and Periyakulam municipalities were founded much later. A committee which reported in 1884 on the extension of local self-government in this Presidency recommended that as a general rule all places which had 10,000 inhabitants and upwards and were also the head-quarters of a tahsildar or deputy tahsildar should be turned into municipalities. Both Palni and Periyakulam came within this description and on 1st April 1886, in spite of the vehement protests of their population, they were constituted municipal towns accordingly. Kodaikanal was made a municipality on 1st October 1899. It is much the smallest in the Presidency.

CHAP. XIV.
THE FIVE
MUNICI-
PALITIES.

Madura
municipality.

Improve-
ments
effected
by it.

The water-
supply
scheme.

The medical and educational institutions maintained by the councils of these various towns have been referred to in Chapters IX and X respectively, and it remains to consider their other permanent undertakings.

The Madura municipal council consisted in 1884 of sixteen members, of whom seven were elected by the rate-payers and the rest nominated by Government. In the next year the number on the council was raised to 24, of whom 18 were elected. Soon afterwards factions arose, and by 1891 disunion had reached such a pitch that Government deprived the council of the power of electing its own chairman. The privilege was restored in 1896. A paid secretary to assist the chairman was appointed in 1898, but the step was not altogether a success and in 1902 the council decided to have as chairman a full-time officer on a salary of from Rs. 400 to Rs. 600. This arrangement still continues. The addition of another *ex-officio* member has now raised the total strength of the council to 25.

The permanent visible improvements effected by this body since it was first established are many. In 1871–72 a municipal office was provided by altering, at a cost of Rs. 5,000, an outlying building belonging to Tirumala Náyakkan's palace. In the same year was put up the clock which adorns one of the two turrets at the east end of the palace. In 1873 the then maternity hospital was extended at a cost of Rs. 2,500 and in July 1876 the branch dispensary, on which Rs. 18,000 had been spent, was opened. In 1884 the causeway across the Vaigai was put in thorough repair, trees were planted in the streets, the People's Park referred to on p. 264, was formed and the first water-supply project (see below) was carried into effect; and at about the same time the council subscribed Rs. 10,000 to the bridge across the Vaigai (see p. 156) which was opened in 1889. The latest notable undertakings have been the opening of the dispensary for women and children in 1894, the laying out of the garden called the Edward Park which was opened on Coronation Day, and the provision of the greater part of the cost of the erection of the excellent new range of buildings for the hospital referred to on p. 172.

The first water-supply project for Madura was suggested as long ago as 1849. The scheme consisted in widening the Pallava-ráyan channel, which takes off from the Vaigai about 4½ miles above Madura, and leading it along a high earthen embankment into a reservoir in the town. The supply would have been very fitful, as the water only reached the channel on the rare occasions when the river was in fresh. It was intended to utilise the water, not only for drinking, but for flushing the side-channels in the streets. An estimate for Rs. 28,600 was sanctioned in 1851. By 1859, Rs 20,000 had been spent, but the work was still unfinished and it was calculated that Rs. 18,800 more than the amount of the original estimate would be required. In 1862, 1863 and 1864 fresh estimates were sanctioned, and the expenditure eventually amounted to Rs. 51,200. The project, however, was never completed. In the seventies several other schemes were suggested or discussed, but none of them ever came to anything.[1]

In 1884 a new scheme, due to Mr. Crole, the then Collector, was carried out. This consisted in sinking a masonry well in the bed of the Vaigai (near the Máya mantapam just above the Vaigai bridge) to tap the copious underflow of that river, and pumping the water thence by steam to an iron cistern placed 27 feet above the ground near the 'elephant stone' (see p. 267) at the southern end of the causeway. Water was also supplied to the golden-lily tank in the Mínákshi temple on the trustees of that institution paying the cost of the pipes. This, the first regular water-supply scheme in the Madras Presidency, was a great success as far as it went. The high floods of November 1884 did some damage to the well and the pipe, but in the next year a bigger pump was put down, another well was sunk and linked with the first, larger pipes were laid and another cistern was put up near Blackburne's lamp (see p. 267). By the end of the year 1887–88 a third well had been made and the pipes had been carried through seventeen streets containing nearly two-fifths of the total population of the town. The outlay had amounted to Rs. 70,000.

The rapid increase in the population of the town necessitated still more water, however, and it became evident that a more comprehensive scheme was essential. Eventually Mr. J. A. Jones, then Sanitary Engineer to Government, designed the project which is now working. This was sanctioned in 1892. The cost of it was Rs. 4,27,050 and Government made a free grant of half this sum and lent the council Rs. 1,96,000 in addition. The project consisted in tapping the underflow in the Vaigai by erecting a barrage wall across the river at a point so far above the town as to be safe from contamination, making a filtration gallery just above this wall, running the filtered water thus collected into a well on the bank, and thence raising it by steam pumps to a point from which it would supply the town by gravitation. The annual charges for the extinction of the loan from Government in thirty

---

[1] See *The water-supply of Madura* by Mr. J. E. O'Shaughnessy, Madras, 1888.

years were estimated to be Rs. 12,868 and for pumping Rs. 19,885, making the total cost of maintaining the scheme Rs. 32,753.

The work was completed in two years and opened on 1st May 1894. But long before it was finished the discovery was made that the barrage wall had been placed by Mr. Jones in a most unfortunate spot. This had been selected chiefly on engineering grounds, because it was believed that the superficial area of the water-bearing strata there was larger than elsewhere; but as a matter of fact a ridge of rocks runs across the river-bed not far above the barrage wall and turns the underflow out of the bed into subterranean ways to the west, through which it eventually finds its way back into the river opposite the town, but *below* the barrage wall. The big well at the spinning-mill near the railway-station taps one of these underground springs and contains an extraordinary supply, but the amount available at the barrage was quite unequal to the demand.

An attempt was made to meet this radical defect in the scheme by carrying the filtration gallery right across the bed at an additional cost of Rs. 22,000. This did but little good, so in February 1895 a collecting channel was excavated for some 1,300 yards upstream from the barrage. This was filled up by a fresh a couple of months later. It was excavated again in July in the same year and the filtration gallery was also covered with gravel, instead of sand, to assist percolation. In 1899 the supply was temporarily increased in the dry season by opening the sand-sluices in the Chittanai anicut and letting some of the Periyár water down the river, but there are many objections to the systematic adoption of this course, and after much discussion an estimate for Rs. 1,32,000 has been drawn up for cutting a trench for some 3,350 yards up the bed, through the ridge of rocks above mentioned, and laying in it an 18-inch stoneware pipe. This is now before the council.

A scheme for the drainage of that part of the town which is bounded by the four Mási streets, the population of which is about 23,000, was completed in 1902. It was designed on the Shone system and provides for leading the sewage into four ejector stations serving an equal number of separate areas and actuated by compressed air supplied through iron pipes from a central station. The sewage thus collected was to be passed into a sealed iron main under pressure and thence through a detritus tank and bacterial filters to a farm of about 177 acres on which sugar-cane and forage crops were to be grown. The estimates amounted to $6\frac{1}{3}$ lakhs and the annual charges, including establishment and provision for a sinking fund, to about Rs. 47,000. Against this had to be set the profit from the farm, which was put at Rs. 29,000 annually.

Government considered that the scheme was clearly beyond the resources of the municipality, and the Sanitary Board accordingly so revised it as to reduce the cost to $3\frac{1}{2}$ lakhs. The reduction was effected by substituting pumping by oil-engines for the Shone system of raising the sewage; by simplifying the treatment of the sewage at the outfall; and by reducing the area of the proposed farm. The Sanitary Board calculated that, adopting these principles, a scheme for the whole town could be carried out for ten lakhs and that the annual maintenance charges would amount to Rs. 63,000. Government have asked the Sanitary Engineer to prepare detailed estimates for such a scheme.

The Dindigul council consists of fourteen members, of whom nine are elected by the rate-payers. This privilege of election was conferred in 1884 and in the next year the council was first given permission to elect its own chairman. The chief permanent improvements carried out in the town have been the construction of the market (first erected in 1872 at a cost of Rs. 3,500 and since added to at a further outlay of Rs. 7,500) and the inauguration of a water-supply scheme.

The first attempt to provide the town with good water was made in 1885 by Mr. Crole, and consisted in pumping a supply from a well sunk in a neighbouring tank to a service reservoir whence it was distributed by pipes. It failed because the water was of bad quality.

In 1890 the Sanitary Engineer proposed a scheme which provided for collecting a supply in an underground tunnel cut in the soft rock to the west of the railway line, and for pumping it thence to the town. The estimate was for Rs. 71,700 and the annual working charges were put at Rs. 5,511. Government sanctioned this in the next year and gave half the cost from Provincial Funds. Work was begun in 1892, but experiments showed that the supply of water in the rock was very doubtful and Government therefore ordered that the tunnel should be made in the first instance from Provincial Funds and should only be charged to the council if it was a success. By 1894 a tunnel 540 feet long had been driven and a supply estimated at 4,000 gallons an hour was obtained, and the rest of the scheme was accordingly put in hand. The work was finished in August 1896 and consists of a gallery 8 feet wide and 511 feet long, with lateral adits, tunnelled through soft rock 44 feet below ground level, two steam pumps, a service reservoir capable of holding 91,000 gallons, and the necessary piping and hydrants.

CHAP. XIV.
THE FIVE MUNICI-PALITIES.
——

Dindigul municipality.

Water-supply.

The yield from the gallery, however, belied its first promise and soon fell to only 64,000 gallons in the 24 hours. It was at first proposed to meet the difficulty by extending the tunnel, but eventually it was decided to dig a new trench in another site, the Odukkam valley. After several trials had been made and several rival schemes projected, Government eventually sanctioned, in 1904, a proposal to cut a trench about 20 feet deep and 400 yards long in the valley, nearly fill this with broken stone in which were embedded three rows of earthenware pipes one above the other, close the top of it with sand, and lead the water thus collected and filtered to the town by gravitation. The estimates amounted to Rs. 51,900 and Government made a free grant of half this sum and lent the council Rs. 16,300 more on the usual terms. The work was completed in 1905 but the supply is disappointing.

Palni
municipality.

The Palni council consists of twelve members, of whom four have been elected since 1897. The chairman is appointed by Government. The council's chief undertaking has been to provide itself with an office at a cost of Rs. 4,000, but in addition a slaughter-house has been built and improvements have been effected to the hospital and the medical officer's quarters. The present water-supply is from the Vyápuri tank, into which the whole drainage of the town flows uninterruptedly. Consequently cholera is common enough, and is sometimes carried hence all over the country by the pilgrims to the Subrahmanya shrine in the town. The richer classes get water brought in from the Shanmuganadi. Schemes for running an intercepting sewer round the foreshore of the tank and for pumping water from the river have been suggested, but they are beyond the means of the council, and the present policy is to endeavour to check the pollution of the foreshore of the tank.

Periyakulam
municipality.

The Periyakulam council is constituted like that of Palni. Except that it has built a small hospital and a choultry, it has done nothing outside the usual routine duties. Drinking-water is obtained from the Varáhanadi, which flows through the middle of the town and receives the whole of the drainage from either bank. The Berijam project, referred to on page 125, will shortly, however, render available a purer supply. A great need in Periyakulam is a bridge (or at least a causeway) across the Varáhanadi. All the heavy traffic from Bódináyakkanúr and the Kambam valley has to cross this river, and is at present often blocked for days together by freshes ; while even when only a little water is passing down, the cart-bullocks have to be shamefully thrashed and goaded to get them through the clinging mud of which the bed consists. The municipality is constructing a suspension bridge for foot-passengers across the river at an estimated cost of Rs. 7,100.

The Kodaikanal council consists of twelve members, none of whom are elected. The drinking-water of the station is at present obtained from wells and springs. In 1902 a scheme for an improved supply was worked out. This included the construction of a storage tank on the Pámbár (the catchment area of which has already been reserved by Government to protect it from pollution) by damming it about 370 yards above the Fairy Falls, and the conveyance of the water by a pipe through the embankment to a cistern just below this, thence along an open channel 1,450 yards in length to a service reservoir on a ridge commanding the place, and thence throughout the station by pipes. Any surplus was to be led into the lake, the supply to which is often less than the evaporation and leakage through the bund. The estimate was Rs. 49,000 and the annual charges, including working expenses and sinking fund, Rs. 4,300. Subsequently it was considered essential that the dam should be of masonry. This raised the cost to Rs. 62,250. The municipal council professed its inability to finance the scheme, and the question of Government assistance is under consideration. The project would not command houses built either along the Pillar Rocks road or in the Tinnevelly settlement, the two directions in which alone any large extension of the station is possible.

CHAPTER XV.

GAZETTEER.

DINDIGUL TALUK—Agaram —Ambáturai—Áttúr—Ayyampálaiyam—Dindigul—
Emakkalápuram—Eriyódu—Kannivádi—Kúvakkápatti—Madúr—Marunúttu
—Palakkanúttu—Sukkámpatti—Tádikkombu — Tavasimadai— Védasandúr.
KODAIKANAL TALUK—Kodaikanal. MADURA TALUK— Ánaimalai—Anuppánadi
—Kodimangalam — Madura—Mángulam — Pasumalai — Sirupálai— Tirup-
parankunram—Velliyakundam. MÉLÚR TALUK—Alagarkóvil—Arittápatti—
Karungálakudi—Kottámpatti—Mélúr - Nattam—Tiruvádúr. NILAKKÓTTAI
TALUK - Ammayanáyakkanúr—Kulasékharankóttai—Méttuppatti—Nilakkót-
tai—Sandaiyúr—Sólavandán—Tiruvédagam—Tóttiyankóttai—Vattilagundu.
PALNI TALUK — Aivarmalai —Áyakkudi—Idaiyankóttai — Kalayamuttúr—
Kíranúr—Mámbárai - Palni—Rettayambádi —Vélúr— Virúpákshi. PERIYA-
KULAM TALUK — Allinagaram — Ándipatti— Anumandanpatti—Ródináyak-
kanúr—Chinnamanúr—Dévadánapatti—Erasakkanáyakkanúr—Gantamaná-
yakkanúr—Gúdalúr—Kambam—Kómbai — Márgaiyankóttai— Periyakulam
— Téváram — Uttamapálaiyam — Vadakarai —Vírapándi. TIRUMANGALAM
TALUK — Ánaiyúr — Doddappanáyakkanúr — Elumalai—Jótilnáyakkanúr—.
Kalligudi—Kílakkóttai - Kóvilánkulam — Kuppalanattam—Mélakkóttai—
Nadukkóttai—Péraiyúr — Puliyankulam—Sandaiyúr — Sáptúr - Tirumanga-
lam—Usilampatti—Uttappanáyakkanúr—Vikkiramangalam.

DINDIGUL TALUK.

CHAP. XV.
DINDIGUL.

DINDIGUL (formerly called the Tádikkombu) taluk occupies the
north-east corner of the district and consists of an open plain of
red land surrounded on the east by the Ailúr hills and the Karandamalais, on the south by the Sirumalais, and on the west by the
Lower Palnis and the little range of rocky heights running south
from the Rangamalai and Karumalai peaks. The taluk slopes
sharply northwards from the pass between the Sirumalais and
Palnis and is drained in that direction by the Kodavanár and its
many tributaries. Next to Palni, Dindigul gets less rain than any
part of the district and it has practically no irrigation channels.
Consequently most of the land is dependent upon local rain, and the
tract suffered severely in the great famine of 1876–78. Nearly a
third of it is cultivated with cholam, and large areas are also cropped
with cambu and sámai. Dindigul tobacco is well known. Like
Palni, the taluk is famous for its numerous wells, and as much as
9 per cent. of its irrigated area is watered by them.

Statistics regarding Dindigul will be found in the separate
Appendix to this volume. After Periyakulam, it is the largest of
the Madura taluks and it contains more people, and also more
Musalmans and Christians, than any of them. The climate is
reputed to be particularly healthy. The chief commercial and
industrial centre is Dindigul, and accounts of this and the other
principal places within the taluk follow hereunder :—

Agaram : Six miles north of Dindigul on the other side of the
Kodavanár, facing Tádikkombu ; population 5,395 ; police-station.

The village is widely known for the festival at its Muttálamma
temple which occurs in September–October and is attended by
crowds from near and far. The building faces the Kodavanár and
architecturally is not remarkable, but the ceremonies at the feast
are curious. This latter cannot take place unless the goddess sig-
nifies her approval, which is revealed by the chirping of lizards on
the northern of the two great demons, eight feet high, which guard
the shrine on either side. If the lizards are silent, no festival
occurs ; and this is a bad omen for the coming north-east monsoon.
If the celebration of the feast is sanctioned, a silver chakram
(quoit), which is kept in a box in the temple and held in great
reverence, is first taken, for several days in succession, to a certain
mantapam, where worship is paid it. Three days before the actual
festival, an image of the goddess is made of clay and this and the
box are escorted to several different mantapams with due formality.
On the Tuesday on which the ceremonies reach their climax the
clay idol and box are taken together to a flower-garden across the
river, the box returns to the temple, and in front of the idol sacrifices
of very many sheep, goats and fowls are made by those who have
taken vows to do so. The mud image is afterwards left to the
mercy of the weather and slowly crumbles away. On the days
following the sacrifices, the assembled crowd is entertained with
such popular plays (acted by Kúttádis) as *Harischandra nátakam*
and so forth.

Ambáturai : Seven miles S.S.W. of Dindigul ; population
5,702 ; railway-station. It stands on the high ground between the
Palnis and the Sirumalais, and is as much as 997 feet above the sea.
Near it is one of the highest points on all the South Indian Railway
and the gradients on either side of this are severe. The village is a
small weaving centre and a dépôt for the products of the adjoining Sirumalai hills, and was formerly the capital of one of the
26 pálaiyams comprised in the Dindigul country at the time of
its cession to the Company. The history of this up to then is
referred to on pp. 70 and 183. It was a small estate some

21 square miles in extent, of which eight square miles were on the Sirumalais. In 1795 it was reported to consist mainly of cultivable dry land and to be paying a peshkash of 1,500 chakrams annually. By 1816 it had been ravaged by the great epidemic of fever, the inhabitants had emigrated in large numbers, the poligar had mismanaged it, and the Collector had resumed it for arrears.

Áttúr: Population 8,704. Lies on the upper waters of the Kodavanár, ten miles south-west of Dindigul, close under the Lower Palnis. The new Áttúr ghát up these hills, now under construction (P. 156), starts from near here. A channel from the river irrigates some 750 acres assessed at Rs. 4,200 and is the only considerable work of its kind in the taluk.

Áttúr is locally very celebrated for its festival to Vandikáliamman, a form of the well-known goddess Káli. Her temple, curiously enough, contains also an image of Muttálamma, and a feast to each of the two goddesses takes place on alternate years, turn and turn about. That to Vandikáliamma is probably the better appreciated of the two. It takes place in the month of Panguni (March–April) and the great day in it is the Tuesday (festivals to Káli are usually fixed for a Tuesday) after the full moon.

Some time before the feast begins, the Pallans of the place go round to the adjoining villages and collect the many buffaloes which have been dedicated to the goddess during the past two years and have been allowed in consequence to graze unmolested and where they willed in the fields. These are brought in to Áttúr and one of them is selected, garlanded and placed in the temple.

On the Sunday preceding the chief day of the feast, the village potter brings some earth to the shrine and it is consecrated and returned to him. From this he manufactures an image of Káli which is taken round the village with all kinds of music and eventually placed in the temple. The people assemble there on the Tuesday and do púja and perform the vows they have taken to the goddess during the past months.

On the Thursday occurs the great sacrificing of the dedicated buffaloes. The one which was garlanded and put in the temple is brought out, led round the village in state and then, in front of the temple, is given three cuts with a knife by a Chakkiliyan who has fasted that day to purify himself for the rite. The privilege of actually killing the animal belongs by immemorial usage to the head of the family of the former poligar of Nilakkóttai, but he deputes certain Pallans to take his place, and they fall upon the animal and slay it. Afterwards twenty or thirty other buffaloes (the number varies with the number of people who have taken vows to carry out this rite) are sacrificed on the same spot. Their bodies are eventually buried in front of the shrine.

This festival is the only one in the district at which any considerable number of these animals is thus offered up. The ceremony is supposed to commemorate the triumph of Káli over the buffalo-headed demon Mahishásura, which event is wonderfully depicted among the sculptures at the ' Seven Pagodas ' in Chingleput district and is fabled to have occurred at Mysore (whence the name of that town) where, on the great rock overlooking the place, is a famous temple to Káli.

On the Friday of the Áttúr feast the image of the goddess which the potter made is taken in procession again and left in a flower-garden (compare the ritual at the festival at Agaram) where sheep, goats and fowls are sacrificed before it. These doings, however, are rather private affairs than part of the real ceremonies. For a week thereafter the temple is shut up and púja is only done outside its doors. Then it is formally purified by the village Panchángi Bráhman (no Bráhman has thus far had any hand in any of the rites) and worship goes on as before. These later doings have the appearance of an apology for the sacrifices which have occurred.

When it is Muttálamma's turn for the festival, no buffalo sacrifices occur, but otherwise the ritual is much the same.

Ayyampálaiyam : A union of 13,881 inhabitants lying eighteen miles in a direct line south-west of Dindigul, in a valley of the Lower Palnis belonging to the Kannivádi zamindari and watered by the Ayyampálaiyam river.

The place is said to get its name from its well-known temple to Aiyanár. It does a great trade with the Lower Palnis in the staple products of that range. The river is prettily fringed with cocoanut and mango topes and is crossed by a dam. Messrs. Turnbull and Keys, in their Survey Account, complain that the wet crops under this work were annually ruined by elephants, though every effort was made to keep them away.

Dindigul, the head-quarters of the division and taluk, is the second largest town in the district, its population numbering 25,182, of whom as many as 3,175 are Musalmans (nearly all of these are Rávutans) and 3,917 are Christians. The place is a municipality and the station of a tahsildar, sub-magistrate, district munsif, subregistrar and bench of magistrates ; is a station on the railway (39 miles north of Madura) ; and possesses a police-station, upper secondary school, hospital, dispensary for women and children, travellesr' bungalow, local fund chattram and a weekly Tamil newspaper. Its medical and educational institutions have been referred to in Chapters IX and X above, and its municipality and water-works in Chapter XIV. The Roman Catholic and American Missions have established stations there and built large churches (that of the former body being an unusually imposing erection) and the Goanese Catholics and the Lutherans have smaller settlements. The town is a pleasant place picturesquely situated between the Palnis and the Sirumalais, and slopes up from the railway-station (which is itself as much as 924 feet above the sea) to the high ground on the north-west where the Sub-Collector's office and house, the district munsif's court, the American Mission compound, the hospital and other public buildings stand close to one another in an open and airy situation among fine trees and amid a climate which is considerably cooler and drier than that of Madura and perhaps than that of any other large town in the district.

The industries of Dindigul include the manufacture of its widely-known cheroots; the making of brass locks and safes and of brass and bell-metal vessels; the collection (for export to Madras) of large quantities of hides and skins, which daily pollute the air along all the many roads leading into the town; and the weaving of fine cloths by Patnúlkárans and coarser fabrics by Séniyans. There is also a considerable trade in the locally grown tobacco and in the products of the Palni hills, such as cardamoms, plantains and coffee. These matters have been referred to in more detail in Chapter VI, and it is sufficient to note here that the town is in a flourishing condition and that its population increased by as much as 25 per cent. in the decade 1891–1901 and by no less than 96 per cent. in the thirty years following 1871.

Dindigul gets its name from, and in olden days owed its importance to, the great isolated, fortress-crowned rock which stands at its western end and dominates the whole of it. This is called the *Tindu-kal,* a word which is said by some (there are several rival etymologies) to mean ' pillow-rock,' from the supposed resemblance of the hill to a native pillow. It may be more justly likened to a huge wedge lying on its side. It is about 400 yards long by 300 wide and lies with its thin end pointing north-eastwards. The top of the thicker, or south-western, end is 1,223 feet above the sea and some 280 feet above the ground immediately round it. The hill is almost absolutely bare of any kind of vegetation, and this gives it (in some lights) a particularly forbidding appearance.

The fortifications, which are on the list of antiquities conserved by Government and are in excellent repair, enclose the whole of the upper part of it and are reached from the thin end of the wedge by a flight of 600 shallow steps cut on the face of the bare rock there. At the top of this flight is the one and only gate into the fort, over which is inscribed, in Persian, the usual Musalman profession of faith and a prayer to the Almighty to guard the place from harm. The walls are of brick and stone and run round the crest of the whole of the rock except in one place at the thicker end which is so precipitous and overhanging as to render artificial protection unnecessary.

The buildings within the enclosure so made are neither numerous nor remarkable. To the west of the main gate are a series of bombproof quarters with barrel roofs, sunk below the level of the walls and placed practically underground. In these, refractory poligars and other state prisoners used to be confined. Above them, in more exposed positions, are two brick erections with steeply pitched roofs which appear to have been magazines and are probably of British construction. Between these latter stand the ruins of a larger building which is said to have been the commanding-officer's quarters in the days of native rule, and just below them are some deep fissures in the rock which contain water in the driest season and one of which is popularly declared to be unfathomable. Lying near one of these pools, below a circular brick bastion containing the foundations of a flagstaff, are two old iron cannon. On the very top of the hill is a dilapidated, empty temple to Abhirámiamman which includes three separate shrines, is of no architectural interest, but contains an inscription of king Achyuta of Vijayanagar, dated 1538 A.D.

In their memoir on the survey of the 'Province of Dindigul,' Messrs. Turnbull and Keys, who wrote in 1815–16 when the memory of such things was fresher, say that Tipu removed the image of Abhirámiamman to the town (where it still remains) so that spies might have no excuse for going through the fortress. They state that both the fortifications on the top of the rock and the works beneath it (see below) were originally built by Muttu Krishnappa Náyakkan of Madura (1602–09) ; that the upper fort was considerably improved in the modern style by Saiyad Sáhib (see p. 70) when he was in charge of the country from 1784 to 1790 ; and that it was thereafter 'entirely altered and systematically strengthened' in 1797–98 by the Company. Wilks confirms their account of Saiyad Sáhib's share in the matter, and states that in the six years previous to 1790 the fort had been 'rebuilt

with excellent masonry, on a new line of defence, not in conformity
to the exact principles of European science, but with a better
attention to flanking defence.'

In 1811, continues the Survey Account, the garrison and
most of the guns and stores were removed owing to the great
epidemic of fever which then swept through the district. In 1813,
the fever having abated, the place was garrisoned afresh, 800 or
900 men being posted there, and it is said that there were troops
in the place as late as 1860. At the time Messrs. Turnbull and
Keys wrote, the lower fort on the south-east side of the rock was
defended by a strong mud wall faced with stones and provided
with eleven bastions and a deep dry ditch. Of all this nothing
now remains except a shapeless earthen mound or two. There
was one entrance to this lower fort, a gate near a small temple,
the brick ruins of which are still standing. Between this and the
rock are the remains of a two-storied brick and chunam building
which was formerly the residence of Saiyad Sáhib, but in 1815–16
had been fitted out as a hospital. The sepoys were quartered in
temporary barracks. Below the south-eastern corner of the rock
was a 'garden house formerly the property of Colonel Cuppage'
and the remains of this still stand in a tope there.

At the opposite end of the rock, facing the 600 steps already
mentioned, is the old Protestant cemetery. Among the tombstones
in it (which have all been *whitewashed* by some Vandal!) are those
of Harriot Hurdis (1802), sister of the famous Collector of that
name; Lieutenant Thomas Wilson (1815), adjutant of one of
the Native Regiments stationed here; Major John Lambe (1828)
of the Honourable Company's service; William Buckley (1834),
ensign in another Native Regiment; Robert Davidson (1841),
Sub-Collector of Dindigul; and the Rev. William Hickey (1870),
a missionary of the S.P.G. who was formerly well known in this
town. Just north of the cemetery is the taluk cutcherry.

South of the rock, near a small mosque and amid a pretty grove
of tamarinds, stands a graceful, white, Musalman tomb, surrounded
with a verandah supported by an arched colonnade, and ornamented
with a dome and dwarf minarets. A Persian inscription in this
shows that it is the grave of Amír-un-nissa Begam, wife of Mír
Razáli Khán Bahádur, the 'Mír Sáhib' of history, who was
husband of Haidar Ali's wife's sister and renter of the Dindigul
country from 1772 to 1782 (see p. 70 above). Mír Sáhib
himself sleeps under the shadow of the great Gurramkonda rock
in the Cuddapah district. The inscription gives the date of Amir-
un-nissa's death as Hijra 1187, which began on 25th March 1773,

and local tradition says she died in child-birth in Saiyad Sáhib's residence above mentioned. There used to be an inam for the up-keep of the tomb, and the hamlet in which it stands is mainly inhabited by Rávutans and is known as Begampur.

Between the fort rock and the town stretched, in days gone by, the parade-ground (still a pleasant, open maidan) and the town (or 'pettah') was itself surrounded by a mud bulwark which has now vanished. The Survey Account says that—

'There were three entrances into the Pettah, the one from Trichinopoly, Caroor and Nuttum by the East Gate; the other from Darapooram, Aravacoorchy and Pylny by the North Gate; and from Madura and Pereacolum, etc., by the South. On this side of the Town the wall runs over two low rocks; the lesser one to the E. stretches to the Nuttum avenue by Punnacolam, a small Tank of irriga-tion which is appropriated to the support of the Begumpore Mosque . . . . . The road leading from the East Gate of the Town is on both sides enclosed by a few Gentlemen's Garden Houses, and by the North Gate stand the ruins of Dr. King's house, which was the finest building in its time, commanding a delightful view of the Town and the adjacent country for a few Miles. A road from it to the East leads to the Darogah's Cutcherry . . . . . On the south of Moat pollium, a small village about four furlongs to the east of Dindigul, chiefly inhabited by herdsmen, are two fine Bunga-lows which are consigned for the residence and Cutcherry of the Collector, who resorts to Dindigul annually for forming the Junima-bundy Assessment of the Country. The head Cutcherry of the Tahsildar is held here, for which a fine building has been erected in the year 1804, on the East side of the village.'

Of this wall and its three gates no traces now survive. Old people in the town remember them, however, and say that the East Gate was some 30 yards west of the west door of the American Church, and crossed the road by the big tamarind there; that the North Gate was just east of the junction of the roads to Palni and Védasandúr; and the South Gate not far from the Begam's tomb. The 'Punnacolum' (Pannaikulam) is now called the Aramanai-kulam. 'Dr. King's house' stood just west of the present hospital, across the road, and a smaller house has been put up on the site of it. 'Moat pollium' (Méttupálaiyam) is now known as Métturáják-kalpatti. The 'two fine bungalows' were the Sub-Collector's old house (which stood within his present compound, but was con-demned in 1881 and replaced by his existing residence) and the bungalow immediately east of it, now unoccupied. North of the back gate of this, across the road, may still be seen the foundations of the tahsildar's old cutcherry, built in 1804.

Until the middle cf the eighteenth century Dindigul fort remained in the possession of the Náyakkans of Madura. One of Taylor's Oriental Historical MSS. says that in the reign of Muttu Vírappa Náyakkan (1609–22) one Mulikan came from Mysore and besieged it, but was driven off by the chief of Kannivádi and the eighteen poligars of Dindigul of whom he was the head. In the reign of Tirumala Náyakkan (1623–59) the Mysoreans again attacked the place and were once more repulsed, this time by Rámappayya, Tirumala's well-known general.

In 1736 Chanda Sáhib seized the territory of the Náyakkans (p. 58) and placed his brother Sadak Sáhib in charge of Dindigul. In the constant wars which followed, the importance of the fort as a strategical point in the only pass between Coimbatore and Madura led to frequent changes in its possessors.

During the troublous times which ensued upon the Marátha attack upon Chanda Sáhib (p. 59) Ráma Náyakkan, an insignificant poligar of Uttamapálaiyam, surprised the place.[1] This was perhaps about 1741. Soon afterwards the Mysore Government sent a force under Birki Venkata Rao into the country, and the officer then in charge of the fort, Mír Imám Ulla, gave it **up to** him without resistance (p. 69).

In 1755 Venkatappa, the Mysorean officer in command of it, reported that the poligars round about were very obstreperous; and Haidar Ali was sent to bring them to their senses. He used Dindigul as his base. It was his first important command, and Wilks[1] thinks that 'this may, perhaps, be considered as the epoch at which the germ of that ambition began to unfold which terminated in his usurpation of the government of Mysore.' The extraordinary ease with which he quelled the poligars has already (p. 70) been mentioned, and for some years afterwards he used Dindigul as a centre for his operations against the Madura country proper. In 1757 he sallied out from it, took Sólavandán and plundered the country up to the walls of Madura; but eventually he was forced back again by Muhammad Yúsuf, Commandant of the Company's sepoys. In 1760 he marched out and attacked Vattilagundu, but was driven home again by the same officer.

In 1767 the place fell for the first time into English hands, the pettah being taken by Colonel Wood's detachment by escalade on the 3rd August and the fort surrendering the next day. The garrison placed there then was left without provisions, money, or instructions; and in the next year it surrendered to Haidar again.

---

[1] Wilks (Madras, 1869), i, 216.

On 4th May 1783 the place once more surrendered to the English
(under Colonel Lang), but was given back to Mysore in 1784 by
the treaty of Mangalore. Tipu Sultan came to Dindigul in 1788
to collect arrears of tribute due from the poligars, and sequestered
many of their estates.

In 1790, on the outbreak of the Second Mysore War, the fortress was besieged by Colonel James Stuart, and, for the first time in its history, made a slight defence. The English had not enough guns nor sufficient ammunition. They silenced the fort's fire on the first day (20th August) and by the evening of the next had made a very indifferent breach. As their ammunition had by that time almost run out, Colonel Stuart determined to escalade, and an assault was made that evening. It was repulsed with loss (Ensign Davidson and six other Europeans being killed), but most of the garrison abandoned the fort during the night, and early the next morning the killadár in command of it capitulated. From that time forth, the place has remained in English hands. It was formally ceded to the Company by Tipu in the treaty of 1792.

Emakkalápuram: A small village of 1,121 souls, lying about eight miles south-east of Dindigul near the Sirumalais. Formerly the capital of one of the 26 pálaiyams comprised in the Dindigul province at the time of its cession to the Company. Family tradition[1] says that the original grantee of the estate was one Kámalakkayya Náyudu, who (unlike the majority of his fellows in this district) came from South Arcot, where he was the headman of Dévanámpatnam, a village now within the Cuddalore municipality. He won the good graces of the Vijayanagar king by taming a vicious charger which no one else could handle, was given Cuddalore as a reward, afterwards accompanied Visvanátha Náyakkan (p. 41) on his victorious expedition into the Madura country and thereafter was put in charge of one of the 72 bastions of the Madura fort and given this pálaiyam of Emakkalápuram. It was a small estate measuring about fifteen square miles, of which five were on the Sirumalais.

Its chequered history up to the time when the British took the country has been given on pp. 70 and 183. In 1795 Mr. Wynch reported that the property, though small, was in first rate order— nearly all its arable land being cultivated ; and that its peshkash had been reduced from 550 chakrams to 450, which latter sum was all that it could afford to pay. About 1816, however, it was resumed for arrears and annexed to the adjoining sequestrated

---

[1] See Mackensie MSS., ii, 141-9, which gives a history of the pálaiyam.

estate of Madúr. The existing representative of the old poligar's family still draws a small pension from Government.

Eriyódu : Twelve miles north-north-east of Dindigul, population 2,266. Now decayed, but formerly the capital of one of the 26 pálaiyams included in the Dindigul province. At the time of Haidar's expedition of 1755 the poligar promised to pay 70,000 chakrams as the price of peace, but defaulted and had his estate sequestrated.

The later history of the pálaiyam is referred to on pp. 70 and 183. In 1795 it was reported to be a ' very fine pálaiyam containing twelve villages' and the Survey Account of 1816 says it occupied 112 square miles of which 30 were hill country. Its owner set the Dindigul Committee of 1796 (p. 185) at defiance and then fled, leaving behind him an irrecoverable balance of 3,436 pagodas. On the 4th August 1796 Government ordered the estate to be forfeited. Thereafter, up to the fall of Seringapatam in 1799, a detached post of the Dindigul garrison, consisting of a company of sepoys under a British officer, was stationed in the place.

Kannivádi: Lies ten miles nearly due west of Dindigul, close under the Palni Hills. It is the chief place in the zamindari of the same name, which is the largest in the district, pays more than twice as much peshkash as any other, and includes the whole of the eastern end of the Lower l'alnis The Survey Account of 1816 says that in those days traces of old buildings and extensive fortifications showed that the village originally stood in the narrow valley about a mile to the west, then entirely deserted except by wild elephants, and that in Pannaimalaiyúr, on the hills above it and approached by a difficult and fortified path, were the remains of buildings to which the zamindars used to flee when harried by the Mysoreans.

The village is not interesting, but the estate has a long history. Until it was bought in a Court sale in 1900 by its present proprietors, the Commercial Bank of India, it was owned by a family of Tóttiyan poligars whose traditions [1] go back five centuries. Like other chiefs of this caste, say these chronicles, the original ancestor of the family (with his two brothers, the first poligars of Virúpákshi and Idaiyankóttai) fled in the fifteenth century from the northern Deccan because the Musalmans there coveted his womenkind ; was saved from pursuit by two accommodating *pongu* trees on either side of an unfordable stream which bowed their heads together to make a bridge for him but stood

---

[1] See the long account in the Maçkensie MSS., iii, 417 ff.

erect again as soon as he had passed ; and settled in this district. A descendant of his, Appaya Náyakkan, won the good graces of Visvanátha of Vijayanagar (p. 41), was granted this estate on the usual terms, cleared it of jungle and marauding Védans and Kallans, and eventually was entrusted with the defence of one of the 72 bastions of the new Madura fort. A later scion of the line, Chinna Kattira Náyakkan, founded Kannivádi. One night (goes the story, which is still very popular) he saw the god of the Madura temple and his wife strolling in the woods. She lingered behind, and he called out to her ' Kanni vádi ! ' (meaning ' Come along, girl! '), and she replied ' Nallám pillai' (or, ' All right, dear.'). The poligar accordingly founded the Kannivádi and Nallámpillai villages in commemoration of this unique experience. Another chief of the pálaiyam was made head of the eighteen poligars of Dindigul who figure so frequently in the old tales as the defenders of this part of the country against incursions from Mysore, and he and his descendants accompanied the Náyakkan rulers of Madura on many of their various military expeditions.

After the decline and fall of the Náyakkans, the Kannivádi poligar, like most of his fellows, aimed at semi-independence. In 1755 (p. 70) Haidar Ali marched to bring them to order, but he was two months before he had cleared away the jungles and obstacles which surrounded the Kannivádi stronghold. At the end of that time the poligar promised to pay three lakhs of chakrams, and produced 70,000 of them on the spot. He was, however, eventually unable to find the remainder, and Haidar sequestrated his estate and sent him under arrest to Bangalore. The property was given back by the English in 1783, resumed again for arrears by Tipu in 1788, and once more restored by the Company in 1790, when it formed one of the 26 pálaiyams at that time comprised in the Dindigul country. The poligar appears to have misbehaved soon after, for he died in confinement in 1793. The chief of Virúpákshi claimed his estate, but by 1795 the property was back in the hands of the original family and was described as ' a very fine little district in capital order.'

For many years thereafter it remained one of the fourteen ' unsettled pálaiyams ' already referred to on p. 194 which always paid the peshkash fixed by Mr. Hurdis in 1802-03, even though this had not been declared permanent and though no sanads had been granted for them. In some ways, however, its case was an exception, for it happened to be under attachment for arrears in 1817-18 when Mr. Rous Peter introduced his reductions in Mr. Hurdis' assessment rates, and these reductions were extended to it and prevailed until it was restored to the poligar's family (on his paying the arrears due on it) in 1842–43, and from then onwards until 1862–63. By the latter year, the poligar was deeply in debt and was compelled to lease his property. In 1867, therefore, when Government ordered (p. 195) that sanads should be granted to certain others of the unsettled pálaiyams on their then existing peshkash, it was feared that to give Kannivádi a sanad would lead to the dismemberment of the heavily-involved estate, and for this and other reasons the case was held over to be further considered when the next occasion for appointing a new poligar should arise. The then proprietor died in 1881, but the estate was still much encumbered and the sanad was again withheld. In 1895 the poligar borrowed some ten lakhs, on a mortgage of his estate, from the Commercial Bank of India; and this institution eventually foreclosed, obtained a decree, and (there being no bidders) itself bought in the property at the Court auction in August 1900. In 1905, after considerable discussion, a permanent sanad for the zamindari was granted to the Bank on the same peshkash which had always been paid, namely, Rs. 38,080-9. The property is not scheduled as impartible and inalienable in the Madras Impartible Estates Act, 1904.

Kúvakkápatti: Fifteen miles in a direct line nearly north of Dindigul; population 1,262. Was formerly known as Palliyappanáyakkanúr, and was the chief village of a small pálaiyam of that name which was one of the 26 estates comprised in the Dindigul province at the time of its acquisition by the Company in 1790. Palliyappa Náyakkan was one of the first owners of this, and is stated in one of the Mackenzie MSS. to have built the mud fort the ruins of which still stand on the east of the village, and the temple and mantapam adjoining it. In Haidar's expedition of 1755 the then poligar surrendered and promised to pay a fine. He broke his word, and Haidar resumed his estate. The later history of the property has been referred to on p. 183. After the Company obtained the Dindigul country, the poligar was again ousted for arrears and in 1795 he was reported not to live on his property and to be much to blame for his neglect of it. One of his descendants still draws a small allowance from Government and his residence enjoys the courtesy title of ' palace. '

Madúr: Seven miles east of Dindigul, population 1,743. Formerly capital of one of the 26 pálaiyams comprised in the Dindigul province. Its history up to the advent of the Company has been sketched on pp. 70 and 183. In 1795 Mr. Wynch reported that it was in bad order owing to the indebtedness of its owner, and it was resumed for arrears in 1796. The poligar then

collected and armed some peons and went about the estate annoying
and intimidating the ryots. The property escheated on failure of
heirs in the same year. It was in a most neglected state, the fields
being overrun with weeds and scrub. It suffered severely in the
great fever epidemic of 1811 ' which swept away the greatest part
of ' its inhabitants, and in 1816 it was stated to be ' almost
desolated.' East of the adjoining village of Rámanádapuram, on a
low rock, is an ancient inscription which has long remained
undeciphered. M.R.Ry. V. Venkayya states that it records the
building of a tank in the time of the Pándya king Maranjadaiyan,
who perhaps belonged to the middle of the ninth century A.D.

Marunúttu: Ten miles in a direct line south-east of Dindigul,
population 512. Formerly the chief village of one of the 26
pálaiyams already several times referred to. The history of this
in pre-British days has been given on pp. 70 and 183. In 1795
it was reported to be a ' well ordered estate,' but in 1798 we find
the poligar charged with murder and other crimes and fleeing
from justice. Soon after, his property was forfeited, and in 1816
Marunúttu village was said to be desolate except for a few
Musalmans in a detached hamlet who .lived by trading with the
people on the Sirumalais.

Palakkanúttu (more usually spelt Palaganuth) is a village
of 4,848 inhabitants in the Kannivádi zamindari 15 miles west of
Dindigul on the Palni road. It contains a chattram, inscriptions in
which show that the part reserved for Bráhmans was built in 1840
from funds raised by Division Sheristadar Chintámani Venkata
Rao, and the non-Bráhman portion in 1843 by the wife of the
zamindar of Áyakkudi. The travellers' bungalow in the village is
located in an old building with an arched roof, half of which is
occupied by the police-station. Local tradition says that it was
constructed by the Robert Davidson who was Sub-Collector of
Dindigul from 1836 to 1837 and again from 1838 to 1841, died at
that town in the last of these years, and lies buried in the cemetery at the foot of the fort rock there.

Gold has long been, and is still, washed from the alluvium and
sand of the red ground at the foot of both sides of the prominent
hill two miles north by west of the travellers' bungalow. It is
found in small particles and in such limited quantities that the
people who search for it do not make more than they would by
manual labour of the ordinary kind.

The Rev. C. F. Muzzy of the American Mission, who first
drew public attention to the matter in 1856,[1] suggested that if

CHAP. XV.
DINDIGUL.

---

[1] M.J.L.S., xvii, 101.

moderately deep shafts were sunk the yield would probably be
greatly increased, but local report says that this has since been tried
by more than one European without success.

Sukkámpatti: Two miles north of Ailúr; population 2,439.
Formerly the chief place of one of the 26 pálaiyams of the Dindigul country. In 1755, during Haidar's expedition against the
owners of these (p. 70), this poligar sent a body of troops to the
help of the chief of Eriyódu, whom Haidar was attacking. These
were cut to pieces, and the poligar was fined 30,000 chakrams for
his audacity. As he did not pay the money, Haidar sequestered
his estate. This was restored by the English in 1783, resumed
again in 1785, given back once more by the Company in 1790, but
again sequestrated for arrears in 1795, being then ' in the greatest
disorder.' On this the poligar, like him of Madúr, armed some
peons and went about for some time harrying the ryots and preventing the collection of the Company's dues. The head of the
family still receives a small pension from Government.

Tádikkombu: About five miles north of Dindigul, population
5,301. The village once gave its name to the head-quarter taluk
of the Dindigul province and the cutcherry was located there. It
possesses a temple to Alagar (Sundararája Perumál) which contains the best sculpture in the taluk. The work is of the later
Náyakkan style and among the inscriptions in the building is a
record dated 1629, in the time of Tirumala Náyakkan. The finest
carving is in the mantapam before the goddess' shrine, which is
supported by a series of big monolithic pillars about twelve feet
high fashioned into very elaborate and spirited representations
of the incarnations of Vishnu and so on. Nearer the shrine is a
smaller and more ordinary inner mantapam. The entrance to this
is flanked on either side by two notable pillars made of a handsome
marbled stone and consisting of a central square column surrounded by eight graceful detached shafts all cut out of one
stone and all of different designs. The roof of this smaller mantapam has eaves quaintly fashioned to represent wooden rafters and
tie-pieces, exactly similar—though smaller and less carefully
executed—to the finer examples of the same artifice to be seen in
the temple at Tiruvádúr (see p. 290). On the east façade of the
main gópuram is another instance of the same unusual work, while
lying about in the temple courtyard are stones which evidently
once formed part of other eaves of this kind and are stated to
have fallen from the deserted shrine in the south-west corner of
this enclosure.

Tavasimadai: Eight miles south-east of Dindigul, close under the Sirumalais; population 1,003. Once the capital of one of the 26 pálaiyams of Dindigul, the history of which has been sketched on pp. 70 and 183 above. It was a very small property and in 1795 was reported to be assessed at a merely nominal peshkash. In 1816 its whole population numbered only 312 souls. Its present inhabitants, like those of several adjoining villages, are largely Roman Catholics. Several burial-grounds of this sect are prominently placed on the wide margins of the road from Kanivaipatti to Dindigul.

CHAP. XV.
DINDIGUL.

The poligar is a Tóttiyan and his family traditions [1] tell the same story of the advent of his forebears to this district as is recounted by other poligars of that caste and has already (p. 106) been referred to.

Tavasimadai means 'pool of penance,' and the legend goes that the ancestor of the family was doing penance by a pool when his family god 'Chotala' appeared and told him to found this village and take his (the god's) name. All the poligars were thereafter called Chotala, and the village so prospered that one of its later owners was raised to the charge of one of the 72 bastions of Madura. The existing representative of the line draws a small pension from Government.

Védasandúr: A union of 7,301 inhabitants, lying twelve miles north of Dindigul. Station of a deputy tahsildar and a sub-registrar. Popular legends say that this part of the country was once inhabited by Védans, a lawless set of people resembling the Kallans, and that the name of the village is a corruption of Véda-sandaiyúr, the prefix being given it to distinguish it from several other places called Sandaiyúr. This last word means 'market village' and Védasandúr still has the second largest weekly fair in the district. In days gone by it was probably even more busy than now, as it lay at the point of junction of the main roads to Palni and was one of the chief halting-places for pilgrims to the shrine there. Messrs. Turnbull and Keys give a graphic description of the crowds which even then assembled in the village, the warmth of the welcome accorded them by the inhabitants (who hoped to derive indirect religious merit thereby) and the pomp and circumstance with which the rich annual gifts to the Palni god sent in those days by the Rájas of Tanjore and Pudukkóttai were escorted through the town in grand processions accompanied by music and dancing-girls.

[1] Mackenzie MSS., ii, 159–66 and Turnbull and Keys' *Survey Account* MS.

CHAP. XV.   The place contains the ruins of an old fort which in 1815 had
DINDIGUL. ' a high cavalier in the centre, commanding a fine prospect of the
surrounding country,' and inside which is now grown some of the
best tobacco in the district; and, just north-west of this, a darga
said to be erected over the remains of Hazarat Saiyad Arab Abdur
Rahim Auliah, concerning whom many fabulous stories are told
but whose fame seems to be on the decline.

KODAIKANAL TALUK.

THE taluk of Kodaikanal, constituted (see. p. 206) in 1889, con- sists of the Upper and Lower Palnis, of which some description has already been given on pp. 3–6 above. The only place in it deserving of separate mention is—

Kodaikanal: This sanitarium stands on the southern crest of the Upper Palni plateau, immediately above Periyakulam town. It averages about 7,000 feet above the sea, the G.T.S. at the Roman Catholic church (one of the highest buildings in it) being 7,209 feet above the sea, and that at Tredis, the Rája of Pudukkóttai's house (one of the least elevated of its residences), being 6,882 feet. The travellers' bungalow at Periyakulam, five miles from the foot of the hills, is 932 feet above mean sea level.

The European houses in Kodaikanal are mostly built round the sides of an irregular basin, roughly a mile and a half long by a mile wide, which is situated on the very edge of the precipitous southern side of the Palnis. From the top of the southern rim of this the plains are seen almost immediately below. Its northern side is high and steep ; on the west it is also bounded by a ridge of considerable elevation ; but on the east the land falls rapidly away to the Lower Palnis, and discloses fine views of that range and of the steep, square-topped peak of Perumál hill (7,326 feet), rising head and shoulders above all his fellows. On the inner slope of the southern rim of the basin is a beautiful hanging wood which is called the *Kodai-kánal,* or 'forest of creepers,' and gives its name to the place. The bottom of the basin was originally a swamp with a small stream wandering through it. In 1863—at the suggestion, and largely at the expense, of Mr. (afterwards Sir Vere) Levinge, then Collector of Madura—this was formed into a lake by banking up the stream. Down into this picturesque sheet of water, from the sides of the basin, run several beautiful wooded spurs on which stand some of the best houses in the place. They cause the lake to assume a shape something like that of a star-fish ; and thus, though nowhere much above half a mile across in a straight line, it is about three miles round, measured along the level road on its margin which follows its many indentations.

Above this ' Lake Road,' round the greater part of the sides of the basin, are two other principal lines of communication—one about half way up the slopes and called the ' Middle Lake Road ' and another still higher up them and known as the 'Upper Lake Road.' These three are connected by many cross roads. There are five chief routes out of the station. To the south-west a new road goes to the 'Pillar Rocks' referred to later; to the west, a track runs past the Observatory to the hill village of Púmbárai, twelve miles away; to the north a footpath leads through the 'Tinnevelly settlement' to Vilpatti, a village perched among impossible precipices not far from a fine waterfall; to the east 'Law's ghát' (begun in 1875 by Major G. V. Law, and already referred to on p. 155 above) winds down to 'Neutral Saddle' at the foot of Perumál hill, the natural boundary between the Upper and Lower Palnis; and to the south is the only practicable route from Kodaikanal to the plains, a steep bridle-path twelve miles long which passes by the small hamlet of Shembaganúr directly below the station and then zigzags down precipitous slopes to the travellers' bungalow at 'Kistnama Náyak's tope' at the foot of the hills.

At Shembaganúr (properly Champakanúr, or 'magnolia village') is a Jesuit theological college, a prominent object from the bridle-path. It is built on land which was acquired by the Jesuit Mission at various dates from 1878 onwards with the idea of forming a great agricultural and industrial school on these hills. Cinchona planting and other agricultural enterprises were tried and failed, and eventually the idea was abandoned. In 1886 a bungalow was built on part of the land; and in 1895 the erection of this college was sanctioned by the mission authorities. It now contains 50 students (20 of whom are French) who undergo a varied course of tuition, lasting seven years, to fit them for work in the various Jesuit missions in India and Ceylon. Kistnama Náyak's-tope (usually called 'the Tope' for short) is said to have been planted by, and named after, a relation of one of the ministers of the Náyakkan kings of Madura who fled to Periyakulam after the downfall of that dynasty. His descendants were village munsifs of Vadakarai continuously up to as late as 1870.

A cart-road goes from the Tope to Periyakulam (five miles) and thence to the nearest railway-station, Ammayanáyakkanúr, 28 miles further east. Visitors to Kodaikanal perform the 33 miles from the station to the Tope in bullock-transits, and thence walk, ride, or are carried in chairs, up the bridle-path. All luggage, supplies and necessaries have to be transported up this latter by coolies, and great are the delays and inconveniences. The proposed Vaigai valley railway from Dindigul to the head of the Kambam valley, and the Áttúr ghát road (both referred to in

Chapter VII above) will, it is hoped, remove in part what is at present the greatest drawback to the sanitarium—its difficulty of access.

CHAP. XV.
KODAIKANAL.

In point of climate, Kodaikanal is considered by many of its admirers to rival Ootacamund. The rainfall, according to the figures of fifteen years,* is greater than that of Ootacamund, but most of it is received during the north-east monsoon when the visitors are absent, instead of with the south-west current of June, July and August, as at Ootacamund. The mean humidity and the mean daily range of temperature are smaller at Kodaikanal than in its rival, and the cold in the wet months

	*Rainfall in inches.	o . of wet days.
January ...	1·12	1
February ...	1·49	2
March	3·75	3
April	5·34	7
May	6·33	9
June	4·16	9
July	3·78	9
August	5·98	12
September ...	6·64	12
October	12·60	16
November ...	8·33	11
December ...	5·67	8
Total ...	65·19	99

is less bleak and searching. The soil is also so gravelly that roads and tennis courts quickly dry again after a shower. The place moreover possesses the advantages that its native bazaar (and its cemetery) are not situated within the basin of the lake and in sight of the residents, and that it commands a view over the plains which is comforting to those who agree with Lucretius that it is sweet to watch, from a safe spot, one's neighbour in distress. Kodaikanal, however, is shut off from the beautiful wild land to the westward by two successive high ridges beyond which few of its inhabitants ever penetrate.

In this wild country, and also nearer Kodaikanal, are very many prehistoric kistvaens and dolmens. The first mention of those on the western, or Travancore, side occurs in the survey memoir of Lieutenant Ward referred to below, and an account of some of the others will be found in the able illustrated article entitled 'Dolmens et cromlechs dans les Palnis,' [1] by the Rev. H. Hosten, S.J., of Kurseong (Bengal) who visited Shembaganúr in 1902, and has very kindly furnished notes of his discoveries. The examples he examined lay chiefly to the south-west of Perumál hill (especially along General Fischer's old trace towards Vilpatti) and at Palamalai. Others are independently

[1] Ch. Bulens, Bruxelles, Rue Terre-Neuve 75, 1905. See also J.A.S.B., 1888, 46-71.

reported to exist at Machúr, Pannaikádu, Tándikkudi, Kámanúr and Páchalúr in the Lower Palnis. Doubtless there are many more.

These monuments present peculiarities not noticed elsewhere. Erected by preference on a level outcrop of rock, each group of dolmens (box-shaped constructions open at one side and made of roughly-dressed slabs of stone) is usually enclosed by rectangular (more rarely, circular) walls made of similar slabs set upright in the ground; the dolmens themselves are larger than usual, an average specimen being found to measure 8 feet by 3 feet and its cap-stone 11 feet by 6 feet; they are sometimes arranged in double parallel rows; to prevent the heavy 'cap-stone from crushing its supports, the space between the several dolmens in each group, and between them and the enclosing walls, is filled in to a height of some three feet with rubble and earth; embedded in this rubble occur stone receptacles, without tops, made of four upright slabs arranged in the form of a square, with a fifth for flooring, and measuring some 3 feet each way and 5 feet in height; and some of the groups are surrounded, outside the enclosing wall of slabs, by small heaps of stone (about $2\frac{1}{2}$ feet square and 1 foot high) placed at regular intervals in the form of a square. Searches within these remains resulted in the discovery of little beyond small fragments of red and black pottery of five or six different patterns (already observed elsewhere and figured in Mr. Bruce Foote's catalogue of the prehistorics at the Madras Museum) and a rust-eaten sickle identical in shape with those found in some of the Nilgiri cairns. No bones were found, nor any cup-marks, swastika designs, inscriptions or sculptures of any kind.

Besides these dolmens, kistvaens (constructions walled in on all four sides and floored and roofed with slabs) occur; at Palamalai was found, buried in the ground and unconnected with any other remains, a large pyriform urn containing two small shallow vases; and in several places are low circles of earth and stones, which may perhaps have been threshing-floors or cattle-kraals.

Round about Kodaikanal are several popular 'sights.' Many rapturous descriptions of all of them are on record and it is unnecessary to add to the list. They include at least three waterfalls within easy reach; namely, the ' Silver Cascade' on Law's ghát, formed by the Parappár stream (into which runs the rivulet issuing from the lake); the ' Glen Falls' on a branch of the Parappár, alongside the path running northwards to Vilpatti; and the ' Fairy Falls' on the Pámbár (' snake river') to the south-west of the station. ' Coaker's Walk' (named after a Lieutenant in the Royal Engineers who was on duty in the district from 1870 to

1872 and made the 1870 map of Kodaikanal) runs along the very brink of the steep southern side of the basin and commands wonderful views of the plains below. On clear days, it is said, even Madura, 47 miles away as the crow flies, can be made out from here. The 'Pillar Rocks' are three huge masses of granite, perhaps 400 feet high, which stand on the edge of the same side of the plateau three miles further on. Between and below them are several caves and chasms, and from the top of them is obtained a superb view of the Aggamalai, the precipitous sides of the Kambam valley and the plains below. Here (and from Coaker's Walk) the 'spectre of the Brocken' is occasionally seen on the mists which drive up from below. 'Doctor's Delight,' a bold bluff about two miles further on, commands a panorama which is claimed to be even finer than that from the Pillar Rocks. 'Fort Hamilton,' $9\frac{1}{2}$ miles from Kodaikanal and on this same southern side of the plateau, is so named after the Major Douglas Hamilton of the 21st N.I. who was obligingly permitted by Sir Charles Trevelyan's Government to spend part of 1859 and (after an interval of service in China) twelve months in 1861–62, all on full pay, in making the series of large sketches of the Palni Hills which are still to be seen in public and official libraries, and in writing the two short reports on the range which were printed in Madras in 1862 and 1864, respectively. There is no 'fort' at the place; only a small hut. Its chief interest lies in the evidences which are visible near by, and were first brought to notice by Major Hamilton, of the former existence there of a great lake. No record or even tradition regarding the formation of this survives. Judging from the traces of its water-line which still remain, it must have been nearly five miles long, from a quarter to three-quarters of a mile wide and from 30 to 70 feet deep. It was apparently formed by the side of a hill slipping down into a valley which runs northwards to the Amarávati river, and damming up the stream which ran at the bottom of it. This stream seems to have eventually cut its way through the huge natural embankment so formed, and thus emptied the lake it had itself once filled. The dam is about 200 yards long and the breach in it is now about 100 yards across and 90 feet deep. Major Hamilton (see the later of his two reports above mentioned) wrote with much enthusiasm of the possibilities of this spot as a site for a sanitarium or cantonment, but it would be most difficult of approach. This latter objection, it may here be noted in parenthesis, is also the answer to the many critics who have railed at the founders of Kodaikanal for having placed it where it stands instead of in one or other of the many (otherwise) superior sites which doubtless exist on the Upper Palni plateau. When the place was originated, the most practicable path up the hills was the existing bridle-road from Periyakulam, and the first arrivals naturally wished to settle as close as might be to the top of this.

The first European who visited the plateau and left any record of his journey was Lieutenant B. S. Ward, who surveyed the Palnis in 1821. His diary shows that he came up from Periyakulam by way of Vellagavi (a small hamlet on the slopes which is said to have been fortified as a haven of refuge by the former poligars of Vadakarai), camped on the 25th May just above the falls of the Pámbár which face the present bridle-path, and went through the Kodaikanal basin. He makes no special mention of this last. An extract from his memoir on the Palni and Travan-core Hills ('the Vurragherry and Kunnundaven Mountains,' as he called them), which has never otherwise been printed, was published by Robert Wight, the well-known botanist, in the M.J.L.S. of October 1837 (Vol. VI).

In 1834 Messrs. J. C. Wroughton (then Sub-Collector) and C. R. Cotton (Judge of the Provincial Court, Southern Division) went up from Periyakulam to Shembaganúr (their visit led to some slight repairs being done to the bridle-path), but Wight himself was the next European visitor to the range who has left any record of his journey. His account appears in Vol. V (pp. 280–7) of the M.J.L.S. He went up in September 1836, apparently by the steep ghát from Dévadánapatti to the Adukkam pass near the peak of that name. He mentions Shembaganúr but not the Kodaikanal basin. His report on the botany of the range has already been referred to on p. 15.

The first people to build houses at Kodaikanal were the American missionaries of Madura. In 1858 so many of them had been compelled to take sick leave and go to Jaffna (their then centre) that the mission actually proposed to purchase a special vessel to carry the invalids and the convalescents backwards and forwards. This idea was eventually abandoned in favour of the suggestion that a sanitarium should be established on the Sirumalais, that range being chosen on account of its propinquity to Madura. Two bungalows were built there, but their occupants suffered so much from fever that in January 1845 the Palnis were examined as an alternative site and in June of the same year two bungalows were begun at the foot of the Kodai-kánal, near the spot on which 'Sunnyside' now stands, and were finished in October.

Not long afterwards, Mr. John Blackburne, Collector of CHAP. XV.
Madura between 1834 and 1847 and the man who had done so KODAIKANAL.
much for the improvement of the revenue system on these hills
(see p. 205), built himself a bungalow about five miles away (see the
survey map of 1890) at the top of the Adukkam Pass. This came
to an untimely end, being burnt down by the first fire which was
lighted in it, but its foundations can still be traced. In 1848–49
Mr. Thomas Clarke (then Sub-Collector and the author of an
excellent report on the Palnis, dated May 1853), Mr. C. R. Baynes
(the District Judge) and Mr. R. D. Parker (Blackburne's successor)
all built themselves bungalows on the high ground just south of
the Kodai-kánal, on the strip of cliff overlooking the plains which
runs from ' Pámbár House ' to ' Roseneath.' Plans of the place
in official records show that Parker's house was built where
Pámbár House now stands ; Baynes' was on the site of the
building next east of this which is now owned by the Roman
Catholic Mission ; and Clarke's was the nucleus of Roseneath. In
this latter Bishop Caldwell lived for many years and it was there
that he died. Soon afterwards, Captain W. H. Horsely, the ' Civil
Engineer,' erected a fourth bungalow between Baynes' and Clarke's,
and the American Mission began the house now called ' Claverack.'
About 1852 a Major J. M. Partridge of the Bombay Army came
up and pitched tents at the bottom of the lake basin. Tempestuous
weather soon drove him to erect some better shelter, and he put
up a rough bungalow on the spot now called, in consequence,
' Bombay Shola.' He had one of the earliest gardens in the
station and is credited with being the first to introduce blue-gums
into it. Of two huge gums which formerly stood near his house,
one still survives and is the biggest in the place. He at one time
proposed to import artisans for the benefit of the community, and
the records show that there was at least one ' shop ' near his
residence.

The above individuals were the pioneers ; their seven houses
were the only ones in the place in 1853, and even by 1861 only
three more had been built. By 1854 Rs. 4,500 had been spent
on, or sanctioned for, the bridle-path, but it was apparently still
in wretched order. A mile of road had also been cut through the
Kodai-kánal by the missionaries and six more miles had been made
elsewhere by other residents. Much correspondence took place
regarding the terms on which the Government should grant the land
on which the houses stood. It was finally ordered that the rules for
the Nilgiris should be applied and an annual charge of Rs. 5–4–0 be
made for the first káni (1·32 acres) occupied, and Rs. 2–8–0 for

every additional káni. Eventually, most of the original grants were converted into freeholds. At present, it may here be noted, the rules in Board's Standing Order No. 21 apply to the grant of sites within the settlement and the sanction of Government is necessary to the sale of them.

The first Governor of Madras to visit Kodaikanal—as the place now began to be named in official correspondence—was Sir Charles Trevelyan, who went up early in 1860 by the bridle-path from the Tope. *More suo*, he wrote a delightful 'minute' recording his impressions of the hills. He stayed at Roseneath, which was still Mr. Clarke's property.[1] Lord Napier also went up later on, in 1871, and tradition says that 'Napier Villa' owes its name to the fact that he stopped there.

In 1860 Mr. Vere Henry Levinge was appointed Collector of Madura. He held the post until 1867 and then retired to Kodaikanal, where he lived (at Pámbár House) until within a few weeks of his death at Madras in 1885. During this latter period he succeeded to the family baronetcy. Both as Collector and after his retirement he took the greatest interest in the station and, as the inscription on the cross erected to his memory just above Coaker's Walk relates, most of the improvements in it are due to him. As has already been stated, he made the lake (mainly at his own expense) and he also completed the bridle-path from Periyakulam, cut the path to Bambadi Shola along the southern crest of the plateau, constructed several roads within the station itself and did much to introduce European fruits and flowers.

Neither time nor space permit of the inclusion here of any history of the growth of the sanitarium from that time forth to the present, but the subject is one which may be commended to the notice of those who have greater knowledge and opportunities. A few isolated facts may, however, be noted. In 1853 the American Mission had begun to build a church on their land near 'Sunnyside.' It was finished in 1856 and an arrangement was made by which the members of the Church of England should also have the use of it. Round about it, a cemetery (now closed) was made. The earliest tomb in this, no doubt, is that of two children who died as early as 1849, but their bodies were removed to the cemetery from the grave near Mount Nebo in which they were originally buried. The church was replaced in 1896 by the new building near the Club, and shortly afterwards it fell down.

---

[1] For this and other items of interest, I am indebted to the Rev. J. E. Tracy's recollections of Kodaikanal in former days.

In 1863 Father Saint Cyr (who was the first of the Roman Catholic missionaries to appreciate Kodaikanal, and in 1860 had bought Baynes' bungalow for his mission) laid the foundations of the existing Roman Catholic church. The site for the Church of England place of worship on Mount Nebo was granted to Bishop Caldwell in 1883. In the same year an estimate was sanctioned for the building of the deputy tahsildar's office. In 1900 the new European cemetery near the ghát path from Shembaganúr, the first thing which catches the eye of the visitor as he approaches this health resort, was finished. It is divided into sections for the use of the various denominations.

In October 1899 Kodaikanal, which was originally merely a part of the village of Vilpatti and afterwards had been made into a Union, was constituted a municipality. It is the least populous of all the Madras municipalities, its inhabitants at the 1901 census numbering only 1,912. This enumeration, however, was taken in March, before the influx of the hot weather visitors (a large proportion of whom belong to the various Christian missions in this and other districts) and their numerous following. The council's annual income averages only some Rs. 9,000, and no very striking undertakings have therefore been possible. The fate of the proposal to supply the place with water from the Pámbár has been referred to on p. 227.

Some two miles from the station, on a hill above the road to Púmbárai already mentioned, is the Observatory. Under the scheme for the re-organization of Indian observatories which came into operation in 1899, the chief work of the Madras Observatory was transferred to this place (which was found to be preferable to either Ootacamund or Kóttagiri on account of its more equable temperature and greater freedom from mists) and the former Government Astronomer, Mr. Michie Smith, became Director of the Kodaikanal and Madras Observatories. The appliances of the new institution are now directed to the prosecution of enquiry in the sciences of terrestrial magnetism, meteorology and seismology, to astronomical observations for the purpose of time-keeping, and, chiefly, to the important subject of solar physics.

MADURA TALUK.

THIS taluk was formerly called after the village of Mádakkulam, which is about four miles west of Madura. It lies in the centre of the south-eastern side of the district and is the smallest of all the taluks. It is an almost featureless plain, drained by the Vaigai. The only hills of note are the southernmost extremity of the Nága-malai and the isolated Skandamalai at Tirupparankunram. The soil is mostly of the red ferruginous variety, but there are some black cotton-soil areas in the south along the Tirumangalam border. The most fertile part is that along the banks of the Vaigai.

Madura receives more rain than most of the other taluks and also benefits very largely from the Periyár water. Consequently paddy occupies nearly two-thirds of the total cultivated area, cocoanut groves are numerous, and the taluk is better protected from adverse seasons than any other. This was not so before the advent of the Periyár irrigation, however, and in the 1876–78 famine it suffered severely.

Statistics about the taluk will be found in the separate Appendix. The density of the population is very much higher than the average for the district, but this is largely due to the presence within it of Madura town.

The more noteworthy places in it are the following :—

Ánaimalai ('elephant hill'): A most striking mass of perfectly naked, solid rock, about two miles long, a quarter of a mile wide and perhaps 250 feet high, which runs from north-east to south-west nearly parallel to the Madura-Mélúr road from the fifth mile-stone from Madura. It consists of grey and pale pink banded micaceous granite gneiss of coarse texture and complicated stratigraphy. The sides are almost sheer and the top rounded, and at its south-western end it terminates in a bold bluff; so that—especially from the Madura side — it bears a very fair resemblance to an elephant lying down. Whence its name. The Madura *sthala purána* goes further and says it is in fact a petrified elephant. The Jains of Conjeeveram, says this chronicle, tried to convert the Saivite people of Madura to the Jain faith. Finding the task difficult, they had recourse to magic. They dug a great pit ten miles long, performed a sacrifice therein and thus caused a huge elephant to arise from it. This beast they sent against Madura. It advanced towards the town, shaking the whole earth at every step, with the Jains marching close behind it. But the Pándya king invoked the aid of Siva, and the god arose and slew the elephant with his arrow at the spot where it now lies petrified.

At the foot of this Ánaimalai, about the middle of its northern side and surrounded by a few chattrams and a lotus-covered tank, is a temple to Narasinga Perumál, of which the inner shrine is cut out of the solid rock of the hill. In front of this stands a long mantapam and the pújári declines to allow Europeans even to look into this, much less to see the entrance to the shrine. The latter is said to measure about six feet in every direction and to have in front of it two pillars similarly cut out of the solid rock. Round about the entrance to it, on the rock, are Tamil and Vatteluttu inscriptions, one of which is dated in the thirty-third year of the Chóla king Parántaka I (906–46 A.D., the 'conqueror of Madura,' see p. 31) and is the only record of his as yet discovered in the vicinity of Madura.[1] The long mantapam is a much more recent erection.

A few yards south-west of this temple, hidden away in a peaceful spot among the trees which cluster round the foot of the great bare hill, is another shrine cut out of the solid rock. It is deserted and consists of an inner recess some $3\frac{1}{2}$ feet by $6\frac{1}{2}$ feet in which are figures of Vishnu (bearing a chank shell) and his wife; an outer porch about 20 feet long, $8\frac{1}{2}$ feet high and 9 feet wide supported on two square pillars with chamfered corners and ornamented with the conventional lotus[2]; and, outside this again, a small platform approached on either side by a flight of half a dozen steps. Within the porch are four figures, two of which apparently represent devotees bringing flowers, and other lesser sculptures. The whole thing—the shrine with its two deities, the porch and its pillars and sculptures, and the two flights of steps—are all cut out of the solid rock. It has been called a Jain shrine, but there seems to be nothing Jain about it.

Still further south-west, however, near the top of the prominent little wooded spur which runs down from the hill, are undoubted relics of the Jains in the shape of sculptures of the tirthankaras on a big boulder. The boulder must have crashed down from the rock above, and now rests so poised on one of its corners that its overhanging portions form a sort of natural cave. There are signs that this recess was formerly improved into a dwelling (probably

[1] Government Epigraphist's report for 1904–05, pp. 4, 40, 50.

[2] Compare the rock-cut shrine at Dalavánúr, *South Arcot Gazetteer*, p. 245.

by Jain hermits) by the erection of rude walls, and the spot was chosen with taste, for in front of it is a flat rock platform which commands the most beautiful view across the green fields, past Madura and its temple towers and palace, away to the Sirumalais and the Palnis in the far distance. The Jains had an eye for the picturesque.[1] On two sides of the great boulder above mentioned, and well out of reach of mischievous herd-boys, are the Jain sculptures. On the northern side is represented a single tirthankara, seated; on the southern, a series of eight others, all quite nude, some standing and some seated, some with the sacred triple crown above their heads, and some surrounded also by attendant figures bearing *chámaras* and other objects. One is a female figure, seated. The series occupies a space perhaps ten feet long by two high. Under it are eight inscriptions in Tamil and Vatteluttu which give the names, either of the figures, or of the villages which were commanded to protect them. Round some of them have been painted backgrounds in elaborate design, and the villagers now worship them as representations of ' the seven Kannimár ' (the virgin goddesses so dear to the Tamil lower classes) and call the spot the *Kannimár-kóvil.*

The Ánaimalai may be climbed from the western end. About half way up it, are some of the sleeping-places cut out of the rock which are usually called *Puncha Pándava padukkai,* or ' beds of the five Pándavas ' (see p. 75); and, further on, a pool which always contains water and is called *Ánaikannu* or ' the elephant's eye,' a big cave in which a tiger is averred to have lived for a long while, and a small teppakulam.

Anuppánadi: Two miles south-east of Madura; population 3,776. Buried in a piece of waste ground to the east of the village are a number of pyriform earthenware tombs, consisting of jars with detachable lids. They appear above the ground singly and in groups and vary considerably in size. One dug up by **Mr. Rea** (whose detailed report upon them is printed in G.O., No. 1663, Public, dated 16th December 1887) measured 1 foot $2\frac{1}{2}$ inches in diameter by 1 foot 7 inches deep, while others were as much as 3 feet 6 inches in diameter. Some of them are made of a coarse, red earthenware and others of thin, glazed, black and red ware. In them were found human bones and numbers of smaller vessels. The latter are often glazed, and the glaze is peculiar, being neither hard nor brittle, and rather resembling a polish than a true glaze.

---

[1] Compare their hermitages at Ádóni and Rayadrug, *Bellary Gazetteer,* pp. 198, 301.

Similar tombs exist in some numbers near Kulasékharankóttai CHAP. XV.
in Nilakkóttai taluk and at Paravai, five miles north-west of Madura MADURA.
near the Vaigai. In some of those at the latter place which were
opened by Mr. Rea a quantity of peculiar beads were found.
Some of these were of a reddish, semi-transparent material, marked
with milky streaks; others were greenish in hue; others of white
crystal; and most of them bore designs in white inlay, lines
having been chased on them and filled in with white enamel.

Kodimangalam : Eight miles north-west of Madura, between
the Nágamalai and the Vaigai; population 1,581. The Siva
temple here contains several inscriptions, but when it was restored
some years back the stones on which they were cut were misplaced,
and they are not easy to decipher. On the slope of the Nágamalai
opposite this village is a sacred stream flowing out of a cow's
mouth cut in stone into a small masonry reservoir. Round about
are a mantapam or two and some carved slabs. The spot is
picturesque and is faced by a fine tope, and on Ádi Amávásya day
(the new moon day in July-August) many people gather there.

The part of the Nágamalai near the adjoining village of
Mélakkál contains several remarkable caves. The best of them
(known as the *Vîra pudavu*) is on the west side of a point in the
range which rises above the general level. Entering the mouth of
this, one descends about 50 feet with the aid of a rope and comes
upon two openings. The eastern of these does not go far, but that
on the west runs for perhaps a quarter of a mile into the hill.
Lights are required and some crawling has to be done. At the
very end is found on the rock a pale watery paste which hardens
quickly on exposure to the outer air. Native druggists declare
that it has wonderful curative properties.

About three-quarters of a mile further along the range to the
north-west is the smaller *puli pudavu*, or ' tiger cave,' and a quarter
of a mile further on again is the ' hyæna cave.'

Madura, the capital of the taluk and district, is the largest
mufassal town in the Presidency, its inhabitants numbering
105,984 in 1901. They then included 3,750 Christians (291 of
whom were Europeans, Americans or Eurasians) and as many as
9,122 Muhammadans, but practically all the rest were Hindus and a
large proportion of these last were Bráhmans. The population
has more than doubled in the last 30 years, for it numbered only
51,987 at the census of 1871, rose to 73,807 in 1881 and to
87,248 in 1891.

Being the chief place in the district, Madura is the head-
quarters of all the usual officers. It stands on the main line

of the South Indian Railway 345 miles from Madras, and from it runs the branch line to Mandapam which is being extended to the island of Rámésvaram and may one day pass across to Ceylon. It possesses a travellers' bungalow, rooms for Europeans at the railway-station, and many chattrams for natives. The chief of these last is that opposite the station which was founded and endowed from funds left by Queen Mangammál and is still called by her name. It has already been referred to on p. 157.

The history of the town is bound up with that of the district, and has already been sketched in Chapter II. The Christian missions in it are referred to in Chapter III; its arts, industries and trade in Chapter VI (some account of the Patnúlkárans who do so much of the weaving is given in Chapter III); its medical and educational institutions (including the ancient Sangams) are mentioned in Chapters IX and X respectively; the jail in Chapter XIII; and the municipal council and the waterworks in Chapter XIV. It is enough to add here that the town is the industrial, educational and religious centre of the district.

Madura stands on the right bank of the Vaigai. In the neighbourhood rise three small but prominent hills, which are called the Ánaimalai, Pasumalai and Nágamalai from their supposed resemblance to an elephant, a cow and a snake respectively, and which are severally referred to on pp. 254, 278 and 7. It lies low and the ground rises away from it on all sides but the south. The G.T.S. on the south *gópuram* of the great Mínákshi temple referred to later is 484 feet above the sea, but this tower is itself some 150 feet above the ground, and the town is thus only about 330 feet above sea-level. It is further hedged about with many plantations of cocoanut palms and other trees and is thus a hot and relaxing place. Statistics of its temperature have already been given on p. 13 above.

It consists (see the map attached) of three main parts—the crowded native town built on and around the site of its old fort referred to below, a series of European bungalows in large compounds (and many smaller houses) lining both sides of the road which runs south-eastwards to the beautiful Vandiyúr Teppakulam and thence to Ramnad, and the new quarter which has recently been established for the residences of officials on the old race-course on the other (north) side of the river. This last is connected with the other two by a bridge over the Vaigai which was completed in 1889 and has been referred to above on p. 156. The view up the river from this is one of the most charming in the district. It is framed on either side by the tall towers of the

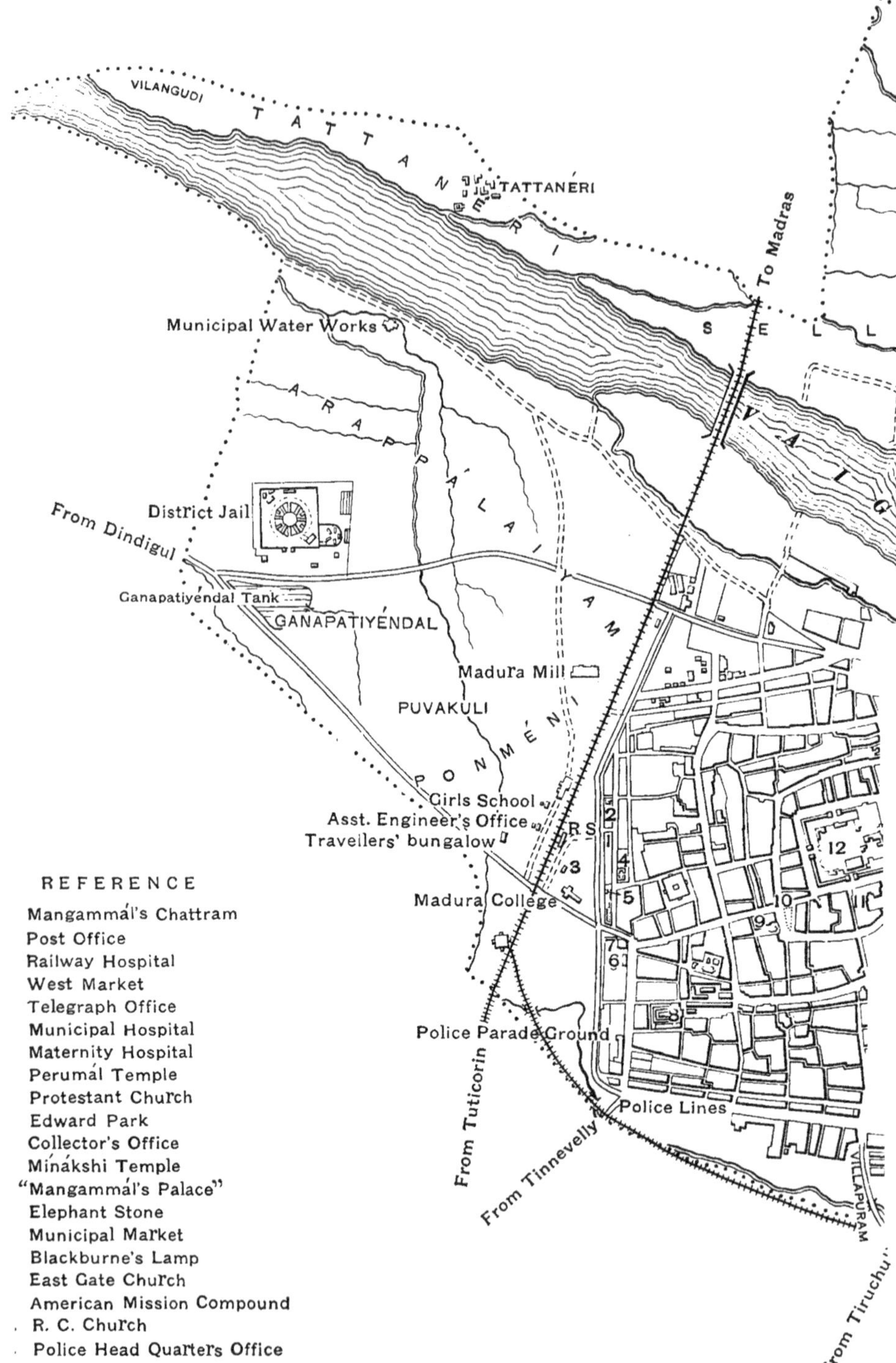

REFERENCE

Mangammál's Chattram
Post Office
Railway Hospital
West Market
Telegraph Office
Municipal Hospital
Maternity Hospital
Perumál Temple
Protestant Church
Edward Park
Collector's Office
Mínákshi Temple
"Mangammál's Palace"
Elephant Stone
Municipal Market
Blackburne's Lamp
East Gate Church
American Mission Compound
R. C. Church
Police Head Quarters Office

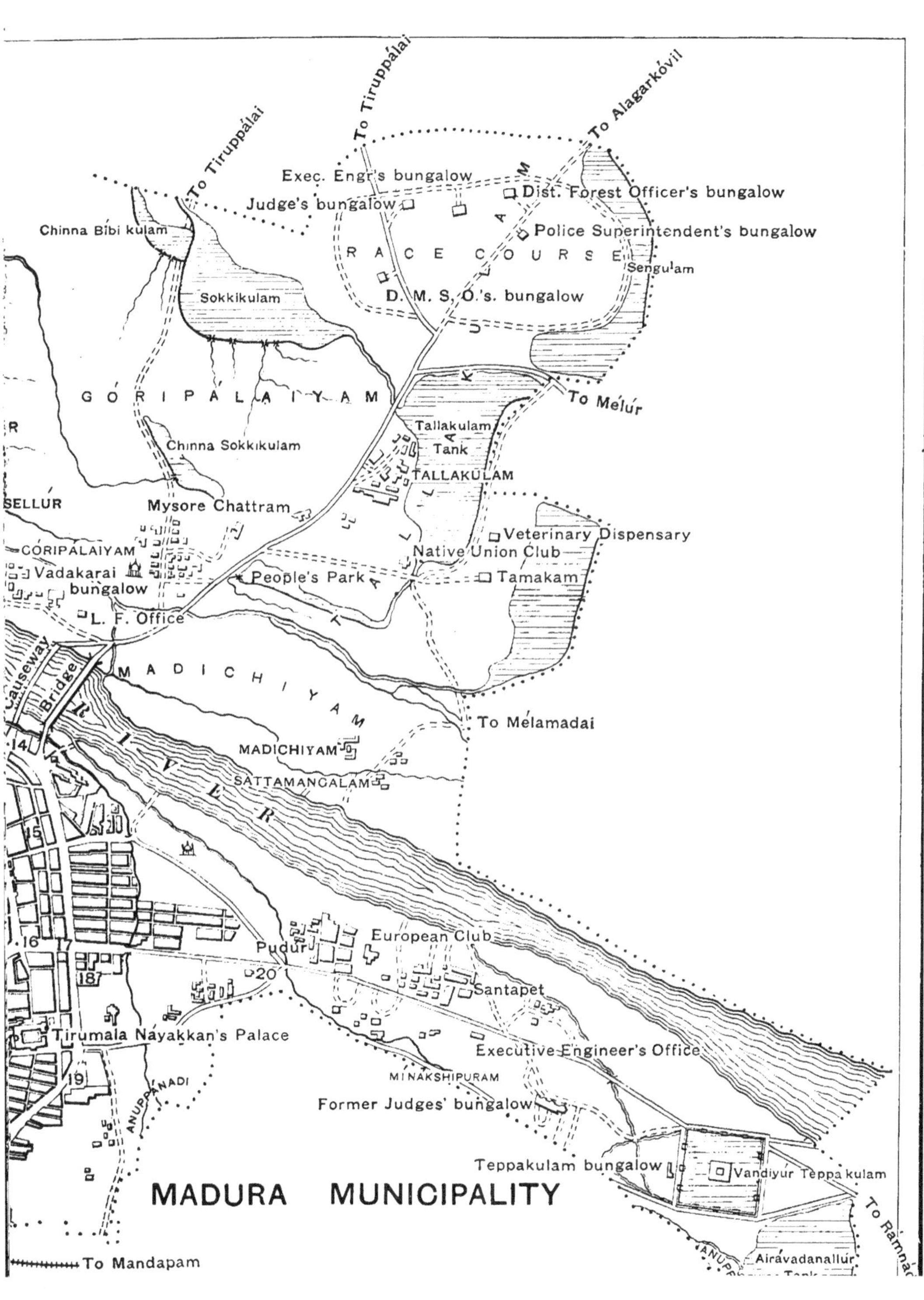

MADURA MUNICIPALITY

great temple and the palms leaning forward over the stream; in the foreground stand the little stone Máya mantapam to which the image of Siva is taken at the great Chittrai feast mentioned later, and a crowd of gaily-dressed people bathing or washing freshly-dyed cloths; further off carts pass slowly across the old causeway and a temple elephant placidly takes his morning bath; while in the ultimate background rises the dim blue sky-line of the Palni hills.

Of the old bungalows along the Ramnad road little that is reliable has been gathered. The history of the European Club (which possesses a racquet-court and swimming-bath) is referred to on p. 172. The house in the compound of which stands the famous banyan tree (shading an area 60 yards in diameter and possessing a main stem 70 feet in circumference) belongs to a branch of the family of the Rája of Ramnad and was for very many years the residence of the Collector of the district and, afterwards, of a series of its Judges. The bungalow facing the Teppakulam was similarly occupied by a series of Collectors and Judges. It now belongs to the Rája of Ramnad, who bought it from the Lessees of Sivaganga. They in their turn obtained it from the family of Mr. Robert Fischer of Madura, to whom it was given by Ráni Káttama Náchiyár of Sivaganga in recognition of services performed in the famous civil suit about the possession of that zamindari which was fought as far as the Privy Council. Who originally built it is not clear. Its swimming-bath is shown by a tablet therein to have been constructed in 1814 by Rous Peter, Collector of the district from 1812 to 1828, and official records show that he built at least a part of the house. The newer south wing was added by Mr. G. F. Fischer, father of Mr. Robert Fischer.

Rous Peter is the best remembered of all the old Collectors of Madura, and vernacular ballads are still sung in his honour. He lived in princely style, was of a most bountiful disposition (both the Mínákshi temple and the Alagarkóvil possess valuable jewels which he gave them) and did great things in ridding the hills round Kannivádi, Periyakulam and Bódináyakkanúr (compare p. 315) of the elephants which in those days infested them and the country below them. The people nicknamed him 'Peter Pándya.' He died in Madura on 6th August 1828 and was buried in the heart of the town outside the then Protestant church. This had been put up the year before [1] (largely at his expense) to replace a small building which had been erected

___
[1] *The Church in Madras*, by Rev. F. Penny (Smith, Elder, 1904), 657 ff.

by public subscription about 1800—'a very plain structure,' according to Ward's Survey Account. In 1874 it was pulled down and the present St. George's Church (consecrated in 1881) was constructed on the site—from designs by Mr. Chisholm the well-known Government Architect—by Mr. Robert Fischer and his sister Mrs. Foulkes in memory of their father Mr. George Frederick Fischer who died in 1867 and is buried beside Rous Peter. The new church was so built as to enclose the two graves, and these now lie behind the altar. The European cemetery proper is near the railway-station and contains tombstones to many soldiers and civilians of the early days of the Company's rule.

The wildest stories about Rous Peter's end are current in Madura and it has been stated in print that he was charged with defalcations and, when a Commissioner came down to make enquiries, committed suicide. Official records [1] tell a different tale. It appears that he kept his own money and Government's mixed together in a manner which Account Codes have now rendered impossible, and sent to his treasury whenever he wanted any cash. In 1819, nine years before his death, he realised that he had drawn more in this way than he was entitled to, and made out a memorandum, the envelope of which was marked 'not to be opened till my death,' admitting this fact and his carelessness, protesting before God his freedom from any dishonest intent, promising to take steps to mend matters, and making over to Government on his demise such part of his property as might be sufficient to make up any deficit which should then appear. His method of endeavouring to replace the missing money was to give his cash-keeper large sums out of the treasury with instructions to trade with it and apply the profits towards meeting the deficiency!

He was ill for a week before his death and his Assistant Collector was apparently with him when he died. The next day the Judge, in taking over his papers officially, came upon the memorandum mentioned above, and the enquiries which resulted disclosed a deficit in the treasury of Rs. 7,79,000. How much of this Rous Peter had himself spent, could never be ascertained; but much of it was shown to have been embezzled by the treasury officials, who had taken every advantage of their Collector's casual ways. Five of these individuals were sentenced to imprisonment—some of them to five years in irons. Rous Peter's estate was confiscated. It was worth between seventy thousand and a lakh of rupees, and included jewels valued at Rs. 10,000,

[1] E.M.C. of August and September 1828 and subsequent papers.

plate to about the same amount, 'innumerable' pictures, and
many guns and rifles.

On the other side of the Vaigai, the first European houses reached are 'Fletcher's bungalow' and the 'Vadakarai ('north bank') bungalow,' both standing close to the head of the bridge. The former was built by the Court of Wards from the funds of the Sivaganga estate for the gentleman whose name it still bears, who was tutor to the then minor zamindar — the last of the 'usurper' zamindars who were ousted by the decision in the great suit already mentioned. It is at present the District Board's office. The latter is known to the natives as 'Cherry's bungalow' and occupies the site of a smaller house put up by the officer of that name who was 'Register of the Zillah' in 1809 and subsequent years and acted once as Judge in 1810. It passed afterwards to the Sivaganga estate, and the high wall which encloses it was built by the zamindar mentioned above when he resided there with the ladies of his family.

Further north, on higher, gravelly ground, are the new bungalows which have been erected for the Judge, Executive Engineer, District Medical and Sanitary Officer, Forest Officer and Superintendent of Police. The idea of moving the residences of these officers from their former unsatisfactory positions on the other side of the river originated with Colonel Kilgour, Superintendent of Police, in 1895 and in the same year Government— one of the Members of which was then Sir Henry Bliss, a former Collector of the district—approved the proposal. Sufficient land was acquired round about the site to prevent any future incursion of native huts, and the five houses were finished by 1902.

It was at first proposed that a residence should also be built in the vicinity for the Collector, in place of the inconvenient (if interesting) native building called the Tamakam in which he now lives. But eventually it was decided[1] to add to that building instead of abandoning it, to construct to the south of it new quarters for the Collector's office and its various branches and for the tahsildar, in place of the badly arranged native buildings in the town now occupied by them, and to erect a new block near the race course for the district and other civil courts which are at present held in the town in Tirumala Náyakkan's palace referred to below. Madura has thus an unrivalled opportunity of laying out a new official quarter, and it only remains to ensure

---

[1] G.Os., Nos. 102, Educational, dated 11th February 1904, and 456, Public, dated 24th June 1905.

that this is not invaded by the usual bazaars and huts. Work on the Tamakam has already been begun.

Tamakamu (or Tamagamu) is a Telugu word, and means [1] a summer-house, or building having a roof supported on pillars but no walls. The oldest part of the Tamakam, the present drawing-room, is just such a building. It is constructed on the top of a square mound of earth (about fifteen feet high and faced outside with stone) and its roof is a masonry dome $21\frac{1}{2}$ feet across supported on the crowns of crenulated arches sprung on to square pillars, and surrounded by three other rows of pillars with similar arching arranged in the form of a square and supporting separate small truncated roofs. Its existing walls are clearly a later addition. The ceiling of the dome is of painted chunam, is exactly similar in design to several of those in Tirumala Náyakkan's palace, and represents an inverted lotus blossom. Who originally constructed this room is not known. Tradition assigns it impartially to both Tirumala Náyakkan and Queen Mangammál, but since these two personages are popularly credited with almost every other undertaking in and about Madura, this goes for little. Rumour also says that it was built as a kind of grand stand from which gladiatorial exhibitions and the like might be witnessed.

It is not until the beginning of the last century that official records throw any light on the history of the Tamakam. In a letter to the Court of Directors, dated London, 2nd June 1826, Sir Alexander Johnston (late Chief Justice of Ceylon, etc.—see *Dictionary of National Biography*) stated that in 1782 his father, Mr. Samuel Johnston, Paymaster at Madura, finding his house in Madura fort very unhealthy, asked the Nawáb of Arcot, then sovereign of the country, to let him have the Tamakam as a residence. The building is referred to in the records as ' an old choultry ' and as ' the choultry called Fort Defiance,' the latter name being apparently due to the fact [2] that it had been an outpost in the siege of Madura in 1764 referred to on p. 66. Sir Alexander said that when this application was made, the place ' had been deserted upwards of a century and was . . . in so desolate and so ruinous a state as to be of no value whatever ' and that the Nawáb accordingly made his father a present of it. Mr. Johnston spent five or six thousand pagodas in clearing the jungle round the building and turning it into a habitation, and lived there with his family till his transfer to Trichinopoly in

---

[1] C. P. Brown's Telugu-English Dictionary, citing the *Dípika*, a Telugu dictionary of 1816.

[2] Vibart's *Hist. of Madras Engineers* (W. H. Allen, 1881), 84.

1787. While he was there the heart of the great Montrose, which was in his keeping, was stolen by Maravan burglars for the sake of the silver casket in which it was enshrined.[1] In a subsequent letter to the Directors, Sir Alexander added that it had been the intention of his parents and of his ' early instructor Colonel Mackenzie (the well-known collector of the ' Mackenzie MSS.'), under whose scientific advice it was laid out,' to turn the building into a place where natives might be instructed in European arts, sciences and literature, and that among the Mackenzie MSS. were two drawings of it, ' the one made by the Colonel before, and the other after, he had repaired and laid out the house for Mr. Johnston.' These drawings would have thrown much light on the interesting question of the extent to which the Tamakam is indebted to Native and European architects respectively, but they are not to be found among the Mackenzie MSS. either in Madras or at the India Office.

When Mr. Johnston was transferred he allowed his friend and successor Mr. Vaughan to occupy the building, which was then commonly known as ' Johnston House.' In 1791 he went to England, where he soon afterwards died without making any disposition of the property.

In 1802 Mr. Hurdis, then Collector, obtained from the Company a grant of the building and the land on which it stood. His application describes the former as ' an old choultry on the top of which Mr. Hurdis is building three sleeping rooms. The body of the choultry in good repair, but the upper part one entire ruin.' In 1806 he sold the property to Government for 2,650 pagodas.

In 1826 in the letter already cited, and again in 1834, Sir Alexander Johnston claimed that the place was his mother's property and not Government's (since Mr. Hurdis had no title) and stated that he wished to recover it to carry out the educational scheme above indicated. The correspondence which ensued [2] shows that the building had been used since its purchase by Government ' as a Court House either for the Judge or Register ' and that two bungalows for the Sadr Amins and a small jail (which was afterwards used as a hen-house and the site of which is now occupied by the Union Club) had been built near it. In 1838 the courts were moved to Tirumala Náyakkan's palace and in

---

[1] For unimpeachable evidence of this curious fact, see Mr. J. D. Rees' *Tours in India*, 1886–90 (Madras Government Press, 1891), p. 63.

[2] Letter to the Secretary at the India House, No. 250, dated 9th February 1838.

1857 the sub-judges were reported to have lived rent-free in the house for many years. One of them, Mr. Phillips, had 'added a room' to it. In 1859 they were required to pay a rent of Rs. 42. In 1864 the District Judge was there.

The Directors' reply (dated 31st August 1839) to Sir Alexander's claim to the house was that, without admitting his title as a matter of right, they were prepared to make it over to him 'for the purpose of its being converted into a place for native education.' No action was however taken on this until 1871, when Sir Alexander's son, Mr. P. F. Campbell-Johnston, suggested that the rent of the building might be applied to endowing a scholarship. Government agreed, and a deed of conveyance and trust was drawn up founding the existing 'Johnston of Carnsalloch scholarships.' These at first consisted of the rent received for the building less the amount expended in keeping it in repair, but the present arrangement is that as far as possible the annual payment to the University of Madras of Rs. 480 for the maintenance of the endowment shall be regarded as a first charge on the rent received.

Thereafter the building was occupied for short periods by different officers and then remained empty for many years. The Government proposed to insist on the Judge living there, and when Lord Napier visited Madura in 1871 he gave personal instructions regarding alterations in it, Mr. Chisholm's estimates for which amounted to Rs. 22,000. But the Judge protested so strongly against being obliged to reside across the Vaigai that nothing was done. In 1877 the place was put in order and occupied for a year by the District Engineer. Mr. C. S. Crole (1882 to 1886) was apparently the first Collector to reside in it and since then his successors have always lived there. As has been stated, it is most inconveniently arranged and until the bridge over the Vaigai was built its situation was equally unfortunate, as when there were floods in the river the Collector's letters and papers had to be sent to him on one of the temple elephants.

Immediately west of the Tamakam is the People's Park, a piece of fenced and planted ground about 70 acres in extent. It was formed in 1883 through the efforts of Mr. Crole with subscriptions received from the Náttukóttai Chettis and some of the zamindars and wealthy natives of the district, and was handed over to the municipality, in whose name patta for it now stands. It was formally opened by Lord Dufferin when he visited Madura in December 1886. The part of it immediately to the north-east of

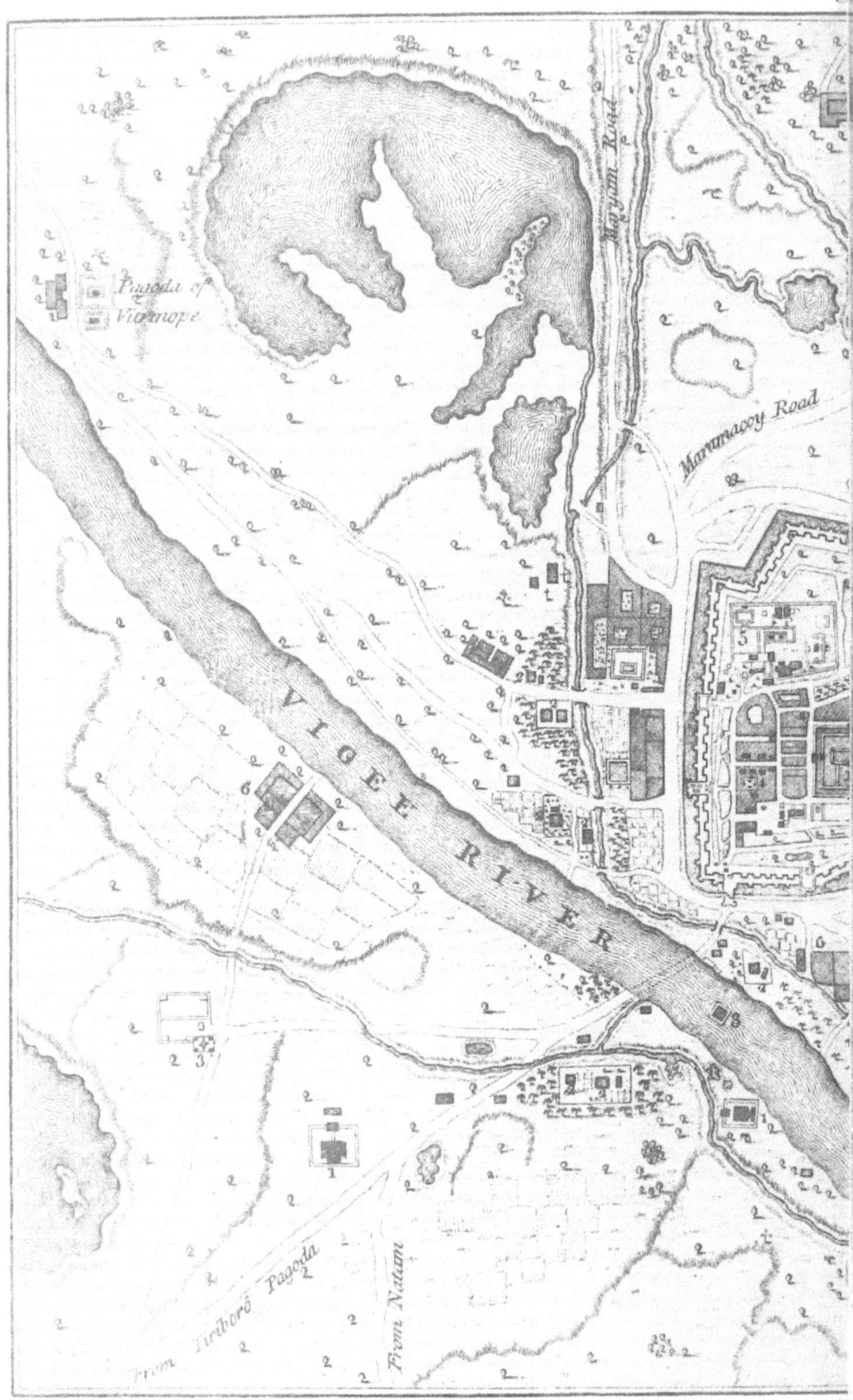

Pagoda of Vitthope
Maranacoy Road
Mayyam Road
VIGEE RIVER
from Tiriboré Pagoda
from Nuttam
East
S O. REG No. 8868
1906 COPIES 500

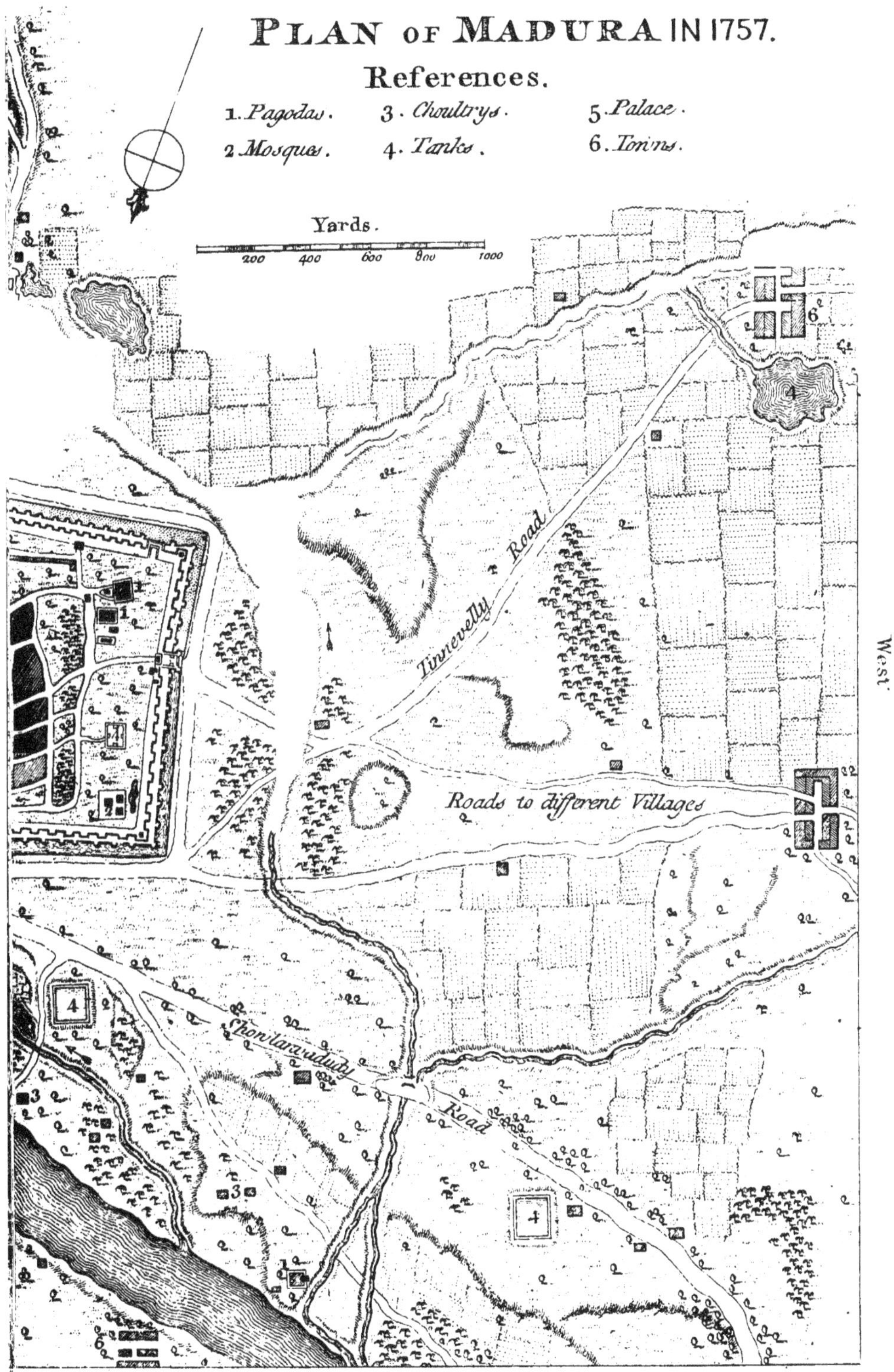

PLAN OF MADURA IN 1757.
References.
1. Pagodas.
2 Mosques.
3. Choultrys.
4. Tanks.
5. Palace.
6. Towns.
Yards.
200   400   600   800   1000
Tinnevelly Road
Roads to different Villages
Showtarrududy
Road
West.
Thos. Jefferys sculp.

the Tamakam was set aside from the outset for agricultural experi-
ments under a Farm Committee, which employed a trained agriculturist and erected sundry buildings. This body effected little of
note and in 1890 it handed over the land and buildings to the
District Board to serve as an agricultural branch of the Technical
institute. The soil is wretched and the scheme was a failure, and
in 1900 the Board gave back the property to the council. In 1904
this latter lent it without charge to the Board for five years for the
use of the Veterinary dispensary which is now located there.
The Union Club for native gentlemen, just west of the Tamakam
compound, was founded under Mr. Crole's auspices in 1883. The
land was granted on patta in that year and the building was
completed in 1884.

Just west of the main gate of the People's Park is the hamlet
of Góripálaiyam in which is the most revered mosque in the town.
In this are two tombs which are traditionally stated to be those of
a king named Allá-ud-din and of his brother Shams-ud-din. It is
not clear who these personages were. A long Tamil inscription on
a pillar within the building (dated 1574–75 and confirming a grant
to the institution of six villages originally given it by one of the
Pándyan kings) calls the place the 'mosque of the Delhi Orukól
Sultan,' but this expression is obscure. The chief peculiarity of
the building is that its domed roof—which is as much as 22 feet
from base to apex and 69 feet in circumference—is (or is declared
to be) made of one single block of stone. It is so covered with
whitewash that proof of the assertion is difficult of attainment.

Returning across the river, one re-enters the native town. This
(see the map above) is laid out on an unusual plan, all the main
streets running roughly parallel with the walls of the great temple
which stands in the centre of it. Thus there is a North Mási street
(so called because the god used to be taken through it in the month
of Mási, February-March) and also a South, East, and West, Mási
street. Similarly there are four Ávani streets rather nearer the
temple, four Chittrai streets just outside it and four Ádi streets
within its walls. The history of the town has already been sketched
in Chapter II, where will be found (p. 64) some account of the
fortifications which formerly defended it. A comparison of the
attached map of the place in 1757 [1] with the plan of it as it stands
to-day will show better than any verbal description the original
position and extent of these defences. It will be noticed that the
number of the bastions was 72, and the inference is that little
radical change had been effected since the time when Visvanátha

[1] Taken from Cambridge's *War in India.*

Náyakkan (see p. 42) first built the fort in 1559. The walls were roughly rectangular and again ran parallel to those of the temple. At the four points of the compass, and at the angle next the river, were gates through the ramparts. A picture in the possession of Mr. Robert Fischer of Madura—copied from one in the India Office and representing the town of Madura from the south-east at the time of a siege by some British force (probably the attack of 1763-64)—gives some idea of the appearance of the walls. They were faced with stone and crowned with a loop-holed parapet of red brick, and closely resembled those still standing at Alagarkóvil. Outside them was a ditch and broad glacis.

They remained in existence until the middle of the last century and are chiefly responsible for the present crowded state of the town and the absence in it of any open spaces worth the name. In 1837 Mr. John Blackburne, the then Collector, proposed to Government that, to improve the health of the place, the ramparts should be thrown into the ditch and the ground levelled by convict labour. This was agreed to, but so many of the convicts were then engaged in cutting the Pámban channel that work went on very slowly. In 1841, therefore, Mr. Blackburne obtained sanction to a different method of procedure. He marked off the rampart, ditch and glacis into sections, and sold these by auction on condition that the purchasers lowered the glacis, threw the ramparts into the ditch (reserving their stone facing for Government) and built the new houses in regular lines and with tiled roofs. In doing this he arranged that each section of land should as far as possible be sold to people of the same or allied castes. Thereafter work proceeded briskly, and soon the town was surrounded with three new sets of four streets, all again roughly parallel with the temple walls, which were called respectively the Velivídi ('outside street'), the North, South, East and West Marrett streets (after the then Assistant Revenue Surveyor) and the North, South, East and West Perumál Maistry streets, after the foreman of works. Blackburne had written to Government that he intended to form 'a handsome boulevard' out of the new ground. Doubtless his new streets were handsomer and wider than any others in the place, but he lost a great opportunity of making a really fine boulevard all round the town which might have done something to provide it with the open spaces it still so badly needs.

Nothing now remains of the old fort except the west gateway and guard-rooms, in and over which the present maternity hospital is built. The gate itself has been blocked up and the building otherwise greatly altered, but three or four of the old embrasures for cannon are still left. Much of the stone taken from the

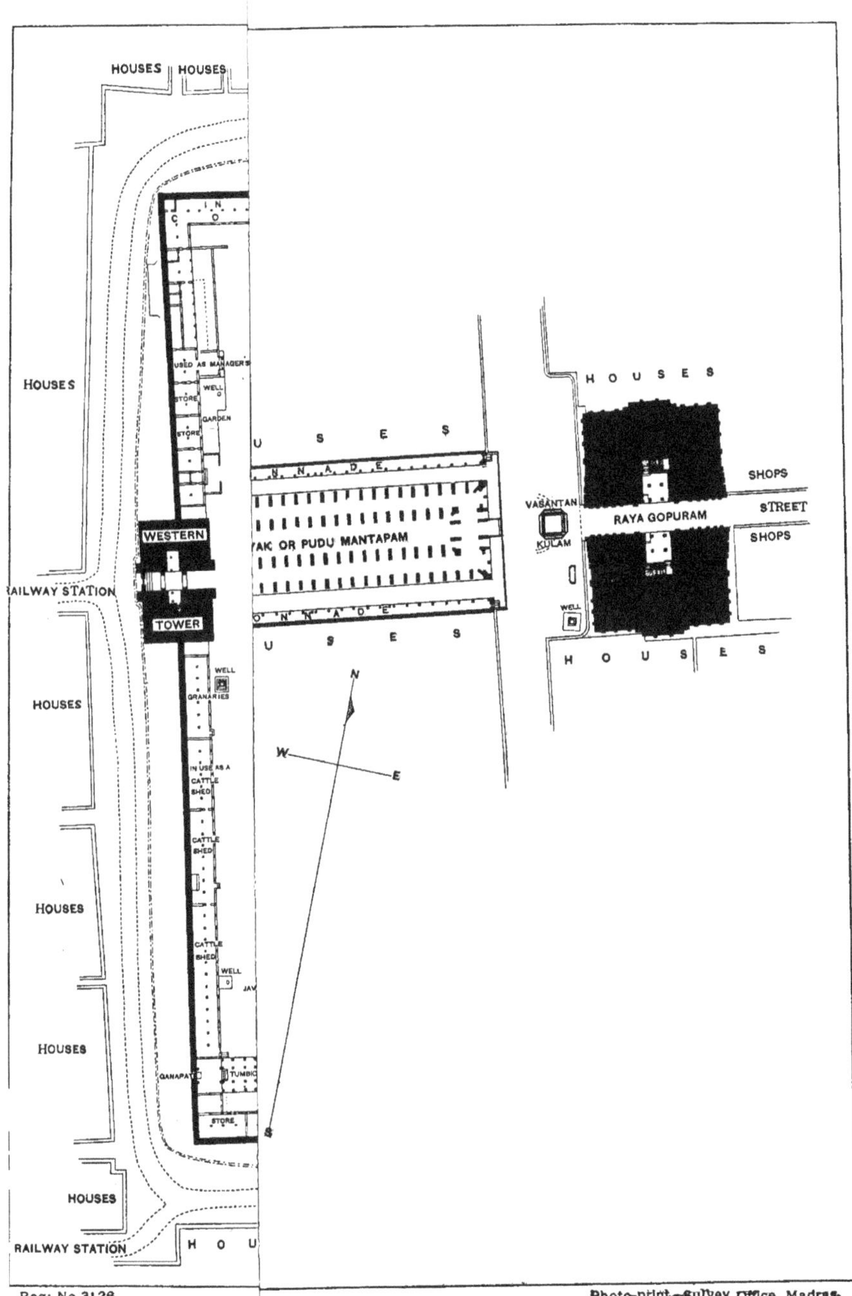
HOUSES
HOUSES
HOUSES
HOUSES
USED AS MANAGER'S
STORE
WELL
STORE
GARDEN
WESTERN
RAILWAY STATION
TOWER
WELL
GRANARIES
HOUSES
IN USE AS A
CATTLE
SHED
CATTLE
SHED
HOUSES
CATTLE
SHED
CATTLE
SHED
WELL
GANAPATI
TUMBIC
STORE
HOUSES
HOUSES
RAILWAY STATION
HOU
HOUSES
AK OR PUDU MANTAPAM
COLONNADE
COLONNADE
N
W
E
S
HOUSES
VASANTAM
KULAM
RAYA GOPURAM
WELL
SHOPS
STREET
SHOPS
HOUSES

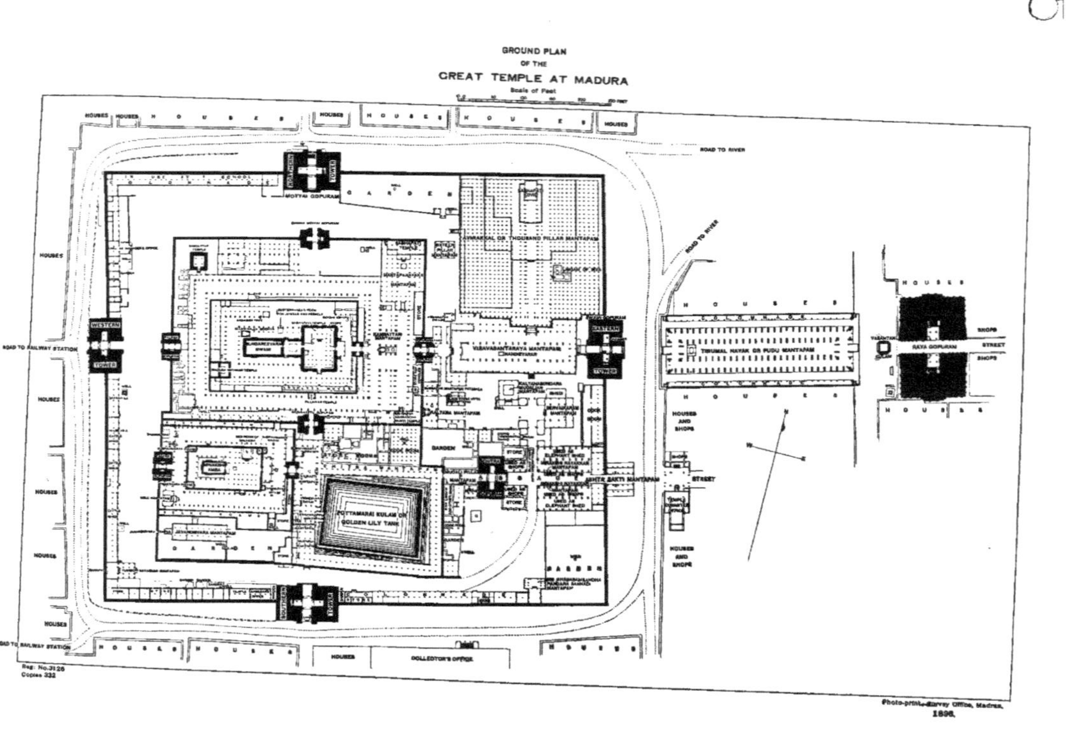

GROUND PLAN OF THE GREAT TEMPLE AT MADURA

ramparts was used for strengthening the causeway across the
Vaigai. The stone figure of an elephant which now faces this was
brought from the palace and set up in its present position as a
memorial of Blackburne's work; and with the same intent the
' Blackburne lamp' was erected near the site of the old east gate
of the fort. The inscription on this says that it was put up ' by a
grateful people,' but the numerous petitions complaining of his
proceedings when he effected these improvements had much to do
with the suspension which subsequently was his lot. He was
eventually restored to his post, but never forgave the authorities.

Troops were stationed in the town for several years after the
fort was demolished. They lived in temporary barracks put up
on the site of the existing lines of the Police Reserve and it is
said that the masonry powder-magazine there was originally
built for them.

It remains to refer to the three buildings for which Madura
is so widely known; namely, the great temple, the tank called
the Teppakulam and the palace of Tirumala Náyakkan.

The temple, as already stated, stands in the centre of the
town. Except the inner shrines, probably none of it is older
than the sixteenth century. The original building of the days
of the Pándya kings was almost entirely destroyed (see p. 38)
by the Musalman troops of Malik Káfur in the invasion of 1310.
The eastern *gópuram* bears an inscription purporting to be of
Pándya times, but the script is modern. The inner shrines are
mentioned by Mánikya-Váchakar (see p. 290), who is thought to
have lived in the fifth century of the present era, and even by
Tamil poets who have been assigned much earlier dates. These
latter call the temple *Velliambalam*, ' the hall of silver '—
probably in contradistinction to *Ponnambalam*, ' the hall of gold,'
the name given to the shrine at Chidambaram. The attached
plan of the existing building gives a clearer idea of its general
arrangement than could be conveyed by any description. It
will be seen that—excluding from consideration for the present
the *Pudu mantapam* and *Ráya gópuram* referred to later--it is
constructed on the system usual with the larger Dravidian
temples. Four high stone walls, in the middle of each of which
is a gateway surmounted by pyramidal *gópurams*, enclose a
nearly rectangular space about 830 feet by 730 feet within which
is a labyrinth of store-houses, cloisters, mantapams and lesser
shrines and the sacred tank, and, in the centre, surrounded by
other walls with more gateways and towers, the inner shrines of
the god and goddess. The god is Siva in his form Sokkanátha

or Sundara, 'the beautiful,' and the goddess, his wife, is Mínákshi, 'the fish-eyed.' The legend regarding them in the local *sthala puránа* says that she was the daughter of a Pándya king who, to the consternation of her parents, was born with three breasts. A fairy, however, told the king that the third breast would disappear as soon as she met her future husband; and it did so when she first encountered Siva. They were wedded accordingly with much pomp. It has been suggested that Mínákshi may have been a local Dravidian goddess whom the Bráhman immigrants found to be too dear to the hearts of the people of the country to be ousted by any of their Áryan deities, and that her marriage to Siva was a method adopted to reconcile and unite the old faith and the new.

Round about the temple, outside the high outer walls, is a neat garden fenced in with iron railings which was laid out in the eighties at the suggestion of Mr. Crole to replace the heaps of rubbish which then occupied this space. The *gópurams* are of the ordinary pattern, the lowest storey consisting of sculptured stone and the upper ones of brickwork profusely ornamented with figures made of brightly painted plaster and representing the more popular of the deities, personages and events met with in the Hindu sacred books. They are unusually lofty and are a landmark for miles round. All of them have been repaired of late years at great cost by the Náttukóttai Chettis who have spent such large sums in the restoration of the Saivite temples of this Presidency. The highest of them is the south *gópuram*, the top of which is about 150 feet above the street below it. The northern tower used to consist only of the brick and stone-work storeys and was known in consequence as the *mottai* (literally 'bald') *gópuram*. Recently, however, a courageous Chetti who cared nothing for the superstition that it is most unlucky to complete a building thus left unfinished, placed the usual plaster top upon it.

Visitors generally enter the temple by the Ashta Sakti mantapam ('porch of the eight saktis,' so called from the images of these goddesses which form part of the pillars inside it) which (see the plan) juts out from the eastern wall. It is noticeable that the door of this is considerably lower than the street. The level of Madura has been much raised in the course of ages. When foundations for new buildings are dug, débris is always met with. In the case of St. George's Church this went down as deep as fourteen feet. At the further end of the mantapam is a doorway on either side of which are images, blackened with frequent oblations, of Ganésa (the elephant-headed son of Siva) and Subrahmanya, his brother, in his form Shanmuga, the six-faced. Passing through the doorway one enters the mantapam of Mínákshi Náyakkan, who is said to have been one of the ministers of Tirumala Náyakkan. This is supported on six rows of tall carved pillars, each of which consists of a single stone. The outer parts of it are used as stables for the temple elephants and the rest is packed with shops and stalls where all kinds of commodities are sold. Both here and in the *Pudu mantapam* these shops so crowd the building as to cloak its architectural beauties, but the temple cash-chest is the richer by some Rs. 17,000 annually from the rents they pay, and the managing body are consequently unwilling to turn them out. At the further end of the mantapam is a doorway surrounded with a brass frame covered with scores of small oil lamps. These are lighted daily from the income derived from certain villages which a former zamindar of Sivaganga presented to the temple for this purpose. Beyond it is the Mudali Pillai mantapam, which is usually known as 'the dark mantapam' and is upheld by various large stone figures executed with great spirit.

Passing through this one reaches 'the golden lily tank,' of the religious efficacy of a bath in which so many stories are told. It is surrounded by a pillared colonnade from one auspicious corner of which the golden tops of the roofs of the two inner shrines can be seen. Its walls were formerly covered with frescoes. These gradually became obliterated by damp and age and were painted out, but parts of the walls have been newly decorated with representations of events from the sacred writings, such as the 64 miracles which Siva is said to have worked in and about Madura. On the western side of the tank is the little chapel of queen Mangammál which has already been referred to on p. 55 above.

Next this is the *Kilikatti* ('parrot') mantapam, so called from the screaming caged parrots which are kept in it. It is upheld by pillars formed of excellent statues—each cut out of a single great block of granite—of *yális* and of the five Pándava brothers. These latter would be more appropriate in a Vaishnava temple than in one dedicated to Siva, and tradition says that they were brought from a shrine to Kariyamánikka Perumál which formerly stood immediately south-west of the *Chinna mottai gópuram* but was demolished. Leading out of this mantapam is Mínákshi's shrine, within which are several smaller chapels to Subrahmanya and Vighnésvara. Passing northwards, the visitor goes towards Siva's shrine through a gateway under the *Nadukattu* ('middle') *gópuram*. Facing this is an image of Ganapati (Pillaiyár) which is said (see below, p. 274) to have been dug up in the great Teppakulam.

Siva's shrine contains several subsidiary buildings which it is not necessary to particularise, a stump which is said to be all that now remains of the legendary forest of *kadamba* trees which is supposed to have formerly covered all this part of the country, and a series of statues of the *Aruvattimúvar*, or 63 Saivite saints. In it are kept the temple jewels, which include a pendant for the god given by a Pándyan king, a head-dress studded with pearls and rubies presented by Tirumala Náyakkan and a pair of golden stirrups which were the gift of Rous Peter—a thank-offering, goes the story, for an escape from an elephant he had wounded. In the covered colonnade surrounding the shrine are little chapels sacred to the Sangattár, or members of the Third Sangam referred to on p. 174, to the nine planets and to the poet-saint Tirugnána Sambandhar whose exploits are mentioned on p. 297. In one corner of it (see the plan) is the Mantapanáyakka mantapam or 'king mantapam among mantapams.' It in no way now deserves this high-sounding name, as it is quite eclipsed by the kambattadi ('foot of the flagstaff') mantapam which adjoins it and surrounds the gilded flagstaff which directly faces the entrance to Siva's shrine. This building was put up in the seventies by the Náttukóttai Chettis and is supported by high monolithic pillars perhaps more elaborately chiselled than anything in the building. Behind the flagstaff are four huge images of Siva dancing, of the fearsome goddess Káli and of Virabhadra in two different shapes, which are again cut out of single blocks of stone. They are done with great spirit and their numerous limbs and elaborate ornaments and attributes make them probably the greatest triumph of technical skill in stone-cutting to be found within the temple walls. Eastward of these images is the great Víravasantaráya mantapam which is said to have been built by Tirumala Náyakkan's predecessor on the Madura throne, Muttu Vírappa (1609–23). It is supported on pillars cut from single blocks of granite and is roofed with long slabs of stone. South of it is the Kalyána ('marriage') mantapam. This has been restored by the Chettis and contains too much varnished woodwork to be pleasing to European taste. In it is conducted the marriage of the god and goddess at the time of the great annual Chittrai festival.

North of the Víravasantaráya mantapam is the 'Thousand-pillared mantapam.' Two shrines built within it reduce the actual number of pillars (all of which are monoliths) to 985, but

Fergusson [1] considers that ' it is not their number but their marvellous elaboration that makes it the wonder of the place ' and declares
that the ' sculptures surpass those of any other hall of its class I
am acquainted with.' It is supposed to have been built by the
Árya Nátha Mudali referred to on p. 42, and an equestrian statue
of him flanks one side of the steps leading up to it. If this legend
is correct, it is (next to the central shrines) the oldest part of the
building.

Passing through the gateway is the eastern tower, and crossing
the street, one enters the *Pudu* ('new') *mantapam,* otherwise
called ' Tirumala Náyakkan's choultry.' It was built by the ruler
whose name it bears (who reigned between 1623 and 1659) as a
summer retreat for the god, and, being formerly surrounded by
a narrow stone water-course designed to cool the air in it, is sometimes called the *Vasanta* ('spring') *mantapam.* It consists (see
the plan) of a rectangular porch 333 feet long and 105 feet wide
(measured on the stylobate) roofed with long slabs of granite
which are supported by four parallel rows of 124 sculptured stone
pillars about 20 feet high. These pillars are all most richly
sculptured and all different in design. Some of them are
ornamented with rearing *yális,* while those near the middle
of the centre aisle are decorated with life-size figures of Tirumala
Náyakkan (with his wives) and his predecessors. At one end
is a porch made of polished black granite. The façade is adorned
with more *yális* or with groups, all cut out of a single block of
granite, representing a warrior seated on a rearing horse the fore
feet of which are supported by the shields of foot-soldiers slaying
tigers or men. ' As works exhibiting difficulties overcome by
patient labour,' says Fergusson, ' they are unrivalled, so far as
I know, by anything found elsewhere.' The whole building is
perhaps the most remarkable of its kind in south India, but the
effect of it is at present sadly marred by the shops and stalls with
which the whole centre aisle is crowded.

East of it is the unfinished *Ráya gópuram* ('king tower')
which Tirumala Náyakkan began and never completed. Native
manuscripts say that he began 64 others (some give the figure as
96) in different places, all at one and the same auspicious moment,
but that many of them were never completed. Unfinished
examples very similar to that at Madura may be seen at Alagarkóvil and Periyakulam. ' Beginning a *Ráya gópuram* ' is a saying
now applied in Madura to the commencement of any hopelessly
ambitious undertaking. The lowest storey of this tower occupies

----

[1] *Indian and Eastern Architecture* (John Murray, 1876), 365.

more than twice the space covered by any of the existing *gópurams* and the sculpture on it is richer and cleaner cut than that on any other. The doorposts of the gateway through it are formed of monoliths over 50 feet high and 3 feet wide, carved with exquisite scrolls of foliage. Had it been finished it would have been the finest *gópuram* in southern India. Having never been conse-crated, it has escaped the whitewash which has spoilt so many of the other buildings in the town.

Here we may take leave of the great Mádura temple. No general view of it will remain in the memory, for there is no point from which more than a small portion of it can be seen, and the chief impression it leaves is wonder at the enormous amount of labour spent upon the immense quantity of elaborate carving in granite which it contains. This granite is supposed to have come from Tirupparankunram. It is not known where the fine-grained black stone which appears here and there in it and in Tirumala Náyakkan's palace was quarried.

The inscriptions in the temple so far deciphered are not of much interest. On the inner parts of it are some grants of Pándyan times. The institution is managed by five dharmakartás appointed by election under the Religious Endowments Act, s ubordinate to whom is a manager. A typical annual budget is roughly as under :—

Receipts.		Expenditure.	
	RS.		RS.
Tasdik allowance	15,773	Daily expenses (lighting, food for the deities, etc.)...	29,637
Inam villages and land ...	45,904	Festivals	4,535
Rent of shops and stalls in the temple	16,862	Establishment (priests, cooks, sweepers, etc., and revenue officials for the	
Rent of cocoanut topes, etc.	3,385		
Rent of land in and about Madura and elsewhere ...	508	care of the temple's land).	21,547
Offerings in the *undial*		Repairs	5,381
boxes	7,245	Legal expenses	3,805
	89,677		64,905

Any surplus is usually laid out in repairs to the fabric, which, notwithstanding the fact that the Náttukóttai Chettis have spent some five lakhs upon the building, are still urgently needed in places.

The chief festivals are the Chittrai, Teppakulam and Ávani-múlam feasts. The first (and chief) of these occurs in the month of Chittrai (April-May) and celebrates the marriage of Siva and Mínákshi. The great event in it is the dragging of the temple car through the four Mási streets, so called because this event originally took place in the month Mási February-March. A very large cattle-fair is held at the same time and the Alagarkóvil god comes to the town. The second feast takes place in Tai (January-February). The images of the god and goddess are floated on a raft (*teppam*) round the Teppakulam, which is lighted with thousands of little lamps for the occasion. This festival was originated by Tirumala Náyakkan after he had built the Teppa-kulam, and is fixed for the anniversary of his birthday. The third feast occurs in August or September and at it a number of the exploits of Siva are commemorated—among them those connected with the life of the saint Mánikya-Váchakar and referred to on p. 290 below.

There are many other temples in Madura, but space does not allow of any detailed account of them. The biggest is that to the Vaishnava deity Perumál in the south-west part of the town. Near it is a tank called the Perumál teppakulam to distinguish it from the other (' Vandiyúr') Teppakulam. The outer walls of this building bear several marks made by round-shot. The central shrine was designed on regal lines, but was apparently never finished. The stone work in this—especially the pierced granite windows, all of different delicate designs, which light the passage round the inner shrine—is as excellent as anything in Madura. The temple to Siva in his form Nanmaitaruvár, ' giver of benefits,' has recently been repaired at great cost by the Chettis. The Patnúlkárans (see p. 109) have their own place of worship, in which priests of the caste officiate. The lower classes largely frequent the shrine to Máriamma, the goddess of small-pox, which stands on the edge of the Vandiyúr Teppakulam. This is hung with cradles presented by women who believe themselves to have obtained children by the grace of the goddess and is decorated with rows of painted clay images of children whom she is held to have delivered from sickness.

This Teppakulam (' raft tank '), which has been several times referred to, is an artificial reservoir made by Tirumala Náyakkan. It is filled by a channel from the Vaigai and lies at the extreme south-east corner of the town. It is almost a perfect square, measuring (along the outside of the parapet walls) 1,000 feet on the north and south and 950 feet on the east and west, and is the largest construction of the kind in south India. The sides are faced all round with cut granite and surmounted by a handsome parapet of the same material, just inside which a granite-paved walk, five feet wide, runs all round the tank. Flights of steps, three on each side, run down at intervals to the water's edge. In the middle of the reservoir is a square island, also faced with cut granite, on which, among green palms and flowering trees, is a small white temple with a tower of the usual kind, flanked, at the four corners of the island, with graceful little mantapams. The whole is exceedingly well-proportioned and graceful in effect. The story goes that this spot was the place at which the bricks for Tirumala Náyakkan's palace were made, and that when the clay for them was being dug out the stone image of Ganapati now in the temple and referred to above was found buried underground. Realizing that the discovery showed that the spot was holy ground, the king turned the excavations into this beautiful tank. The legend at least affords an explanation for the construction of such an undertaking so far from the town.

The ruins of Tirumala Náyakkan's palace stand near what was once the south-east corner of the old fort. The map of the town in 1757 already given shows what an immense area the buildings originally covered. Only one block of them now survives. The destruction of them was begun by Tirumala's own grandson Chokkanátha, who ruled from 1662 to 1682. He held his court at Trichinopoly, and, to provide himself with a dwelling there, ruthlessly removed thither all the best portions of his grandfather's splendid residence, but only succeeded in constructing a building which has remained quite unknown to fame. The plan of 1757 shows the arrangement of the chief parts of the original building; a vernacular paper translated on pp. 157–9 of Vol. II of Taylor's *Oriental Historical Manuscripts* gives a lengthy description of these; the two drawings made by Daniell in 1794 which are reproduced in M. Langlès' *Monuments anciens et modernes de l'Hindoustan* (Paris, 1821) show portions which have now entirely disappeared; a painting in the library in the Tanjore palace and another in the possession of Mr. Fischer and referred to above show other similar parts; and from the roof of the one block which survives may be seen the tall Ten Pillars, a small dome among the Patnúlkárans' quarter, and the site of the old Naubat khána (or band stand) which were all once included in the original building. But these materials are not sufficient to enable us to reconstruct the palace as it stood in the days gone by. One thing only is certain, namely that, in spite of the current belief to the contrary, the Collector's present office near the temple and the building called 'Mangammál's palace' where the taluk cutcherry and other offices are now located were entirely distinct from it.

The Naubat khána, it may here be noted, was so dilapidated in the fifties that the American Mission declined to take it as a gift; it was then restored by Mr. George Fischer for the use of a school; and was taken by Government in 1858 for the use of the new Zilla school. When the new building for this latter was put up, the Naubat khána was used for some time as the police head-quarter office. It was eventually sold as being past repair and the Patnúlkárans' primary school now occupies its site.

The one block of the palace which now survives consists of two oblong buildings running east and west *en échelon* and connected at one corner. The smaller of these is 135 feet long, half as wide (including the cloisters on either side), and about 70 feet in height. 'It possesses,' says Fergusson, whose book contains an inadequate engraving of its interior, 'all the structural propriety and character of a Gothic building.' The roof is a pointed arch of brickwork strengthened by granite ribs springing from a double series, one above the other, of other pointed arches supported on columns. Behind the upper series of these arches runs a gallery resembling the triforium of an English cathedral. Tradition says that this room was Tirumala's sleeping apartment and that his cot hung by long chains from hooks in the roof. One night, says a favourite story, a Kallan made a hole in the roof, swarmed down the chains and stole the royal jewels. The king promised a jaghir to any one who would bring him the thief, and the Kallan then gave himself up and claimed the reward. The king gave him the jaghir and then promptly had him beheaded. For many years this chamber was used as the District Court and portraits of two former Judges, Sir Philip Hutchins and Mr. Thomas Weir, still hang in it. It is at present occupied by one of the Sub-Courts.

The larger of the two buildings is even more impressive. It consists of a great open courtyard, 252 feet long and 151 feet wide, round which runs a roofed arcade of great beauty, supported on tall stone pillars 40 feet in height connected by foliated brick arches of much elegance of design ornamented with Hindu designs carried out in the fine shell-lime plaster which almost resembles marble. Round three sides of this court, at the back of the arcade, runs a very handsome line of lofty cloisters, 43 feet wide and upheld by three parallel rows of pillars supporting arches some 26 feet high. In the middle of two sides of this are large domes built on pillars of the same height as those of the outer arcade, and an upper gallery runs all round it. On the fourth side of the court the cloister is much deeper and finer, being altogether 105 feet wide, supported on five rows of huge pillars and roofed with three great domes, the central and largest of which measures 60 feet in diameter and is 73 feet above the ground. In front of it stands a magnificent portico, the pillars of which are 55 feet high to the spring of the arches.

The vernacular MS. above referred to calls this building the *Swarga Vilásam* and says—

'This pavilion is so constructed as to cause it to be said that in no other country is there a court equal to it, by reason of its splendid ornaments, their excellence, number, extent, curious workmanship, and great beau y. To the west, in the midst of a great dome-shaped hall, is a square building of black stone, inside which is a chamber made of ivory. In the middle of this is a jewelled throne, on which the king is accustomed to take his seat at the great nine-nights' festival surrounded by all his banners or ensigns of royalty, and before which all kings are accustomed to do homage.'

Behind this domed chamber are three other rooms which, though small, are noteworthy for the tall pillars of black marble which uphold their roofs.

The whole construction has been declared by competent authority to be the largest and most perfect specimen of palace architecture existing anywhere south of a line drawn from Bombay to Calcutta.

M. Langlès' volume already referred to shows that the palace was an absolute ruin before the British acquired the Madura country. He says that it was utilised as barracks, and the Survey Account of 1821 states that part of it was occupied then by a paper factory worked by convict labour. In 1837 Mr. Blackburne reported that it was used by the weavers for their work, and obtained leave to demolish the great walls (40 feet high, 900 feet long on the east and west and 660 feet on the north and south) which surrounded it and which threatened to collapse. In 1857 it was stated that almost every part of the building was so cracked as to be dangerous and that the only really safe part of it was the inner cloister. The courts of the District Judge, Sub-Judge, Sadr Amin and Munsif were, however, held in it and the Zilla school occupied the north-east corner of the cloisters. The amount required to restore the place was estimated at two lakhs. In 1858 heavy rain did much damage and brought down the west wall of Tirumala Náyakkan's bed-chamber and the Judge reported that portions of the building fell so frequently that approach to his court was positively dangerous and that the Sub-Judge and Munsif had had to move elsewhere.

In 1868 Lord Napier, the then Governor of Madras, wrote an emphatic minute on the necessity of restoring ancient ruins in general and this palace in particular, and Mr. Chisholm, the Government architect, was sent down to report on the possibility of saving what remained of the building. His account led the Government to decide to repair the palace to render it suitable for the Revenue, Judicial and municipal offices of the town, and a first instalment of Rs. 10,000 for this purpose was entered in the budget for 1870–71. Thereafter annual allotments were made for continuing the work. Lord Napier took the greatest personal interest in the matter and in 1871, after visiting the place, recorded an elaborate minute regarding the offices which were to be located in it. By 1882 Rs. 2,13,000 had been spent, iron ties had been inserted to hold the structure together, the ruined portions had been rebuilt or rendered safe, the plaster-work and painting had been restored on the original lines and the entrance on the east side of the great courtyard had been surrounded with an ornamental gateway. This entrance had been cut through the solid brickwork in comparatively recent times. Mr. Chisholm found evidence to show that the original opening had been on the west, behind the three great domes.

Various public offices were then located in the restored portions, and to accommodate them the cloisters were partitioned off into sets of rooms with ugly dwarf walls which quite spoilt their appearance. The next year a committee of local officers settled the best methods of distributing the remaining available space and much correspondence ensued as to the desirability of placing the Collector's office in the building. By 1886 a sum of Rs. 3,31,000 had been spent on, or sanctioned for, the palace, and shortly afterwards the Collector's office was at length moved into it. The space available was, however, found to be quite insufficient and eventually it was removed back to its former quarters.

The palace, indeed, is in no way suited for public offices. The ventilation is insufficient, the acoustic properties poor, the lighting bad and the surroundings insanitary; while, owing to the echoes in the great courtyard, the noise made by the crowds who attend the various courts and offices renders it most difficult to hear in any of them. Consequently, as already stated above, a new court-house is to be built on the other side of the Vaigai, north-west of the Mysore chattram, for the Judge (who now holds court under the great dome) and the other judicial officers who are located in the palace; and new quarters are to be constructed on a site to the south of the Tamakam for the Collector's office and its various branches, the Madura Deputy

Collector and the tahsildar. The only offices then left in the palace will be those of the Registration department. These will be located in the three rooms west of the great dome and all the dwarf walls and partitions will be removed from the cloisters. This part of the old palace will thus, after the lapse of perhaps a couple of conturies, be restored to almost its original grandeur.

Mángulam: Twelve miles north-east of Madura ; population 3,075. To the south of it stands the Pándava-muttu hill, in the rock on the western side of which are cut three small shrines adjoining one another. They are about $3\frac{1}{2}$ feet deep and 7 feet high and look as if they had been originally intended to be connected together so as to make a rock-cut temple of the usual kind. There are no inscriptions or sculptures at the spot.

A mile east of the village is Kalugumalai, on a rock on the top of which are some of the shallow excavations which (see p. 75) are called *Pancha Pándava padukkai* or ' beds of the five Pándavas.'

Pasumalai: A small hill of quartz rock, standing two miles south of Madura, from which most of the metal for mending the streets of the town is quarried. The name means ' cow hill,' and the legend about the place in the Madura *sthala purána* says that the Jains, being defeated in their attempt to destroy Madura by means of the serpent which was turned into the Nágamalai (see p. 7), resorted to more magic and evolved a demon in the form of an enormous cow. They selected this particular shape for their demon because they thought that no one would dare kill so sacred an animal. Siva, however, directed the bull which is his vehicle to increase vastly in size and go to meet the cow. The cow, seeing him, died of love and was turned into this hill.

The hill, it may be mentioned, bears no resemblance to a cow or to any other animal. It consists of two rounded heights joined by a lower saddle. On one of these is a shrine to one of the many *grámadévatas* at which sheep are periodically offered up, and beneath the other is the extensive compound of the American Mission, within which are built the high school referred to on p. 176 above, a church, a theological seminary and numerous subsidiary buildings.

Sirupálai (or Siruválai) contains 663 inhabitants and is situated eight miles north-north-west of Madura. It is the chief of the four villages which make up the small zamindari of the same name. This was one of the ' unsettled pálaiyams ' referred to on p. 194 above and no sanad has yet been granted for it. Nor, since it has passed out of the possession of the family of the original holders, is it scheduled in the Impartible Estates Act of 1904. It was sold in 1861 in satisfaction of a decree of the civil courts obtained by creditors of the then zamindar, Achyuta (*alias* Vasuvacha) Ráma Kavundan, an Anuppan by caste, and passed successively to Marudamuttu Pillai, Tavamunia Pillai, Mr. T. M. Scott (a barrister at Madura), Mr. E. Scott (his son), Father F. Rapatel, s.j. (who bought it in 1893 on behalf of the Madura Jesuit Mission) and Chidambara Chetti, the present registered holder, who purchased it from the mission in 1900.

Tirupparankunram: Four miles south-west of Madura; population 4,528 (largely Kallans); a station on the main line of the South Indian Railway. The village is built at the foot of a hill which rises 1,048 feet above the sea and is called Skandamalai, or 'Subrahmanya's hill' from the famous temple to that deity which stands at the foot of it. The Musalmans, however, say that the name is properly Sikandarmalai after a fakir called Sikandar who is buried at the top of the hill. The place was formerly a sort of outpost of Madura, figures more than once in the wars of the eighteenth century, and still contains traces of fortifications. The granite of which the hill consists is a handsome variety with pink and grey bandings which is much prized as building material, and tradition says that it was largely employed in the construction of the Madura temple. A flight of steps, gradually degenerating into mere footholds cut in the rock, runs up the hill to the tomb of the fakir. About half way up, on the southern face of the hill, on the overhanging side of an enormous hummock of bare granite at the foot of which is a deep cleft full of water, are carved, side by side, two panels about $2\frac{1}{2}$ feet long and 2 feet wide representing nude, standing, Jain figures in the customary position with their hands hanging straight down by their sides and surrounded by female attendants, some smaller figures and a cobra or two. They are some eighteen feet from the ground and must have been sculptured from a scaffolding. This has saved them from mutilation.

A little further along the same south side of this hummock is a small shrine to Kási Visvésvaralinga. The cleft here widens out to a considerable pool of great depth, and on the rock on the far side of it are carved in a line, in deep relief, representations of the lingam and certain of the Hindu gods. The pújári has to swim across the pool to cover them with the daily oblations and flowers. The water contains numbers of small fish which come for food when called by the *bairágis* who frequent this spot.

On the very top of the hill is the tomb of the fakir Sikandar. It lies in a crevice between two boulders in which the holy man is said to have lived and died. In front of it is a new porch supported by pillars of Hindu style and crowned with a brick dome and minarets constructed after the Musalman fashion which are still unfinished. The visitors to the building are as mixed as its architecture, the place being frequented by both Hindus and Musalmans.

At the foot of the southern side of the hill is a rock-cut temple (commonly called the Umaiyándan kóvil) which must once have been the finest of its kind in the district. It measures about 19 feet by 17 feet and 9 feet in height, and at the west end of it is a separate shrine 8 feet square. It was originally supported by four pillars, but the two in the centre have now disappeared (probably through fires having been lighted round them) and the two outside have been disfigured by being built into an ugly wall which now runs across the face of the temple. The place is dedicated to Natarája or Siva dancing in competition with Káli (the form in which he is worshipped at Chidambaram) and the central portion of the back wall is occupied by what must once have been a most spirited sculpture of the deity, flanked on either side by the drummer and by Káli. This, however, has also been almost entirely destroyed. To the east of this group is an image of Subrahmanya with his two wives and in the separate shrine to the west is a representation of Siva in the uncommon form of Ardhanárísvara, or half man and half woman. Almost all the eastern side of the temple is occupied by a long inscription which has been assigned [1] to king Máravarman Sundara Pándya I, who (see p. 35) came to the throne in 1216 A.D. It records the grant of lands and endowments to this temple in the sixth year of his reign. Outside the shrine, on the face of the rock cliff in which it is excavated, are a series of sculptures of rishis and deities.

The big temple to Subrahmanya stands close under the northern foot of the hill and its innermost shrine is cut out of the solid rock. In front of this are a series of mantapams, built at different levels, one below the other. The lowest or outermost of these is an exceedingly fine example of this class of work. Its roof is of great stone slabs and is supported on 48 tall, carved, monolithic pillars, which are from 20 to 24 feet high but the sculpture on which is clogged with the usual colour wash. It has three aisles, the middle one of which (measured from the inside edges of the pillars) is as much as 24 feet wide, and it occupies a total area 116 feet by 94 feet. These mantapams are said to have been built by Tirumala Náyakkan, and a statue of him stands at

---

[1] *Ep. Ind.*, vi, 314.

the side of the shrine. A well within the temple, called the *Sanyásikulam,* contains water which is held in such repute as a remedy for diabetes and other diseases that it is carried all the way to Madura and sold there. The building contains several inscriptions. One of these says that in 1792 A.D. a regiment of Europeans seized the town and were forcing their way into the temple when the priests, fearing that its holiness would thus be destroyed, prevailed upon one Kutti to throw himself down from the gópuram. Kutti did so, the regiment withdrew, the place was saved and Kutti (who evidently survived) was given a grant for his heroic action. In olden days it was a not uncommon practice in Madura, says Blackader,[1] for the constant quarrels between the native rulers and the temple priests to be settled in a similar way. A man climbed up one of the *gópurams* and vowed that unless the quarrel was ended by a certain time he would throw himself down. Neither side cared to be held guilty of his blood, and each accordingly did all in its power to heal the breach.

Velliyakundam : Eight miles north-north-east of Madura ; population 1,294. The chief of the thirteen villages which make up the small zamindari of the same name. This estate, which is some 3,300 acres in extent, was one of the ' unsettled pálaiyams' referred to (p. 194) above, but a sanad has since been granted for it. It is not scheduled in the Impartible Estates Act, 1904, as in 1882 it passed from the family of the original owners by a court sale to the present registered holder, Mínákshi Náyakkan.

---

[1] *Archæologia,* **xv**, 453.

MÉLÚR TALUK.

MÉLÚR is the easternmost taluk of the district and slopes gradually towards the south-east. The southern part of it is a flat and somewhat uninteresting plain which is now being rapidly turned into wet land with the aid of the Periyár water, but the northern portion is picturesquely diversified with the spurs of the Ailúr hills, the Karandamalais, the Nattam hills and the Alagarmalais, and is a pleasant country covered with tiny patches of rice-cultivation under little tanks and wide areas of dry crops growing on vivid red soil among red, wooded hills. The villages here are usually hidden away among groves of fine trees, especially tamarinds, and on every scrap of waste land scrub and bushes flourish luxuriantly. The soil is apparently particularly suited to the growth of trees, and the magnificent white-barked figs which line the road west of Nattam are the finest in all the district.

Over a fifth of the taluk, a higher proportion than in any other, is covered with forest. The soil is all of the red ferruginous variety and is the poorest in the district. None of the dry land is assessed at more than Rs. 1-4-0 per acre (in no other taluk except Kodaikanal is this the case) and as much as nine-tenths of the wet land (a higher proportion than in any other part of Madura) is charged as little as Rs. 3-8-0 or less. Mélúr, however, receives a heavier rainfall than any part except the Palni hills, and the Periyár water reaches most of the south of it; consequently as much as two-fifths of the taluk is cultivated with paddy and it is better protected from famine than any other except Madura. The population has hitherto increased very slowly, the proportional growth both in the decade 1891–1901 and in the thirty years from 1871 to 1901 being smaller than in any taluk except Tirumangalam; but as the use of the Periyár water extends, a change in this respect may be looked for.

Statistics on other matters regarding the taluk will be found in the separate Appendix. Below is some account of the more interesting places in it :––

Alagarkóvil: A temple to Vishnu in his form Alagarsvámi, ' the beautiful god ', which stands close under the southern end of the hill called (after it) Alagarmalai, twelve miles north-west **of Madura town.**

Round about this temple, in days gone by, was a considerable CHAP. XV.
fortified town; and the remains of the palace of Tirumala MÉLÚR.
Náyakkan which still stand near it show that it was a favourite
place of residence of the rulers of Madura. It is now absolutely
deserted; owing, it is said, to its feverishness.

The spot is most picturesque. Running out southwards from
the foot of the hill and surrounding not only the temple but the
ruins of the old town and palace, runs a high rectangular fort
wall, measuring some 730 yards by 400, faced with stone and
crowned with battlements of dark red brick exactly like those
shown in the picture of Madura fort above (p. 265) referred to.
A stone gateway passes through this, in front of which a broad
street, flanked on either side by high mounds made of the débris of
former houses and by a ruined shrine or two, runs straight to the
temple and the old palace. These stand close under the Alagar
hill and the red brick of the main *gópuram* of the former building
contrasts effectively with the dark green of the wooded slopes
behind it.

Passing up this street one sees first, on the western side, a
carved stone mantapam which is supposed to have been built by
Tirumala Náyakkan and contains several life-size statues, two of
which are said to represent that ruler and his wife. The ' fair
round belly' for which he was notorious is realistically and
unflatteringly depicted. A little further up the street are the
ruins of his palace, an erection of brick and chunam which was
roofed with the domed and vaulted structures used in the palace
at Madura and is consequently in the last state of decay. Facing
it is the temple car-stand and gorgeous new car. Further on is a
big mantapam which belongs to the Kallans of this part of the
country. It is lofty, and contains many excellently sculptured
pillars and a frieze of well-executed carvings of episodes in the
various incarnations of Vishnu, but all these are clogged up with
whitewash. Westward of it is the *Ráya gópuram*, or ' king tower,'
an imposing unfinished mass which is said, like its counterpart at
Madura, to be due to the great Tirumala, embodies the best stone-
carving in all the place, has hitherto escaped the whitewash brush,
but is choked up with débris, covered with trees, plants and
creepers and requires only a few more years of neglect to be an
absolute ruin. West of it again, is the *Vasanta mantapam* or
' spring porch,' a building forming a hot-weather retreat for the
god and containing a square central mantapam surrounded by a
stone channel designed to hold cooling streams, and a shady
cloister the walls and ceilings of which bear frescoes illustrative of
the Vaishnava scriptures.

Retracing his steps to the Kallans' mantapam, the traveller reaches at length the Alagarkóvil itself. This is surrounded with a high wall, over the main (eastern) entrance through which rises a *gópuram*. In front of this entrance, however, is a notable peculiarity. A flight of eighteen steps runs down from it at the foot of which is a big wooden gate which is sacred to Karuppanasvámi, the most popular of all the less orthodox gods of the Madura district. He is known here as 'Karuppan of the eighteen steps.' The gate and steps are held in especial veneration by the Kallans who are so numerous in the adjoining villages. The gate is spattered from top to bottom with sandal-paste; on either side of it is a collection of great iron bill-hooks and spears (some of them 12 ft. long) which are the favourite weapons of Karuppanasvámi and have been presented to him in accomplishment of vows by devotees whose undertakings he has blessed; and mingled with these are the cradles given him by women to whom he is supposed to have granted offspring. The gate is commonly resorted to when solemn affirmations have to be made. It is believed throughout the taluk that the man who swears to a falsehood here and passes through Karuppan's gate with the lie upon his lips will speedily come to a miserable end, and many a civil suit is settled by the parties agreeing to allow the court's decree to follow the affirmations which are made in this manner.

Just to the south of the gate, is a stone bearing a modern (1842) inscription relating how Pachaiyappa Mudali (the well-known benefactor of Pachaiyappa's College at Madras and other charities) gave the annual interest on a lakh of pagodas for feeding pilgrims to the temple. North of it is the every-day entrance to the spacious Alagarkóvil quadrangle, which measures 90 yards by 50. This is a striking place. On two sides of it towers the wooded hill; it is paved throughout with stone; round the sides of it stand several little mantapams and two old circular granaries called Ráma and Lakshmana, formerly used to hold the offerings of grain made to the god; and in the middle of it, faced by a long, much whitewashed, three-aisled mantapam of the Náyakkan period, upborne by 40 pillars shaped into fearsome yális and other figures, is the holy of holies. This has an uncommon circular apse lighted, it is said, by windows of pierced stone all of different design. In it is kept the wooden image of the god, the processional image (an unusually handsome affair heavily plated with gold), another image, about 15 inches high, made of solid gold and most beautifully chased, and the temple jewels, some of which are the gift of Rous Peter (see p. 259) and bear his name.

In the god's bedchamber adjoining, stands a rare and antique bedstead, said to be the gift of Tirumala (whose statue stands at the entrance to the room), which from all accounts (Europeans cannot, of course, see it) must be nearly unique. It is said to be 12 feet long by 10 feet wide and about 15 feet high; to stand on a pedestal of sculptured black stone, inlaid with small ivory figures, supporting four pillars carved from similar stone and ornamented with small detached shafts and figures in ivory; and to be covered with a domed wooden roof elaborately inlaid with ivory work carved in most intricate and minute designs.

Of late years, under the present energetic executive, much has been done to bring the Alagar temple and its surroundings into the state of repair which its considerable wealth (its income is some Rs. 16,000) demands. The quadrangle has been cleared of rubbish and earth, the inner *gópuram* above the entrance to the shrine has been repaired, the main *gópuram* is shortly to be similarly treated, the fort wall is being patched and a big teppa'kulam near the main gate through this is being rebuilt.

On the hill above the temple, to the north and perhaps two miles away, is a clear and cool natural stream, called the Núpura Gangai, which flows over a little waterfall into a reservoir surrounded by a *vasanta mantapam* and thence down the mountain side to the temple. Pipes have recently been laid to bring this to the different parts of the building and its surroundings and this is a great boon to the pilgrims at festivals. No other water is ever used for bathing the god (who is said to turn black with displeasure if such an innovation is attempted) and when he makes his annual journey to Madura this water is always carried with him.

This journey takes place at the time of the Chittrai (April-May) festival at Madura, when Siva is married to Mínákshi. Alagar is carried in state in a great palanquin, halts at each of the numerous mantapams which line the 12 miles of road to the town, and eventually stays for the festival at Tallákulam, the village just north-east of the Vaigai bridge. Before he starts, his palanquin is halted at the gate of Karuppanasvámi, who is held to be in some way his servant, and a list of the jewels he is taking with him is publicly recited. When he gets back, the same list is re-read in the same place in token of the safe return of these valuables. The religious enthusiasm exhibited throughout the whole of this state progress needs to be seen to be believed.

The popular story accounting for the visit says that Alagar is the brother of Mínákshi, comes to her wedding, arrives too late for the ceremony, and so returns home in dudgeon without entering the town. This has no canonical authority. There is no real connection between Alagar's journey and the wedding ; and before Tirumala Náyakkan's reign they took place at different times, the former occurring in the month Chittrai (April-May) and the latter in Mási (February-March). Tirumala combined the two for the convenience of the numerous pilgrims by fixing the wedding festival in Chittrai, in which month it still occurs.

Alagarsvámi is held in special veneration by the Kallans who are so numerous in the neighbouring villages and is often popularly called the Kallar-Alagar. The men of this caste have the right to drag his car at the car-festival and when he goes on his visit to Madura he is dressed as a Kallan, exhibits the long ear lobes characteristic of that caste, and carries the boomerang and club which were of old their favourite weapons. It is whispered that Kallan dacoits invoke his aid when they are setting out on marauding expeditions and, if they are successful therein, put part of their ill-gotten gains into the offertory (*undial*) box which is kept at his shrine.

Arittápatti: About midway between Mélúr and Alagarkóvil and a mile south of the road connecting them. Population 1,654. One of the many villages which have been transformed by the Periyár water-channels, paddy-fields now occupying what a few years ago was all dry land.

Hidden away in a solitary spot in the long, low line of bare, broken, hills which lies to the west of the village site and is called the Perumálmalai, is a neat little rock-cut Siva temple which faces west. It consists of an inner shrine about 8 feet square and 7 high containing a lingam; a little porch in front of this measuring some 9 feet by 5 and including, on either side of the entrance to the shrine, a *dvárapálaka* (door-keeper) carved in high relief, standing in an aggressive attitude and armed with a formidable club ; and on either side of this porch, less deeply recessed, two niches containing figures, again in high relief, of Ganésa and of some individual bearing a big club round which twines a cobra. The whole affair—shrine, lingam, *dvárapálakas* and images—is all cut out of the solid rock, and the sculpture is much better than in the usual run of this class of temple. In front, stands a detached *nandi* (Siva's bull) of more modern date. There appear to be no inscriptions in the immediate neighbourhood.

Karungálakudi: Eight miles north of Mélúr on the Trichinopoly road ; population 2,075. About a mile to the south of the village are still left a few dolmens. They were formerly numerous. To the south-east of it, on the floor of a natural shelter made by an

overhanging rock, are cut out some *Pancha Pándava padukkai*, or
' beds of the five Pándavas' (see p. 75). Others, it may here be
mentioned, are to be seen to the north-west of Kílavalavu, seven
miles south by east on the Mélúr-Tiruppattúr road. Karungálakudi
also contains one of the oddest of the many curious solid granite
hills which abound in this part of the district—a huge sugar-loaf
peak, the western side of which is one smooth, unbroken, bare slope
of sheet rock. Nearly due west of the village site, on the opposite
side of the road and on the top of a low hummock of rock, stands
the prominent temple of Tiruchunai, an old Saivite shrine which
contains ten or a dozen inscriptions of Pándya times.

see p. 75

Kottámpatti : Fourteen miles north of Mélúr on the Trichinopoly road ; population 2,126 ; police-station, local fund chattram
and an ancient travellers' bungalow (it was in existence in 1817)
in a pleasant compound. The village was formerly a place of
importance owing to its being one of the stages on the pilgrim road
to Rámésvaram, but the railway has now diverted this and other
traffic and the trunk road which runs past the place from Madura to
Trichinopoly is full of ruts and holes which would disgrace a village
bandy-track.

Iron ore is more plentiful in this neighbourhood than perhaps
anywhere in the district. A mile east of the travellers' bungalow
it crops out in the form of silicate in a hill of quartz, the whole of
which is coloured by it.[1] It is seen again in a tank three-quarters
of a mile west of the bungalow, and again four miles still farther
west it forms a hill of ironstone some 50 feet high and nearly half
a mile long. It then vanishes, but reappears about a mile to the
westward again, where it rises into a ridge in a small hill, forms
several prominent points, again vanishes, reappears once more about
a mile still west in long ridges, and forms the topmost peak of a
hill some 600 feet high. The whole line of the outcrop is thus
eight miles long, in which distance it forms an important part of
seven considerable hills and, where it has been excavated, strews
much of the low ground with its fragments. In 1855 several native
blast furnaces were at work in this part of the taluk extracting the
metal from iron ore and iron-sand.

About a mile to the north-east of Kottámpatti, through dense
groves of cocoanut and other fruit trees, runs the Pálár, a jungle
stream of some local importance. Four miles beyond it, a striking
object from the village, rises the steep scarp of Piránmalai hill in
the Sivaganga zamindari. At the foot of this is a well-known

[1] The account which follows is based on pp. 119–20 of Dr. Balfour's *Report
on Iron ores* (Madras, 1855) which in its turn was founded on material contributed
by the Rev. C. F. Muzzy of the American Mission at Madura.

temple to Subrahmanya and two other shrines, all of which contain ancient inscriptions, and also a rich *math* in charge of a non-Bráhman Pandára-sannadhi; and on the top of it are five or six sacred pools, a stone mantapam, a Musalman place of worship strongly built of big bricks, the ruins of masonry fortifications and a long iron cannon of curious design.

Mélúr: Eighteen miles north-east of Madura on the road to Trichinopoly; population 10,100; union; head-quarters of the taluk and so the station of the tahsildar and stationary sub-magistrate and of a sub-registrar; a centre of the American Mission; weekly market; travellers' bungalow, police-station, local fund chattram. The Periyár project has brought new life to the town, which is now a rising agricultural and commercial centre.

It is known to history as the head-quarters of the turbulent Kallans of the ' Mélúr-nád,' whose exploits are referred to in the account of the caste on p. 93 above, and Muhammad Yúsuf Khán established a fort there to overawe them. All trace of this has now vanished, but Ward's Survey Account shows that it stood round about the present travellers' bungalow, to the north-east of the village. After the English took control of the district, a detachment of native infantry was kept in Mélúr for some years, and perhaps the bombproof buildings there and at Kottámpatti which are now used as travellers' bungalows are relics of this occupation. In the compound of the former stands the finest banyan in the district— perhaps in the Presidency—a huge tree which shades a roughly circular space some 75 yards in diameter and which has a much taller and thicker top than its well-known rival in Madura.

Nattam: Twenty-three miles north-north-east of Madura by a road which in bygone years was the main route to Trichinopoly but is now in very second-rate order. Population 7,796; union; station of a sub-registrar who is also a special magistrate under the 'Towns Nuisances Act; travellers' bungalow (at Vélampatti, half a mile to the west); police-station. In the eighteenth century the village possessed a fort and was a regular halting-place between Trichinopoly and Madura, and it appears frequently in the histories of the wars of that period. It was then the head-quarters of a zamin estate. This escheated to Government at the beginning of the last century for lack of legal heirs. There are ruins of old wells and buildings to the west of the village. The place used to be notorious for its fever, but is now healthy enough and boasts a thriving manufacture of oil (some of it made in iron mills of European pattern) from ground-nut and gingelly seed.

The village gives its name to the scattered, stony 'Nattam hills' which surround it, and to the 'Nattam pass' which leads to Madura between the Alagarmalais and the eastern spurs of the Sirumalais. Both these were formerly great strongholds of the 'Nattam Colleries' (Kallans) who figure so prominently in Orme's history. In 1755 the expedition under Col. Heron which had been sent to quiet Madura and Tinnevelly (see p. 62) met on its return with a most serious reverse in this Nattam pass. Orme describes the place as 'one of the most difficult and dangerous defiles in the peninsula' as it 'continues for six miles through a wood, impenetrable everywhere else to all excepting the wild beasts and Colleries to whom it belongs.' The advance party of the expedition saw no enemy in this pass and so went on and halted at Nattam. The main body followed and had got well within the defile when one of the gun tumbrils stuck in the mud. This blocked the other tumbrils, the three guns of the rear detachment of artillery and all the baggage, which was at the tail of the column. Col. Heron foolishly allowed the rest of his men to proceed, and they were soon two miles ahead of the blocked portion. This latter was guarded by only 100 men, of whom only 25 were Europeans.

The Kallans now burst upon this small body from all sides. The guns opened fire on them, but they 'nevertheless maintained the attack for some time with courage and with a variety of weapons; arrows, matchlocks, rockets, javelins and pikes; every one accompanying his efforts with horrible screams and howlings.' Eventually they pushed right down to the road, stabbed the bullocks which drew the tumbrils and broke open these vehicles.

In them they found what was probably the cause of the whole attack—some little brazen idols which the expedition had taken from the temple at Kóvilkudi, six miles east of Madura. 'The confused outcries of the enemy were on a sudden changed to one voice, and nothing was heard on all sides but continual repetitions of the word *swamy*, meaning gods, which expression they accompanied with violent gesticulations and antic postures, like men frantic with joy.' But the recovery of the idols did not end the fight, and it was not until dark that the section got through the pass to the main body of the detachment; and then only with the loss of many men and more followers and the whole of its baggage and stores. Col. Heron was recalled to Madras, court-martialled, and cashiered.

Tiruvádúr: Six miles south of Mélúr; population 2,499. Picturesquely situated on a fine tank, across which is a beautiful view of the Alagar hills. The road runs along the embankment of this. On top of one of the sluices stands an unusual stone image of a centaur-like being which is supposed to protect the tank. Close under the embankment, behind a shrine to Pidári, is a small building made of old stones bearing fragments of inscriptions, which marks the place where one Venkammál committed *sati* on the pyre of her murdered husband. This meritorious deed, say the people, has ever since brought prosperity to Tiruvádúr.

The tank flanks the north and west sides of the village and these were further strengthened in former days by a stone-faced rampart topped with a red brick parapet similar to that at Alagarkóvil (p. 283) and protected by semi-circular bastions. Extensive remains of these are still standing. Within these fortifications is the village and its old Siva temple. This latter contains an architectural freak which is not uncommon in this district but is nowhere carried out in so bold a manner. The wide stone eaves of the imposing ruined mantapam just within the gateway (the sculpture throughout which is unusually good) are made of huge blocks of granite, some six feet long, the upper sides of which are fashioned into a most graceful double curve while the under portions are carved, at immense expense of time and energy, to represent long, thin wooden rafters radiating from a central point above the building and strengthened by purlins executed in complete relief. Similar eaves surround the porch to the south of the inner shrine of this temple and (until it was recently repaired) were also to be seen in another mantapam in the north-east corner of the inner enclosure. The remains of these last are lying about the temple courtyard.

Tiruvádúr was the birth-place of the famous Saivite poet-saint Mánikya-Váchakar (' he whose utterances are rubies '), the author of the sacred poems known as the *Tiruváchakam*. The site of his house is still pointed out and there is a shrine to him within the temple. He is thought by some[1] to have lived as early as the middle of the fifth century, and the current traditions regarding his life are known and repeated throughout the Tamil country. A Bráhman by caste, he rose, it is said, to be Prime Minister to the Pándya king of Madura. But his mind turned ever to higher matters and a crisis was at last reached when he handed over to a holy guru (who was really Siva in disguise) the whole of an immense treasure with which his royal master had sent him out to buy horses for the cavalry. The tale was carried to the king, who instantly summoned Mánikya-Váchakar to the capital. Siva bade him go as directed and assure his master that

---

[1] *Christian College Magazine*, N.S., i, 144 ff. Dr. Pope's *Tiruvaçagam* (Clarendon Press, 1900) gives a translation of his poems and the main events of his life.

the horses would shortly arrive; and then, in one of those fits of playfulness which so endear him to his adherents, the deity transformed a number of jackals into splendid horses and himself rode at their head into the town of Madura. The Pándya king's displeasure vanished at the sight and Mánikya-Váchakar was forgiven; but the same night the supposed horses all resumed their original shapes, escaped from the royal stables and ran howling through the Madura streets back to their native jungles. Mánikya-Váchakar was thrown into prison, but Siva again intervened and sent a mighty flood down the Vaigai which threatened to overwhelm the capital. The whole population was turned out to raise an embankment to keep back the waters and every man and woman in the place was set to build a certain section of this. One aged woman could not complete her task quickly enough, so Siva assumed the guise of a labourer and set himself to help her. At that moment the king came along to inspect the work and, seeing this section behindhand, struck the supposed cooly with his stick. Now Siva is the world, and when he was struck every man and woman in the world—the king himself included—felt the blow; and the king thus knew that Siva was on the side of Mánikya-Váchakar and at once released his minister.

Mánikya-Váchakar thereafter renounced mundane affairs, travelled round as an ascetic to the more famous shrines of the south, singing their praises in the polished verses which are even now recited in them, settled at length near Chidambaram, and finally attained beatitude within the shrine of the great temple there.

In Madura his memory is kept green at the festivals at the Mínákshi temple. Every year at the Ávanimúlam feast, the story of the jackals is acted and a live jackal is brought into the temple and let loose with much ceremony; and the people go in a body to a spot on the bank of the Vaigai near the municipal waterworks and similarly enact the story of the raising of the dam, one of the temple priests taking the part of Siva and shovelling earth and another representing the Pándya king and striking him.

NILAKKOTTAI TALUK.

THIS new taluk is surrounded with hills. It is bounded on the greater part of its northern and eastern sides by the Sirumalais and the Alagarmalais, and on much of its southern and western frontiers by the Nágamalai, the end of the Ándipatti range and a corner of the Lower Palnis. It is also well watered. The country round Vattilagundu is irrigated by the almost perennial Manjalár, and the Vaigai runs all along the southern part of the taluk. The important Peranai and Chittanai dams across this latter river are both situated within the taluk, and much of the southern part of it is irrigated by the Periyár water which the former of them renders available for cultivation.

Detailed statistics for Nilakkóttai are not yet available. The more interesting villages in it are the following :—

Ammayanáyakkanúr : Four miles east of Nilakkóttai and 786 feet above the sea. Contains a chattram, a travellers' bungalow and a railway rest-house, and is the station at which passengers for Kodaikanal alight—bullock-tongas taking them thence to Krishnama Náyak's tope at the foot of the ghát[1]—and the point of export for the produce of the Kannan Dévan Hills in Travancore. The battle fought here in 1736 (see p. 58) decided the fate of the Náyakkan dynasty and delivered its territories into the hands of Chanda Sáhib.

The village is the chief place in the zamindari of the same name, which pays the fourth largest peshkash in the district and includes the plateau and the western slopes of the Sirumalai hills. Family tradition [2] says that the original ancestor of the zamindar's family was one Mákkaya Náyakkan, who was owner of a pálaiyam in the Vijayanagar country and commanded one of the detachments which accompanied Visvanátha's expedition thence to Madura in 1559 (see p. 41). For his services he was granted this estate and put in charge of one of the 72 bastions of the new Madura fort. His property appears originally to have included villages round Védasandúr and some rights over the pálaiyam of Palliyappanáyakkanúr (Kúvakkápatti), but when the Mysoreans took

---

[1] Full details regarding distances, charges, baggage and arrangements generally, will be found in the South Indian Railway *Guide.*

[2] In one of the Mackenzie MSS.

Dindigul the former were detached and the latter was made
independent.[1] During Haidar's operations of 1755 against the
Dindigul poligars (see p. 70) the owner of Ammayanáyakkanúr
assisted him and so escaped the punishment which overtook most of
his fellows. The estate was however sequestrated for arrears by
Tipu in 1788, but restored by the Company in 1790. In 1796 the
poligar gave trouble, declining either to pay up his arrears of
peshkash or to keep the road to Madura free of dacoits, and the
forfeiture of his property was proposed.

The subsequent history of the family has been largely a
chronicle of debt, mismanagement and litigation. In 1846 the
property was leased to M. Faure de Fondclair, who built the
bungalow the ruins of which stand a little to the north of the
railway-station, started the planting of coffee on the Sirumalais, but
(according to a report by the Collector) dealt so oppressively with
the ryots there that several of the hill villages were deserted and
much land went out of cultivation. He died in 1853 (he is buried in
the Roman Catholic church at Madura) and in 1856 his claim against
the estate was cleared off and the property leased again to a Chetti
of Dévakkóttai.[2] In 1870 another lease to one Ádimúlam Pillai
was executed, but this was afterwards set aside by the courts. A
permanent sanad was granted for the zamindari in 1873. A
subsequent gift of the estate to his wife made by a later zamindar
in 1891 was set aside in 1894 by the High Court, which declared
the property inalienable and impartible.[3] The present proprietor,
Rámasvámi Náyakkan, succeeded in 1905. A decree for $1\frac{1}{4}$ lakhs
has been passed against him and a receiver has been appointed
to take charge of the estate.

'A peculiar custom called *dáyádi pattam* regulates the succession
to this pálaiyam.[4] On the demise of the pálaiyagár for the time
being, the estate devolves, not on his heir according to the Mitákshara
law, which, in the absence of a special custom, governs this part of
southern India, not on the eldest son according to the rule of primoge-
niture, which obtains in the other pálaiyams in the district owned by
persons of the Kamblar (Tóttiyan) caste, but on the *dáyádi*, or cousin,
of the deceased pálaiyagár who is senior in age and who is descended
from one of the three brothers who originally formed a joint Hindu
family. These three brothers were named (1) Petala Náyak, (2) Cha-
kala Náyak, and (3) Chinnalu Náyak, and of the three branches

---

[1] Historical memorandum of 1796 in the Collector's records.

[2] Records in O.S. No. 13 of 1892 on the file of the West Sub-Court of
Madura.

[3] I.L.R. (Madras), XVIII, 287 ff.

[4] *Ibid.*, 289.

springing from them the second is now extinct. Thus·the class of kindred in which the heir has to be found is that of the descendants of the two branches, and the person to be selected as pálaiyagár from that class is the one who is the oldest or senior in years.'

This curious custom is accounted for by the following tradition : One of the poligars, named Ponniya Náyakkan, died, leaving a wife Kistnammál and an infant son Lakkayya. Hearing that her late husband's brother, Kámayya Náyakkan, was plotting to murder her and her child and seize the estate, Kistnammál had him assassinated. His wife Errammál was overcome with grief, committed *sati* on his funeral pyre, and pronounced a hideous curse against any direct descendant who should thenceforth succeed to the estate. The stone slab bearing representations of a man, a woman and a child which stands within the little enclosure a couple of hundred yards north-east of the railway-station, is said to mark the spot where the *sati* was committed and is still paid periodical reverence by the zamindar's family.

Kulasékharankóttai: Population 3,023. Lies nine miles south-east of Nilakkóttai at the foot of the southernmost spur of the Sirumalais. On this spur are two curious cavities in the rocks, opening one out of the other, which have at some time, for some unknown purpose, been roofed with a large mass of concrete and so formed into two chambers. The villagers have always held that there was hidden treasure in these, and an old man who was 90 years of age in 1887 related to the then Collector, Mr. E. Turner, how sixty years before he ánd some others had dug down into them. When they entered, the foremost of the party fell down and died, and, thinking that he had been killed by a devil, they gave up the enterprise. Mr. Turner reported the story to Government, who directed him to examine the place with the Archæological Superintendent. An entrance was dug into the chambers and the toe-ring and bones of the man above referred to (who had doubtless been suffocated by the foul air of the place) were found, but nothing else.

Méttuppatti: A village of 488 inhabitants belonging to the Ammayanáyakkanúr zamindari and lying six miles south of Nilakkóttai, on the south bank of the Vaigai. The Peranai dam (near which is a Public Works department bungalow) lies partly within its limits and partly in Pillaiyárnattam.

About a mile north of Méttupatti is a hill called Siddharmalai ('sages' hill') on the top of which is a very ordinary Siva shrine. A path running from this down the southern side of the hill leads to some odd sculptures representing a pair of feet, a balance, a

trident and other objects enclosed in a rectangular border, above
which is an inscription as yet undeciphered. The spot is known
locally as the Pancha Pándava pádam, or 'feet of the five
Pándavas.' A little west of it are five 'Pándava beds' of the
usual description, round about which are more inscriptions. Near
the Kannimár kovil, lower down the hill, is cut upon the rock a
figure of an armed man which is popularly declared to represent
Karuppanasvámi and is reverenced accordingly by the local Kallans.
Tradition says that this hill was once the abode of sages and
recluses and that they cut these unusual figures about it.

Nilakkóttai: A union of 5,269 inhabitants; head-quarters
of the tahsildar of the taluk and of a sub-registrar; contains a
chattram.

The place was the chief village of the estate of the same
name which was one of the 23 pálaiyams of the Dindigul province.
According to one of the Mackenzie MSS.[1] the founder of the
pálaiyam came from the Vijayanagar country before the time of
Visvanátha Náyakkan and built the mud fort from which the
village is named and the remains of which still stand about a
quarter of a mile to the south of it. His successors (sculptures
of some of whom are still to be seen in the Ahóbila Narasimha
shrine in the village) strengthened this fort, built temples and
assisted the Náyakkans of Madura in their military expeditions.
The history of the estate after Dindigul became a province of
Mysore has already been referred to on pp. 70 and 183.

After the Company acquired the country, the poligar (Kulappa
Náyakkan) fell into arrears with his tribute, and in 1795 his estate
was accordingly resumed. He then openly rebelled and on 11th
December 1798 attacked the Nilakkóttai fort (one of the strongest
in all the Dindigul country) with a force of six or eight thousand
Kallans from the Ánaiyúr country armed with 'small jingalls,
matchlocks, spears, cudgels and bludgeons.' Messrs. Turnbull
and Keys (one of whom was inside the fort at the time) give
a graphic account of the affair in the Survey Account. The fort
was garrisoned with a company of sepoys under a subadar and
300 *sibbandi* peons under the tahsildar, a Musalman. After some
hours' hard fighting, they succeeded in putting the attackers to
flight. The same night three more companies of sepoys arrived
from Dindigul, and the next day the Collector and another
company from Madura. These pursued the poligar, but failed to
catch him. A reward of Rs. 1,000 was then put upon his head,
but with no better success. Three years later, however, the

---

[1] Vol. II, 216.

poligar, dressed as a mendicant, presented himself before the Collector, threw himself at his feet, and besought the protection of the Company. The Collector procured for him an allowance of 30 pagodas a month and permission to reside in his former capital. In 1805 the then Collector (Mr. Parish) made over to him a large sum which had accrued to the estate during his absence from it, and with this he bought back his old property and Vattilagundu as well. Seven years later, however, the peshkash on these was again in arrears and they were once more resumed. The poligar was granted an allowance and a descendant of his, who lives within the mouldering walls of the old fort, still draws a pension from Government.

Sandaiyúr: Ten miles in a direct line south-west of Nilak-kóttai; population 460. Formerly the chief village of the estate of the same name, which was one of the 26 pálaiyams of Dindigul. The history of this property up to the time when the Company acquired that province has already been referred to on pp. 70 and 183. The poligar, Gopia Náyakkan, afterwards gave considerable trouble. In 1795 he laid claim to the pálaiyam of Dévadánapatti, the owner of which had just died, declined to pay any peshkash unless his claim was admitted, raised nearly 200 armed peons and plundered Vattilagundu and Ganguvárapatti. The Collector accordingly seized his estate and it was shortly afterwards formally sequestered.

Sólavandán: A union of 13,556 inhabitants standing on the left bank of the Vaigai twelve miles north-west of Madura; sub-registrar's office; railway-station. The union includes the two villages of Mullipallam and Tenkarai which adjoin one another on the opposite bank of the river.

Sólavandán is said to mean 'the Chóla came' and the old name of the village is shown by inscriptions to have been Chólántaka-Chaturvédimangalam, the first part of which means 'destruction to the Chólas.' Hence tradition has it that the town was the scene of a defeat of the Chólas by the Pándya kings of Madura, but when this occurred is not clear. The numerous inscriptions of Pándya rulers in the Perumál temple at Sólavandán and in the Múlanátha shrine at Tenkarai seem to show that the village was a favourite with those monarchs. In 1566 Visvanátha's minister, Árya Náyakka Mudali (see p. 12), brought a number of his caste-men (Tondaimandalam Vellálas) from near Conjeeveram and settled them in Sólavandán, building for them 300 houses, a fort and a temple and providing them with a guru, slaves, artisans and Paraiyans. Their descendants are even now found in considerable numbers in the place and are chiefly congregated in a portion of it which is still called Mudaliyárkóttai, or 'the Mudaliyár's fort.'

In later times, during the wars of the eighteenth century, the CHAP. XV.
fort here became of importance, since it commanded the road NILAKKÓTTAI.
between Madura and Dindigul. In 1757 Haidar Ali of Mysore
marched out of the latter town, took this place without opposition
and marched up to the walls of Madura, plundering as he went.
He was soon afterwards beaten back by Muhammad Yúsuf, the
Company's Commandant of sepoys, and the latter subsequently
strengthened Sólavandán to prevent a repetition of his incursion.

Besides commanding the Madura-Dindigul road, Sólavandán
was for centuries an important halting place for pilgrims travelling
to Rámésvaram. Queen Mangammál built a chattram here for
these people and endowed it generously. It still exists (see
p. 157) and bears her name, but now that the pilgrims usually go
by rail direct to Madura it is no longer as much used as in the
old days, and part of its income has been diverted to the maintenance of a chattram opposite the Madura railway-station.

Nowadays Sólavandán is chiefly known for its numerous plantations of cocoanuts and the richness of its wet lands. These
spread for a long distance on either side of the railway and are a
prominent object from the train as one approaches Madura from
the north. The advent of the Periyár water has made them more
valuable than ever and they command very high prices. In the
tanks among them is the best snipe-shooting in the district.

Tiruvédagam : On the left bank of the Vaigai, twelve miles
north-west of Madura ; population 1,488.

The name is said to mean ' the place (*agam*) of the sacred (*tiru*)
leaf (*édu*)', and the Madura *sthala purána* tells the following story
accounting for it : Kubja (' the hunchback ') Pándya, king of
Madura (the *Periya Puránam*, see p. 29, calls him Nedumáran)
became a Jain and persecuted all his Saivite subjects. His queen,
however, remained in secret a fervent adherent of Siva, and
through her means Tirugnána Sambandhar, the famous Saivite
poet-saint, was induced to visit the city. The king was afflicted
at this time with a serious fever which none of his Jain priests
could remedy, and at last he was induced to send for the priest of
the rival religion. He was cured by Tirugnána Sambandhar not
only of his fever, but also of his hunchback, and he changed his
name accordingly to Sundara (' the beautiful ') Pándya, became a
Saivite again, and decreed the death of all Jains. But these
latter prevailed on him to first agree to a trial of strength between
them and Tirugnána. Prayers of the two faiths were written on
palm-leaves and thrown into a fire, but the Jain texts were all
consumed and the Saivite scriptures remained untouched. Prayers

were then similarly written on other palm-leaves and thrown into the Vaigai to see which would first sink. Those of the Jains quickly disappeared, but those of Tirugnána floated away up-stream, against the current, until they were out of sight. This confirmed the king's determination to have done with the Jains, and he impaled all who declined to become converts to Saivism. Afterwards a search for Tirugnána's leaves was made, and they were found in a grove of bilva trees, where also a lingam was for the first time discovered. The king accordingly built a temple on the spot and round about it grew up the present village of Tiruvédagam.

'Tirugnána Sambandhar's *math* ' in Madura town, a prominent building to the south-east of the temple, is said to be built on the site of an older *math* in which the saint stayed during this affair and to have been afterwards called by its present name in celebration of this victory. It is now presided over by non-Bráhman Pandára-sannadhis, who appoint their own successors, and on its walls are the portraits of a long series of these individuals ; but tradition says that it was once a Bráhman institution. In it is a small shrine dedicated to Tirugnána, before which the *óduvárs* morning and evening recite the sacred verses of the'saint.

Tóttiyankóttai: Six miles west-south-west of Nilakkóttai, population 190. Once the chief village of another of the 26 pálaiyams already several times mentioned (see pp. 70 and 183). It was eventually resumed again by the Company, apparently for arrears. As the name of the place implies, the poligar was a Tóttiyan by caste. The estate always suffered from its compara-tive propinquity to the marauding Kallans of Ánaiyúr in the Tirumangalam taluk ; one of its chiefs had once to flee from them and in 1816 the poligar lived shut up in his fort to be secure from them.

Vattilagundu (*alias* Batlagundu) is a union of 10,665 inhabi-tants lying seven miles west of Nilakkóttai at the junction of the road from Dindigul with that between Ammayanáyakkanúr and Periyakulam. It is a regular place of halt on the journey from the railway to the latter and the Palni hills, and contains a local fund chattram and a travellers' bungalow. The latter looks west-wards over a stretch of rich paddy land and up to the Kodaikanal cliffs, and is one of the pleasantest halting-places in the district. The wet fields in these parts are watered by channels from the Manjalár, which is an almost perennial stream, and the rice called 'Vattilagundu sambá' is so much prized that the crop is said to

be sometimes bought in advance before ever the seedlings are
planted.

Vattilagundu formerly boasted ' a considerable fort,' the twelve
bastions and five gates of which were still standing when the
Survey Account of 1815–16 was written. In 1760 this was the
scene of some sharp fighting between Haidar Ali's troops from
Dindigul and the forces of the Company in Madura under
Muhammad Yúsuf, the Commandant of the sepoys. The latter
captured the place in July, making a breach with cannon and then
storming it, but were themselves at once attacked by reinforcements
from Dindigul. Their detachments outside the walls were driven
back after six days' hard fighting, and subsequently the fort itself
fell after a stubborn resistance. Shortly afterwards Muhammad
Yúsuf in his turn was reinforced from Madura, and he set himself
to win back the place. He was completely successful, driving the
Dindigul forces out of their camp, capturing their artillery and
reoccupying Vattilagundu.

PALNI TALUK.

THIS lies in the north-west corner of the district and 45 per cent. of it is made up of zamindaris. It was formerly called the Aiyampalle taluk. Along the whole of its southern boundary run the Palni hills, and it slopes northwards away from these and is drained by the three parallel rivers—Shanmuganadi, Nallatangi and Nangánji—which flow down from their slopes. The wet land under the first of these is some of the best in the district and as much as 8 per cent. of the irrigated fields of the taluk are assessed as highly as Rs. 7-8-0 and over per acre. Palni contains some patches of black soil, but red earth occupies a higher proportion of it than of any other taluk except Mélúr. This land is much of it infertile, and nearly one-half of the dry fields are assessed at as little as 12 annas and under per acre. Also, the taluk receives less rain than any other. Consequently in bad seasons it is poorly protected and it suffered severely in the great famine. In ordinary years it is saved by its numerous wells, which water as much as nine per cent. of its irrigated area and the cultivation under which is carefully conducted, and only $9\frac{1}{2}$ per cent. of the assessed land, a smaller figure than in any other taluk, is unoccupied. The chief crop is cholam, which is grown on nearly a third of the total cultivated area, and next come horse-gram and the smaller millets.

Statistics relating to the taluk are given in the separate Appendix. Below are accounts of its chief towns and villages :—

Aivarmalai, 'the hill of the five,' is a prominent height, 1,402 feet above the sea, which rises abruptly from the surrounding country nine miles west of Palni and is crowned by a little shrine to Ganésa. The people say it was a resting-place of the five Pándava brothers, and hence its name. On the north-east side the rock of which it consists overhangs and form a natural shelter 160 feet long and 13 feet high. This has now been bricked up and formed into shrines for such popular deities as Draupadi and so on ; but it was doubtless originally a Jain hermitage, for above it, on the face of the overhanging rock, in a long horizontal line about 30 feet from end to end and arranged in six groups, are cut sixteen representations of the Jain tirthankaras, each some eighteen inches high, which constitute the best preserved relic of the Jains in this district. Some of the tirthankaras are standing, others are seated ; some have a hooded serpent above their heads, others one on either side ; some have the triple crown above their heads, others nothing at all ; some are supported on each side by a person bearing a *chámara* (fly-whisk), others are unattended. Round about them are cut several short Vatteluttu inscriptions, parts of which are defaced by lamp-oil. These have not so far been translated.

Áyakkudi : Four miles east of Palni. A union of 14,725 inhabitants and the chief village of the zamindari of the same name. This latter, which includes a considerable area on the Palni hills, is the second largest in the district, and the proprietor of it is also owner of the large estate of Rettayambádi.

According to the traditions of his family [1] his original ancestor (like those of other Tóttiyan zamindars of the district, see p. 106) quitted the northern Deccan in the fifteenth century and came south into the territories of Vijayanagar. There he was granted a pálaiyam near the well-known temple of Ahóbilam in the present Anantapur district, since when Ahóbilam (often corrupted into 'Óbila' and the like) has been a common name in the family.

One of his descendants accompanied the expedition of Visvanátha (p. 41) to Madura and was granted this estate and appointed to the charge of one of the 72 bastions of the Madura fort. He built Palaya (' old ') Áyakkudi, and Pudu (' new ') Áyakkudi was founded some time afterwards. His successors built forts and villages, cleared the forest, kept the wild elephants from molesting pilgrims to Palni, brought the Kallans and other marauding peoples to order, constructed tanks and temples, and accompanied the Náyakkans of Madura on their various military expeditions.

When the Company acquired the Dindigul province the estate was in some way an appanage of the Palni pálaiyam, and in 1794 the two poligars were engaged in open hostilities. In 1795 Áyakkudi was ordered to be detached and separately assessed, and in consequence the Palni poligar openly rebelled and Áyakkudi began arming. The latter chief was eventually arrested and confined in the Dindigul fort. In 1796 the estate was handed back to the family, and ten years later the then head of it purchased Rettayambádi at a sale for arrears of revenue.

Both properties were included for many years among the 'unsettled pálaiyams' of the district (see p. 194). They were

---

[1] Mackenzie MSS., Local Records, vol. 42, 449, and Wilson, 417.

managed by the Court of Wards from 1851 to 1860 during the minority of the then proprietor Jánakiráma Náyakkan. He died in 1868 and his paternal uncle, Muttukondama Náyakkan, succeeded. In 1872 this man turned ascetic and resigned the property to his eldest son, Ahóbila Kondama. The next year this latter was granted a permanent sanad for this estate and for Rettayambádi. Thereafter, he rapidly fell deeply in debt and in 1879 he leased the property to the Chettis for nineteen years. Later on he transferred the estates to a nephew; but a son (Ahóbila Kondama Náyakkan) who was subsequently born to him contested the transfer in the courts and was eventually placed in possession by a decree of the Privy Council in 1900. The property has since been again mortgaged (with possession) to a Chetti.

The customs at the succession of a new heir are curious. When the zamindar is on his death-bed the heir is bathed and adorned with flowers and jewels, is taken to the dying man, and receives at his hands the insignia of ownership. He then goes in a procession with music and so on to a mantapam, where he holds a levée and is publicly pronounced the rightful successor. He is not permitted to see the corpse of his predecessor nor to exhibit any sign of grief at his death.

Idaiyankóttai: Lies on the northern frontier of the taluk and on the left bank of the Nangánji some 21 miles by road from Dindigul; population 3,044. In 1815 remains of its old fort, a construction about 200 yards square defended by sixteen bastions, were still visible close to the river.

It is the chief village of the impartible zamindari of the same name. According to the family traditions among the Mackenzie MSS., the original ancestor of this family (like those of several others of the zamindars of this district) came to Madura with Visvanátha (p. 41) and for his services was granted this estate and placed in charge of one of the bastions of the Madura fort. The history of the estate in the eighteenth century has already been referred to on pp. 70 and 183, from which it will be seen that it escaped the numerous resumptions and restorations which were the usual lot of its fellows, and was one of the four of the 26 pálaiyams of Dindigul which were not under attachment at the time that the Company acquired that province in 1790. It formerly belonged to the district of Aravakurichi in Coimbatore, and was added to Dindigul by Haidar Ali.

In 1792 the then poligar gave the English some trouble, setting out to plunder in the Coimbatore district, and Mr. Hurdis wa͟s obliged later on to resume the estate for arrears. These were afterwards paid, and the estate was restored. Thereafter for many years it was one of the ' unsettled pálaiyams ' of the district and it was not granted a permanent sanad until 1871, when Muttu Venkatádri Náyakkan was the proprietor. This man died in 1872 and his son Lakshmipati followed him and held the estate until his death on 3rd October 1902. His son and heir was then a minor fourteen years old, and the estate was accordingly taken under the management of the Court of Wards, which is still administering it.

Kalayamuttúr: Three miles west of Palni on the Udamalpet road ; population 5,499.

In 1856, 63 gold coins of Augustus and other Roman emperors were found in a small pot buried in the ground near the Shanmuganadi here. [1] A mile west of the village, on the southern side of the road, are a few kistvaens of the usual kind and size in fair preservation, and there are eight more to the north of Chinnakalayamuttúr, on either side of the road. These latter are propitiated by the villagers, especially in cases of difficult labour ; they are daubed with the usual red and white streaks of paint and in front of them are some of the little swings which are so often placed before shrines in gratitude for favours received.

Kíranúr : Ten miles north of Palni ; population 3,973. A prosperous village lying in the valley of the Shanmuganadi and inhabited largely by Rávutans, who grow betel under the river channel, trade with the Coimbatore district and keep several of the bazaars in Ootacamund. It is an ancient place, and the inscriptions on the Siva temple to the east of it record grants by Chóla kings who flourished as long ago as 1063 A.D.

Mámbárai : A small impartible zamindari of only three villages which lies on the northern frontier of the taluk 21 miles north-east of Palni. There is no village of the name.

According to one of the Mackenzie MSS., the original ancestor of the zamindar's family, about whose prodigious personal strength several fabulous tales are narrated, was granted the pálaiyam by Visvanátha Náyakkan (see p. 42) and afterwards accompanied the later Náyakkan rulers of Madura on several of their military expeditions.

The ͏estate once belonged to the Aravakurichi district of Coimbatore, but was transferred by Haidar Ali to Dindigul and formed one of the 26 pálaiyams comprised in that province when it was acquired by the Company in 1790. Its history up to that year has been referred to on pp. 70 and 183.

---

[1] M.J.L.S., xvii, 114.

Thereafter it remained for a long while one of the 'unsettled pálaiyams' of the district, and it was not granted a permanent sanad until 1872. The present proprietor's name is Venkataráma Náyakkan and he lives in Attapanpatti. He succeeded in 1888 on the death of his father, Kumára Kathiráya. Náyakkan, in August of that year. As he was then only eight years old, the estate remained, until he attained his majority, under the management of the Court of Wards.

Palni : Head-quarters of the taluk and a municipality of 17,168 inhabitants. The proposals which have been made regarding the improvement of the water-supply of the place are referred to in Chapter XIV. The town is known throughout the south of the Presidency for its temple to Subrahmanya referred to below. It is the head-quarters of the tahsildar and stationary sub-magistrate and of a sub-registrar, and contains a hospital, several chattrams, and a travellers' bungalow belonging to the temple authorities. It has always been a great centre of trade with Coimbatore on the one side and the Palni Hills on the other.

Palni is one of the most charmingly situated places in all the district, standing 1,068 feet above the sea on the edge of the great Vyápuri tank and looking across this towards the mouths of the two largest valleys in the Palnis and the bold cliffs which separate them. Framing the eastern side of this beautiful prospect, rises the steep, rocky hill (450 feet high) on the top of which is built the famous temple to Subrahmanya in his form Dandáyudhapáni, or 'the bearer of the baton.' Round this hill runs a sandy road adorned at intervals with many mantapams, several of which contain great stone images of the peacock, the favourite vehicle of Subrahmanya. Up it, is built a winding flight of stone steps on which are cut the names and footprints of many devotees, and which is flanked at frequent intervals by mantapams and lesser shrines, and crowded in typically oriental fashion with pilgrims passing up and down to the temple, begging ascetics smeared with holy ash, a few gorgeous peacocks and many most impudent monkeys. A story is told[1] about Queen Mangammál of Madura and these steps. One day when she was going up them, she came upon a young man who, perceiving her, retreated in confusion. She called out graciously to him *Irunkól!* or 'Pray wait!' and he and his sons' sons thereafter always took this word as their name. At night the path is lighted at intervals with lamps (a favourite form of showing devotion to the god is to maintain one of these for a certain period) and the effect from below is most picturesque.

---

[1] *Indian Antiquary*, x, 365.

Architecturally, the building on the top of the rock is not
noteworthy, there being no sculpture in it which is above the
ordinary. It consists of the usual outer wall enclosing a central
shrine surrounded by smaller buildings and entered from the west
by a gateway beneath a brick and plaster *gópuram*. The best
reward for the climb is the view of the great Palni Hills and the
rich cultivation

> Spread like a praying-carpet at the foot
> Of those divinest altars.

The fading of the evening light of a quiet October day across
the green rice-fields, the groves of palms and the vast, silent range
beyond is a memorable sight. The belt below the hills, though very
fair to the eye, is exceedingly malarious; and Aiyampalle (which
of old gave its name to this taluk) and Bálasamudram (once the
fort and residence of the poligar of Palni referred to later) are now
entirely deserted, their fields being tilled by people who live in
Palni and return home every evening.

The *sthala purána* of Palni gives the widely known legend
regarding the founding of this temple : Agastya, the famous rishi,
created the hill Sivagiri on which the shrine stands and the neighbouring, slightly lower, eminence now called Idumbanmalai; did
penance on them for some time ; and then went to Mount Kailása
to visit Siva. On his return to his home at the southern end of
the Western Gháts, he sent his demon-servant Idumban to bring
these two hills thither. Idumban fixed them to either end of a
kávadi (the pole by which burdens are slung across the shoulder)
but when he began to lift them he found that Idumbanmalai went
up in the air while Sivagiri remained immovable. Thinking the
latter must be too heavy he put two big boulders (still to be seen)
on the top of the former to make the balance better. Sivagiri,
however, was still immovable, so he went to it to see what was
the matter.

Meanwhile, on Mount Kailása, Siva had offered a pomegranate
to whichever of his two sons, Subrahmanya and Ganésa, could
travel round the world the quicker. Subrahmanya mounted his
peacock and set off at a great pace, but Ganésa (whose elephant-
head and portly figure handicapped him heavily in such a contest)
took thought and then walked slowly round his father and claimed
that as Siva was all-in-all he had by so doing travelled round the
world and won the fruit. Siva admitted his contention and gave
him the pomegranate. Subrahmanya eventually completed his
journey and was very wroth when he heard how he had been
outwitted. His father attempted to console him by saying *Palani*,

'thou art thyself a fruit,' (whence the name of this town), but he went angrily away to Tiruvávinangudi (near the foot of Sivagiri, where there is now a considerable temple) and later on to Sivagiri itself.

When Idumban went to this hill to see why it would not move, Subrahmanya was there and was much annoyed at being disturbed. He accordingly slew Idumban. Agastya, however, hurried up and at his intercession the god restored the demon-servant to life and promised that in future the first worship on the hill should always be performed to him. This is still done—at the little temple to Idumban which stands about half way up the steps leading to the top of Sivagiri.

This story in the *sthala purána* explains why pilgrims to this Palni temple very generally bring with them a *kávadi* on their shoulders. The custom has since, however, been copied at many other shrines to Subrahmanya. The tale also shows, what is in other ways clear, that the Tiruvávinangudi temple is older than that on Sivagiri. This latter is, indeed, a comparatively modern erection. A M.S. in the Mackenzie collection, which is confirmed by local accounts, states that a Canarese non-Bráhman Udaiyár first set up a small shrine on Sivagiri, and that for some time he conducted the worship in it. Eventually, in the time of Tirumala Náyakkan, he was induced by that ruler's general Rámappayya, who visited this town, to hand over to the Bráhmans the actual performance of the púja, and was given in return certain duties of superintendence and a right to receive certain annual presents and to shoot off, at the Dasara festival, the arrow which symbolises Subrahmanya's victory over Idumban. His descendants have ever since performed this rite. Many of them are buried at the foot of the steps leading up to the hill. The present heir of the family, Bhóganátha Pulippáni Pátra Udaiyár, is a minor.

The Tiruvávinangudi shrine is now being completely rebuilt by the Chettis, and the new sculpture in it, executed in the fine-grained granite quarried on Idumbanmalai, is excellent. There is also good modern stone-work in the Siva temple in the middle of the town itself, but much of this has been pitiably defaced by the greasy oblations which have been poured over it.

Pilgrims come to the shrine on Sivagiri from all over the Presidency and especially from the West Coast. As has been said, they usually bring *kávadis* with them. Milk and other offerings are carried in sealed vessels on either end of these, and the former is duly poured over the god's image. Fanciful stories are current telling how the milk keeps sweet for days and weeks on the

journey when brought for this sacred purpose, and how fish cooked
for the god when the pilgrim sets out leap alive from the sealed
vessels when they are opened for the first time before the shrine.
Messrs. Turnbull and Keys' Survey Account of 1815–16 says
that in those days if by any chance the milk and so on brought up
in the sealed *káradis* were found not to be fresh, it was held to be
a sign of the impiety of the pilgrim, who was expected to atone by
severe bodily penance. Penances are still in fashion at the shrine.
Pilgrims occasionally take a vow to wear a ' mouth-lock ' for
several days before going to the temple. This instrument consists
of a piece of silver wire which is driven through both cheeks,
passes through the mouth and is fastened outside, in front of the
face. Another similar ordeal consists in passing a small skewer
through the tip of the tongue.

Curiously enough, Musalmans also believe in the efficacy of
prayer to this shrine. Rávutans go to the little door at the
back (east) of it and make their intercessions and offer sugar in
the mantapam immediately inside this. They explain their action
by saying that a Musalman fakir, called Palni Bává, is buried
within the shrine.

Palni was formerly the capital of an extensive estate of the
same name which was one of the 26 pálaiyams included in the
Dindigul province at the time of its acquisition by the Company in 1790. According to one of the Mackenzie MSS.,[1] the
original founder of the family was a relation of the ancestor
of the Áyakkudi poligar and came with him from Ahóbilam
in Anantapur. ' Sinnóba ' (*i.e.*, Chinna Ahóbilam) is a name of
frequent occurrence in the family. He was given an estate by
Visvanátha Náyakkan and put in charge of one of the 72 bastions
of Madura. He founded the fort of Bálasamudram, just south of
Palni, which was thereafter the residence of the family, and he and
his successors did much for the extension of the Palni temple and
the improvement of the country. The more recent history of
the pálaiyam has already been referred to on pp. 70 and 183
above. During his expedition of 1755 Haidar Ali plundered
it of everything valuable and compelled its owner (who had fled)
to agree to pay a fine of 1,75,000 chakrams. After the British
took the country the then poligar, Vélǎyudha Náyakkan, gave a
great deal of trouble. In 1792 he was plundering in the Coimbatore
district ; in 1794 he was engaged in open hostilities with his
neighbour Áyakkudi, who was in some way dependent upon him ;
and in the next year he took umbrage at a proposal of Government

---

[1] Local Records, vol. 42, 499, and Wilson, 417.

to detach this latter estate and assess it separately, and was reported to have armed 1,000 men and to be marching on Bódináyakkanúr. On the 7th October 1795 Captain Oliver surprised and captured him in his fort at Bálasamudram ; and the achievement was considered of such importance that Oliver and his detachment were thanked in general orders and the jemàdar of the party was promoted and given a gold medal inscribed ' Courage and Fidelity. By Government, 7th October 1795.' [1]

A week later the poligar, nothing abashed, wrote the Collector an indignant letter complaining that Captain Oliver had attacked, wounded and confined him, just because he wouldn't pay his peshkash. In November, however, the Collector was warned that a plan was afoot to kidnap him and keep him in confinement as a hostage for Véláyudha's release ; in December Captain Oliver reported that the poligar's Aiyangár ' pradháni ' (chief minister) had attacked him in Palni with 800 men ; and in the next month this man had to be driven off by a force from Dindigul under Colonel Cuppage. In 1796 the estate was forfeited for this rebellion, and Véláyudha was confined ·on the Dindigul rock and subsequently deported to Madras, where he eventually died. But as late as 1799 Virúpákshi, Kannivádi and other poligars were conspiring to reinstate his son, Vyápuri, as chief of Palni.

Rettayambádi : A zamindari lying to the west of Palni town and including a considerable area on the slopes of Palni hills. According to one of the Mackenzie MSS.[2], the original founder of the family (who were Tóttiyans by caste) fled (with the ancestors of the Palni and Áyakkudi poligars) from the Musalmans of the north, because these wanted to marry the girls of his caste, and took service under the Vijayanagar kings. Like the founders of other zamindaris in this district, he afterwards accompanied Visvanátha on his expedition against Madura and for his services was granted an estate. His son did much for the temple on Aivarmalai above mentioned, clearing the way up to it, establishing a water-pandal for the refreshment of pilgrims and granting the inam (still in existence) for the upkeep of the worship in it. His successors built Old Rettayambádi and New Rettayambádi (to the south of Páppanpatti), both of which have now disappeared. The later history of the estate has already been referred to on p. 183. It was in some way dependent upon the Palni pálaiyam and in 1795 it was paying an annual tribute to the poligar thereof. When Palni was forfeited for rebellion in 1796, it was

---

[1] Wilson's *History of the Madras Army*, ii, 249.
[2] No. 17-5-52.

accordingly placed under the management of the Collector. Ten
years later it escheated for failure of heirs (other accounts say
it was resumed for arrears) and was sold. It was bought by the
then poligar of Áyakkudi and still belongs to his descendants.
But, like the rest of his property, it has now been leased to the
Chettis. A permanent sanad for it was granted in 1873.

Vélúr : A village of 4,224 inhabitants lying about ten miles
east of Palni, which gives its name to a small zamindari which
was granted a permanent sanad in November 1871 but, since it
was not in existence prior to the passing of Regulation XXV of
1802, has not been scheduled as impartible and inalienable in the
Madras Impartible Estates Act, 1904. The present owner of the
estate, whose name is Perumál Náyakkan, lives in Sattirapatti (a
hamlet of Vélúr which contains a sub-registrar's office, a chattram
and a bungalow belonging to the zamindar in which travellers
are permitted to halt) and is commonly known in consequence as
' the Sattirapatti zamindar.' The history of the property has
already been referred to on pp. 195–6. In 1806 it was sold
for arrears and was bought by the ancestor of the present
holder.

Virúpákshi : Lies 13 miles east of Palni on the bank of
the Nangánji ; population 1,911. It possesses the biggest
weekly market in the district, people from the adjoining Lower
Palnis flocking to it in large numbers and exchanging the produce
of their villages for the necessaries which the hill country does
not provide. Adjoining the market is the Forest rest-house, and
in front of this stands a shrine to Karuppan which is equipped
with even more than the usual number of pottery horses, etc., and
of wooden swings. Close by, a road two miles long leads to the foot
of the Palnis and from the end of this a much-used path runs up
the slopes to Páchalúr and other hill villages. Another path
branches off to the two falls of the Nangánji (*Kíl talakuttu* and
Mél talakuttu, as they are called) the upper of which is so prominent from the main road to Palni. They are worth seeing. The
lower one is only some 30 feet high, but the force of the water
flowing over it is strikingly indicated by the big pot-holes on its
brow and the deep pool below. Round about it are several little
ruined temples to the seven Kannimár (virgin goddesses) and
other deities, which are almost overgrown, now, with jungle.
Above it, the river is turned into a channel ingeniously carried,
by blasting and walling, along the steep side of the hill and
thence to the Perumálkulam. Alongside this channel runs the
path to the higher fall. This is a wild spot. The river winds

down a deep wooded cleft in the great hills and at length tumbles over a sheer cliff of solid rock 150 feet high into a very deep rock pool. The cliff consists of a black stone which is oddly marbled with white streaks, has been curiously chiselled in several places by the great force of the water, and the clefts in which are tenanted· by many wild bees and blue pigeons. Beneath it, are more rocks, marbled in several colours and worn to a glassy smoothness by the river. Even when little water is passing over it, this fall is worth a visit and when the Nangánji is in flood the scene must be most impressive. As the only good path leads up the bed of the river, it would not then however,'be an easy place to approach.

Virúpákshi was once the chief village of one of the 26 pálaiyams which made up the Dindigul province when it came into the possession of the Company in 1790. The ruins of the ' palace ' of the old poligars may still be seen to the east of the road already mentioned which runs to the foot of the hills. Captain Ward's Survey Account and one of the Mackenzie MSS.[1] give the early history of their family. The founder of it was one of the Tóttiyans who fled to Vijayanagar in the circumstances already narrated on p. 106 above, came to Madura with Visvanátha's expedition, and was granted an estate for his services. A later head of the family assisted Tirumala Náyakkan of Madura against the Musalmans and was granted the following assortment of rewards, which compares oddly with the unsubstantial honours accorded to present-day warriors : ' An ornament for the turban ; a single-leaved golden torie or diadem ; a necklace worn by warriors ; a golden bangle for the right leg ; a chain of gold ; a toe-ring of gold ; a palanquin with a lion's face in front ; an elephant with a howdah or castle ; a camel with a pair of naggars of metal ; a horse with all its caparisons ; a day torch ; a white ensign ; a white umbrella ; an ensign with the representation of a boar ; a green parasol ; white handkerchiefs to be waved ; white fleecy flapping sticks.'

Another of the line had a vision telling him that the pool below the *Kíl talakuttu* was a favourite bathing-place of the seven Kannimár, and so he built the shrine to them there. He also made the Perumálkulam, and doubtless the ingenious channel to it already mentioned. His descendants founded Páchalúr and other villages on the hills and effected many similar improvements.

---

[1] Local Records, vol. 42, 495, and Wilson, 417.

In 1755 Haidar attacked the place because the poligar was
in arrears with his tribute, and imposed a fine of 75,000 chakrams upon it. The later history of the estate has already been
referred to on pp. 70 and 183. Narrated in detail, it would
be found to consist chiefly of resistance to the authorities and
quarrels with the neighbouring pálaiyams. After the Company
obtained the country the poligar, Kuppala Náyakkan, grew
particularly contumacious. In 1795 he claimed possession of
Kannivádi, the owner of which had just then died, and rejected
the Collector's customary presents and barred his march into this
part of the country. The next year he annexed 22 villages to which
he had no right. With the weakness which characterised its dealings with the poligars in those days, Government not only did not
punish him for this, but actually said he might keep the mesne
profits up to the date when he (at last) handed them back. This
leniency did not cause him to mend his ways and in 1801 Colonel
Innes, who then commanded at Dindigul, had to march against
him in force.[1] On the 21st March Virúpákshi and two adjoining
strongholds were taken without loss and the poligar fled. On
the 27th his horses, baggage and elephants were seized at Vada-
kádu (on the hills to the east of Virúpákshi) and on the 4th
May he himself was captured. Ward's Survey Account says
that he and his accomplices were hanged on a low hill near Dévadánapatti (7 miles east of Periyakulam) on gibbets the remains of
which were still visible at the time when he wrote (1821). The
Mackenzie MSS. say the hanging took place in Virúpákshi
and that 22 members of the family were confined on the
Dindigul rock. The pálaiyam was forfeited. Some descendants
of the poligar still draw an allowance from Government.

[1] *History of Madras Army*, iii, 30-2.

PERIYAKULAM TALUK.

THIS was once called the Tenkarai taluk. It is the biggest in Madura, but much of it consists of hill and forest and more than half (a higher proportion than in any other taluk) is made up of zamindaris. It lies in the south-western corner of the district and its limits correspond with those of the beautiful Kambam and Varushanád valleys referred to on page 6 above. A long, narrow strip of country, running north-east and south-west, is completely shut in by the Palnis and the Travancore hills on the north and west, and by the Varushanád and Ándipatti range on the east. Down the centre of this run the Suruli and the Vaigai, and the Periyár water which now flows into the former of these has conferred great prosperity upon the southern part of the taluk, much fresh land being brought under wet cultivation and two crops being grown on existing rice-land where only one was formerly possible. Over two-fifths of Periyakulam (a higher proportion than in any other taluk except Tirumangalam) is covered with black soil, but the land rises rapidly away from the rivers in the centre of the taluk and these higher portions consist of red land which can only be irrigated from wells. Some of this (that round about Ándipatti, for example) is dotted with boulder-strewn granite hills rising out of wide expanses of dry crops, and bears the most striking resemblance to parts of the Mysore plateau. At present cholam occupies a larger area than paddy, and over a fifth of the assessed land (a higher percentage than in any other taluk) is unoccupied. The density of the population is also lower than anywhere else, but this is largely due to the existence within the taluk of so much hill and forest, and the proportional increase in the number of the inhabitants both in the decade 1891–1901 and in the thirty years ending with 1901 was higher than in any other part of the district. The recent opening out of the neighbouring Travancore hills to the cultivation of tea, coffee and cardamoms has doubtless had much to do with this growth, as the estates export their produce through this taluk and draw most of their labour and supplies from it.

Statistics regarding Periyakulam appear in the separate Appendix to this book. The more interesting places in it are the following : —

Allinagaram : Eight miles south-west of Periyakulam on the road to Uttamapálaiyam; population 6,436. Less than two miles south of it the Téniyár and Suruli meet, and, after flowing together another two miles, join the Vaigai. About a mile south of the village, at the junction of the main road with the lesser lines leading to Bódináyakkanúr and Usilampatti, is the rapidly rising village of Téni, which ten years ago consisted of little besides the chattram originated by the Téváram zamindar which is still its principal building, but now possesses the biggest weekly market in all the taluk.

Ándipatti : Ten miles in a direct line south-east from Periyakulam on the road from Téni to Usilampatti; population 7,899; contains a chattram, a dispensary and a Siva temple of some celebrity in which are inscriptions. It has given its name to the range of hills to the east of it, but otherwise is not interesting. The land on all sides of it is under dry cultivation, a paddy-field being a rarity.

Anumandanpatti : Two miles south-west of Uttamapálaiyam, on the road to the Periyár; population 2,692. About a quarter of a mile south-east of the village and east of the road, in the middle of a small grove, stands a sculptured stone slab which is called *annamárkal,* or ' the brothers' stone.' It is between three and four feet high and bears a representation of two armed men. Facing it is a second stone on which are a few Tamil letters, almost obliterated. The villagers say that the brothers were two Maravans. They found out that their sister was carrying on an intrigue with a man of another caste, lay in wait for her as she was coming back from visiting him, and slew first her and then themselves. The stone facing the sculptured slab is supposed to represent the sister. The stones are now regularly worshipped and on the trees around them are hung bundles of paddy placed there by grateful ryots as a thanksgiving for good harvests.

Bódináyakkanúr : Lies fifteen miles in a straight line south-west of Periyakulam at the mouth of a deep valley between the Palnis and the Travancore Hills down which flows the almost perennial Téniyár. It is a union of 22,209 inhabitants and the head-quarters of a sub-registrar (who is also a magistrate under the Towns Nuisances Act) and of the zamindari of the same name. The town is a rapidly-growing place, the population having increased by 26 per cent. in the decade 1891–1901 and by 69 per cent. in the thirty years following 1871. This is due to the fact that through it passes the track which goes north-westwards up the narrow valley of Kóttakudi to the foot of the Travancore hills and to the bottom of the wire ropeway which has been erected by the important company which has opened out so much land for tea, coffee, and cardamoms on the Kannan Dévan hills in Travancore. All the produce of these estates passes down the ropeway and through Bódináyakkanúr to the railway at Ammayanáyakkanúr, and nearly all the grain and other necessaries required for the numerous labourers and staff on the properties goes up to the hills by the same route. A proposal to constitute the town a municipality has been negatived, see p. 221.

The Bódináyakkanúr estate is one of the most ancient in all the district. According to the traditions of the family, its original founder, a Tóttiyan named Chakku Náyakkan, emigrated to this part of the world from Gooty in Anantapur-district early in the fourteenth century, to avoid the Musalmans of the Deccan who were then passing southwards. A long list of his many successors is still preserved. He is reputed to have first come to the notice of the powers in this country by slaying a ferocious wild boar for the destruction of which the Rája of Travancore, who then ruled in these parts, had long in vain offered a large reward. He overcame it in single combat and brought it half alive and half dead to the Rája, who was so delighted with his prowess that he gave him many presents and marks of honour, and conferred this estate upon him on condition that 100 *pons* should be paid each time thesuccession devolved on a new heir. This sign of vassalage has survived down to modern times, and whenever a new zamindar of Bódináyakkanúr succeeds, he sends a present of money to the Mahárája of Travancore and receives in return a gold bangle and other gifts. On the last of these occasions (in 1879) an elephant was added to these.

Chila Bódi Náyakkan, who is said to have come into the property in 1487, similarly attained fame by his personal strength and bravery. He overcame one Mallá Khán, an athlete who was champion of all the Vijayanagar territory, and the then king conferred many fresh honours upon him and directed that his estate should be known thenceforth as Bódináyakkanúr. After Visvanátha (p. 41) had conquered the Madura country, the then poligar, Bangáru Muttu, was appointed to the charge of one of the bastions of the new fort at its capital. He was of a devout disposition and did much for the Siva temple at Periyakulam, building, among other additions, the porch which is still called the Bódináyakkanúr mantapam. Another of the line who is still remembered is the Rája Náyakkan who succeeded in 1642. A representation of him is sculptured in the local Subrahmanya temple and his portrait appears in the entrance hall of the zamindar's palace. He was so devout that when a blind girl went to the goddess Mínákshi at Madura and prayed to have her vision restored, that deity gave her back the sight of one eye and told her to go to Ráju Náyakkan to get the other cured. The poligar's faith was such that he was able to work this miracle, and he was ever afterwards known as Kan-kodutta Ráju, or ' Ráju the eye-restorer.'

These ancient fables are merely a specimen of more which might be added to show the antiquity of the family and the estimation in which it once was held. Its subsequent doings have sometimes been less exemplary. After the Dindigul country fell into the power of Mysore, the then poligar refused to pay tribute and in 1755 he was attacked by Haidar Ali and forced to flee. His estate was confiscated. Its later history up to the acquisition of the Dindigul country by the Company in 1790, when it formed one of the 26 Dindigul pálaiyams, has already been referred to on p. 183. In 1795 the then poligar, Tirumala Bódi Náyakkan, aided by his neighbour of Vadakarai, resisted the Collector's march through this part of the district and fired upon his peons. He was reported to have armed over 600 men. He subsequently repented and was restored to favour and in 1807 we find his son helping Rous Peter (see p. 259) in his elephant-shooting expeditions and being presented in return with a gold jewel and an elephant-calf. Thereafter the estate remained for many years one of the ' unsettled pálaiyams ' referred to on p. 194. In the fifties of the last century the then poligar, Bangáru Tirumala Bódi, built the existing most effective anicut across the Téniyár, and he also made the tank which bears his name and the zamindars' present palace. He died in October 1862, leaving an infant son Kámarája Pándya, and the estate was under the Court of Wards until the boy attained his majority in October 1879. He was granted a permanent sanad for his property in 1880. He is remembered for the great graft mango topes he planted along the banks of the Téniyár. After his death in 1888 his widow Kamulu Ammál, the present zamindarni, succeeded.

In 1889 Kandasámi Náyakkan, her husband's cousin, filed a suit claiming the zamindari. In consideration of his relinquishment of his pretensions, the village of Bhútipuram was granted him, and this was separately registered and assessed in 1897. In 1896, in somewhat similar circumstances, the village of Dombáchéri was ordered by the courts to be separately registered and assessed. Other litigation as to the possession of the zamindari is still proceeding. Until a few years ago the property was mortgaged with possession to **Mr. Robert Fischer** of Madura, but it has now been redeemed. In 1900 the zamindarni gave the town its present hospital.

Chinnamanúr: Twenty-two miles south-west from Periyakulam along the road to Uttamapálaiyam; a prosperous union of 10,270 inhabitants. It is said to get its name from a Chinnama Náyak, who flourished in the time of Queen Mangammál of Madura and founded the place and brought Bráhmans to it. Bráhmans are still prominent among its inhabitants. So are Musalmans, and they have a fine new mosque. Much land to the west of the village is grown with paddy irrigated from a channel from the Suruli river. Half a mile to the north-west, among some more rice-fields and surrounded by a grove, is the Rájasimhésvara temple, in which there are several inscriptions as yet undeciphered and the car festival at which is largely attended. It is said to have been founded by a Pándya king named Rájasimha, who fled hither to escape a Musalman invasion of his territories.

Dévadánapatti: Seven miles east-north-east of Periyakulam, on the road to Ammayanáyakkanúr; population 6,310; travellers' bungalow. It lies close under the Murugumalai spur of the Palnis and from it runs the easiest path to the fine fall of the Manjalár on that range. The place is widely known for its temple to Kámákshi Amman, the peculiarity about which is that its shrine, which must never be roofed with anything but thatch, is always kept closed, the worship being done in front of its great doors. The pújári (a Tóttiyan by caste, who possesses a copper record purporting to be a grant to the temple by Tirumala Náyakkan) is declared to have a vision telling him when the roof needs repairs and he then fasts, enters the shrine blindfolded and does what is necessary.

Dévadánapatti was once the chief village of one of the twenty-six pálaiyams of Dindigul the history of which, up to the acquisition of the province by the Company in 1790, has already been referred to on p. 183. It was ownerless for many years, was claimed by the poligar of Sandaiyúr in 1795 and escheated to Government soon after for want of heirs. The remains of the poligar's old fort may still be traced about a mile to the north of the village on the right bank of the Manjalár.

Erasakkanáyakkanúr: Four miles east of Uttamapálaiyam, on no main road; population 7,079. Chief village of the zamindari of the same name, which includes a considerable area at the foot f the slopes of the High Wavy Mountain. The correspondence regarding the boundary dispute connected with part of this will be found in G.O., No. 1287, Revenue, dated 20th November 1882, and the previous papers. The zamindari was one of the 26 pálaiyams of Dindigul the history of which has been alluded to on pp. 70 and 183. After the Company acquired that province it was for many years one of the ' unsettled pálaiyams,' see p. 194. Between 1858 and 1863 it was under the management of the Court of Wards. The present proprietor is the widow of the last holder and is named Akkalu Ammál.

Gantamanáyakkanúr: A zamindari which includes the south-east corner of the taluk and the beautiful Varushanád valley. It was one of the 26 pálaiyams of Dindigul, and after the country was acquired by the Company continued for many years as one of the ' unsettled pálaiyams.' Hardly anything seems to be on record about its early history, but a fragment among the Mackenzie MSS. states that its founder came from the Deccan and was placed in charge of one of the bastions of Madura by Visvanátha Náyakkan.

So much of it consists of unprofitable hills that it has never been in a particularly flourishing condition, In 1795 the Collector reported that it was ' in very bad order'; Ward's Survey Account of 1821 notes that several of the villages lying near the hills (Rájadáni and Teppampatti for example) showed signs of having once been better off, and mentions the constant ravages of the elephants in parts of the estate: in 1862 the Collector said that the poverty of the soil, the unhealthiness of the country and the incapacity of the proprietor had resulted in the ryots being heavily in arrear with their assessments and at open enmity with their landlord; and finally in April 1896 fifteen of the twenty-one villages of the estate (the peshkash on which was Rs. 10,653 out of a total of Rs. 13,415) were sold in execution of a decree obtained by the Commercial Bank of India and were purchased by the Court of Wards on behalf of the minor zamindar of Ettaiyápuram in Tinnevelly. In 1897 these were separately registered and assessed under the name of the Vallanadi sub-division of the estate. Vallanadi (otherwise called Gantamanáyakkanúr) was the capital of the property, and the zamindar has accordingly removed his residence to Teppampatti. Ward's Survey Account says that in the hills east of this village in a narrow valley is a stream called Máváttu (' the mango spring '), which flows down from a ruined temple over a fall about 100 feet high, and has the property of ' petrifying ' articles placed in it. The head waters f the Suruli are stated to possess a similar power.

The Varushanád ('rain country') valley is so called from the old village of that name which stands almost in the middle of it, buried in the jungle, on the right bank of a fine bend in the Vaigai river there. In 1821 there were still some 30 families living in this place, but it is now practically deserted except that a Rávutan who is the renter of the forest produce of the valley lives there with his coolies for part of the year. Local tradition declares this desolation to be the result of a curse pronounced by a shepherd who was cruelly ill-treated by a former zamindar, but the malariousness of the place is sufficient to account for it. The ruins of old Varushanád include the remains of a temple, a stone-faced tank, a stone oil-mill, a stone trough ten feet long and several curious stone pillars (*málai*) similar to that referred to in the account of Márgaiyankóttai below, and also several neglected tanks and a breached anicut. North and north-east of them, similarly overrun with jungle, lie the ruins of Narasingapuram, another deserted village, and its mouldering fort.

Gúdalúr: A union of 10,202 inhabitants, lying about 38 miles south-south-west of Periyakulam and five from the head of the Kambam valley. East of it is a Forest rest-house. Many of its people belong to the Canarese-speaking caste of Káppiliyans. In former days, it is said, the town was much larger than it is now, and foundations of ruined houses are often dug into in its outskirts. Ward's Survey Account of 1821 says that the village was then 'almost in ruins' and contained only 30 families. This place and Kambam (see below) were of old respectively the chief villages of two estates which were included in the 26 pálaiyams of the Dindigul province. When Haidar Ali of Mysore marched in 1755 to reduce the refractory Dindigul poligars to order, the owners of these two properties came to his camp and agreed to pay their arrears. Both of them broke their promises and fled; and their pálaiyams were consequently confiscated and ever after remained part of the Sirkar land. When the Company acquired the Dindigul country in 1790, the Rája of Travancore declared (see p. 184) that both estates belonged to him, and a great deal of correspondence and trouble occurred before he at last handed them over. It appears that the ancestors of the present chief of Púniyár in Travancore held the Gúdalúr pálaiyam, and the Alagar temple in the town is said to have been built by them. When, last year, it was re-opened after the completion of the recent extensive repairs to it, the present chief came down for the *kumbhábhishékam* ceremony.

Kambam: A union of 12,737 inhabitants six miles south-south-west of Uttamapálaiyam on the road to the Periyár;

travellers' bungalow. A large proportion of its people are Canarese-speaking Káppiliyans. Local tradition says that the Anuppans, another Canarese caste, were in great strength here in olden days, and that quarrels arose between the two bodies in the course of which the chief of the Káppiliyans, Rámachcha Kavundan, was killed. With his dying breath he cursed the Anuppans and thenceforth they never prospered and now not one of them is left in the town. A fig tree to the east of the village is shown as marking the place where Rámachcha's body was burned; near it is his tank, the Rámachchankulam; and under the bank of this is his *math* where his ashes were deposited. Not far off is the new cattle shed which the Káppiliyans have built for the breeding-herd already referred to on p. 20 above.

The early history of Kambam is similar to that of Gúdalúr already sketched above. The Púniyár chief is said to have built the two dilapidated temples which stand in the ruined fort to the east of the town and are now being repaired. One of these was originally founded, goes the story, because a goddess appeared there to a wandering bangle-seller. She asked him to sell her a pair of bangles and he, taking her for an ordinary mortal, slipped two on her wrists. To his amazement she then held out her other two arms and asked for a second pair for them, and he then realized who his customer really was.

At the northern end of the place, west of the main road, are two stones bearing representations of armed men. They are apparently memorials to departed heroes, similar to the *círakals* so common in the Deccan. One of them has been surrounded with a brick building and a visit to it is said to be a good remedy for malaria. Close by are two kistvaens. In the fields, stands a group of five little shrines which are said to mark places where *satis* were committed.

Kómbai: Four miles north-west of Uttamapálaiyam, close under the great wall of the Travancore hills which here shuts in that side of the Kambam valley; population 6,211. The well-known Kómbai (or 'poligar') dogs came originally from here and can still with some difficulty be obtained. No one takes much interest in breeding them now, but old papers say that in days gone by the poligars of this part of the country valued a good dog so highly that they would even exchange a horse for one. On the small hill south of the village which is crowned by a conspicuous banyan stands a little shrine near an immense overhanging rock.

The village gave its name to an estate which was one of the 26 pálaiyams of Dindigul referred to on pp. 70 and 183 above. Its early history is unknown. Unlike the majority of their *confrères* in this district, who are Telugu Tóttiyans by caste, its poligars were Canarese Káppiliyans, and there is a vague tradition that they came from the Mysore country *viâ* Conjeeveram. There are many members of their caste in the neighbourhood still. After the Company acquired the Dindigul province the then poligar, Appáji Kavundan, became troublesome, and in May 1795 he was stirring up disturbances in this Kambam valley. Eventually the estate was resumed and an allowance was granted to the dispossessed proprietor. A descendant of his still draws a pension.

Márgaiyankóttai : Four miles north-north-east of Uttama-pálaiyam; population 2,929. East of it, under a small brick mantapam, is perhaps the best executed of the many ' *málai* stones ' which are common in these parts and are memorials of the dead erected by the Tóttiyans. *Málai* means ' garland ', and the name is due to the fact that floral tributes are (or should be) periodically placed upon such stones. Most of them are slabs with carving on only one side, but this one is square, and each of its four sides bears three sculptured panels one above the other.

Round these *málai* slabs is a sort of Tóttiyan mausoleum, a plain slab being erected whenever a member of the family dies. In a small grove in Uttappanáyakkanúr in Tirumangalam taluk is one used only by the Tóttiyan zamindars, in which are placed the memorial slabs of the zamindars of that village and also of Doddappanáyakkanúr, Jótilnáyakkanúr and Elumalai.

Near the Márgaiyankóttai *málai* stone is a *sati* stone of the pattern usual in this district, representing the husband and the devoted wife seated side by side, each with one leg tucked under them and the other hanging down.

Periyakulam : A municipality of 17,960 inhabitants; head-quarters of the tahsildar and of a district munsif, a sub-magistrate and a sub-registrar; contains a bungalow ' belonging to the Bódináyakkanúr estate which Europeans may occupy with per-mission, and a chattram. The place is most picturesquely situated on the palm-fringed banks of the Varáhanadi, with the great wall of the Palnis immediately north of it. It is an important centre for the trade of that range, the foot of the bridle-path to Kodaikanal being only five miles to the north of it. The scheme for supplying it with water has been referred to on p. 226 above,

The town consists of three villages, Tenkarai, Vadakarai and Kaikulánkulam, of which the first (as its name implies) is on the south bank of the river and the other two on the north. All these are overcrowded and intersected only by narrow lanes, and the town has a bad name for cholera. In 1882 a fire swept through the huddled houses and burnt 300 of them with all their contents, the heat and smoke preventing any chance of saving property in such cramped quarters. New building-sites have, however, been recently acquired by the municipality to the east and south and are being sold as need arises. There are, however, two pleasant roads in the place; namely, those which run westwards to the hills on either side of the river. The northern of these passes through some excellent topes and the other runs along the bank of the picturesque river, past the more open quarter where the public offices.stand, to the Siva temple (which contains inscriptions of Chóla times), the Periyakulam (' big tank ') which gives the place its name (by the north corner of the embankment of which stands perhaps the biggest tamarind in the district), and the Chidambara tírtham, a small, comparatively modern, stone-faced tank supplied through a cow's mouth, which is a popular place for the morning's bath.

Téváram: Seven miles north-west of Uttamapálaiyam, population 10,293. Chief village of the small zamindari of the same name, the present holder of which is Bangáru Ammál, daughter of the last proprietor and a Tóttiyan by caste. This was another of the 26 pálaiyams of Dindigul referred to on pp. 70 and 183. After the Company acquired that country it remained for many years one of the ' unsettled pálaiyams ' mentioned on p. 194, but it was eventually granted a sanad.

Uttamapálaiyam: Lies twenty-eight miles south-south-west of Periyakulam down the Kambam valley road on the left bank of the Suruli, the bridge over which was built in 1893; a union of 10,009 inhabitants; station of the deputy tahsildar and of a sub-registrar; travellers' bungalow. The name means ' best estate ' and is declared to have been given to the place by the Pándava brothers (less venturesome authorities say by Haidar Ali of Mysore) in recognition of its excellent position and climate. It is the first large town down the valley which is benefited by the Periyár water, and since this was let into the Suruli the place has rapidly increased in wealth, importance and size. The growth in the population in the ten years ending with 1901 was 22 per cent. and in the 30 years from 1871 to 1901 as much as 57 per cent.

The Kálahastísvara temple in the town is said to get its name from the fact that a fervent devotee of the well-known shrine at Kálahasti in North Arcot was informed in a vision that he need no longer continue to travel the long journey to that place, since the god could be worshipped at this spot with equal efficacy. He accordingly founded and named this temple. An inscription in the building testifies to a gift to it by Queen Mangammál and the authorities possess a copper grant in its favour made by the last of the Náyakkans, the Vangáru Tirumala referred to on p. 56 above. Near its main entrance is a stone slab on which is cut a figure of Garuda (the celestial kite and enemy of all serpents), two crossed triangles with a circle in the middle of them, and certain mystic letters. People who were bitten by snakes are declared to have formerly derived much benefit from walking thrice round this and striking their foreheads against the circle after each circumambulation, but a *bairági* moved the stone to see if there was any treasure hidden under it, and its virtue has since departed.

At the Draupadi shrine there is an annual fire-walking ceremony. Curiously enough, a Bráhman widow is the only person who is allowed to give the idols their annual cleansing. Near the building is a mantapam said to have been erected by a Kallan who came to rob it but was struck blind as he approached. South of the town, west of the main road and perhaps a quarter of a mile from the travellers' bungalow, are two *sati* stones.

Just north of it, on the flat face of one of a series of huge boulders near the Karuppan temple, is one of the best series of sculptures of nude Jain tirthankaras to be found in the district. They are arranged in two rows, one above the other, and there are long Vatteluttu inscriptions round about them. In the upper row are eleven figures, two about eighteen inches high and the others rather smaller. Some are standing and others are sitting in the usual cross-legged contemplative attitude; some have hooded serpents above their heads and some the triple crown; some are unattended and others have smaller figures on either side of them. In the lower row are eight more figures of a very similar description. The space covered by the whole series is some twenty-one feet by ten.

Vadakarai ('north bank') now forms part of that portion of Periyakulam municipality which lies north of the Varáhanadi, but it was once the chief village of a pálaiyam of the same name. According to one of the Mackenzie MSS, the original founder of this was Rámabhadra Náyaka, a Balija by caste, who came from the Vijayanagar country with Nágama Náyakkan (p. 41). He seems to have been greatly trusted, as he was appointed to act for the latter while he was away on a pilgrimage to Benares; subsequently helped to arrange matters between him and his son; and was eventually made collector of the revenue of Madura. Later on he showed much personal bravery in an attack on the fort of Kambam, pressing forward notwithstanding a wound in the face and being the first to plant a flag on the ramparts. For this exploit he was granted the Vadakarai estate. A successor of his was subsequently given charge of one of the 72 bastions of Madura. One of the best remembered of the poligars who followed is the Máchi Náyaka who succeeded in 1519. He is said to have obtained an addition to his estate by his prowess in shooting an arrow across the Teppakulam in Madura in the presence of Tirumala Náyakkan and all his court, an achievement which none of the other poligars could equal. The event is still annually celebrated in Vadakarai by a general beat for small game (known as 'Máchi Náyak's hunt') followed by a visit to his tomb in Kaikulánkulam. A later Máchi Náyaka is stated in the Mackenzie MS. to have helped Tirumala Náyakkan about 1638 against the rebellious Sétupati of Ramnad referred to on p. 48; and his paternal uncle and successor Náráyanappa Náyaka is said to have assisted Chokkanátha Náyakkan in his expedition against the Tanjore Náyakkan mentioned on p. 50.

CHAP. XV.
PERIYA-
KULAM.

When the Mysoreans threatened Dindigul (p. 69), the then poligar of Vadakarai summoned a council of his commanders to devise measures of defence. It was not a success, as Gantama-náyakkanúr said that Vadakarai was taking too much upon him, and invaded his property and cut off his head (whence the two families still decline to dine together), but tradition has it that the Mysore people bore the matter in mind and confiscated the Vadakarai estate when they eventually captured the country.

The subsequent history of the pálaiyam has already been referred to on pp. 70 and 183. In 1759 its owner assisted Bódináyakkanúr in opposing the Collector's march through this part of the district. In 1859 it was resumed for arrears of peshkash and the poligar was granted an allowance which descends to the eldest son. He had considerable property independently of the pálaiyam and when, in 1881, his son died, leaving an heir (the present holder, M.R.Ry. V. Rámabhadra Náyudu) who was a minor, the Court of Wards managed his estate until he attained his majority in December 1894. He has since distinguished himself as a patron of education, a protector of the beautiful topes planted by his forebears in the neighbourhood, an experimenter in scientific agriculture, and the chairman of the Periyakulam municipal council.

Vírapándi : Thirteen miles south-south-west of Periyakulam ; population 3,960. On high ground about a mile to the south of it, overlooking an anicut and bridge (built in 1893) across the Suruli, and commanding beautiful views of the Palnis and Travancore hills, stands a travellers' bungalow. The land near the river is a sheet of rice-fields, but the high ground in the east is some of the most barren in the district. The Siva temple, which is of no architectural merit, is dedicated to Kannésvara Udaiyár, 'the lord protector of eyes,' and the story goes that it was built because Vira Pándya, a Pándya king of Madura who· was blind in one eye, had a vision that if he built it his sight would be restored. The king afterwards lived for some time in the village and it obtained its present name in consequence.

The Máriamman shrine near the bridge over the Suruli is famous throughout the taluk, and at its annual festival great crowds assemble and very many fowls and goats are offered up. Ward's Survey Account of 1821 says that in those days hook-swinging took place at it. Another village in the district where this ceremony was once regularly performed is Nallamaram in the south of the Tirumangalam taluk. The last swinging there occurred only a dozen years ago.

TIRUMANGALAM TALUK.

THIS lies in the centre of the southern side of the district and is bounded on the west by the Varushanád and Ándipatti range and on the north and north-east by the Nágamalai. It drains south-eastwards into the Gundár. It is an uninteresting, level plain, broken only by a few isolated granite hills, of which over three-fifths (a far higher proportion than in any other taluk) are covered with the fertile black cotton-soil. Cotton is accordingly the chief crop of the taluk and occupies over a quarter of the cultivated area. Thirty per cent. of the dry land in Tirumangalam is assessed at as much as Rs. 2 per acre and another 22 per cent. at Re. 1-8-0, while of no other taluk in the district is more than 5 per cent. assessed at Re. 1-8-0 or over. Only 10 per cent. of the assessed area is unoccupied. On the other hand there are practically no irrigation channels in the taluk and very few wells; and consequently much less of it is protected against adverse seasons than is the case in any other part of the district. The taluk suffered severely in the great famine of 1876-78 and between the censuses of 1871 and 1881 its inhabitants decreased by over 15 per cent. The growth in the population in the period between 1871 and 1901 was smaller than in any other part of the district and in the decade 1891-1901 the number of the people remained practically stationary.

Ánaiyúr: Three and a half miles east of Usilampatti. Formerly a village of note, it is now only a hamlet of Kattakaruppanpatti. A considerable Siva temple (which in general plan resembles on a larger scale that at Vikkiramangalam referred to below) and crumbling walls and houses to the west of this testify to the byegone importance of the place. The name means 'elephant village' and the story goes that Indra's celestial white elephant (which was turned into an ordinary black one for trampling under foot a garland given Indra by a rishi) recovered its colour and high estate by bathing in the golden-lily pool attached to the temple here, lived in the village afterwards and eventually died within the shrine. The temple is consequently dedicated to Airávatésvara, or 'Siva of the white elephant.' In 1877, it is said, some fragments of ivory were unearthed within the building and served, in popular estimation, to put the story beyond the possibility of question. Ánaiyúr was formerly a great stronghold of the western Kallans, and figures prominently in this connection in the old reports. The country round about it is still largely peopled with this caste.

Doddappanáyakkanúr: Chief village of the zamindari of the same name; stands in the Ándipatti pass through the Ándipatti hills; population 6,584. The zamindari consists of two villages some 20,000 acres in extent, of which over 11,000 acres are made up of forest on the Doddappanáyakkanúr hill, 3,445 feet in elevation. It was one of the 'unsettled pálaiyams' referred to on p. 194, but a sanad was eventually granted for it. The present proprietor, Kadirasvámi Doddappa Náyakkan, succeeded to the estate on the death of his father on 15th November 1904, and is a minor under the guardianship of his mother. The property is very heavily in debt, but has not yet been actually mortgaged.

Elumalai: Twenty miles west by north of Tirumangalam, near the foot of the Ándipatti hills; population 5,414. It is the principal village of the small zamindari of the same name. This was purchased from the last holder, Errachinnamma Náyakkan, by the present proprietor Vadamalai Tiruvanáda Sundaradása Tévar (who is a relation of the zamindar of Séttúr in Tinnevelly district and lives in that village) and was registered in his name in May 1895. As it has passed from the family of the original owners, it is not scheduled in the Impartible Estates Act, 1904. Nor has any sanad apparently been granted for it.

Jótilnáyakkanúr: Seven miles south by west of Usilampatti; population 1,413. Chief village of the small zamindari of the same name, which contains two villages about 5,500 acres in extent of which 3,600 acres are forest. This was one of the 'unsettled pálaiyams' referred to on p. 194, but a sanad was eventually granted for it. The zamindars are Telugu Tóttiyans by caste and their family name is Jótil Náyakkan. The present proprietor, Gurunátha Jótil Náyakkan, is a minor under the guardianship of his mother and succeeded on the death of his father in October 1902.

Kalligudi: Nine miles south by west of Tirumangalam; population 3,270; sub-registrar's office, railway-station and local fund chattram. The place is a centre for cotton, which is grown on the black soil round about it. In the low hills to the west of it a very beautiful granitoid gneiss is quarried, which is pale greyish or pinkish-white in colour and banded with laminæ consisting mainly of rather pale red or pink garnets of small size with a few spangles of mica.

Kílakkóttai: Three miles south by east of Tirumangalam; population 630. Chief village of the small zamindari of the name, which is only some 1,750 acres in extent. This was another of the ' unsettled pálaiyams ' and a sanad was granted for it in 1872. It is not scheduled in the Impartible Estates Act as it has passed from the family of the original proprietors. In 1886 it was registered in the joint names of Sátappa Chetti and Muttu Rávutar Kavundan, who owned, respectively, two-thirds and one-third of it. Subsequently the former sold his share to the latter, and the whole estate was registered in this latter's name in October 1894. The property has since passed to one Annámalai Chetti of Dévikóttai.

Kóvilánkulam: Twenty miles in a direct line from Tirumangalam in the extreme south of the taluk; population 2,180. West of it is a slab of black stone on which is carved an image of one of the Jain tirthankaras about $3\frac{1}{2}$ feet high and 2 feet broad. The figure is represented sitting in the usual cross-legged contemplative attitude and is worshipped by the villagers.

Kuppalanattam: Eleven miles due west of Tirumangalam; population 923. Noteworthy for more Jain antiquities. On the northern face of the hill called Poigaimalai, about a mile southwest of the village, is a natural cave at the entrance of which are carved in relief on the rock a series of Jain tirthankaras. They are in three groups. The first contains four figures measuring about 2 feet by $1\frac{1}{2}$ feet represented in the usual sitting position, with triple crowns above their heads and attendants on either side. The second group is made up of three standing figures and one seated, which measure about four inches by three inches and are again adorned with the triple crown. The third group comprises a standing image, about a foot high, with an attendant on either side of it. The place is called the Samanar-kóvil or ' Jains ' temple ', but the images are regularly worshipped and are, indeed, so smeared with oil that the details of them can with difficulty be made out. On the top of the Poigaimalai is an insignificant Vishnu shrine.

Mélakkóttai: Two miles south by west of Tirumangalam; population 1,007. Chief village of the small zamindari (about 1,800 acres in extent) of the same name. This was another of the ' unsettled pálaiyams ', but a sanad was granted for it in 1872. The zamindars are Canarese Anuppans by caste, and their family name is Súrappa Kavundan. The present proprietor, Immadi Achuráma Súrappa Kavundan, succeeded to the estate in 1874 and in 1898 mortgaged it to K. Ranga Rao, a Bráhman landholder of Madura.

Nadukkóttai: Two miles south of Tirumangalam; population 263. Chief village of another small zamindari (about 2,000 acres in extent) which was also one of the ' unsettled pálaiyams.' The zamindars are again Anuppans by caste and their family name is Periya Súrappa Kavundan. The estate is now leased to the same gentleman who holds Mélakkóttai.

Péraiyúr: Seventeen miles south-west of Tirumangalam; a union with a population of 3,510; sub-registrar's office and chattram. It is the chief village of the zamindari of the same name. This estate and Sandaiyúr and Sáptúr referred to below were transferred from the Tinnevelly district in 1859 and their history differs somewhat from that of the other zamindaris in Madura. The Tinnevelly pálaiyams were permanently settled early in the last century, the peshkash ranging from 54 to 57 per cent. of the computed income of the larger estates and from 41 to 49 per cent. of that of the smaller ones in which the expenses of management were relatively heavier. Further details will be found in the Appendix to the well-known Fifth Report of the Committee on the affairs of the East India Company.

Péraiyúr is the second largest zamindari in the taluk, comprising 30 villages with an area of about 21 square miles. The proprietors are Telugu Tóttiyans by caste and their family appellation is Tumbichi Náyakkan. The hill near Péraiyúr which goes by this name is called after them. The present holder, Nágayasvámi Tumbichi Náyakkan, succeeded in 1889.

Puliyankulam: Thirteen miles south-south-west of Tirumangalam; population 1,160. Chief village of the small zamindari known as Mádavanáyakkanúr, *alias* Puliyankulam, *alias* Mádavanáyakkanúr-Puliyankulam. This comprises three villages and is about 2,700 acres in extent. It was another of the ' unsettled pálaiyams ' and was granted a sanad in 1872. The proprietors are Tóttiyans by caste and their family name is Mádava Náyakkan. The present proprietor has leased the estate to one Kántimatinátha Pillai of Tinnevelly.

Sandaiyúr: Twenty miles south-west of Tirumangalam; population 1,381. Chief village of the zamindari of the name, which comprises fifteen villages aggregating about 8,700 acres in extent. This was one of the three estates transferred from Tinnevelly and mentioned in the account of Péraiyúr above. A sanad was granted for it in 1804. The then zamindar having protested against the peshkash proposed, the estate was taken under Government management for some time in order that its capabilities might be ascertained with accuracy. The present holder, Krishnasvámi Kulappa Náyakkan, succeeded in 1898.

Sáptúr: About 22 miles west-south-west of Tirumangalam; population 2,649. The chief village of the zamindari of the same name, which is the largest in the taluk and comprises an area of about 123 square miles including a large portion of the eastern slopes of the Varushanád hills.

Until 1859 the estate belonged to the Tinnevelly district, and (as already stated in the account of Péraiyúr above) its history differs from that of other Madura zamindaris. In 1795 [1] the then poligar, who went by the family name of Kámaya Náyakkau, withheld his tribute and committed other irregularities and his estate was accordingly taken from him and managed by the Collector. He fled to the neighbouring hills and from thence so intimidated and harassed the inhabitants of the pálaiyam and the officials who were administering it that in 1799 Mr. Lushington, Collector of Southern Poligar Peshkash, with the concurrence of Government, offered a reward for his capture. He was seized in July 1800 and after a formal trial by a special board of officers, was convicted and executed in October of the same year. The estate continued for some years more under the Collector's management and in 1803 was restored to the late poligar's son, to whom a sanad was granted, on a fixed peshkash.

In January 1886, on the death of the then zamindar, the property was placed under the Court of Wards owing to the minority of the heir. This boy died at Madras of an hereditary taint on the last day of 1887 and was succeeded by his younger brother Rámasvámi Kámaya Náyakkan. The latter came of age in 1902 and was then placed in possession of the property, which he now holds. The zamindari is admittedly impartible (see the case reported in I.L.R., XVII Madras, 424) and has been scheduled as such in the Impartible Estates Act, 1904.

Tirumangalam: Head-quarters of the taluk and a union of 8,894 inhabitants; stands on the north bank of the Gundár thirteen miles by road south-west of Madura, is a station on the railway and possesses a sub-registrar's office, local fund dispensary, travellers' bungalow, chattrams, a large weekly market on Fridays and a station andchurch of the American Mission. The Madura Mínákshi Ginning and Pressing Co. erected a factory here to deal with the local cotton (for the export of which Tirumangalam is a centre), but it was a failure and is to be sold. Árya Nátha Mudali established a number of Tondaimandalam

___

[1] See Mr. Lushington's letter in the Fifth Report of the Select Committee on the affairs of the East India Company.

Vellálas here at the same time as he founded the similar colony at Sólavandán referred to in the account of that place above, and several families of this caste still live in the town. The antiquities of the place include seven nameless *sati* stones of the usual pattern (some placed in small masonry buildings) among the dry fields just north-west of the travellers' bungalow; a few pyriform tombs (similar to those mentioned in the account of Anuppánadi above) at Senkulam, about a mile to the north-west of the town; and a small mantapam, called the *nagará* (drum) *mantapam*. This last is said to have been one of a series which Tirumala Náyakkan established all along the road from Madura to his palace at Srívilliputtúr, and provided with drummers to pass the word as soon as the god at Madura had had his meals, so that Tirumala could begin his own.

Usilampatti : Seventeen miles north-west of Tirumangalam; a union of 6,335 inhabitants and the head-quarters of the deputy tahsildar and a sub-registrar; contains a good chattram. The Wednesday market here is the most important in the taluk and the second largest (next to that at Virúpákshi) in all the district. It is held in a large tope, on one side of which a good range of stalls has been erected, and is attended by people from as far off as Sólavandán, Tirumangalam and Periyakulam. The town is a comparatively modern place, and owes its new importance to its being the deputy tahsildar's station and possessing this large market.

Uttappanáyakkanúr: Five miles north of Usilampatti; population 3,828. Chief village of the small zamindari of the name, which is about 26 square miles in extent. This was one of the ' unsettled pálaiyams ' referred to on p. 194, but was granted a sanad in 1880. It was under the management of the Court of Wards from 1866 to 1879. The present proprietor, Muttukrishnasvámi Uttapa Náyakkan, is the brother of the last holder and succeeded in 1897.

Vikkiramangalam : Fourteen miles in a direct line north-north-west of Tirumangalam; population 2,596. In its hamlet Kóvilpatti stands a ruined Siva temple which contains some of the best stone-carving in the district and is on the list of buildings conserved by Government. In this are several inscriptions, translations of some of which have been published,[1] but they do not show the age of the building. The lingam is usually kept in a private house in the village and is only placed in the shrine

---

[1] See report of the Government Epigraphist for 1894.

on special occasions. The whole of the outer walls and base of this shrine are sculptured with much elegance of design and minuteness of detail and it is surrcunded on both sides and behind with a *prákára* (arcade) supported ou twelve well-carved pillars. In front of it is a portico upheld by four piers and a mantapam containing twelve more in three rows of four each.

INDEX.

A

Hazarat Saiyad Arab Abdur Rahim
Auliah, darga of, 244.
Heimpel. Mr. J., 149.
Hemingway, Mr. F. R., 25 note.
Hemitragus hylocrius, 23.
Hemp-drugs, 212.
Heron, Col., 62, 88, 181, 289.
Hickey, Rev. William, 234.
Hides and skins, 150.
' High Wavy ' mountain(*Bf*), 7, 11, 140, 316.
Hill villages, settlement of, 205.
Hills, 3–10.
Hindu Permanent Fund, 131.
Hindus, 80–111, 176.
Hindustáni, 79.
History of the district, 25–71.
Hodgson, Mr., 191.
Hoisington, Mr., 78.
Honey tax, 179, 190, 205.
Hook-swinging, 324.
Horse-gram, 113, 114, 118.
Horsely, Captain W. H., 251.
Hospitals, 171, 172, 316.
Hosten, Rev. H., 247.
House-tax, 179, 189, 220, 221.
Houses, 5, 81.
Hoysala Balálas, 34, 35, 36.
Hultzsch, Dr., 27 note.
Humidity, 14.
Hurdis, Harriot, 234.
Hurdis, Mr. Thomas Bowyer, chattram
inams resumed by, 158; the collector-
ship of, 186; his reports on the Dindigul
country, 194, 197; his settlement of
the district, 197–201; and of the hill
villages, 205; list of inams compiled by,
206; tomb of the sister of, 234; ob-
tains grant of the Tamakam, 263;
Idaiyankóttai estate resumed by, 302.
Hutchins, Sir Philip, 275.
Hyæna cave, 257.

I

Ibn Batúta, 28 note.
Idaiyankóttai (*Db*), not resumed by Haidar
or Tipu, 70, 183; plundering raids of
poligar of, 184; resumed for arrears,
194; sanad granted to, 195; poligars'
relationship to Kannivádi family, 238;
described, 302.
Idaiyans, 92, 96.
Idumban, 305, 306.
Idumbanmalai, 305, 306.
Idylls, ten Tamil, 28.
Ilaiyáttakudi, sub-division of Náttukóttai
Chettis, 100.
Iluppaikudi, 100.
Imám ulla, Mír, 69, 236.
Imburán, 147.
Immadi Achuráma Súrappa Kavundan,
327.
Impartible Estates Act (1901), 196.
Imports, 151.
Inams, 157, 186, 197, 200, 206.

Income-tax, 213.
Indian Antiquary, (v), 106; (viii), 29 note;
(x), 304 note; (xv), 110; (xx), 26 note.
Indigo, 115, 147.
Indigo-vats, 179, 189.
Industries, 144–151, 232.
Inheritance, among Idaiyans, 97; in the
estates of Ammayanáyakkanúr, 293;
Áyakkudi, 302; and Bódináyakkanúr,
314.
Innes, Colonel, 311.
Inscriptions at, Aivarmalai, 301; Alagar-
kóvil, 284; Anaimalai, 255, 256;
Ándipatti, 313; Chinnamanúr, 316;
Dindigul, 233, 234; Góripálaiyam, 265;
Kálahasti, 31; Kíranúr, 303; Kodai-
kanal, 252; Kodimangalam, 257;
Kóvilpatti, 330; Madura, 267, 272;
Mandasór, 110; Palakkanáttu, 241;
Periyakulam, 321; Pillánmalai, 288;
Rámanádapuram, 211; Siddharmalai,
295; Sólavandán, 296; Suchíndram,
31; Tádikkombu, 242; Tanjore, 30;
Tiruchunai, 287; Tirupparankunram,
280, 281; Tiruvádúr, 290; Uttamapá-
laiyan, 322.
Inscriptions of, Achyuta, 40, 233; Déva
Ráya II, 40; Kulóttunga I, 32; Kulót-
tunga III, 34; Mangammál, 322;
Maranjadaiyan, 241; Máravarman
Sundara-Pándya I, 35, 280; Nandivar-
man Pallavamalla, 30; Narasimhavar-
man I, 29; Parántaka I, 31, 255;
Pulakésin II, 29; Rájádhirája I, 32;
Rájéndra Déva, 32; Simhavishnu, 29;
Tirumala Náyakkan, 44, 242.
Iron, ore of, 9, 15, 287; smelting of, 137,
179, 189; import of, 151; oil mills of,
288.
Irrigation, in the district, 121–130; on the
Palnis, 4, 6, 205.
Irrigation cess, 125.
Irunkól, 304.
Irwin, Mr. Eyles, 68.
Ixora parviflora, 142.

J

Jackals, 19, 291.
Jails, 217.
Jains, 29, 74, 254, 278, 297; their antiqui-
ties, 75; at Aivarmalai, 300; Ánaimalai,
255; Kóvilánkulam, 327; Kuppalanat-
tam, 327; Tirupparankunram, 279;
Uttamapálaiyam, 322.
Jakkamma, 107.
Jallikat, 20, 83, 90.
James, Father, 77.
Jánakiráma Náyakkan, 302.
Játi Kavundan, 108.
Jawádi hills, 213.
Jellicut, 83.
Jemaul Saheb, 63.
Jervis' *Narrative of a Journey to the Falls
of the Cauvery*, 23.

Jesuit Mission of Madura, 75-77, 279.
Jesuit priests, letters of. See *La Mission du Maduré.*
Jesuit theological college, 243.
Jewellery, 82, 95, 103.
Jivitham, 197, 199.
Johnston, Sir Alexander, 262-264.
Johnston, Mr. Samuel, 262, 263.
Johnston of Carusalloch scholarships, 264.
Jones, Mr. J. A., 223.
Jótilnáyakkanúr (*De*), 195, 320, 326.
Journal of the Asiatic Society of Bengal (xiv), 28 note.
Judges, list of, 218.
Jungle conservancy department, 133, 135.
Justice, administration of, 214-219.

K

Kadirasvámi Doddappa Náyakkan, 326.
Kudukkáy, 141.
Kämpfer, Mr., 170.
Kaikólans, 145, 146.
Kaikulánkulam (*Cd*), 321, 323.
Kailása pudavu, 11.
Kaittiyankóttai (*Eb*), 25.
Kákatíyas, 36.
Kal Tachchans (stone masons), 99.
Kálahasti, 31, 322.
Kálahastísvara, 322.
Kálam crops, 115
Kalayamuttúr (*Cc*), 25, 26 note, 220, 303.
Kalés Déwar, 36.
Káli, 230.
Kalkatti Idaiyans, 96.
Kallans, cows used for ploughing by, 20; their ravages, 66, 184, 196, 197; precautions taken from fear of, 81; dress of the women of, 82; jallikat cattle of, 83; popular gods of, 85, 286; described, 88-96; economic condition of, 130; ním oil used by, 150; earth-salt made by, 210; crime of, 216, 275; numerical strength of, 279, 284; their strongholds at Mélúr, 288; Nattam, 289; and Ánaiyúr. 295, 298, 326.
Kal'ar-Alagar, 198, 286.
Kalligudi (*Df*), 215, 326.
Kalugumalai, 278.
Kalvárpatti (*Db*), 25.
Kalyáni, 31.
Kámákshiamman, 99, 316.
Kámalakkayya Náyudu, 237.
Kamandalanadi river, 10.
Kámanúr (*Cc*), 248.
Kámarája Pándya Náyakkan, 315.
Kámaya Náyakkan, 329.
Kámayya Náyakkan, 294.
Kambalattúr, 106; Chinna, 103.
Kambam valley, scenery of, 5; drainage of, 11; climate of, 14; cattle-breeding in, 20; forests in, 132, 133, 136, 139, 141, 142; road to, 155; malarial fever in, 169; disturbances in, 185; troops stationed in, 197.

Kambam village (*Ef*), elephants caught near, 23; prehistoric burial places in, 25; Visvanátha's expedition against, 43; timber dépôt at, 134; resumed pálaiyam, 183; former taluk, 184; claimed by Travancore, 184, 185; union, 220; described, 318; attack on the fort of, 323.
Kambliyán, 97.
Kamela powder, 147.
Kammálans, 99.
Kampana Udaiyár, 38.
Kamudi, 10, 167.
Kamulu Am bál, 315.
Kanakasabhai Pillai, Mr. V., 26, 27, 83, 175.
Kánappér, 28.
Kandasámi Náyakkan, 315.
Kángayam, 103.
Kangu Valaiyans, 97.
Kaniyambádi, 213.
Kan kodutta Ráju Náyakkan, 315.
Kannan Dévan Hills, tea and coffee cultivation in, 73; cardamoms exported from, 151, their produce passes through Bódináyakkanúr, 152; and Ammayanáyakkanúr, 292; aerial ropeway to, 155, 314.
Kannáns (brass-smiths), 99, 151.
Kannapatti, 151.
Kannésvara Udaiyár, 324.
Kannimár, 86, 256, 309, 310.
Kaunivári (*Dc*), forests of, 134, 136; *dupatis* made in, 145; dispensary at, 173; history of, 183; claimed by Virúpákshi poligar, 185; sanad granted for. 195, 196; not included in the Impartible Estates Act, 196; its chief drives off Mulikan of Mysore, 236; described, 238; elephants in the hills near, 259; poligar conspires to reinstate Palni poligar, 308; claimed by the Virúpákshi poligar, 311.
Káutimatinátha Pillai, 328.
Kapádapuram, 28, 174.
Káppiliyans, cattle breeding of, 20; Canarese spoken by, 73; described, 108; numerous in Gádalúr, 318; and Kambam, 319; caste of poligar of Kómbai, 320.
Kár paddy, 115.
Karadi Valaiyans, 97.
Kárai-katti Valaiyans, 97.
Káraikkál, 58.
Karaiyapatti (*Fd*), 210.
Kárakkat Vellálans, 5.
Karaudamalais, 8, 133, 137.
Kariyamánikka Perumál, 269.
Karumalai (*Db*), 9.
Karumalaiyan, Pulaiyan deity, 104.
Karungálakudi (*Fd*), 25, 286, 287.
Karuppansvámi, *chóvadis* connected with the worship of, 81; god of the Kallans, 85, 93; his shrines at, Alagarkóvil, 284, 285; Méttuppatti, 295; Virúpákshi, 309; and Uttamapálaiyam, 322.
Kási Visvésvaralinga, 279.
Kattakaruppanpatti (*De*), 325.
Káttama Náchiyár, Ráni of Sivaganga, 25.

Peter Pándya, 259.

Peter, **Mr.** Rous, collectorship of, 192 ; assessments reduced by, 201 ; reduces peshkash of Kannivádi, 239 ; account of, 259–261 ; his presents to Madura temple, 270 ; and to Alagarkóvil, 284 ; elephant shooting expeditions of, 315.

Petrifaction of objects by water, 11, 317.

Phillips, Mr., 264.

Píchi Pulaiyans, 104.

Pidári shrine, 290.

Pigeons, blue, 310.

Pillaiváli estate, 150.

Pillaiyárnattam, 294.

Pillaiyárpatti, 100.

Pillar Rocks, 227, 246, 249.

Pilluvari, land, 189 ; tax, 205.

Piramalaináḍ Kallans, 93.

Piránmalai, 100, 287.

Plantains, on the Lower Palnis, 4, 114 ; on the Sirumalais, 8, 114 ; grown on wet lands, 116 ; and in cleared forest land, 132, 138 ; export of, 151 ; rates of assessment for, 205.

Plantations, 140.

Pliny, 26.

Plough-tax, 179, 205.

Podiyil mountain, 32.

Podunáttu Idaiyans, 96.

Poigaimalai, 327.

Police, 216.

Poligar system, 42, 180, 216.

Polyandry, 95.

Pon-Amarávati, 33.

Pondicherry, 77, 150.

Pongu tree, 106, 108.

Ponikáḍu tax, 189, 205.

Ponméni (*Ee*), 215.

Ponnammál, 86.

Ponniya Náyakkan, 294.

Poppy heads, 212.

Population, 72, 162, 166.

Porandalár, 124, 125.

Poruppu tax, 189, 200.

Poruppu villages, 197, 199.

Prehistoric peoples, 24.

Proctor, Mr. George, 68.

Proprietary Estates Village Service Act, 207.

Provincial Court of Appeal, 214, 215.

Pterocarpus Marsupium, 138, 140.

Ptolemy, 26, 28.

Public health, 168–173.

Pudu Áyakkudi (*Cc*), 301.

Pudu mantapam at Madura, 3, 49, 271.

Pudukkóttai State, known as Tondamana, 33 ; its part in the war of Ramnad succession, 56 ; boiling oil ordeal in, 107 ; new Tamil sangam supported by the Rája of, 175 ; salt arrangements with, 210 ; arrack and toddy made in, 211, 212 ; supply of opium and hemp-drugs to, 213 ; house at Kodaikanal of the Rája of, 245.

Pulaiyans, 4, 103, 104.

Pulakésin II, 29.

Puli pudavu cave, 257.

Puliyankudiyár, 80.

Puliyankulam (*Df*), 195, 328.

Pámbárai (*Dc*), 5, 17, 19, 246.

Púniyár chief, 318, 319.

Punnacolum tank, 235.

Puranánúru, 27.

Q

Quartz, 14, 15.

Quilon, 31, 37.

R

Rágalápuram (*Ec*), 25.

Ragi, 83, 113, 114, 118.

Railway cess, 159.

Railways, 158.

Rainfall, 13, 160, 247.

Rája of Ramnad, 130, 259.

Rájadáni (*Ce*), 317.

Rájádhirája I, 32.

Rájádhirája II, 33.

Rájarája I, 31.

Rájarája III, 34.

Rájarája-Pándi-nádu, 31.

Rájasimha Pándya, 316.

Rájéndra Chóla I, 31.

Rájéndra Chóla III, 36.

Rájéndra Déva, 32.

Rájéndra Idaiyans, 96.

Ráju Náyakkan, 314.

Ráma Náyakkan, 236.

Rámabhadra Náyaka, 322.

Rámabhadra Náyudu, M.R.Ry. V., 178, 323.

Rámachcha Kavundan, 319.

Rámanádapuram (*Ec*), 241.

Rámappayya, 236, 306.

Rámasvámi Kámaya Náyakkan, 329.

Rámésvaram, mosque founded by Malik Káfur at, 37 ; pilgrim roads to, 43, 44, 157 ; cholera propagated from, 168.

Ramnad, 56, 187, 214.

Ranga of Vijayanagar, 45.

Ranga Krishna Muttu Vírappa Náyakkan, 42, 53.

Ranga Rao, K., 327.

Rangamalai (*Db*), 9.

Rangoon, 130.

Rapatel, Father F., 279.

Ráshtrakútas of Málkhéd, 31.

Russums, 198.

Ratnasvámi Nádár, M.R.Ry. T., 211.

Ravikkai, 82.

Rávutans, described, 79 ; *dupatis* made by, 145 ; engaged in tanning, 150 ; mats woven by, 151 ; trade of, 152 ; literacy of, 176 ; numerous in Dindigul, 231, 235 ; and Kíranúr, 303 ; their offerings to the Palni shrine, 307.

Ráya gópuram, 49, 271.

Rea, Mr., 256, 257.

Receiver of Assigned Revenue, 68.